Knock 'em Dead helps you find jobs *and* turn the interviews into job offers

"I just wanted to say thank you! After reading your book and following its precepts, I got my dream job within two months! (And I've been searching for almost a year!)"

—**J. B. D.**

"I landed a job that was over double the salary of my previous job, on the same day as I interviewed, which is very, very rare in a state job. *Knock 'em Dead* really says it all. I was able to negotiate to the absolute top end of the starting pay [because] of my resume, cover letter, and interview and the chapter on salary negotiations. Your book was extremely helpful in presenting the best part of me."

—**S. J., KANSAS**

"The interviews nowadays are much tougher than they were four or five years ago. I am so thankful that I had heard about you! I heard of your book right after I bombed out on three interviews. I read and studied it. The first interview that I went on after doing this ended up in a job being offered to me! The interviewer told me that I was the best interviewee she'd seen! Thanks a million for writing your book."

—**K. P., HOUSTON, TX**

"Your book changed my life!! It really did. It shaped the way that I went about getting back into the workforce and the way that I see myself and what I bring to a company. Thank you!"

—**R., LITTLETON, CO**

"One of my most-admired authors in the career advice space. Martin always challenges me to think about career development issues in new and innovative ways."

—**THE WALL STREET JOURNAL'S ALEXANDRA LEVITT ON HER WATERCOOLER WISDOM BLOG**

Knock 'em Dead helps people from everywhere get great jobs anywhere

"I'm a graduating senior from Johnson & Wales University. I read your book, *Knock 'em Dead*, which has helped me score many offers in just the past weeks."

—**D. T., HONG KONG–BOUND**

"I have used the UK version of *Knock 'em Dead* to successfully improve my career prospects. This is the best job-hunting book on the market bar none; keep up the good work."

—**PAUL BREMNER, LONDON UK**

"WOOOOOOOOHOOOOOOOOO!!!!! It worked!! I got the job!!!!!!!!!!!!!!!!!!!!!!!!!!!!!!!!!!!! I luv u Martin!"

—**A., EDMONTON, CANADA**

Knock 'em Dead works for career changers

"[After leaving the Army] I bought all three of your books, *Knock 'em Dead Resumes, Cover Letters*, and *The Ultimate Job Search Guide*. I read each book cover to cover. I followed each step in your books and I got an entry-level job of my dreams. I was prepared because of your books. Thanks!"

—**K. G.**

Knock 'em Dead is inspirational

"I've been a reader of the *KED* books for quite some time. You've made a difference in my life and saying 'Thank you' doesn't begin to express my gratitude."

—T. S.

"You helped me get a job a couple years ago; now I've just accepted a new job. Thank you again for everything you do and all the people you help; I've read your books so many times you feel like a friend. You've been an inspiration to me again and I could not take this job in good conscience without acknowledging your contributions. Take care and God bless."

—T. F., HOUSTON, TX

Knock 'em Dead is motivational

"*Knock 'em Dead: The Ultimate Job Search Guide* inspired me. I have turned my job search into multiple interviews and offers in just a couple of months. The motivation and positive energy will steer you to stay focused on getting the best job offer! Thank you, Martin!"

—E. R., NEW YORK, NY

"*KED* has been a rock in turbulent emotional waters. It is amazing to see the changes that have occurred so far, I can't wait to see what comes next."

—R. L.

Knock 'em Dead helps professionals at all ages and stages of their career

"I wanted to let you know that I've just landed a National Account Manager job. I can't thank you enough; your help and support in my job search was invaluable."

—K. S., IN

"I just got a new job and $16K raise using your approaches—at my venerable age: Number of years employed: thirty-four."

—S. S., LITTLE ROCK, AR

More praise from *Knock 'em Dead* users

"My husband has been wondering why I'm laughing out loud reading a book on job search. Your book is not only imparting valuable advice it is a very refreshing read, sprinkled with humour."

—M. W., TORONTO, CANADA

"My recommendation to job seekers everywhere: Buy it, read it, and use it. It works. Using the techniques in it has led to three initial interviews within the first week of putting it into action. I just wanted to thank you for your excellent book."

—J. R., SAN ANTONIO, TX

KnOCK DEaD 'em

THE ULTIMATE JOB SEARCH GUIDE 2013

MARTIN YATE, CPC
New York Times bestselling author

Adamsmedia
Avon, Massachusetts

To your successful job search

ACKNOWLEDGMENTS

Knock 'em Dead is now in its twenty-eighth year of publication and has become a staple of job searchers around the world. My thanks to the ongoing encouragement of the Adams Media sales team, Beth in PR, and Peter in editorial. Special thanks go to my publisher Karen Cooper, and to Will Yate for his perceptive editorial guidance.

Published by
Adams Media, a division of F+W Media, Inc.
57 Littlefield Street, Avon, MA 02322. U.S.A.
www.adamsmedia.com

ISBN 10: 1-4405-3682-1
ISBN 13: 978-1-4405-3682-3

Printed in the United States of America.

10   9   8   7   6   5   4   3

This publication is designed to provide accurate and authoritative information with regard to the subject matter covered. It is sold with the understanding that the publisher is not engaged in rendering legal, accounting, or other professional advice. If legal advice or other expert assistance is required, the services of a competent professional person should be sought.
—From a *Declaration of Principles* jointly adopted by a Committee of the American Bar Association and a Committee of Publishers and Associations

Many of the designations used by manufacturers and sellers to distinguish their product are claimed as trademarks. Where those designations appear in this book and Adams Media was aware of a trademark claim, the designations have been printed with initial capital letters.

This book is available at quantity discounts for bulk purchases.
For information, please call 1-800-289-0963.

CONTENTS

Part II Get the Word Out...129

Job search is all about getting into conversations with the people who can hire you as quickly and as often as you can. Powerful networking techniques to *quadruple* your hit ratio on every job posting.

CHAPTER 7: Making Contact...131

Study the best strategies for making contact with employers, from e-mailing resumes to making calls. Here's how to introduce yourself to employers, get past gatekeepers, and handle initial interview questions and objections to your candidacy. Effective tactics for getting *useable leads from every* conversation you have.

CHAPTER 8: Ace the Telephone Interview...157

Telephone interviews are a common screening device. How to prepare for the scheduled telephone interview and to be ready for the unexpected call. Headhunter tactics for turning the telephone interview into a face-to-face meeting.

CHAPTER 9: Dress for Job Interview Success...163

You never get a second chance to make a first impression at a job interview; so unless you dress the part, don't expect an offer. Here are men's and women's **guidelines for correct professional dress.**

CHAPTER 10: Body Language...177

Learn the **seven techniques for body language success** during a job interview. Learn to employ positive body language messaging that can help your entire career.

CHAPTER 11: The Curtain Rises on the Job Interview...187

First impressions are the strongest. Here are **twenty small preparations** you can make before you walk into the interviewer's office that will help calm your nerves and psych you up for a successful interview.

Part III Great Answers to Tough Interview Questions...191

Hundreds of tough job interview questions, what's behind them, and how to develop powerful, honest answers.

CHAPTER 12: The Five Secrets of the Hire...195

Knowing how an interviewer thinks is a critical element of the job search that is frequently overlooked. Here are the five secrets of the hire, showing you how to get inside the hiring authority's head. Master them now and they will serve you throughout your career.

CHAPTER 13: The Other Side of the Desk: Why Interviewers Do the Things They Do, and How to Respond...201

Learn the questioning techniques an interviewer uses to find out whether you will fit into the department and the company, whether you are a **team player**, and whether you are going to be a management headache.

CHAPTER 14: How to Knock 'em Dead: Great Answers to Tough Interview Questions...213

The greatest fear is fear of the unknown. Learn about the toughest questions an interviewer can throw at you: **what's behind the question**, what are they looking for in an answer, and how you can give an honest and winning answer without sounding like a snake-oil salesman.

CHAPTER 15: "What Are You Like to Work with, Mr. Jones?": Questions of Manageability and Team Spirit...229

Learn the right way to answer questions an interviewer asks to find out whether you will fit into the company and department, and, most important, whether you are a good person to work with, and will fit into the team.

CHAPTER 16: How to Handle Stress and Illegal Questions...243

Your worst nightmare can come true at a stress interview, but once you learn that these questions are just amplified versions of much simpler ones, you'll remain cool and calm. Also: a vital discussion on handling illegal interview questions, what mock-meetings, role-playing, and in-basket tests are looking for, and how to handle them.

CHAPTER 17: Welcome to the Real World...261

For the entry-level candidate, some special interview questions specifically tailored to discover your business potential when real-world experience is lacking.

CHAPTER 18: Strange Venues for Job Interviews...269

Learn the tips that will help you master job interviews in noisy, distracting hotel lobbies, in restaurants, at poolside, and in other **unusual settings**. Includes an essential review of table manners that you'll remember for the rest of your career.

CHAPTER 19: How to Ace the Psychological Tests...275

We are all professional schizophrenics! Approaching psych tests casually can be hazardous to your professional health. How to prepare for them, what's behind the questions, and techniques for answering correctly in the heat of the moment.

CHAPTER 20: The Graceful Exit...285

All the critical dos and don'ts to ensure that the lasting impression you leave is the right one.

WHY *KNOCK 'EM DEAD?*

You didn't come to this book because everything is good in your professional life. You came because these are times of upheaval, crisis, and change. Managing a successful career isn't easy, so I'm not going to waste your time.

You are somewhere in the middle of a half-century work life, in which, statistically speaking, you are likely to change jobs about every four years (not always by choice) and have three or more distinct careers.

Add an awareness that recessions causing widespread job loss rear their ugly heads every seven to ten years (I have worked in career management through five of them in the past thirty-five years), and you can see that smart career management strategies and a firm grasp of practical job search tactics are critical to your survival and happiness. *In the context of your whole work life, career management and job search skills are the most important skills you can ever develop, bar none.*

All the advice you've been given about careers—get an education, choose a career, settle down and do a good a job; patience and loyalty to the company will be rewarded with job security and life success—all the promised rewards of running straight and true have proved themselves a crock.

We live in a global economy where voracious political and corporate greed has turned your life into a disposable commodity to be used and discarded. It is time for a radical shift in your career management strategy. You need to move from hapless employee at the whim of financial currents beyond your control to enlightened professional who puts the pathway to personal success in its proper context.

What's this context? Those job changes coming round every four years or so add up to twelve or more over fifty years, with perhaps three of them involving the greater challenges concerned with career change.

This means professional change is constant; professional change is a given. You need to recognize that your career is not a fixed thing that came as a gift with the purchase of your college diploma. Instead, it's a critical aspect of your life, and it needs management. Face this and you can begin to change your situation, today and forever.

It's Time for Enlightened Self-Interest

Enlightened self-interest means placing *your* financial survival front and center in your life. I want you to start to think of yourself not as a person looking for a job, but as a company, a financial entity that must maintain a steady cash flow over half a century. Start to think of yourself as MeInc, a corporation that must always plan and act in its own best interests; in doing so, you will begin to see this job search and the management of your career in a new light.

As a corporation, MeInc has products and services that are constantly under development. These are the bundle of skills that define the *professional you* and are positioned and sold to your targeted customer base: those employers who hire people like you.

The success of MeInc depends on how well you run your company, which means that just like every successful company in the world, you must have ongoing initiatives for:

R & D: Your identification and development of products and services that will appeal to your customers. This translates to skill building in response to market trends; it also relates to your development of job search, interview, and career management skills.

Strategic Planning: The development of effective career management strategies that make you more visible and more desirable for the times when you must look for work, and strategies you pursue when employed to make your job more secure and to encourage professional growth with that company, as you continue with strategies that build your credibility and visibility within your company and profession.

Marketing and PR: The establishment of personal credibility for the services you deliver, and the positioning of these services so that your professional credibility becomes visible to an ever-widening circle of potential customers.

Sales: A state-of-the-art sales program to sell your products and services, including resume, job search, and interviewing tactics.

Now, this may or may not be your first job search, and it almost certainly won't be your last, but it can be the last one that you begin in confusion. This can be the last time you have no clear idea of your options or how best to pursue them.

In these pages you will learn how to achieve your goal of a successful and happy professional life as I show you the best ways to find job openings, effectively turn them into interviews, and transform not one but sometimes many of those interviews into job offers.

This intelligent approach to job search will not only help you land jobs but will also show you how to achieve greater success *within* each of those jobs. This book has been updated and expanded every year for more than twenty-five years, always reflecting the changing needs of the job hunter in changing times. People who used this book all those years ago tell me they still use it today. They tell me it is why they are VPs at *Fortune* 500 companies or why they own their own companies and how it changed both their sense of self and their life for the better.

This is not because *Knock 'em Dead* or any of my fourteen career books is some motivational quick fix. Instead, what this book gives you is an infinitely flexible, completely down-to-earth plan of attack for your job search, which also happens to make sense as a blueprint for a successful professional life. That just happens to be something no one else has really thought through the way I have, but then I've been at it as my chosen mission for more than thirty years. This is what I think about every day of my life: no hidden religious or political agendas, just me talking to you, using all my insights about work and careers to help you get out of a tough spot in your life and into a better place for the future, so you understand how it works and how to play the game.

No one ever thought to give it to you straight. I will because I understand, and I care about your well-being. Change and the unexpected are constants in professional life today, and I have an intelligent approach to dealing with these issues. Follow the job search advice in these pages, and you will make that next step up the professional ladder. Follow the strategic career management advice in these pages and you will be in far greater control of your destiny.

I update this *Knock 'em Dead* book every year because too much of what I find online and in bookstores lacks real insight into vitally important issues: your financial survival and success.

Twenty-five years and millions of copies later, *Knock 'em Dead* has become a time-tested and proven commodity both here in America and in many countries around the world. If you want to make sense of your career, I have a carefully coordinated approach for making this job search and your professional life a success, and I'm here to help.

Sincerely,
—**Martin Yate, CPC**

PART I
THE WELL-STOCKED BRIEFCASE

THIS SECTION WILL show you how to discover, define, and package your skills, and how to put together a comprehensive plan of attack that uses all the most effective job search techniques.

ONCE UPON A TIME, long ago, there lived a man who spent his days watching life go by. He lived in a town ravaged by bears, and one of his dreams was that if he could shoot bears, he could travel the world as a bear slayer. Every day he sat on his porch and waited for a bear to go by. After weeks of watching and waiting, he thought he might go looking for bears.

He didn't know much about them, except that they were out there somewhere. Full of hope, he loaded his musket, and headed for the edge of the forest, raised his rusty old single-shot musket, and fired into the trees. Then, disappointed, he went back to sit on the porch.

Because our hero couldn't tell dreams from reality, he went hunting unprepared and earned exactly what he deserved: nothing. The moral is: when you go bear—or job—hunting, get a grip on reality, and don't go off half-cocked.

Out there in the forest of the professional world are countless opportunities. Even in times of severe economic downturn—and remember they are cyclical and likely to come by every seven to ten years throughout your career—there are always jobs out there. Yes, they are harder to find, and yes, the competition is tougher, but someone is going to find those jobs and land those job offers. It can be you.

All companies share two things in common: They are in business to make money; and things go wrong, so they hire problem solvers to fix them. This is an important life lesson. Think about your current job; you were hired to cope with certain problems within your area of expertise: to *anticipate* and *prevent* them from arising and when they cannot be prevented, to *solve* them. At some elemental level, *everyone, in every profession and at every level, is paid to be a problem solver.* There are three lessons you should take away from this:

Lesson One: Companies are in business to make money; they have loyalty only to the bottom line. They make money by sales and by being efficient and saving time. If they save time, they save money and have more time to make more money; we call this productivity.

Lesson Two: Companies and MeInc are exactly alike. You both want to make as much money as possible in as short a time as possible: Think efficient systems and procedures, and *multitasking* (time management and organization). Think of focus and goal, not task and activity.

Lesson Three: There are buyer's markets (advantage: employer) and there are seller's markets (advantage: employee). Job offers put you in a seller's market and give you the whip hand.

Lesson One tells you the three things every company is interested in. Lesson Two teaches you to recognize that MeInc has the same goals as any company. Lesson Three reminds you that anyone with any sense wants to be in a seller's market.

If you look for jobs one at a time, you put yourself in a buyer's market; if you implement my advice in *Knock 'em Dead*, you can generate multiple job offers (even in a tough economy) and put yourself in a seller's market. This means making sure MeInc is ready with a properly packaged product and integrated sales process.

In this first part of the book you will:

- Learn to evaluate market needs and package your professional skills for those needs.
- Discover how to identify *every* company in your target location that could be in need of your services.
- Get connected to the most influential people in your profession, so that you'll have personal introductions at many prospective companies.
- Implement an integrated job search plan of attack.

While I will cover each of these areas in sequence, I recommend that you mix and match the activities. In other words, when working on your resume starts to drive you nuts, switch to researching your target market, or building your professional networks. An hour of one activity followed by an hour of another will keep your mind fresh and your program balanced.

CHAPTER 1

THE REALITIES OF A JOB SEARCH

JOB SEARCH ISN'T nanotechnology; you'll find a commonsense logic in everything I show you and wonder why you didn't see it before. You can get your job search moving onto a new trajectory this week, and reap the rewards for the rest of your career. You can do this.

Everyone feels crappy when they are looking for a job—you aren't the only one—but while there used to be a stigma about looking for a job, times have changed. Job change is an integral part of modern life. It comes around about every four years, making change and job search a constant factor for everyone.

Because everyone understands this, once you organize and follow the plan of attack, you will find many, many people are ready to give you a helping hand if they can.

We live and work in a time of immense change. When you were born, there still existed a world in which hard work, dedication, and sacrifice led to long-term job security and a steady, predictable climb up the ladder of success. The world you now work in is entirely different: Companies still expect hard work, dedication, and sacrifice, but their only loyalty is to the profit imperative. You are expendable.

Different times require different strategies for today's job search and for your long-term career success. The job security and professional growth our parents were raised to expect as the norm is a thing of the past. Here are the realities you're facing, expressed in numbers:

50–4–3–7–10
A **50**-year work life
Job change about every **4** years
3 or more distinct careers
Economic downturns every **7–10** years

KNOCK 'EM DEAD TIP

Changing careers at the same time as you change jobs adds another level of complexity to the process because you are leaving behind many of the skills that usually help you land that new job. If a career change is part of your job search—for example, if you are changing from a career in finance to one in education—go to Career Management Issues on the *Knock 'em Dead* website, *www.knockemdead.com*. Read the additional commentary you find on those pages and then come back to this page and proceed.

Integrate the job search advice into the long-term career management plan I outline in these pages and you need never again be caught flat-footed, urgently needing a job to put food on the table.

Along the way, we'll discuss many long-term career management initiatives that are also essential parts of your job search plan of attack. For example, you'll learn about credibility, visibility, and professional branding. These are all issues that can have great impact on your job search and even greater impact on your long-term career management initiatives.

Not surprisingly, the process starts with your resume. The resume creation process helps you focus on the job you want and package your skills effectively. It's the first step in turning your dreams into realities, and as you'll see, the resume techniques you'll learn in Chapter 3 to help you land a new job can also be leveraged to get you promotions on that job; but first things first.

How Business Works

Companies exist to make money for the owners, as quickly, efficiently, and reliably as possible. They make money by selling a product or service, and they prosper by becoming better and more efficient at it. When a company saves time, it saves money, and then has more time to make more money; this is called productivity.

If a company can make money without employees, it will do so, because that means more money for the owners. Unfortunately for the owners, a company requires a complex machinery to deliver those products and services that bring in revenue. You can think of any and every job as a small but important cog in this complex moneymaking machine, and every cog has to be oiled and maintained; this costs money. If the company can redesign its machinery to do without that cog (automation) or can find a cheaper cog (outsourcing that job to Mumbai), of course it is going to do so.

There are two reasons jobs exist. First, as I've said, every job is a small but important cog in the corporation's complex moneymaking machine: It exists to help the company make money. Second, the company hasn't been able to automate that job out of existence because in your area of technical expertise, problems arise.

Consequently, the company hires someone who has the *technical skills* to solve the problems that typically occur within an area of specific expertise. The company hopes to hire someone who knows the territory well enough to predict these problems and prevent many of them from arising in the first place.

It doesn't matter what your job title is, you are always hired to be a problem solver with a specific area of expertise. Think about the nuts and bolts of any job you've held: At its heart, that job is chiefly concerned with the *anticipation, identification, prevention, and solution of problems*. This enables the company to make money for its owners, as quickly, efficiently, and reliably as possible.

These aren't the only factors that are critical to your success and that all jobs have in common. In the next chapter you'll learn about a specific set of *transferable skills* and *professional values* that all employers are anxious to find in candidates, whom they then hire and promote just as quickly as they can find them.

CHAPTER 2
THE TRANSFERABLE SKILLS AND PROFESSIONAL VALUES THAT GUARANTEE A SUCCESSFUL JOB SEARCH AND CAREER

THERE ARE A SERIES of *transferable skills* and *professional values* that are admired by employers the world over. Referred to as *transferable skills* because they can be applied in any job and at any level, and as *professional values* because they describe habits and priorities that translate to any career and job title, they are at the heart of all professional success.

In fact, the predominance of behavioral interviewing techniques used in job interviews is due to their ability to determine your possession of these *transferable skills*. This is a topic we will address thoroughly and on which you will become an expert by the end of the book.

Transferable Skills and *Professional Values*

As you learn about the *transferable skills* and *professional values* that all employers seek in all employees and that identify those people who will become most successful in the professional world, four things will happen:

1. When you identify one of these *transferable skills* or *professional values* as something you possess, you will integrate it into your *personal brand*. It will appear in your resume and become a conscious part of everything you do in your professional life.
2. When you identify one of these *transferable skills* or *professional values* as something that you *do not* possess or that needs development, it should immediately become part of your professional development program.
3. These skills and values underlie your long-term survival and success; you will develop *all of them* and ensure that they are reflected in your attitude to your career. This is going to set you apart from the vast majority of your competitors in this job hunt.
4. These skills are the building blocks of success, and this awareness will positively impact the success of your career as you move forward through the years.

Although they can be developed in school or in almost any activity to which you are dedicated to doing well, the *transferable skills* and *professional values* that are most desirable to employers are largely developed as a result of your experiences in the workplace. Remember that first day on your first job, when you eventually got up the courage to go forage for a cup of coffee? You found the coffee machine, and there was a handwritten sign stuck on the wall reading:

YOUR MOTHER DOESN'T WORK HERE
PICK UP AFTER YOURSELF

You thought, "Pick up after myself? Gee, that means I can't behave like I do at home and get away with it," and so you started to observe and emulate the more successful professionals around you. You behaved in a way that was appropriate to the environment, and in so doing you demonstrated *emotional intelligence*. Over time, you developed many new ways of conducting yourself at work in order to be accepted as a professional in your field. You weren't born this way. You developed a behavioral profile, a *professional persona* that enabled you to survive in the professional world.

Some people are just better than the average bear at everything they do, and they become more successful as a result. It doesn't happen by accident; it is a result of their having acquired the set of *transferable skills* and *professional values* that underlies professional success: skills and values that employers all over the world in every industry and profession are anxious to find in candidates from the entry level to the boardroom. Why this isn't taught in schools and in the university programs that cost a small fortune is unfathomable, because these skills and values are the foundation of every successful career. They break down into these groups:

1. *The Technical Skills of Your Current Profession.* These are the technical competencies that give you the *ability* to do your job—those skills needed for a task and the know-how to use them productively and efficiently.

   These *technical skills* are mandatory if you want to land a job within your profession. *Technical skills*, while transferable, vary from profession to profession, so many of your current *technical skills* will only be transferable within your current profession.

2. *Transferable Skills That Apply in All Professions.* This set of skills underlies your ability to execute the *technical skills* of your job effectively, whatever that job might be. They are the foundation of all the professional success you will experience in this and any other career (including dream and entrepreneurial careers) that you may pursue over the years.

3. *Professional Values.* These are a set of beliefs that enable all professionals to make the many judgment calls required during the working day to ensure that the best interests of the department and the employer are always promoted. They complement the *transferable skills* and together form a firm foundation for a successful professional life.

A Review of Transferable Skills and Professional Values

As you read through the following breakdown of each *transferable skill* and *professional value*, consider your own varying strengths and weaknesses. You may, for example, read about *communication*, and think, "Yes, I can see how communication skills are important in all jobs and at all levels of the promotional ladder, and, hallelujah, I have good communication skills." Take time to recall examples of your *communication skills* and the role they play in the success of your work.

You might also read about *multitasking skills* and realize that you need to improve in that area. Whenever you identify a *transferable skill* that needs work, you have found a *professional development project* improving that skill. Your attention to those areas will repay you for the rest of your working life, no matter how you make a living.

Here are the *transferable skills* and *professional values* that will speed the conclusion of this job search and your long-term professional success. You'll find that you already have some of them to a greater or lesser degree, and if you are committed to making a success of your life, you'll commit to further development of all of them.

Transferable Skills

Technical
Critical Thinking
Communication
Multitasking
Creativity
Teamwork
Leadership

Professional Values

Motivation and Energy
Commitment and Reliability
Determination
Pride and Integrity
Productivity and Economy
Systems and Procedures

Transferable Skills

Technical

The *technical skills* of your profession are the foundation of all success; without them you won't even land a job, much less succeed in your career. Technical skills speak to your *ability* to do the job, those essentials necessary for success in the day-to-day execution of your duties. It means you know which skills and tools are needed for a particular task and possess the know-how to use them productively and efficiently. These *technical skills* vary from profession to profession and do not necessarily refer to anything technical *per se* or to technology skills.

However, it is a given that one of the *technical skills* essential to every job is technological adaptivity. You must be proficient in all computer- and Internet-based applications relevant to your work. Even when you are not working in a technology field, strong *technology skills* will enhance stability and help you leverage professional growth.

When people are referred to as "professionals," it means they possess the appropriate *technical* and *technology skills* necessary for success in their profession and have interwoven them with the other major *transferable skills*. Staying current with the essential *technical* and *technology skills* of your chosen career path through ongoing professional education is going to be an integral part of your growth and stability. That's why the education section toward the end of your resume can be an important tool in developing your *professional brand*: It speaks to your technical competence and your commitment, exemplified by your continuing pursuit of professional skills.

According to a recent study by a recruitment metrics company, 60 percent of the jobs available by 2015 will require skills held by 20 percent of the population. Technology constantly changes the nature of our jobs and the ways in which they are executed. As a result, if you want to stay employable, you need to stay current with the skills most prized in your professional world.

In addition to the *technical skills* that are specific to your job or profession, there is a body of skills that transcend industry lines. These skills will not only enhance your employability in your current profession but will ease your transition should you ever change your career—something that the statistics say you will do three or more times over the span of your work life.

Employers are always on the lookout for employees who, in addition to the must-haves of the job, possess the *written communication skills* to write a PR piece or a training manual; who know how to structure and format a proposal; who are able to stand up and make presentations; or who know how to research, analyze, and assimilate hard-to-access data.

Some of the *transferable technical skills* sought across a wide spectrum of jobs include:

- Selling skills: Even in non-sales jobs, the art of persuasive communication is always appreciated, because no matter what the job, you are always selling something to someone.
- Project management skills
- Six Sigma skills
- Lean Management skills
- Quantitative analysis skills
- Theory development and conceptual thinking skills
- Counseling and mentoring skills
- Customer Resource Management (CRM) skills
- Research skills
- Social networking skills

There are also *technology skills* that have application within all professions in our technology-driven world. It is pretty much a given that you need to be computer literate to hold down any job today, as just about every job expects competency with Microsoft Word and e-mail. Similarly, Excel and PowerPoint are becoming skills it is risky not to possess.

Any employer is going to welcome a staff member who knows his way around spreadsheets and databases, who can update a webpage, or who is knowledgeable in CRM.

Some of the *technology skills* that enhance employability on nontechnological jobs include:

- Database management
- Spreadsheet creation
- Word processing
- Building and designing of presentations
- E-mail and social media communication

Eventually, more and more of these skills will become specific requirements of the jobs of the future, but until then, possession of these skills will add a special sauce to your candidacy for any job.

You can find useful links for professional development at:
www.knockemdead.com
www.mindtools.com/pages/main/newMN_ISS.htm
www.mindtools.com/page8.html
www.mindtools.com/pages/main/newMN_TED.htm

Communication

Without *communication,* you live in silence and isolation. With *communication,* you make things happen in your life.

As George Bernard Shaw said, "The greatest problem in communication is the illusion that it has been accomplished." Every professional job today requires *communication skills*; promotions and professional success are impossible without them. Good verbal *communication skills* enable you to accurately process incoming information and also to present outgoing information persuasively and appropriately to your audience and message, so that it is understood and accepted.

But *communication* embraces much more than listening and speaking. When the professional world talks about *communication skills*, it is referring to four primary skills and four supportive skills.

The primary *communication skills* are:

- Verbal skills—what you say and how you say it.
- Listening skills—listening to understand, rather than just waiting your turn to talk.
- Writing skills—clear written communication, essential for any professional career. It creates a lasting impression of who you are.
- Technological communication skills—the way you communicate and your ability to navigate the new communication media.

The four supportive *communication skills* are subtler, but, nevertheless, they impact every interaction you have with others. They are:

- Grooming and dress—they tell others who you are and how you feel about yourself.
- Social graces—these are demonstrated by how you behave around others. If your table manners are sketchy, odds are you'll never sit at the CEO's table or represent your organization at the higher levels.
- Body language—this displays how you're feeling deep inside, a form of communication mankind learned before speech. For truly effective communication, what your mouth says must be in harmony with what your body says.
- Emotional IQ—your emotional maturity in dealing with other adults in professional settings.

Develop effective *communication skills* in all these areas and you'll gain enormous control over what you can achieve, how you are perceived, and what happens in your life.

You can check out resources for developing each of these skills at *www.knockemdead.com*.

Verbal Skills

www.wordsmith.org/awad/index.html
www.mindtools.com/page8.html
www.stress.about.com/od/relationships/ht/healthycomm.htm

Listening Skills

www.mindtools.com/CommSkll/ActiveListening.htm

Writing Skills

www.collegeboard.com/student/plan/boost-your-skills/123.html
www.mindtools.com/CommSkll/WritingSkills.htm
www.smashingmagazine.com/2009/06/28/50-free-resources-that-will-improve-your-writing-skills/
www.essortment.com/all/howtoimprovew_rgka.htm

Body Language

www.helpguide.org/mental/eq6_nonverbal_communication.htm#improving
www.positivityblog.com/index.php/2007/09/10/how-to-improve-your-social-skills/

Social Graces

www.windowscollective.net/social_graces.html

Dress and Grooming

www.tips.learnhub.com/lesson/2800-tips-on-business-dress-etiquette-and-grooming
   (guys, remember to scroll down)
www.womeninbusiness.about.com/od/businessattireforwomen/Business_Attire_for_Women.htm
www.deed.state.mn.us/cjs/dress.htm
www.positivelyminnesota.com/JobSeekers/Creative_Job_Search_Guide/The_Job_Interview/Communicate_Your_Best_Image.aspx

Emotional Intelligence

www.psychology.about.com/lr/emotional_intelligence/337325/1/

Critical Thinking

You know to come in from the rain, right? Then you know *critical thinking* impacts everything you do in life.

Life and the world of work are full of opportunity, and every one of those opportunities is peppered with problems. With *critical thinking skills,* you can turn those opportunities into achievement, earnings, and fulfillment. This is the professional-world application of all those problem-solving skills you've been developing since grade school: a systematic approach to uncovering all the issues related to a particular challenge that will lead to its solution.

Critical thinking, analytical, or problem-solving skills allow the successful professional to think through logically and clearly define a challenge and its desired solutions and then evaluate and implement the best solution for that challenge from all available options.

You examine the problem and ask the critical questions:

- What's the problem?
- Who is it a problem for?
- Why is it a problem?
- What is causing this problem?
- What are the options for a solution?
- What problems might a given solution create?
- What is the most suitable solution?

You look through the factors affecting each possible solution and decide which solutions to keep and which to disregard. You look at the solution as a whole and use your judgment as to whether to use it or not. Once you have decided on a course of action, you plan out the steps, the timing, and the resources to make it happen.

- How long will it take to implement this solution?
- How much will it cost?
- What resources will I need?
- Can I get these resources?
- Will the solution really resolve the problem to everyone's benefit?
- Will this solution cause its own problems?

Einstein said that if he had one hour to save the world, he would spend fifty-five minutes defining the problem. It's a thought worth remembering, because a properly defined problem always leads to a better solution, and 50 percent of the success of any project is in the prep. *Critical thinking* is an integral part of preparation.

Check out these links to learn more about developing your *critical thinking skills*:

www.litemind.com/problem-definition/
www.mindtools.com/pages/main/newMN_TED.htm
www.mindtools.com/pages/main/newMN_TMC.htm
www.virtualsalt.com/crebook3.htm

Multitasking (Time Management and Organization)

With *multitasking* (time management and organization) *skills,* you can bring your dreams to life. Without them, you will forever spin in underachieving circles. There are two types of people in the world: the task-oriented, who let tasks expand to fill all the time allotted to them, and the goal-oriented, who organize and prioritize and strive to get all work completed in an orderly manner and as quickly and efficiently as quality will allow. Sometimes the only difference between these two types is that one group learned how to *multitask.* You get one guess as to who has the most successful and fulfilled life. The ability to *multitask* increases productivity; this ability is based on the sensible expedient of ordering your activities based on their priorities, the time of day, and consistently efficient use of every moment of your time. The people who do this, often characterized as high achievers and goal-oriented because they get so much done, are just people who have learned how to organize themselves and consequently work with more purpose. The result is that they can *multitask* and seriously outperform their peers.

If you're effective at *multitasking*, you make a *To Do* list, then prioritize each task with an A, B, or C:

- The As absolutely must be done today. "A" priority activities always get your full attention; the other activities fill in around them. Just remember, your boss's priority is *always* your priority!
- It would be good to get the Bs done today. These are the first activities to fill in around your A priorities.
- C items need to get done, but they're either not urgent or are someone else's priority, not yours. These fill in odd moments unless approaching deadlines move them to B status.

Having a physical *To Do* list handy means you always have work to do, and referring to it keeps you maximally productive and on-track. Make a habit of this for twenty-one days and you will see *big* changes in your productivity.

Another *multitasking* technique that encourages productivity without increasing effort is the Daily Plan/Do/Review cycle. Always set aside time at the end of the day to review what happened:

- What went well and why?
- What didn't go so well, and what can you do about it?
- What new projects have landed on your desk?
- What is their A/B/C priority?

Look at each "A" priority separately and identify exactly where you will jump in on this project tomorrow, what you hope to achieve, and the tools you'll need to do so. "A" priorities frequently include large and complex projects, so where will you begin? Break the big task into smaller action steps, things that you can get done tomorrow. This skill is at the very heart of your ability to achieve professional success. Developing *multitasking* (time management and organization) *skills* enables you to do the things you have to do when they ought to be done in an organized and professional manner. Check out this link to learn more about developing this skill, and how it relates to resume, job search, and other career management issues: *www.mindtools.com/pages/main/newMN_HTE.htm.*

Creativity

There's a difference between *creativity* and just having ideas. Ideas are like headaches: We all get them once in awhile, and, like headaches, they usually disappear as mysteriously as they arrived. *Creativity*, on the other hand, is the ability to develop those ideas and the strategic and tactical know-how that brings them to life.

Creativity in the professional context is the generation of new ideas as they relate to a specific situation, challenge, or goal. It is a skill that can be learned and applied to anything you do in life. The ability to bring life to your professional *creativity* comes from:

- Your *critical thinking* skills, applied within an area of technical expertise.
- Your *multitasking* (time management and organization) *skills,* which combine with your *critical thinking skills* and *technical* expertise, enable you to break down your challenge into specific steps, each one of which is small enough that some meaningful progress can be made on them today.
- Your *communication skills,* which allow you to explain your approach and its component building blocks persuasively to your target audience.
- Your *teamwork skills,* which are a factor whenever others are needed to bring the idea to fruition.
- Your *leadership skills* come into play as you bring your new ideas forward.

Creative approaches to challenges can take time or can come fully formed in a flash, but the longer you work on developing the supporting skills that bring *creativity* to life, the more often they *will* come fully formed and in a flash.

Here are five rules for building *creativity* skills:

1. Whatever you do in life, engage in it fully. Commit to developing competence in everything you do, because the wider your frame of reference for the world around you, the higher octane fuel you have to propel your ideas to acceptance and reality.
2. Learn something new every day. Treat the pursuit of knowledge as a way of life. Absorb as much as you can about everything. Information exercises your brain and fills your

mind with the ever-widening frame of reference that allows you to make creative connections where others won't see them.

3. Catch ideas as they occur. Note them in your smartphone or on a scrap of paper. Anything will do, so long as you capture the idea.

4. Welcome restrictions in your world. They encourage creativity: Ask any successful writer, artist, musician, or business leader. Restrictions in time, money, or resources are all negative in initial impact, but they become the realities under which you must operate. Consequently, the professional defines those restrictions very carefully and then proceeds with the work under these new guidelines. From a production point of view (and creativity is all about giving abstract ideas some concrete form), restrictions make you think harder about the essentials and building blocks of your task. When you can take complex ideas and reduce them to their elemental parts, you have a real understanding of that task. Similarly, restrictions increase the need for simplicity in design, function, and expression, and simplicity leads to elegance no matter the project at hand. Restrictions are part of life; you can whine or suck it up and get on with the job.

5. Don't spend your life glued to Facebook or TV. You need to live life, not watch it go by out of the corner of your eye. If you do watch television, try to learn something or motivate yourself with science, history, or biography programming. If you surf the Internet, do it with purpose.

Building *creativity* skills enables you to bring your dreams to life; and the development of each of these interconnected *transferable skills* will help you do it.

Teamwork

If you become a successful leader one day, it will be due to the fact that you were a great *team player* first; that's the way it works. The professional world revolves around the complex challenges of making money, and such challenges require teams of people to provide ongoing solutions. This, in turn, demands that you work efficiently and respectfully with others who have totally different responsibilities, backgrounds, objectives, and areas of expertise.

Teamwork asks that a commitment to the team and its success come first. This means you take on a task because it needs to be done, not because it makes you look good. The payback, of course, is that management always recognizes and appreciates a *team player*.

As a *team player* you:

• Always cooperate.
• Always make decisions based on team goals.

- Always keep team members informed.
- Always keep commitments.
- Always share credit, never share blame.

Teamwork skills are especially important if you intend to be a leader, because all successful leaders need to first understand the critical dynamics of *teamwork*. It is only by being a *team player* that you will understand the subtleties of what makes a team pull together and function productively as a unit, and how to recognize and encourage those who display a team spirit; so if you intend to be a leader, learn to be a *team player*.

Check out this link to learn more about developing your *teamwork skills*: *www.hku.hk/cepc/taccasu/ref/teamwk.htm*

Leadership

"A leader has two important characteristics; first, he is going somewhere; second, he is able to persuade other people to go with him." The guy who said this, Maximilien Robespierre, was a principal figure in the French Revolution and literally changed the world. As you develop *teamwork* skills, which is a must if you ever hope to lead, notice how you are willing to follow true leaders and how you don't fall in line with people who don't respect you and who don't have your best interests at heart.

When you are credible, when people believe in your competence and believe you have everyone's success as your goal, those people will follow you; you accept responsibility, but "we" gets the credit. When your actions inspire others to think more, learn more, do more, and become more, you are on your way to becoming a leader.

Leadership is the most complex of all the *transferable skills* that you will develop to make a success of your professional work life. It is a combination and outgrowth of all the other *transferable skills*:

- Your job as a leader is to make your team function, so your *teamwork skills* give you the smarts to pull your team together as a cohesive unit.
- Your *technical* expertise, *critical thinking*, and *creativity skills* help you correctly define the challenges and their solutions.
- Your *communication skills* enable your team to understand the task and its goals; there's nothing more demoralizing than a leader who can't clearly articulate why we're doing what we're doing.
- Your *multitasking* (time management and organization) *skills* enable you to create a practical blueprint for success, and they help your team to take ownership of the task and deliver the expected results.

Leaders aren't born; they are self-made. And just like anything else, it takes hard work. That's the price you pay to achieve this or any other serious goal.

For advice on how to further develop this skill, check out the following links:

www.mindtools.com/pages/main/newMN_LDR.htm
www.crfonline.org/orc/ca/ca-2.html
www.top7business.com/?id=2113
www.businessballs.com/leadership.htm
www.career-success-for-newbies.com/developing-leadership-skills.html

Professional Values

Motivation and Energy

Employers realize that a *motivated* professional will do a better job on every assignment. *Motivation* expresses itself in a commitment to the job and the profession, an eagerness to learn and grow professionally, and a willingness to take the rough with the smooth.

Motivation is invariably expressed by the *energy* you demonstrate in your work. You always give that extra effort to get the job done right.

Commitment and Reliability

Commitment to your job, to making a difference with your presence every day, to your company and profession, to the role your job plays in the larger issues of company success, and the empowerment that comes from knowing how your part contributes to the greater good . . . these are desirable *professional values*.

Commitment is also a demonstration of enlightened self-interest. The more you are engaged in your career, the more likely you are to join the inner circles that exist in every department and company, enhancing opportunities for advancement. At the same time, this dedication will repay you with better job security and improved professional horizons.

Your *commitment* expresses itself in your *reliability*. Showing up is half the battle; the other half is your performance on the job. This requires following up on your actions—not relying on anyone else to ensure the job is done and done well—and it also speaks to your reliability as a *team player* committed to the greater good of the team.

Determination

Your *determination* speaks of a resilient professional who doesn't get worn down or back off when a problem or situation gets tough. It's a value that marks you as someone who chooses to be part of the solution rather than standing idly by and being part of the problem.

The *determined* professional has decided to make a difference with his presence every day, because it is the *right* thing to do.

The *determined* professional is willing to do whatever it takes to get a job done, even if that includes duties that might not appear in her job description.

Pride and Integrity

Pride in yourself as a professional means always making sure the job is done to the best of your ability; this, in turn, means paying attention to details and to time and cost constraints. *Integrity* means taking responsibility for your actions, both good and bad, and it also means treating others, within and outside of the company, with respect at all times and in all situations. With *pride* in yourself as a professional with *integrity*, your actions will always be in the ethical best interests of the company, and your decisions will never be based on whim or personal preference.

Productivity and Economy

Always work toward enhanced *productivity* through efficiencies of time, resources, money, and effort. Most problems have two solutions, and the expensive one isn't always the best. Ideas of efficiency and *economy* engage the *creative* mind in ways that others would not consider.

Systems and Procedures

This is a natural outgrowth of all the other *transferable skills* and *professional values*. Your *commitment* to your profession in all these ways gives you an appreciation of the need for *systems and procedures* and their implementation only after careful thought. You understand and always follow the chain of command. You don't implement your own "improved" procedures or encourage others to do so. If ways of doing things don't make sense or are interfering with *economy* and *productivity*, you work through the system to get them changed.

Long-Term Security and Success

Development of *transferable skills* and *professional values* supports your enlightened self-interest, because honing them will repay you with better job security and improved professional horizons. Anyone seen to embody these *transferable skills* and *professional values* in their professional persona will be known and respected as a consummate professional. The more you are engaged in your career and the more effective you become because of your *transferable skills* and *professional values*, the more likely you are to join the inner circles that exist in every department and company; and that's where the plum assignments, raises, and promotions live.

That you have these admirable traits is one thing; that *I* know you have them, well, that's another matter. You need to:

- Develop these skills and values.
- Make them a living dimension of your *professional brand*.
- Understand how each enables you to do every aspect of your job just that little bit better.
- Reference them subtly in your resume and other written communications.
- Reference them appropriately in your meetings with employers as the underlying skills that enable you to do your work well.

Examples of your application of these skills or the impact of these values on your work can be used in your resume, cover letters, and as illustrative answers to questions in interviews. But most important, when these skills become a part of you, they will bring greater success to everything you do.

CHAPTER 3
HOW TO BUILD A KILLER RESUME

YOUR CURRENT RESUME doesn't work, and here's how to fix it.

*Y*our resume is the most financially important document you will ever own. When it works, the doors of opportunity open for you. When it doesn't work, you don't either, so writing that resume is a job that deserves your full attention. Your resume establishes an achievable goal for your search, opens the doors of opportunity for interviews, prepares you for the questions interviewers will ask, and acts as a powerful ambassador at decision time.

A good resume is not simply a recitation of all the things you have done in your work life. In fact, if your resume is just recitation of all the things you happen to think important, it is likely sitting unread in countless resume databases.

The impact of technology on the workplace causes the nature of all jobs to change almost as rapidly as the pages on a calendar. In the not-so-distant past, someone would have reviewed your resume almost as soon as it was received. Today, resumes no longer go straight to a recruiter or manager's desk; they are more likely to go to a resume database. This means that before a human being reviews your resume, it must be chosen from that resume database as worth reviewing. Since some of those databases contain over 30 million resumes, you can see that decrepit old resume needs a complete overhaul.

Recruitment and Resume Banks

When recruiters access resume databases, they always do so with a specific Job Description (JD) in mind. This is important to know, since:

1. Job postings invariably reflect the exact wording of the Job Descriptions they come from, so these postings contain the words and phrases the company uses throughout the recruitment and selection cycle.
2. Consequently, these are the words and phrases recruiters use when searching resume databases.

Here's how the process works: You and I want to hire an accountant, so, among other resources, we might look in the CareerBuilder.com database. To access the database, we need to define the job title, so we type "accountant" into the dialogue box, specify a location, and click on the keywords (supplied by most resume banks) that we feel best describe that job. We also add words of our own that do not appear in the keyword choices.

Once programmed to search for a specific set of words, the software scours the database and builds a list of all the resumes that contain *any* of those descriptors or keywords. It then weights the list. Those resumes with the most frequent use *and* greatest total number of keywords rise to the top of the list. Mentioning keywords in a Core Competency section at the front of your resume, and then repeating them within the context of the jobs in which they were used, *doubles* your keyword count.

This is the *first* keyword test your resume *must* pass: Because *recruiters very rarely go beyond the top twenty resumes in a database search*, not enough relevant keywords means that no human will review it.

The *second* keyword test your resume *must* pass is when your resume gets in front of recruiters' eyes. The first scan takes about fifteen seconds. No relevant keywords/phrases likely means no second read.

The next read is a little more careful. The reviewers are *looking to see if the resume's claims really hang together and tell the story of the job they are trying to fill*. Recruiters and HR typically plow through enough resumes to create a "long list" of up to six candidates.

Here it may land in front of the manager who actually has the authority to hire you, but: *Managers hate reading resumes*—they just want to hire someone and get back to work. You get that? *Managers hate reading resumes—they just want to hire someone and get back to work.*

In fact, no one likes to read resumes; try reading six of them in a row and feel your brain melting into a gelatinous goop. Bear this in mind, because we will use it to great advantage.

Only those resumes that pass these tests get a more thoughtful reading, one that carefully evaluates the resume against the JD's requirements; this is the first time your credentials are seen as representing a living, breathing human being.

A resume that tries to cram in everything you have done without any real focus is doomed to fail any and all of these initial hurdles, and failure at any of these points means no interviews and no job offers. So you can continue doing the same unproductive activities, or you can rethink your approach.

Get Inside the Employer's Head

Fortunately, after much thought I have devised something that I feel is nothing short of a life-changing solution to this huge challenge: Before writing your resume, you are going to get inside the employer's head and examine what she looks for when hiring. What I am going to show you will deliver:

- A template for the story your resume *must* tell to be successful
- An objective tool against which to evaluate your resume's performance
- A complete understanding of where the focus will be at interviews
- A very good idea of the questions that will be heading your way and why
- Relevant examples with which to illustrate your answers
- A behavioral profile for getting hired and for professional success throughout your career
- A behavioral profile for not getting hired and for ongoing professional failure

Start with Simple Common Sense

Your resume will always be more effective if it begins with a clear focus on, and understanding of, a specific target job. When you have this focus you can look backward into your work history for those experiences that best position you for the target job. This will enable you to tailor a killer resume.

The big question is: how do you do this? The answer is what I call the Target Job Deconstruction process.

Target Job Deconstruction (TJD)

Step #1 Decide on a Primary Target Job

Focus on a specific and realistic target job, one in which you can succeed based on the skills you possess today. Some people think you change jobs to get a promotion, but this is largely incorrect, especially in a tight job market. *People get hired based on their credentials, not their potential.* Most people don't get promotions to the next step up the professional ladder when they change jobs, because that would mean coming onboard as an unknown quantity in a job they've never done.

Typically, most professionals accept a position similar to the one they have now, but one that offers opportunity for growth once they have proved themselves. The most common exception is an employee already doing that higher-level job but without the title recognition. Also, sometimes you can combine experience and credentials from a number of jobs into a new configuration. This is always more likely to happen when the economy is on the upswing. In down economies, there are just too many thoroughly qualified candidates for an employer to warrant the risk, because with every hire the hiring manager's performance comes under scrutiny.

So of all the jobs you can do—and we can all do more than one—decide on the one that will be *the easiest sell for you and the easiest buy for the employer.* This will be:

  • A job you can do and that you can justify on paper
  • A job you can convince skilled interviewers that you can do
  • A job in which you can succeed

Let's look at "a job in which you can succeed." The ability to do 70 percent or more of the job will usually get you in the running for the selection cycle in any economy. You'll be able to deliver on the job's requirements and have room for professional growth, making such a target job a good choice. Less than this and you may need to reconsider your target job or anticipate a longer job search to reach your goals.

If you have more than five years of experience, there are probably a couple of jobs you can do. More than fifteen years' experience, and there could be half a dozen jobs in which you can succeed. Carefully evaluate and rank these jobs based on their availability, remuneration, fulfillment, and potential for growth or shrinkage. This way you will target a "primary job" based on practicality and common sense. If you ultimately decide you want to go after that White Water Rafting Guide job because you once owned a canoe . . . well, at least you'll be doing it with your eyes open, knowing that you won't have most of the required skills, and that your search will take considerably longer.

This does not mean you cannot pursue any of those other jobs for which you have the desire or some of the qualifications. However, be sensible, create your primary resume with a single "primary target job" in mind, and make that job one you can nail!

Targeted Resumes for Different Jobs

One general resume covering all the skills you possess for all the jobs you can do doesn't work anymore; you have to have a resume focused on a single target job. This means that you have to create individual resumes for each of the different jobs you want to pursue; fortunately this isn't nearly as hard as it sounds. Once you have tailored a *primary* resume to your job search, you can quite easily customize it for any of those other jobs you are interested in. There is usually considerable overlap in the deliverables of the different jobs for which we are qualified, so you can take that primary resume, make a copy, retitle it, and make the necessary changes to give the secondary resume a specific focus. To determine what changes to make, go through the TJD process for each additional job-targeted resume and you will quickly maximize the impact potential of each one; you won't have to start from scratch, and you'll have customized resumes for each opportunity.

Step #2 Collect Job Postings

Collect a half-dozen job postings for your chosen primary target job; if you want to save some time, try one of the job aggregators, or spiders (so-called because they *crawl* the web looking for suitable jobs based on your search criteria), listed below, each of which will search thousands of job sites for you. Some are free, and some are for a fee, but they all work similarly. The home page has a couple of dialogue boxes: one for a job title and one for a geographic area. If you cannot find half a dozen jobs in your target location just try another major metropolitan area: for the purpose of TJD it doesn't matter where the jobs are located.

- *www.indeed.com*
- *www.worktree.com*
- *www.jobbankusa.com*
- *www.jobster.com*

Put them in a folder on your desktop and also print them out.

From the collected Job Descriptions we will carefully define exactly the way employers think about, prioritize, and express their needs when they consider that particular job. The result will be a template that describes your target job *the way employers themselves think about, prioritize, and describe it.*

Step #3 Look at Your Job from the Other Side of the Desk

This is where you deconstruct your collection of JDs so that you understand exactly how employers *think about, prioritize, and describe the deliverables of your job.*

1. Start a new MSWord document, and name it "Primary TJD" or something similar.
2. Under the subhead "Target Job Titles," cut and paste all the variations on the job title you are pursuing from your collection of job postings.
3. Add a second subhead entitled: "Experience/Responsibilities/Skills/Deliverables/Etc."

Review your collection of job postings and find one requirement that is common to all six; of these six choose the most complete description of that particular experience/responsibility/ skill/deliverable and paste it under the second subhead and put the number 6 in front of it to signify that it is common to all six job postings. Underneath this, list additional keywords used in the other five job postings to describe this same requirement.

For this step you may find it easier to work with the printed copies, since your kitchen counter is bigger than your computer screen ;-).

Repeat these steps for any other requirements that are common to all six of your collected job postings, placing the number 6 alongside each one.

4. Repeat this process with requirements that are common to five of the six job postings, then four of the six postings . . . and so on down the line.

At the end of this first part of the TJD process you will be able to read the document and say to yourself, *"When employers are looking for _____, these are the job titles they use; this is the order in which these needs are prioritized; these are the skills, experiences, deliverables, and professional behaviors they look for; and these are the words with which they describe the deliverables of the job."*

As you read through your TJD document, the story your resume needs to tell will be laid out before you, and some of those promises I made a few paragraphs back will begin to sound a little less like smoke and mirrors.

Step #4 Identify What's Missing

Add to your TJD any additional skills/experiences you believe are relevant to this job. There are plenty of job descriptions that don't tell the whole story. In some companies, even publicly traded multinationals, the Job Descriptions can be maddeningly vague because the company hasn't paid close enough attention to the hard skills of the job. Furthermore, in many companies, job descriptions won't go into all the nuts and bolts of a particular job because they all have to be approved by the Legal Department before they see the light of day. This is part of an overall corporate cost-containment policy designed to protect against the release of JDs that might aid individual or class-action lawsuits brought by disgruntled employees. How can I be sure of this? I used to be a director of human resources in Silicon Valley. I've overseen this process.

If you know a specific skill is mandatory for this job, feel free to add it at the bottom of your list. Job postings can also be vague or poorly thought through, which is why you collect a number of them and add responsibilities that you know belong.

KNOCK 'EM DEAD TIP

If you are new to the professional world and cannot bring personal awareness of a job's needs to the TJD process, you might want to do a little additional research to ensure that your resume has the proper focus.

For further insight into a specific target job, visit the Occupational Outlook Handbook pages at *www.bls.gov/oco/home.htm*, which give detailed analyses of hundreds of jobs. After that, talk to people who are actually doing the work and have them deconstruct the job for you along the lines discussed. Check the section on networking for ways to identify and reach out to the right people.

Step #5 Problem Solving

At their most elemental level, all jobs are the same—all jobs focus on *problem identification, prevention, and solution*; this is what we all get paid for, no matter what we do for a living.

Go back to your TJD and start with the first requirement. Think about and note the problems you will typically need to *identify, prevent, and/or solve* in the course of a normal work day as you deliver on this requirement of the job; then list specific examples, big and small, of your successful *identification, prevention, and/or solution to the problems*. Quantify your results when possible.

Repeat this with each of the TJD's other requirements by identifying the problems inherent in that particular responsibility. Some examples may appear in your resume as significant professional achievements, while others will provide you with the ammunition to answer all those interview questions that begin, "Tell me about a time when . . . ."

Step #6 Achievements

Make a list of your greatest solo professional achievements from each of the jobs you have held, quantifying the results where you can, to demonstrate the value of your work. Add to this list examples of team achievements to which you contributed.

Once you have made this list, come up with a couple of examples of projects that went wrong and couldn't be fixed; you need these to illustrate your answers to questions that might well be asked about projects that went wrong. Ideally, you want examples that are in the past, where the *going wrong* was less than catastrophic and where other people were involved, so you weren't solely responsible. In every example you must be able to illustrate what you learned from the experience.

Interviewers are fond of asking you questions about the following:

- Things that didn't work out well (but did in end)
- Things that didn't work out well ever, and what you learned
- Unpopular decisions you have had to make
- How you developed new processes (because existing ones didn't work or weren't efficient)
- How you improved something that was already working well
- How you fixed something that was broken

Being ready with appropriate answers for tough questions in these areas takes some thought. Now—as you do the TJD and as you gather information about your experience in the coming resume questionnaire—is a good time to think about examples to use in answer to these questions.

Come back to these examples as you are preparing for an interview. This may seem like a lot of work, but the better prepared you are, the more job offers you will land and the better companies you will land those job offers with.

Step #7 A Behavioral Profile for Success

Interviewers always have an image of the person they want to hire (and the person they don't). This is not about height, weight, and hair color; it's a composite behavioral profile of the best people they've known in the job. It's what hiring managers want to find and will hire when they see it.

Have you ever thought about the behavioral profile that defines success in your area of expertise and then measured yourself against it? Doing so can help you define the professional you want to be and the persona you want to show to the professional world. Not understanding how your behavior can help or hinder your success usually means that you are unwittingly sabotaging future potential.

Work your way through each of the responsibilities itemized in your TJD one by one, profiling the *best* person you ever saw doing that aspect of the job and what made her stand out. Describe how she went about the work, skills hard and soft, interaction with others, general attitude and demeanor, and anything else that sticks out in your mind about that person, and you'll get something like: *Carole Jenkins, superior communication skills, always asking questions and listening, a fine analytical mind, great professional appearance, and a nice person to work with; she'd do anything for anyone.* Do this for each one of the job's deliverables and you will have a detailed behavioral profile of the person all employers want to hire and everyone wants as a colleague: *You will have a behavioral profile that will help you land job offers and, just as important, a behavioral profile for professional success.*

Step #8 A Behavioral Profile for Failure

Now think of the *worst* person you have ever seen for each of the requirements and what made that individual stand out in such a negative way. Describe the performance, professional behaviors, interaction with others, and general attitude and demeanor of that person and you'll get something like: *Jack Dornitz, insecure, critical, passive aggressive, no social graces.* You are describing the person that all employers want to avoid and no one wants to work with; and *you will have a behavioral profile for long periods of unemployment and professional suicide.* Then compare yourself against this profile and see if there is anything you need to change or work on.

Step #9 Transferable Skills and Professional Values

The final step of the TJD is to review each of the skills/responsibilities/deliverables of the job one last time to identify which of the *transferable skills* and *professional values* help you execute your responsibilities in each of the target job's requirements.

Once you complete and review your TJD, you will have a clear idea of the way employers think about, prioritize, and express their needs for this job; you'll know what they'll need to ask about at interviews and, beyond the hard skills, exactly the person they will hire. Yes, it will take time and it would be easy to cut corners or just skip it, but this is your career and this is your life: Make the choice that is right for your long-term success and happiness.

The more immediate result will be to give you a template for the story your resume has to tell and an objective tool with which to evaluate your work. And when you apply what you learn from the TJD exercise to your professional life, it will increase your job security as it opens doors to the inner circles that exist in every department and company.

Resume Building

Once you have a clearly defined target job, you can look back into your work history and pull out the experiences that best reflect your ability to do this job. The following questionnaire will help you assemble all the data you will need for a productive resume.

You can find an electronic version of this questionnaire at *www.knockemdead.com* on the resume advice pages. The electronic document will expand to fit your needs.

Resume Questionnaire

In answering the questions, don't worry about grammar or perfect expression (that comes later), but do take the time to think about the issues. Be descriptive—don't just say you were a manager; say that you were a manager with fifty-five direct reports in Decatur and a further fifteen in Mumbai. Be specific whenever possible: Mention full budgetary responsibility (with dollar amount) plus selection, development, discipline, and termination responsibilities. Wherever you can, illustrate with real-world examples, and quantify those examples in terms of money earned or saved, time saved, and productivity improved. Round these examples down, rather than up. Always identify your role as a team member when appropriate. This makes your claims more believable.

Contact Information
Name
Address
E-mail
Home telephone *(recommend alternate #)*
Cell
Current job title
Variations on this job title
Operational area *(sales, finance, R & D, IT, supply chain, etc.)*
Industry/market sectors *(technology, pharma, financial services, etc.)*

Education and Skills
Postsecondary education *(You might not use all this but do collect it.)*

Degree	Major
Concentration	Minor
Graduation date	GPA

GPA major	Major
GPA minor	Minor
Ranking	GPA
Honors, scholarships	GPA major
Special accomplishments	GPA minor
International studies	Ranking
Degree	Honors, scholarships
Concentration	Special accomplishments
Graduation date	

Professional Education

(Ongoing professional education signals commitment to success.)

Course name
Completion date
Duration
Certification
Sponsoring organization

Professional Credentials Not Covered Elsewhere

Professional memberships and affiliations (*American Management Association, American Marketing Association, etc.*)

Organization
Leadership role

KNOCK 'EM DEAD TIP

Active membership in a professional association is a key tool for career resilience and success. If you don't know where to start, come to the association page on the Internet resources area at *www.knockemdead.com*.

Technological Skills

(*List all that apply to you.*)

No one gets ahead today without technological competence. Capture your fluency here, and update regularly. That alphabet soup of technology just might help your resume's performance in database searches.

Professional Accomplishments

(*You can also include your work on projects that resulted in copyright and patents, so long as you make clear your real contribution.*)

Awards and recognition
Public speaking/presentations
Profession-related publications
Patents and copyrights

Global Experience, Cultural Diversity Awareness

In a global economy, any exposure here is relevant, and it doesn't have to be professional in nature. That you were an Army brat and grew up in ten different countries can be a big plus. Just name the countries, not the circumstances.

Foreign Languages

Community, Civic Involvement

(*List all organizations and any special projects/activities/leadership roles.*)

Other Activities

This should include all the activities with which you fill your out-of-work hours. Your resume may include those activities that can say something positive about the professional you. For example, in sales and marketing just about all group activities show a desirable mindset. Bridge might argue strong analytical skills, and the senior executive who still plays competitive lacrosse and runs marathons is crazy not to let the world know.

Valuable Profession-Related Skills Developed Outside of Your Professional Work

Military Service

Rank
Discharge
Promotions
Decorations
Honors

Professional Development Courses

Achievements

What professional capabilities/skills do you feel have most contributed to your professional success?

What professional behaviors (analytical or *communication skills*, for example) do you feel have most contributed to your professional success?

Employment History

(To ensure a proper focus I strongly advise that you complete your TJD exercises before looking back at your work history.)

Current position	Standing (division, public, private)
Company	Industry/market sector
Employment dates	What does your company do?
Location	

EXAMPLE:

Squanto Corporation, Inc., Orlando, FL

1997 to present

$500 million company

One of the largest resort and vacation sales/development companies in the United States.

In rapid growth through international expansion, strategic M & A, industry rollup, and IPO.

EXAMPLE:

Worldwide Director of Operations, Entertainment Imaging, 1998–2006

Selected to re-engineer and revitalize this $65 million business unit with accountability for thirty-two direct reports in four cities across the United States. Established strategic vision and developed operational infrastructure. Managed Supply Chain, Logistics/Distribution, Forecasting, System Integration, Project Management, Contracts Administration, and Third-Party Site Operations.

Or, more simply:

> **EXAMPLE:**
> DryRoc, Inc. Indianapolis, IN, 2004–present
> Production Director
> Drove production for world's largest wallboard plant, with 258 employees working in multiple shifts.

Your Title

Review your TJD to identify the ways in which your job and your department as a whole are expected to contribute to the bottom line (making or saving money, improving productivity, and so on).

> **EXAMPLE:**
> Internal auditor: to contain costs by audits to ensure adherence to company policies and financial reporting procedures.

The PSRV Process

All jobs revolve around *problem identification, prevention, and solution.*

At some level every job exists for four major reasons:

1. To identify potential problems and avoid them
2. To identify and solve the problems that arise daily as an integral part of the job
3. To identify and avoid or solve the major problems that occur in every business on a regular basis
4. To identify opportunities for contributing to the bottom line

Develop examples of problem identification and opportunity initiatives, both small and large, for every job title you have held. The more you come up with the better, because they will add weight and reality to your resume and show that you think with employers' needs in mind, which will boost your resume's punch. All examples are valuable; those most relevant to your target job are most valuable.

To help you bring out the information that will be most useful to you in your resume and in interview situations, you can apply the PSRV process (you might know this as STAR—same process, different acronym).

- Identify a **Problem**.
- Envision your **Solution**, including strategy and tactics.
- Take note of the **Result** of your actions.
- Understand the **Value** of this to the company (usually in earnings or productivity enhancements).

Now describe four typical or notable problems with which you have been involved on your last (or current) job. Analyze each in terms of PSRV and include the following information:

Company
Employment dates
Location
Standing (division, public, private)
Industry sector
What does the company do?
What were you hired to do?
Title you report to
Your title
Department/unit
Leadership or membership of executive teams, project teams, or committees
Responsibilities/deliverables
Quotes, praise, and endorsements from management

Repeat the process for other employers so you have a range of examples.

Putting It All Together

The TJD process gave you a clear idea of the way employers think about, prioritize, and express their needs for this job; as such, it provided a template for the story your resume needs to tell and an objective tool with which to evaluate your work. Next you filled out the questionnaire, which helped you gather all the raw data that you will shape to match the employer priorities uncovered by the TJD. Because all jobs at their heart are about problem identification and solution, you went through your work history using the PSRV process to help identify examples of problems you have surmounted; this helps you figure out what exactly it is you've been doing for forty hours a week all these years, how it contributes to the company's bottom line, and how to pack this information into trenchant, high-impact sound bites for your resume. Now it's time to decide on a resume format that fits your work history.

Three Standard Resume Formats

There are three standard types of resume:

1. **Chronological:** The most frequently used format. Use it when your work history is stable and your professional growth is consistent within a profession. The chronological format is exactly what it sounds like: It follows your work history backward from the current job, listing companies, dates, and responsibilities.

2. **Functional:** A functional resume concentrates on the skills and responsibilities that you bring to the target job, and it de-emphasizes when, where, and how you got that experience. It is useful when changing careers, returning to the workplace or the profession after an absence, or when current responsibilities don't relate to the job you want. It is written with the most relevant experience to the job you're seeking placed first and de-emphasizes jobs, employment dates, and job titles by placing them toward the end.

3. **Combination:** A combination of chronological and functional resumes. Use this format if you have a steady work history with demonstrated growth and if you are continuing your progression within an industry or profession. It often starts with a brief performance profile, then lists job-specific skills relevant to the objective, and segues into a chronological format that lists how, where, and when these skills were acquired.

Check your resume against these six resume rules:

Rule One: Always have a target job title.

Place a target job title at the top of your resume, right after your contact information. This will help your visibility in database searches and will give human eyes an immediate focus. Use the most common job title for your target job title; because different employers use different titles for the same job, you want to use a title specific enough to put you in the running. One way you can make a job title "specifically vague" is to add the term "specialist" (Computer Specialist, Administration Specialist) or "management" (Operations Management, Financial Management).

Anna Seeger • 2567 Central Park Street • Arlington, Virginia 22205
646.555.5555 • Marcompro@gmail.com

Corporate Communications Management

Performance Profile

Strategic communications professional with . . .

Rule Two: Always have a Performance Profile or Career Summary.

Following your target job title, give a summary of your capabilities as they relate to the demands of the target job. You can title this section Career Summary or Performance Profile.

I suggest you stay away from Job Objective or Career Objective for two very good reasons:

1. Your needs will not help your ranking in the database searches.
2. At this stage no recruiter has the slightest interest in what you want.

If you do need to state a specific job objective—for example if you are at the start of your career and have absolutely no experience—follow the advice in the following paragraphs for what you should put here.

I like the new term Performance Profile for this important section of your resume because it captures the essence of the *professional you* as it relates to your TJD, and until everyone and their dog starts using the phrase it subtly positions you as a "performer" and separates you from other applicants.

No more than five lines of unbroken text, this section can be followed by a second similar paragraph or short list of bullets. Your intent is to capture your ability to do the target job. For what to put in this section, refer back to your TJD exercise and rewrite the major priorities as your Performance Profile. This will help your resume's database visibility and will create immediate resonance when read by the recruiter. Always note any bilingual skills here, since we live in a global economy.

CORPORATE COMMUNICATIONS MANAGEMENT

Performance Profile

Strategic communications professional with nine years' experience developing effective, high-impact, and cost-efficient media outreach plans for consumer, business, and policy audiences in media, entertainment, and technology practice areas. Experienced in managing corporate and crisis communications. Goal- and deadline-oriented with five years' experience managing internal and external communications team members. Adept at working with multiple teams and stakeholders.

If you are starting your career and have no relevant experience, that's okay—your chief competitors will be in the same boat. You can tilt the game in your favor by starting your objective with "The opportunity to" and then, referring back to your TJD exercise, rewriting the target job's major priorities as your job objective. This will make a big difference in your resume's productivity.

Rule Three: Always have a Core Competencies section if the list of your core skills creates a block of type longer than five lines.

Large blocks of text are less likely to be read by human eyes, especially if those eyes are older (which the hiring manager's probably are) or tired (which the hiring manager's definitely are). Depending on your skills, you may even consider a separate Technology Competencies section. This helps database visibility because it guarantees you are using the words employers use. You can repeat many of them again in the body of your resume in the context of each job in which you used them, further increasing your visibility. For the human eyes that see your resume, each word or phrase acts as a headline for a topic to be addressed at the interview and increases the odds of that interview happening.

You can also use keywords in these sections that won't fit in the body of your resume; this will result in better performance with the database spiders and bots. Here's an example of a Core Competencies section followed by a Technology Competencies section.

—CORE COMPETENCIES—

Strategic Planning ~ Full-Cycle Project Management ~ Technical & Application Standards ~ IT Governance Process ~ Technical Vision & Leadership ~ Architecture Roadmaps ~ Technical Specifications & Project Design Best Practices ~ Teambuilding & Leadership ~ Standards & Process Development

TECHNOLOGY COMPETENCIES	
Hardware	Sun Servers; HP-UX; AIX; p-Series; Windows Server
Operating Systems	Sun Solaris; AIX; HP-UX; Linux; z/OS; OS/400
Languages	C / C++; COBOL; Visual Basic; Java; Unix; Korn Shell Scripting; Perl; Assembler; SQL*Plus; RPG
Databases	Oracle; DB2; SQL Server; Microsoft Access; Informix Visio; HP Service
Applications	MQSeries; Tuxedo; CICS; Microsoft Project, Word, Excel, Outlook, PowerPoint, Sharepoint, and Visio; HP Service Desk; Provision; Telelogic Doors; Change Synergy; Rational System Architect; Rational System Developer; Visual Studio; CA Clarity; LiveLink
Other	Cobit 4.1

Rule Four: Never put salary on a resume.

It does not belong there. If salary information is requested for a specific opening, put it in your cover letter and don't tie yourself to a specific figure; give a range. If you are earning too little or too much, you could rule yourself out before getting your foot in the door. For the same reason, do not mention your desired salary. For details on developing a realistic salary range, see Chapter 22, "Negotiating the Job Offer."

Rule Five: Keep your resume focused.

The standard for resume length used to be one page for every ten years of experience, and never more than two pages. However, as jobs have gotten more complex, they require more explanation. The length of your resume is less important than its relevance to the target job. If the first page of your resume is tightly focused and contains a target job title, Performance Profile, Core Competencies, and perhaps career highlights section, you will have the reader's attention. If the first page makes the right argument, the rest of your resume will be read carefully. A longer resume also means that much more space for selling your skills with relevant keywords and more opportunities to establish your *professional brand*. You should still make every effort to maintain focus and an "if in doubt, cut it out" editing approach.

Rule Six: Emphasize your achievements.

Make your achievements, problem-solving skills, and *professional brand* the focus of your resume.

Here's a resume template, showing the basic component parts of a productive resume.

An excellent final test for your revamped resume is to first reread your TJD and then read your resume from front to back. If it clearly echoes your TJD, then you are likely to have a productive resume. If it doesn't, you'll readily be able to tell where your content needs fine-tuning.

RESUME CONTENT TEMPLATE

Name
Mailing address (if appropriate) • Telephone & cell phone • E-mail address

Professional Target Job Title
This helps database visibility and gives focus to human eyes about what they will be reading.

Performance Profile/Career Summary
No more than five lines of unbroken text can be followed by a second similar paragraph or short list of bullets. Your intent is to capture your ability to do the target job. What goes in here? Take the most common requirements from your TJD exercise Step 3 and rewrite as your performance profile. This will help your resume's database visibility and will create immediate resonance with the recruiter. Always note bilingual skills, since we live in a global economy.

Core Competencies
Specific and detailed. This is a bulleted list of keywords that you identified in Step 3 of the TJD. It can be as long as you like. This list gives the reader an immediate focus ("Oh, she can talk about this and this") and each word can be repeated in the context of the job where it applied.

Technical Competencies
An optional category, depending on your needs.

Professional Experience
Company name and location
Job title and employment dates
(Repeat this format as many times as necessary.)

Education
This may come at the front of the resume if these credentials are critical, especially relevant to the Target Job Description, or highlight your greatest strength.

Licenses/Professional Accreditations
This may come at the front of the resume if these credentials are critical, especially relevant to the Target Job Description, or highlight your greatest strength.

Ongoing Professional Education

Professional Organization/Affiliations

Publications/Patents/Speaking Languages

Military Service

Extracurricular Interests
If they relate to the job

References Available on Request
Employers *assume* that your references are available. Only end your resume with this if there is no better use of the space. Never list references on your resume.

> **KNOCK 'EM DEAD TIP**
> Once you are on that new job, keep a low profile for three to six months while you learn the culture of the company, get up to speed with all your job's deliverables, and determine who is in the inner and outer circles of your department and why. Acquire allies by your commitment to doing a good job and by your behavior with the group that will most support your career goals. Quietly identify the next step up the promotional ladder at this or any other company, and then start working toward it. Promotions don't come as a reward for loyalty and tenure; they come as a result of capabilities.
>
> Identify that next job, collect six to twelve job postings for it, and complete a TJD on the position. Then do a gap analysis: identifying the gaps between what you can do and what the next job requires. These gaps become your professional development program.

Resume writing is a major topic all on its own, so you can find more help:

- On the resume advice pages at *www.knockemdead.com*
- In the latest edition of *Knock 'em Dead Resumes*
- With a professionally written resume from the credentialed resume writers at *www.knockemdead.com*

Integrating a Professional Brand Into Your Resume

Your *professional brand* should be communicated throughout your resume, but especially with opening and closing brand statements. The first place you begin to establish a *professional brand* is with your Target Job Title (TJT), where you consciously decide on the job that best allows you to package your skill sets and create a *professional brand*.

Target Job Title and Branding Statement

Your TJT and subsequent brand statement give the reader a focus for what this resume is about and what to expect. The brand statement is a short phrase following the TJT that defines what you will bring to this job. It says, in effect, "These are the benefits my presence on your payroll will bring to your team and your company." Put this statement after your TJT and you have a succinct brand statement, or, if you prefer, "value proposition."

Notice the following brand statements focus on the benefits brought to the job, but do not take up space identifying the specifics of how this was done.

Professional brand statements often start with an action verb: "Poised to," "Delivers," "Dedicated to," "Bringing," "Positioned to," "Building."

Chronological Resume

Jane Swift, 9 Central Avenue, Quincy, MA 02169. (617) 555-1212 jswift@careerbrain.com

SUMMARY: Ten years of increasing responsibilities in the employment services industry. Concentration in the high-technology markets.

EXPERIENCE: Howard Systems International, Inc.
2004–Present

Management Consulting Firm
Personnel Manager

Responsible for recruiting and managing consulting staff of five. Set up office and organized the recruitment, selection, and hiring of consultants. Recruited all levels of MIS staff from financial to manufacturing markets.

Additional responsibilities:
- Coordinated with outside advertising agencies.
- Developed P.R. with industry periodicals—placement with over 20 magazines and newsletters.
- Developed effective referral programs—referrals increased 32 percent.

EXPERIENCE: Technical Aid Corporation
1996–2004

National Consulting Firm. MICRO/TEMPS Division

Division Manager	2001–2004
Area Manager	1998–2001
Branch Manager	1996–1998

As Division Manager, opened additional West Coast offices. Staffed and trained all offices with appropriate personnel. Created and implemented all divisional operational policies responsible for P&L. Sales increased to $20 million dollars, from $0 in 1990.

Additional responsibilities:
- Achieved and maintained 30 percent annual growth over seven-year period.
- Maintained sales staff turnover at 14 percent.

As Area Manager, opened additional offices, hiring staff, setting up office policies, and training sales and recruiting personnel.

Additional responsibilities:
- Supervised offices in two states.
- Developed business relationships with accounts—75 percent of clients were regular customers.
- Client base increased 28 percent per year.
- Generated over $200,000 worth of free trade-journal publicity.

As Branch Manager, hired to establish the new MICRO/TEMPS operation. Recruited and managed consultants. Hired internal staff. Sold service to clients.

EDUCATION: Boston University
B.S. Public Relations, 1995.

Pharmaceutical Sales Management Professional

Poised to outperform in pharmaceutical software sales. Repeating records of achievement with major pharmaceutical companies.

Senior Operations/Plant Management Professional

Dedicated to continuous improvement ~ Lean Six Sigma ~ Start-up & turnaround operations ~ Mergers & change management ~ Process & productivity optimization ~ Logistics & supply chain

Bank Collections Management

Equipped to continue excellence in loss mitigation/collections/recovery management.

Mechanical/Design/Structural Engineer

Delivering high volume of complex structural and design projects for global companies in manufacturing/construction/power generation.

Account Management/Client Communications Manager

Reliably achieving performance improvement and compliance within financial services industry.

Marketing Communications

Consistently delivering successful strategic marketing, media relations, and special events.

Administrative/Office Support Professional

Ready, willing and competent: detail-oriented problem solver, consistently forges effective working relationships with all publics.

Senior Engineering Executive

Bringing sound technical skills, strong business acumen, and real management skill to technical projects and personnel in fast-paced environment.

Edit for Consistent Brand Messaging

Review the body copy of your resume to see that the messaging supports the professional brand you have defined. Refer to the list of action verbs for words that you can add to a statement and further clarify your brand. Make sure your branding is front and center in the following sections of your resume:

- Performance Profile
- Performance/Career Highlights
- Professional Experience

Closing Brand Statement

You will occasionally see a resume closed with a third-party endorsement:

I've never worked with a more ethical and conscientious auditor.

—Petra Tompkins, Controller

This endorsement can act as a closing brand statement: a bold statement clarifying the value proposition of the product (that's you, that's the brand). It's a great way to end a resume. If you have just the right kind of supportive quote, use it, but suitable quotes aren't always as readily available as we would like.

However, you can achieve an equally powerful effect with a final comment of your own, a comment that relates to your *professional brand* and is written in the first person to make it conversational and different from the voice of the rest of your resume. Most resumes are written in the third person, allowing you to talk about yourself with a semblance of objectivity. Moving into the first person for a final comment at the resume's end acts both as an exclamation point and a matching "bookend" for the brand statement at the beginning. For example:

I believe that leadership by example and conscientious performance management underlie my department's consistent customer satisfaction ratings.

You Must Have a True and Truthful Brand

You have to be able to deliver on the brand you create. It must be based on your possession of the *technical skills* of your profession, plus those *transferable skills* and *professional values* that you take with you from job to job.

It is all too easy to overpromise, and while the employer might initially be attracted by the pizzazz of your resume, whether or not you live up to the value proposition determines the length and quality of the relationship.

If a box of cereal doesn't live up to the brand's hype you simply don't buy it again. The same logic applies with your career, but the stakes are higher: Sell yourself into the wrong job with exaggerations or outright lies and it is likely to cost you that job, plus the possibility of collateral career damage that can follow you for years.

Your Cover Letter

Conversations have to happen before any hiring decision is made, which means that *getting into conversations with the people who can make a decision to hire you* is the primary focus of every smart job search.

1. Because the majority of resumes typically end up in resume databases, where cover letters often can't help you, learning to use the more personal approaches where a cover letter can make a difference will greatly impact the productivity of your search. When you identify hiring managers by name (advice on how to do this coming up), you can avoid the resume databases altogether, and when you have a name, your cover letter is a very effective marketing tool.
2. Many resume banks and corporate websites have a place where you can upload or paste a cover letter along with your resume, and employers look more favorably on candidates who take the extra step.

In a professional world where *communication skills* are a must for any job, your cover letter introduces you, puts your resume in context, and demonstrates your *writing skills*. In fact, from your first contact with an employer to the day you start that new job, there are a number of opportunities to use letters/e-mails to advance your candidacy. There are different types of cover letters for different situations: follow-up letters after telephone and face-to-face interviews, and resurrection, negotiation, acceptance, rejection, and resignation letters to name a few. It's a bigger topic than can be handled here, and for proper coverage you should get the latest edition of *Knock 'em Dead Cover Letters* with over 125 examples covering all these categories and more; you can also find job search letter templates at *www.knockemdead.com*. In the mean time, here is a very effective form of cover letter.

The Executive Briefing

This is a type of cover letter I developed many years ago, which continues to get rave reviews from users year in and year out. You can use its striking format to clearly link skills to employer needs or to quickly customize an application when your resume doesn't tell the whole story.

An executive briefing enables you to customize your resume quickly to any specific job and is especially helpful on the other side of the desk—for overworked recruiters, hiring managers, HR professionals, or administrative assistants, who may not understand all the requirements of a specific job function. It is a powerful focusing tool for any harried resume reader. Furthermore, the executive briefing allows you to update and customize a more general resume with lightning speed without derailing the rest of your day's mission or missing out on an opportunity.

Like many great ideas, the executive briefing is beautiful in its simplicity. It is a cover letter on your standard letterhead/e-mail with the company's requirements for the job opening listed on the left side and your skills—matching point-by-point the company's needs—on the right. See the example on the following page.

An executive briefing sent with a resume provides a comprehensive picture of a thorough professional, plus a personalized, fast, and easy-to-read synopsis that details exactly how you can help with current needs. Using the executive briefing as a cover letter for your resume will greatly increase the chance that your query will be picked out of the pile in the human resources department and hand-carried to the appropriate manager.

The use of an executive briefing is obviously not appropriate when the specific requirements of a job are unavailable.

We have covered a lot of territory in discussing how to put together a killer resume, because *your resume is the most financially important document you will ever own.* Furthermore, the processes through which you develop a compelling resume (TJD, questionnaire, and PSRV) are also crucial in defining the professional persona you present to the world; this is almost as important as having a resume that tells a compelling story. Additionally, the process has prepared you for just about all the questions you are likely to be asked at an interview; this will become apparent when you start learning about how to turn job interviews into job offers.

EXECUTIVE BRIEFING SAMPLE

Executive Briefing
From: A1coordpro@earthlink.net
Subject: Assessment Coordinator
Date: February 28, 2010 11:18:39 PM EST
To: jobs@pepsi.com

Dear HR Staff,
Your advertisement on the *New York Times* website on February 27, 2012, for an **Assessment Coordinator**, seems to perfectly match my background and experience. As the International Brand Coordinator for Kahlúa, I coordinated meetings, prepared presentations and materials, organized a major off-site conference, and supervised an assistant. I believe that I am an excellent candidate for this position, as I have illustrated below:

YOUR REQUIREMENTS	MY QUALIFICATIONS
Highly motivated, diplomatic	Successfully managed project teams involving different flexible, quality-driven professional business units. The defined end results were achieved on every project.
Exceptional organizational skills and attention to detail	Planned the development and launch of the Kahlúa Heritage Edition bottle series. My former manager enjoyed leaving the details and follow-through to me. Coverdale project management training.
College degree and six years of experience	B.A. from Vassar College (1998). 6+ years relevant business experience in productive, professional environments.
Computer literacy	Extensive knowledge of Windows and Macintosh applications.

I'm interested in this position because it fits well with my new career focus in the human resources field. Currently, I am enrolled in NYU's adult career planning and development certificate program and working at Lee Hecht Harrison.

My resume, pasted below and attached in MS Word, will provide more information on my strengths and career achievements. If after reviewing my material you believe that there is a match, please call me. Thank you for your consideration.

Sincere regards,

Jane Swift

CHAPTER 4
HOW TO BUILD A PROFESSIONAL BRAND

CUSTOMERS ARE FIERCELY loyal to brands they like, and those brands become wildly successful.

What was once called a reputation is now called a brand, and we are told that anyone can have one. My colleague Dr. Jim Bright, author of *Chaos Theory of Careers*, notes that you can brand a swine but it still has to be processed before anyone wants to eat it. Branding is really just a buzzword for building a reputation, and it cannot be done as quickly as most of the branding merchants will tell you.

You can brand objects, but people are more difficult, because people change within themselves almost constantly, and they change jobs and careers so frequently that the brand has to be flexible, has to be able to evolve without losing its identity.

Branding

As you commit to greater involvement in the evolution and management of your professional destiny, you have to look at your career with the same consideration for objectivity and strategic development that an established corporation uses for its sustained growth. You have decided to develop new *transferable skills* and polish existing ones, have moved along a path to more consciously integrating your *professional values* into how you think about and conduct your professional life, and after considerable self-analysis you have a killer resume focused on a target job.

Your job search is a major sales campaign, and the final preparations before launch must include tweaking your marketing communications documents to ensure the product you are taking to market is clearly defined, with enough distinctive features to differentiate you from others. At this point you should have a more thorough knowledge of the product you are taking to market than you have ever had before, so now is the time to consider ways to further define your legitimate *professional persona*, the face you show to the world of work, and the supporting documents that position you (resume, letters, e-mails). When you do this in a conscious manner, it gives people a distinct way to look at you, and if the promises made by your *professional brand* are substantiated by your work habits, your reputation/brand will grow.

Beware of Instant Brand Promises

Considerable rubbish has been written about personal branding by a legion of freshly minted branding coaches with few or no credentials in career management or advertising and no understanding of the damage that can be wrought by irresponsible quackery. In some of the coaching communities that straddle the netherworlds of professional culture it is generally believed that to say something is to make it true. Who am I to say this isn't okay in a "personal brand" and your personal life? But your professional life and your *professional brand* are a different matter, because what you say in speech and writing will be examined, and when the truth is seen to be exaggeration, hyperbole, or outright fabrication, it *will* destroy that relationship and sour potential employers. Besides, people get around: Large professions become small communities as the years roll by, so you must be respectful of the collective memory of your professional community.

You Must Have a Relevant and Truthful Brand

It is all too easy to brand professional attributes that are of little interest to your target market, and just as easy to overpromise on, or overlook, attributes that are of interest. If you rush to create a *professional brand* with limited appeal, it's your own fault for not taking the time to understand what your target market wants.

If you overpromise, the employer might initially be attracted by the pizzazz of your resume, but when you aren't able to live up to its promises, or are seen as all thunder and no lightning in your job interviews, it will backfire.

If a box of cereal doesn't live up to the brand's hype, you simply don't buy it again. But sell yourself into the wrong job and it is likely to cost you that job and haunt you for years with collateral career damage. You have to be able to stand behind and deliver on the brand you create.

Branding Is a Long-Term Marketing Strategy

Branding is the process by which you consistently draw attention to the ways your product is special: the sum of these special attributes creating the brand. Differentiating the message that defines the professional you and keeping that message consistent and visible in all you say, do, and write is what constitutes a *professional brand*.

Think of your *professional brand* as a thoughtful way of defining how you want to be seen in your professional world. When you create a professional brand as part of an overall career management strategy, it gives *you* focus and motivation, and over time offers *others* an easy way to differentiate you.

The Geico Gecko Didn't Happen Overnight

A brand is the public face that makes MeInc memorable. All the most outstanding commercial brands have a distinct personality: That green gecko with the funny English accent immediately springs to mind.

The question is, what came first, Geico or the gecko? The product came first; the insurance giant was successful *before* the gecko became a household name, because the *finely tuned* personality that makes it so memorable *backs a solid product*.

The personality of a commercial brand can be created quickly: That quirky gecko was created and launched inside of twelve months. But, the engaging public face of Geico only came to us from the blood, sweat, and tears of (at least) four large, highly creative teams of advertising pros, and at the cost of many millions of dollars.

Branding means creating a distinctive and memorable image of your *professional persona* as a means to an end: imprinting that *professional persona* onto the collective memory of the professional community (your customer base).

If you want a brand that helps you succeed professionally, you must consider what your customers want (they don't want a lizard with a funny accent), and then develop a brand that *resonates with the priorities of those customers*. A well-conceived brand can give momentum to a product, but don't put the cart before the horse: *A great product comes before the packaging*. To be successful, the public face you create in developing a *professional brand* needs to be based on a firm foundation of the skills, behaviors, and values desirable to your customers.

If it takes a major corporation like Geico the brainpower of hundreds of top creative professionals in two companies, tens of millions of dollars, and a year to define their brand, maybe you should give yourself at least as much time and effort for your brand development. If a big company takes this long you will need *at least* as long.

It's easy to mistake all the hype about branding for an instant solution to all your professional challenges, but brand development takes time because you have to get it right. Your priority for this year and this job search is to build the core of your brand: those *transferable* and *technical skills* and *professional values* that your customers *want most, want now, and will always want*. Get the basics down, own them in everything you do, and identify yourself as such in your marketing materials; beyond this, let your brand/reputation evolve over time.

The product comes first. Focus on building the backbone of your brand so that you embody a product worthy of branding: one that *resonates with the priorities of your customers*. No one gets hired or promoted because their winning personality trumps their lousy skills. But if you are patient, when your brand supports a product built to meet the needs of your customers, it can make a real contribution to your credibility, visibility, and ultimately your long-term success, because *people are fiercely loyal to brands they like and those brands become wildly successful, sometimes for generations*.

What Do Your Customers Want?

When it comes to your reputation/*professional brand*, you want employers to have strong, positive associations with you. You want them to identify you with the *transferable skills* and *professional values* that together spell competence, performance, and reliability, making you different and desirable. Throughout your career your brand should position you as someone who's current, committed, easy and pleasant to work with, and a thorough professional.

Start with the first rule of advertising, marketing, public relations, and sales: *Sell to the customers' needs*. Look through their eyes and see the world as they do, and you'll see what they value. Take a moment to write down the messages you have absorbed so far about what your customers value. Your list will read something like this:

MY POTENTIAL CUSTOMERS:
- Have technical competency in the skills of the profession *(Technical Skills)*
- Have competency with the technology applications of the profession *(Technical Skills)*
- Embody *Motivation and Energy, Commitment and Reliability, Determination, Pride and Integrity, Productivity, Systems and Procedures*
- Enjoy competency with the inner working and nuances of the profession and industry *(Secrets of the Hire)*

HIGH-PERFORMANCE EMPLOYEES:
- Possess *Technical Skills, Critical Thinking, Communication Skills, Multitasking Skills, Creativity, Teamwork, Leadership, Motivation and Energy, Commitment and Reliability, Determination, Pride and Integrity, a commitment to Productivity, an adherence to Systems and Procedures*

And especially:

- Are goal- vs. task-oriented people *(Professional values of Motivation and Energy, Determination, Productivity)*
- Possess *Multitasking Skills* based on sound time management and organization skills
- Resolve and prevent problems *(Critical Thinking and Creativity)*

RELIABLE EMPLOYEES:
- Have *Technical Skills, Critical Thinking, Communication Skills, Multitasking Skills, Creativity, Teamwork, Leadership, Motivation and Energy, Commitment and Reliability, Determination, Pride and Integrity, a commitment to Productivity, an adherence to Systems and Procedures*

CURRENT, UP-TO-THE-MINUTE PEOPLE:
- Possess *Technical Skills*
- Have *Motivation and Energy*
- Offer *Commitment*
- Have *Pride*
- Display *Productivity*

COMMITTED WORKERS:
- Have *Technical Skills, Critical Thinking, Communication Skills, Multitasking Skills, Creativity, Teamwork, Leadership, Motivation and Energy, Commitment and Reliability, Determination, Pride and Integrity, a commitment to Productivity, an adherence to Systems and Procedures*

CONSUMMATE PROFESSIONALS POSSESS ALL OF THE ABOVE AND ESPECIALLY:
- *Pride and Integrity*
- *Systems and Procedures*
- *Communication*
- *Teamwork*
- *Critical Thinking*

First Impressions Are the Strongest

You are a unique individual and bring a special combination of these *transferable skills* and *professional values* to your work, and you also differentiate yourself from others in how you are seen to behave, by:

- Your dress
- Your social graces
- Your body language
- Your emotional maturity

We discussed these earlier in the book as supporting components for the four primary *communication skills*. Place dress, social graces, body language, and *emotional maturity* in this larger context of the branding that occurs in all professional interactions, and these are the primary behaviors—along with how you listen and express yourself—with which you build a reputation and a brand.

The Competitive Difference Questionnaire

To help you analyze what it is that makes up the unique package that is the *professional you* and learn how to express it in your professional brand, I've created the Competitive Difference Questionnaire. You can find a link to download an MSWord version of this questionnaire at *www.knockemdead.com*.

The Competitive Difference Questionnaire

List and prioritize the *transferable skills* and *professional values* that best capture the essence of the professional you.

_____
_____
_____

Which of the *transferable skills*, and *professional values* have you marked for further professional development? What are you going to do about it?

_____
_____
_____

What skills/behaviors/values or other characteristics do you share with top performers in your department/profession?

_____
_____
_____

What have you achieved with these qualities?

_____
_____
_____

What makes you different from others with whom you have worked?

_____
_____
_____

What do you see as your four most defining professional skills/behaviors/values and how does each help your performance?

_____
_____
_____
_____

How do your most defining professional traits help you contribute to the team?

_____
_____
_____

How do your most defining professional traits help you contribute to your departmental goals and your boss?

_____
_____
_____
_____

Why do you stand out in your job/profession?

_____
_____
_____

If you realize you don't stand out and you want to, explain in a few sentences why the people you admire stand out. What plans do you have for change?

_____
_____
_____

In what ways are you better than others at your workplace who hold the same title?

_____
_____
_____

What excites you most about your professional responsibilities?

_____
_____
_____

What are your biggest achievements in these areas?

_____
_____
_____

What do your peers say about you?

_____
_____
_____

What does management say about you?

_____
_____
_____

What do your reports say about you?

_____

_____

_____

What are your top four professional skills?

Skill #1: _____

Quantifiable achievements with this skill:

_____

_____

_____

Skill #2: _____

Quantifiable achievements with this skill:

_____

_____

_____

Skill #3: _____

Quantifiable achievements with this skill:

_____

_____

_____

Skill #4: _____

Quantifiable achievements with this skill:

_____

_____

_____

What are your top four leadership skills?

Skill #1: _____

Quantifiable achievements with this skill:

_____

_____

_____

Skill #2: _____

Quantifiable achievements with this skill:

_____
_____
_____

Skill #3: _____

Quantifiable achievements with this skill:

_____
_____
_____

Skill #4: _____

Quantifiable achievements with this skill:

_____
_____
_____

What do you believe are the three key deliverables of your job?

_____
_____
_____

What gives you greatest satisfaction in the work you do?

_____
_____
_____

What *value* does this combination of *transferable skills*, *professional values*, and achievements bring to your targeted employers?

_____
_____
_____

Now compile endorsements. Looking at each of your major areas of responsibility throughout your work history, write down any positive verbal or written commentary others have made on your performance.

_____
_____
_____

_____

_____

_____

After rereading your answers, make three one-sentence statements that capture the essence of the professional you and your competitive difference.

_____

_____

_____

Take these three statements and rework them into one sentence. This is your competitive difference:

_____

_____

Making Use of Your Brand

What you have in the questions and your answers to the Competitive Difference Questionnaire are the components and expression of your brand. You made three one-sentence statements that capture the essence of the professional you and your competitive difference.

The three one-sentence statements should capture all that is best about you, and the *spirit* of them should echo the content of your resume and job search letters. In conversation with recruiters and employers and in answers to interview questions they can play the same role, not so much being spouted verbatim—that would come across as phony and overbearing—but rather as the special sauce you bring to everything you do. Finally, you rework them into one sentence *and this is your competitive difference and the signature of your brand.*

What you do with the final result of the questionnaire takes real objectivity. Looked at this way you might say, "Well, it's a beginning, but if this is the best I've got to say right now, maybe letting the world know won't have the desired effect." It is much better to come to this *emotionally mature* decision and engage yourself in developing the *transferable skills* and *professional values* that will underlie a valid brand and help build your reputation, than it is to be premature.

It's worthwhile to reiterate the importance of truth in branding. Recently a large soft-drink manufacturer that made a "healthy" drink was sued. It turned out that the so-called healthy drink wasn't, in fact, any healthier than a regular soft drink. Consumers were fooled into buying it, and sued. You won't be sued for lying or exaggeration, but the financial loss caused could still be significant due to lost opportunities, now and in the future.

In the same way that a commercial brand has to deliver on its promises, so you have to be able to deliver on the promises associated with your brand. If your brand says that you're a great communicator . . . you'd better be. If your resume says you can program in five computer languages, you'd better really have that ability. If not, you'll be very quickly found out. And your job won't be the only thing you'll lose. Your reputation will be injured, perhaps irreparably. You'll lose credibility, which is central to your professional success.

So avoid the temptation to overpromise. Make your brand truthful, and work hard to improve those parts of it that are weak and strengthen those parts that are outstanding. The benefits are incalculable.

Integrating a Professional Brand Signature Into Your Resume

When your competitive difference statement is valid and powerful you might think of using it as a brand signature in written communications like your resume and job search letters. It can become a presence throughout your resume, but especially with opening and closing personal or brand statements.

The first place you begin to establish a professional brand is in your Target Job Title, where you consciously decide on the job that best allows you to package your skill sets and create a *professional brand*.

Target Job Title and Branding Statement

Your TJT followed by a brand statement gives the reader a focus for what you and your resume are about and what to expect. The brand statement is a short phrase (perhaps the final sentence you wrote on the Competitive Difference Questionnaire) following the TJT that defines what you will bring to this job. It says in effect, "These are the benefits my presence on your payroll will bring to your team and your company."

Your resume is headed with contact information, then immediately followed by the TJT and brand statement, both of these usually being centered on the page. Professional brand statements often start with action verbs: "Poised to," "Delivers," "Dedicated to," " Brings," "Positioned to."

Senior Operations / Plant Management Professional
Dedicated to continuous improvement ~ Lean Six Sigma ~ Start-up & turnaround operations ~ Mergers & change management ~ Process & productivity optimization ~ Logistics & supply chain

Account Management / Client Communications Manager
Reliably achieving performance improvement and compliance within financial services industry

Administrative/Office Support Professional
Ready, willing and competent: detail-oriented problem solver, consistently forges effective working relationships with all publics

Edit for Consistent Brand Messaging
Review the body copy of your resume to see that the messaging supports the *professional brand* you have defined, especially in these areas:

- Performance Profile
- Performance/Career Highlights
- Professional Experience

Your resume might also end with a closing brand statement. To learn more about integrating a *professional brand* into your resume, see *Knock 'em Dead Resumes*, current edition.

Use Your Brand to Maintain Visibility

This packaging and positioning of the professional you, inherent in the branding process, goes beyond this job search. Part and parcel of achieving long-term career success is establishing credibility and a gradually increasing visibility within your department, your company, your local professional community, and perhaps ultimately your profession on a national or international basis. Your steadily evolving brand supports your growing credibility and visibility.

The *professional brand* built into your new resume is the profile you should keep posted on your professional networking sites on an ongoing basis. This increases your credibility within your profession and visibility to the recruitment industry, making you more desirable as an employee and increasing your options.

Your Professional Brand and the Long Haul

A commitment to building your capabilities over time is smart thinking: enlightened self-interest in a new insecure world of work. Change is constant in everyone's career, so while we talk about developing an initial professional brand identity as part of your job search strategy, it isn't "mission accomplished" once you've landed a new job.

Always think of your ongoing commitment to building professional capabilities and credibility as the nexus of your career management strategies: Greater credibility and visibility will result from this. Think of branding as the marketing department of MeInc continuing to evolve the packaging to keep the ever-developing product current and respected in its market.

Now it's time to launch your job search in earnest. The focus of a successful job search is to *get into conversations with people in a position to hire you as quickly and as frequently as possible*. You achieve this by integrating networking into every job search strategy and tactic, because networking is the fastest and easiest way to get into those conversations with the right people.

CHAPTER 5
NETWORKING AND THE SUCCESSFUL JOB SEARCH

EFFECTIVE JOB SEARCH strategy first demands an understanding of how companies recruit, and that you integrate networking tactics into every aspect of your plan of attack.

Getting into conversations with the people who can actually offer you a job is the only way you are going to get hired. The more ways you have of getting into these conversations, the sooner your job search will be over. This is what we will concentrate on in the next two chapters. When networking strategies are integrated into your job search, they can quadruple your odds of getting an interview from any job posting you respond to, or from any opening you discover through your networking activities.

Companies plan their staffing needs up to twelve months in advance, so the interviews you go on *this* year were mostly planned and budgeted *last* year. Hiring budgets usually open at the start of a new calendar year, with hires staggered throughout the year. The early part of every year usually has plenty of job opportunities because of this strategy—so if you read this book in November, you should be diligent about working on your job search right through the holiday season!

However, because we live in such a huge economy, there are always jobs available, at any time of year and in any economic climate; you just need to know how to find them. Even in the depths of the 2009–10 recession, every month saw at least 4 million jobs posted on the Internet. So whatever the economy, don't give up; just develop the tools to compete more effectively.

The cost of hiring and training a new employee runs into thousands and often tens of thousands of dollars, so the entire recruitment process is cost/productivity-conscious (okay, so tell me something in business that isn't). Consequently, the people involved in a specific search—the hiring manager, along with the assigned HR and recruitment professionals, all want the same thing: good hires, fast hires, and hires made as cheaply as possible.

Understanding how and why these recruitment activities are performed in the sequence they are will help you focus your job search efforts on the tactics that most consistently result in job interviews. It's all about economy, speed, and value.

Remember as you read this that the primary focus of your job search activities every day is to *get into conversations with the people who can hire you as quickly and as often as possible.*

Internal Hires

Put yourself on the other side of the hiring manager's desk for a few moments. Naturally, you want to hire from within, because it's cheap, you are dealing with known quantities, and internal promotions are motivational. So you obviously start the recruitment process by asking yourself, your peers, and your staff who within the company can do this job. Many jobs are filled this way.

Knowing this can give you a head start on the competition whenever you hear about internal promotions and transfers at your own or other companies. A job filled from within usually means another job opening has been created by the vacuum, and with the right kind of network, you can identify these jobs and get introductions to the titles hiring for these positions.

Who Do You Know?

When a hiring manager can't make an internal hire, he will logically ask, "Who do I know, and who do my people know?" Recruiters will review all the resumes in the company's database and try to recall any promising candidates who have been interviewed in the past for similar positions.

KNOCK 'EM DEAD TIP
Remember that dream job where you came in second? The social networking strategies addressed here will enable you to stay in touch with the recruiters and hiring managers, keeping you visible for just such occasions.

HR may also create an internal job posting (often tied to cash incentives for employee referrals) and actively consider people known to employees and the recruitment team through their involvement in the professional community. This will include contacts made through online social networks, professional associations, and alumni societies. Developing a networking presence will help you become visible to recruiters and increase the chances of your hearing about these jobs in the *hidden job market*.

These are the first steps of any recruitment campaign because they are fast, cheap, and because employees who come to the company "known by us" in some way are seen to be better hires, and thought to get up-to-speed more quickly and stay with the company longer.

Even when companies go beyond these recruitment approaches and start advertising with job postings and using headhunters, they still prefer to hire people who come to them directly or through referral networks. You really can make these direct connections happen when you are adequately connected to your professional community.

For you, the questions are obvious:

1. How do I get better connected to my (local) profession?
2. How do I get to know, and be known by, more of my colleagues?

Recruitment Advertising

The next and more expensive step is to advertise for candidates. Companies start by advertising on the company website and then move on to commercial job banks. A small number of hires come directly through the company's own website (we'll address how to identify websites of all companies in your target location in the next chapter).

Next in importance—after hires made from a company's own website—come hires made from specialty job sites that focus on a specific profession. A recruiter's preference for advertising on specialty sites and searching their resume databases makes sense: She can expect more consistently suitable candidates, and fewer unqualified resumes to wade through.

Last comes the big job boards, like Monster and CareerBuilder.

Yet even when these recruitment strategies are being used, companies still prefer to hire the candidate who comes to them directly or as a referral. For you, this means that the most effective job search tactic is networking. You just have to learn a completely new way of doing it.

Nothing Happens Without Conversation

The quickest way to get past the living hell of this job search is to *get into conversation, as quickly and as often as possible*, with the holders of those job titles that have the authority to hire you. Keep that sentence in the front of your mind at all times and I guarantee that you will always receive the highest possible return on your job search time investment.

The most effective way to make this happen is to beef up your networking expertise and expand your professional networks. This means getting better connected to your professional communities so that you can find and reach out to the people in a position to hire you, and make it easier for them to find you.

When you connect with your professional community, you get to know, and become known by, all the most dedicated and best-connected professionals in your target location, and perhaps across the entire span of your profession.

There are four types of networks that can be helpful to the success of your job search. They include four distinct types of network:

1. Social networking
2. Professional associations
3. Alumni networks
4. Community networks

The first three are predominantly professional in nature. The last one can be a mixture of friends, family, community, hobby, and religious networks. Community networks are made up predominantly of social contacts but can still provide connections within your desired professional communities. We will address each of these networks in turn, and discuss how best to leverage your involvement with them.

Social Networking

For corporate recruiters and headhunters, social networking sites are honey pots, offering millions of qualified candidates. For you, social networks provide a reliable pathway to millions of jobs through the people connected to them. Social networking competency is a must for any cutting-edge job search plan of attack. Through the thousands of social networking sites, you can reach out to friends, colleagues, and specific categories of strangers who might have your ideal lead.

Plus, the more connected you are, the greater your odds of locating opportunities in the hidden job market. The connections you make can lead to referrals and introductions to hiring managers, and in many instances you'll be able to bypass the job sites and their resume banks entirely. You can search a social networking site's database by zip code, job title, company, or any keywords of your choice. The database will pull up the profiles of people who match your requirements and allow you to initiate contact directly, through your common membership in groups, or through the chain of people who connect you.

Here's an example about a job hunter who was also changing careers: A soldier cycling out of the military sought my help in her search for a new civilian career. I took her to *www.linkedin.com*, the premier professional networking site. First, to find other individuals with a similar background, I plugged the word *army* into the dialogue box and hit enter. The result was more than 4,000 profiles of people who shared her military experience. (That was six years ago; the same search today produces 539,000 profiles. LinkedIn has been growing steadily and will continue to do so.) We then tried a search using the phrase "*information technology*" (reflecting her desired career change) and got 39,000 profiles (today it is well over 1 million). While both these potential networks would have relevance to her job search, it got even better when we combined the keywords: "*information technology* and *army*." This pulled up 908 profiles (today more than 26,000) of people who shared her life experience and who had, in about half of the profiles we reviewed, already made the transition into her desired profession. This means she could have productive conversations with an enormous number of people, each of whom would likely be relevant to her job search.

Developing good social networking skills is not difficult and can be a great asset to any job search:

1. They can increase your odds of finding a job opening and turning it into an interview by up to 400 percent.
2. When you are employed and engaged in a confidential job search, social networks allow you to make yourself visible, but because this is not a resume bank, you do it without an "I'm for sale" sign.
3. When you are cycling out of one profession and into another, you can use social networking sites to build a network of people who do the target job in your chosen profession and, whenever possible, people who have made a similar transition. If you are involved in a job search that involves career change, go to *www.knockemdead.com* and read the "Career Change" article.

Maintain your social networks once you land that next job on your professional path. This keeps you visible both within your professional community and among the corporate recruiters and headhunters who may call you down the road with unexpected opportunities. You don't have to accept them, but isn't it better to have to turn down an offer than not to get it at all?

Which Social Networks Are Right for You?

Social networking can get you useful introductions to people throughout your profession, the country, and the world—people who might know of jobs at their own companies or who can introduce you to people who do. Social networking enables you to reach out into an almost limitless community of like-minded professionals.

You'll find networking sites that cater to an almost limitless array of special interests. Sites that cater to the multilingual or to recognized minority groups can connect you with people of similar skills and backgrounds—people who may know of opportunities ideal for your skill sets. It is good to connect with others who share your interests or background, not just for the joy and support it can bring to your life, but because recruiters haunt these sites too!

In a global economy, people with language skills have a special edge, so sites that encourage bilingual professionals can help you leverage those language skills with any global company searching for multicultural awareness in its employees.

There are thousands of social networks and the list is growing every day. The more these sites proliferate, the more specialized they become. It is a good idea to have a presence on two of the biggest, LinkedIn and Facebook. Beyond this, go to *www.wikipedia.org* and type in "social networks" for a complete listing.

LinkedIn: The Center of Professional Networking

By far the most important networking site for professionals is LinkedIn. Use it correctly and it may well help you land your next job and sustain your professional growth. While the following discussion is focused on how best to leverage LinkedIn, everything I say applies equally well to any other networking sites you join.

When you first join a networking site, your goals are twofold: You want to be found and you want to find people who can help you. At LinkedIn, as with any social networking site, there are certain steps to take that help you get the most out of the social networking experience.

- Sign up and create a profile: This makes you visible to others so that they can find and connect with you.
- Connect with people you know or have worked with in the past: This is the core of your network.
- Expand your network by joining the special interest groups that exist on all social networking sites, and connect with other members of those groups whose acquaintance could prove mutually beneficial.
- Join the Knock 'em Dead Secrets & Strategies group: It's a friendly, vibrant group that exists to help you with job search and career management issues.
- Link with me personally.

Social Networking Profile/Resume

Social networking sites are honey pots for corporate recruiters and headhunters, and you are the honey. Because of this, you should shape the information you make available about yourself. Your first step is to create a profile that will make you visible and attractive to these recruiters and to the professional peers who will be looking for you, just as you are soon going to be looking for them.

How to Create a Killer LinkedIn Profile

The profile you create will give you visibility with search engines and enable others to find you. Remember that there could well be 200 million LinkedIn users (half of them in the U.S.) by the time you read this! Also, recruiters and hiring managers who have already seen your resume increasingly like to check out your social profile(s) to find out more about you. This is why— once you are satisfied with your profile and *not* before—I suggested adding hyperlinks to it at the end of your resume.

Have your primary resume handy: You can cut and paste a lot of it directly into your profile. Your profile can become much richer and deeper than your target job–focused resume, but using your resume as the backbone of your profile gives you immediate visibility and credibility. LinkedIn provides a tool for cutting and pasting information, but resumes have sophisticated formatting needs, and the LinkedIn tool has problems.

Alternatively, you can use the freemium application box.net to upload/cut and paste your resume. It works far better than the LinkedIn version. It is then available to a recruiter to download, print out, or forward. For privacy reasons, you may wish to remove your exact address. However, remember that recruiters have relocation issues to contend with, so if you remove it, you'll need to identify yourself by city or area of state.

Your LinkedIn profile, and any other social networking profiles you subsequently develop, are your public face and, along with your resume, your most important marketing tool. They deserve careful thought and effort.

Use a First- or Third-Person Voice?

Although the conventional wisdom on social networking sites is to use the first person exclusively, don't follow this advice in your profile. Instead, stick with the third person, as you do in your resume. If you feel strongly about it, you can use the first person when you get to the end and talk about your hobbies and interests.

Now that we have the preliminaries out of the way, let's walk through the process of building your profile as it will appear on the LinkedIn page. (Remember, the process on other sites will be similar.)

Headline

The first thing anyone sees about you is your name and a brief headline. Start with the target job title from your *primary* resume. You will then have about ten words with which to describe who you are professionally. For maximum impact, use the highest frequency keywords you discovered during the TJD process. As you now know, these are the words most likely to be used by recruiters searching for someone like you; the same tools that got your resume before recruiters' eyes will get your LinkedIn profile before their eyes.

Summary

You have a huge amount of space in this section, and, consequently, your summary can grow over time as you develop the rest of your profile.

To begin with, you need to give recruiters the right information to find you. Social networking sites provide more space than your tightly focused, job-targeted resume, and you need to take full advantage of this. Start by adding those five or so lines from your *primary* resume's Performance Profile. Add to that any additional information from the Performance Profiles of additional resumes you might have created.

Some people writing on this topic suggest writing about your interests here. I strongly disagree. This information is irrelevant to all but the most interested parties and giving it to them up front is likely to cost you readers. LinkedIn has provided a space for this, so those personal interests should appear in the proper place: at the end of your profile.

Work Experience

Like a traditional chronological resume, the experience section of your profile begins with your current job and work experience. Again, you can cut and paste the entry from your primary resume first, then add to this with additional information from any other resumes.

When everything is pasted/uploaded, review the entry and see if there is additional experience you would like to add. You have plenty of space here, so as long as your entries for each job start with the most important information from your *primary* resume, you can add additional supporting information at the end of each entry.

Whatever you do, don't be lazy and just list your current job: It gives the impression that you have only had the one job. LinkedIn will tell you that you're twelve times more likely to be found by recruiters when you have more than one job listed, perhaps because those other jobs allow you to weight your profile with enough relevant keywords to be found in recruiters' database searches.

Remember this when you get to the very next section, which allows you to add the core, professional, and technical competencies from your resume. The inclusion of keywords that are likely to be used in a database search helps make you more visible.

However, you can increase this visibility by taking the time to include the keywords that relate to competencies you developed on each particular job. This helps recruiters see your claims of professional competencies in context and will dramatically increase the frequency of keyword usage. Do this with each job and you will have an optimized profile that is readily visible in any search.

Professional and Technology Competencies

Adding a professional and technology competencies section to your LinkedIn profile has the same benefits as adding it to your resume: It makes your profile more visible in database searches and your skills more readily accessible to readers.

Click on *Edit Profile*, then look for the *Add Skills* link. You can paste up to fifty skills in the dialogue box.

Education

Cut and paste the information from your resume. However, unlike your resume, you might want to consider listing high school as well: LinkedIn says that this increases your networking opportunities, and it makes sense in this context.

Certifications

Add all your professional certifications, and because this is a networking site, you can add certifications related to activities outside of your professional life, such as your scuba diving or ballroom dancing certifications.

Interests

Finally, the place where it is appropriate to add something about your outside interests! If someone has read this far, learning that I enjoy history, historical fiction, kayaking, ballroom dancing, am an obsessed collector of phonographs, prohibition-era cocktail shakers, art-deco chrome, and am the world's worst bass player might be of interest, because it gives me an additional dimension. While earlier in my profile this would only be a distraction, in the right place it makes me more well rounded.

Associations and Awards

Include membership in any associations or societies. List profession-related organizations and professional awards first, then follow with groups and awards related to your personal interests.

Reading List

Remember that your audience is potentially recruiters and hiring managers wanting to know more about you. Be sure your list includes at least 50 percent profession-oriented materials.

Headshot

While a headshot on a resume is inappropriate, it is pretty much expected with a social networking profile. Springing for a professional headshot is the best option, but if this isn't possible, you can probably do a passable job with the help of a friend.

Review professional-looking headshots on LinkedIn, because you'll be looking at the size yours will be, and you can evaluate what works and what doesn't. You'll notice the distance they seem to be taken from and the plain, light-colored backgrounds that work best. You'll notice with headshots that work, the subject is looking directly into the camera and smiling.

Spelling, Punctuation, and Grammar

The same considerations you applied to spelling, punctuation, and grammar in your resume also apply here. If you have problems creating your profile or editing it, at *www.knockemdead .com* we create LinkedIn profiles for our resume clients and also offer a separate social networking profile editing service, similar to the one we offer for resumes.

Save Your Work

As with all things computer-related, if you don't back up your work, somewhere along the line you are going to lose it. My recommendation is to save everything in a Microsoft Word document *and to back up that document.*

Expand Your Network Through Group Membership

Once you have reached out to connect with all current and past colleagues, professional acquaintances, and coworkers, it is time to start expanding the depth and breadth of your network with people you don't know, but who, by virtue of their titles and where they work, you feel might be able to help you now or in the future.

LinkedIn has thousands of special-interest groups where you can find exactly the people you are looking for, and any member is allowed to join up to fifty of these groups. You are allowed to reach out to someone directly only if you know each other or if you have a shared interest, and being a member of the same group counts as that shared interest. So group membership allows you to reach out and establish relationships with a very significant cross-section of your professional community. Once you have established contact, you have free and clear communication.

Who Do You Connect With?

Intelligent networking means you look to form relationships with people in your profession and industry at many levels. Almost anyone in your industry or location can be useful regardless of title or experience, but the people of most interest will likely fall into these categories:

1. *People who hold job titles that are one, two, or three levels above your own, because these are the people most likely to have relevant jobs and be in a position to hire you, now or in the future.*

   With people in this group, you can initiate contact by sending an e-mail to introduce yourself and asking them to look at your profile. If this proceeds to a conversation and interviews, fine; if not, you can instead ask the person to connect you to others. There is a whole chapter on the specifics of making contact in a few pages.
2. *Those with the same job title as you, and ideally within your target industry and location.*
3. *Those one job title below yours, and ideally within the target industry and location.*
4. *Those whose job titles identify them as people with whom you would interact on a regular basis, but who have different functions and might work in different departments.*

You can initiate relationships by asking for advice; many people will give you a few minutes of their time. You will develop the best relationships, though, by reaching out to others with help and advice, because when you offer good things, forging a relationship with you becomes important to the other person.

The challenge then becomes how to encourage a relationship that shares introductions and job leads. The answer is logical and painless: *Use the job leads you hear about that are inappropriate for your own use.*

It's a not-so-funny thing about a job search: When you are fresh out of school, no one is hiring entry-level workers; they all want you to call back in five years. Five years later, when you are once again looking for a job, they either want someone fresh out of school or with ten years' experience.

In a job search, you constantly come across positions that aren't right for you but that could be just what someone else is aching to hear about. Offer these leads to others as part of your introduction. Here's how it can work: Sometimes you have to send an e-mail stating why you want to make contact, and sometimes you can communicate immediately—it depends on a number of variables. In the first instance, you send an e-mail simply stating you have a job lead that your contact might find interesting.

In the second instance, when you can make direct contact, state your business: "I am involved in a strategic career move right now, and I have come across a job that isn't right for me but could be perfect for you. I'll be happy to pass the lead on, and perhaps you have heard about something that would suit me. I am cycling out of the army and into the private sector and have been looking for jobs in IT in the _____ area. If you'd like to talk, let's exchange telephone numbers."

Build your own database of the jobs that are not suitable for you and pass them on to all those people above and below you in your profession who will make perfectly symbiotic networking partners.

KNOCK 'EM DEAD TIP
You will find social networking sites especially important when you are involved in or are planning a career transition. If you know you are cycling out of one profession and into another, you can use social networking sites to build a network of people who do the target job in your chosen profession and, whenever possible, people who have made a similar transition. If you are involved in a job search that involves career change, go to *www .knockemdead.com* and read the "Career Change" article.

Other Ways to Use Your Connections

When you find an online job posting that seems like a good fit, you are usually faced with uploading your resume into a corporate or headhunter database . . . and then waiting and waiting for a response. Now, your social networks can deliver direct contact with the people who can hire you or the people who know the people who can hire you. On all of your social networking sites, there are people who work at your "companies of interest" or have done so in the past. Search for them, using the company name in your keyword search, then look for job titles one, two, and three levels above your own and for titles at your rank and one to two levels below it.

In all these instances, once you have identified profiles of desirable titleholders and confirmed that they are members of at least one shared group, you can approach them to connect. You can do this based on your common professional interests, or with an e-mail stating your professional interests and attaching a resume. Check out *Knock 'em Dead Job Search Letter Templates* at *www.knockemdead.com* for sample letters.

For titles at or below your level in the target company, you can reach out by saying that you that you have heard about an opening at the company and hope to get some inside information before you apply and/or explain that you might have unearthed some interesting opportunities which, though not right for you, might be of interest to your interlocutor. If you make time to visit the company website before any conversation, you will be well informed and make a good impression when you talk to each other.

The more you reach out, the better your reputation becomes and the more others will reach out to you. However, a word of caution: Social networking is a great tool, but a single tool nevertheless; it is most effective when integrated into a comprehensive job search plan of attack.

Many Other LinkedIn Resources

Most social networking sites offer an array of tools for your professional networking activities:

- Job postings from employers and headhunters
- Reminders of when to follow up with a call or e-mail to nurture your relationships
- Thousands of special-interest groups
- Links to job sites
- Offline social events to meet and mingle in person

KNOCK 'EM DEAD TIP

If you grew up with social networking, there are probably details of your wilder times available online for the world to see. You need to go back and clean up this digital dirt. As I write this 2013 edition of *Knock 'em Dead*, I have just returned from an appearance at a major convention for college career services and corporate campus recruiters. It was noted at the conference that upward of 40 percent of recruiters are using publicly available online data about short-list candidates as a screening tool. Twenty-five percent said they would reject a candidate based on this information. This means we all have to police the image we have online, so delete those once-amusing pictures of you projectile vomiting at a frat party.

Smart Networking: Strategies and Tactics

There are more network options than you can cultivate, so you'll need to put all these networks through your personal filters to judge which ones are most relevant to you. Your goal should be to integrate networking into your life so that it is less of a chore and more a part of the joy of living. You plant the seeds when you initiate a new relationship, but you don't harvest the best fruit immediately. Networking can and does bear fruit right away, but your harvest will get richer as time passes and you tend your networking contacts.

Professional Associations

One of the best things you can do for this job search and your long-term career success is connect with your professional community, both online and offline in your local area.

Professional associations have monthly meetings in most major metropolitan areas, plus regional and national get-togethers every year. The local meetings are of immediate interest, and, unless you work on a national level, membership in the local or state chapters of a national association will be quite sufficient for your needs—and cheaper, too. When you join a local chapter of a recognized national association and attend the local meetings, you get to know, and be known by, the most committed and best-connected people in your profession in your target marketplace. Your membership will help you stay attuned to what is going on in your profession, as associations offer ongoing training that makes you a more knowledgeable, and therefore a more desirable, employee. Of course, almost everything that is happening locally is also happening in the association's online groups.

The professional association is a new "old boy" network for the modern world. Your membership becomes a link to millions of colleagues, most of whom will gladly talk to you based on your connection through the association.

All industries and professions have multiple associations, any one of which could be valuable depending on your needs. For example, if you are in retail, you could join any of some thirty national associations and fifty state associations. Together these associations represent employees of more than 1.5 million retail organizations, which in turn provide employment for more than 14 million people. Most other associations offer similarly impressive networking potential.

If you fit the profile of a special interest or minority group, you will also find professional associations that cater to another dimension of the *professional you*. These include—but are by no means restricted to—associations for African Americans, Latinos, Asian Americans, professionals with disabilities, and women. If you can find a niche association that's a fit, it represents a whole new network for you; and besides, companies actively recruit identifiable minorities. A good place to start online is the Wikipedia.org professional associations page. In your local library, check out the *Encyclopedia of Associations* (published by Gale). Alternatively, you can try a Google search for relevant keywords. For example, "legal association" will generate listings of associations for the legal profession. If you belong to any identifiable minority, use that in your Google searches as well. For example, "Asian legal association" will generate a listing of local associations specifically for Asian professionals working in the legal field.

The Value of Volunteering

It is easier to get to know people than you might think. All professional association members are there, at least in part, to advance their careers through networking. Once you have the lay of the land, volunteer for one of the many committees that keep associations running. It's the best way to meet people and expand your sphere of influence, as you can reach out to others while you engage in your volunteer association activities. Committee involvement doesn't take much time because volunteer associations invariably employ the "many hands make light work" approach: They are structured to function with the help of full-time professionals like you who have mortgages to pay and families to support.

When you join an association, you'll benefit greatly from attending the meetings, because this is where you will meet other professionals in your field. But don't just attend the meetings; get involved. Associations are largely volunteer organizations and always need someone to set out chairs or hand out paperwork and nametags. The task itself doesn't matter, but your visible willingness to be an active participant most certainly does, and will get you on a first-name basis with people you would probably never meet otherwise.

Given the nature of association membership, you don't have to go straight from introductions to asking for leads on jobs. In fact, it can be productive to have initial conversations where you do not ask for leads or help in your job search, but where you make a contribution to the group; this is always preferable because others are more likely to help you when they see you making an effort toward the common good.

There is a good argument that, from a networking point of view, the bigger the committee, the better. Membership and program committees are among the best to join. However, involvement in any committee will serve your needs, because being on one will enable you to reach out to those on other committees. If you join the conferences and events committee, you can initiate contact with just about anyone in your professional world: "Hi, Bill Parsons? I'm Becky Lemon with the conference committee of the local association. I'd like to invite you to a meeting we are having next week on . . . ."

Don't join committees for which you lack the experience to be a productive member, unless you make it clear that the reason you want to become a part of that team is for professional development—if this is the case, expect to become the designated water carrier, at least initially.

If you volunteer and become active in an association, the people with whom you come in contact will begin to identify you as a team player. This perception can be instrumental in landing that new job and surging ahead in your career.

Association Databases and Directories

Access to the association database (and sometimes a printed association directory) comes with your membership and delivers a superb networking resource for telephone and e-mail networking campaigns. You can feel comfortable calling any other member on the phone and introducing yourself: "Hi, Brenda Massie? My name is Martin Yate. We haven't spoken before, but we are both members of the Teachers' Federation. I need some advice; can you spare a minute?"

Your mutual membership, and the commitment to your profession that it bespeaks, will guarantee you a few moments of anyone's time, a courtesy you should always return.

You can also use your association membership directory to generate personal introductions for jobs you have heard about elsewhere. For example, you might have found an interesting job posting on *www.careerbuilder.com*, or perhaps on a company website, with the request that you upload your resume; this is where your networking can pay big dividends. Apply just as the website where you found the job requested, then return to your membership directory and find people who work for that company. A judicious call or two will frequently get you a personal referral and some inside information on the opening, and you have just *doubled your chances of landing that interview*. Once you have an interview scheduled, these same contacts can help you prepare for the interview with insider knowledge about the company, the department, and the hiring manager.

Newsletters

Professional associations all have online newsletters, and many have a jobs section that appears on their website and is linked to the newsletter. Companies post job openings with associations because they know the applicants will be qualified. For this reason, you will often see job postings that don't appear anywhere else. In down economic times, a savvy corporate recruiter will use an association website to skim the cream of available talent while at the same time screening out the less committed.

You will also notice that association members write all the articles in the newsletters. As everyone likes to have their literary efforts appreciated, telling a member you have read an article that he has written gives you a great introduction to a networking call or letter.

Active association membership puts you on the radar of all the best-qualified and best-connected professionals in your area.

KNOCK 'EM DEAD TIP
List professional associations at the end of your resume under a "Professional Affiliations" heading. This is guaranteed to get a second glance, as it signifies professional awareness. Employers and headhunters will sometimes use words like *association*, *club*, and *society* in their keyword searches, so association membership will also help get your resume pulled up from the databases for investigation by human eyes.

Alumni Associations

Almost every school, from Acme Welding to Wellesley College, has an alumni association, and being a member of your alma mater's can play a pivotal role in your professional life. Historically, alumni associations have existed primarily to raise money from alumni for the school, but in these changing times, they increasingly see career outreach as a cost-efficient way to stay in touch with alumni.

So, that means good things for the future, but what about now? If you are an alumni member, you have access to the alumni association membership database, which puts you in touch with other graduates. People like to extend their help to those with whom they share a college experience.

Additionally, going to the meetings and occasionally volunteering for some tasks are activities that will ease you into collegial relationships with men and women on every rung of the corporate ladder—people who are in a position to boost your career.

Alumni associations all have online newsletters, and many include information about job openings. An increasing number even have semiformalized job-hunting networks in which alumni are encouraged to pass on their companies' employment needs. As a member of an alumni association, you can also cultivate an informal relationship with the school's career services department. Even when your school days are in the misty past, don't forget these people and the valuable resource they represent.

Build an Alumni Database

Your alumni association is a valuable network waiting for you to become involved and leverage its contacts intelligently. Whenever you upload your resume as a response to a job posting, cross-check your alumni database first for members who hold a job title one to three levels above your own, and second for those at or below your level. Using the same approach we discussed with professional association contacts, *you can again double your chances of that job posting turning into an interview* by getting an introduction or referral from a fellow alumnus.

If you don't know the URL of your alma mater, go to *www.utexas.edu/world/univ/.* For community college URLs, you'll find an excellent resource at: *www.mcli.dist.maricopa.edu/cc/.* Another site with job search relevance is: *www.Classmates.com.*

Company Alumni Associations

In recent years larger, more widely dispersed companies have seen increased value in maintaining contact with ex-employees, since these people provide a source for future hires or leads on future hires. Corporate HR departments are doing this through online corporate alumni associations. Go to *www.job-hunt.org* for more than 250 corporate alumni associations.

KNOCK 'EM DEAD TIP
The site *www.alumni.net* will lead you to company, university, high school, and other alumni associations all over the world.

Your Past Managers and Other References as a Networking Resource

It is a major mistake not to speak to your references at all or only at the end of your search, when a job offer is imminent. While as a rule we are confident that our references will speak well of us, the fact is that some might bear us no good will. It isn't wise to discover this by trial and error, as one potential offer after another bites the dust. If these are people you know well and who you *believe* will speak well of you, why not confirm it and leverage that good will throughout your job search?

KNOCK 'EM DEAD TIP

For a discussion of how to handle your references when you are under serious consideration for a position, or have received and accepted an offer based on successful reference checks, see Chapter 22, which deals with negotiating the job offer.

At the very start of your job search, you should identify as many potential references as possible. The more options, the better the odds of coming up with excellent references. There are other reasons: References can represent great networking resources; everyone you ask to be a reference for you will be flattered, and they are prime candidates to offer introductions for jobs at their current company. With a little research, you can identify any suitable jobs with the company at which this reference works, putting you in a prime position to ask for a referral or introduction.

KNOCK 'EM DEAD TIP

Of course, when employed, do not use current managers and coworkers as references. It could cost you a job. If you have never worked anywhere else, you can track down people who have already left your current employer. If you explain your situation, they may act as references for you.

At the beginning of your job search, excellent references, though important, are simply an added bonus. Your real agenda is to use these contacts as another tactic within your overall networking strategy.

The process is simplicity itself, starting with an introduction: "John, this is _____. We worked together at Citibank between 2002 and 2006. How's it going?" It is appropriate here to catch up on gossip and the like. Then broach the subject of your call.

"John, I wanted to ask your advice. [Everyone loves to be asked for an expert opinion.] We've had some cutbacks at Fly-By-Night Finance, as you probably heard," or "The last five years at Bank of Crooks and Criminals International have been great, and the _____ project we are just winding down has been a fascinating job. Nevertheless, I have decided that this would be a perfect time for a strategic career move to capitalize on my experience."

Then, "John, I realize how important references can be, and I was wondering if you would have any reservations about my using you as one?" It's better to find out now if John doesn't want to be a reference, rather than down the line when it could blow a job offer. The response will usually be positive, so you can then move to the next step. "Thanks, John, I hoped you would say that. Let me update you about what I have been doing recently and tell you about the type of job I'm after." Give a capsule description of what you've done since you worked together and specifically what you can do. Remember that talking too much about what you want in a dream job only reduces your chances of receiving leads. You might also ask John if he would take a look at your resume for you. There are two reasons for this:

1. It gets your resume in his hands so he can pass it on to others.
2. It gives you a reason to follow up with John in two or three weeks, when you can ask for job leads again.

Notice these reasons do *not* include getting feedback on your resume, although you will often get it. Why don't I cite this as a reason? If you ask someone their opinion about your resume, in trying to be helpful, they will come up with subjective suggestions that have no basis of understanding of the world in which your resume must perform. If you completed the Target Job Deconstruction exercise suggested earlier, you already have objective criteria against which to judge the quality of your resume. And if you followed the detailed resume writing directions in Chapter 3 and elaborated on in *Knock 'em Dead Resumes*, then you've checked the story your resume tells against your TJD, and it has all the component parts—the right focus, prioritization of information and keywords—that will make your resume as powerful as your experience will allow.

So while you already have objective benchmarks against which to judge your resume, this doesn't mean you shouldn't listen to suggestions and thank the person who gives them—just that every breeze shouldn't sway you in a new direction. Show appreciation for any advice you receive by following up your call with a thank-you e-mail (see *Knock 'em Dead Cover Letters* for samples).

With the scene set in this manner, you can network with each of these potential references every month or two, either for input on a particular opportunity or to ask for other intelligence relevant to your search. This might include leads or information about a specific company; for example, "Tina, do you know anyone who went to work at _____?"

Personal/Community Networks

Personal networking should mean more than just annoying the heck out of your friends until they stop taking your calls. If you are like most people, your friends and acquaintances would like to help, but they don't know how. And because these personal networks are rarely that large, they are easily exhausted. Here's a new way to think about and leverage the personal and community networks we all share.

While networking should become an integral part of your life, it will always move into higher gear when strategic career moves are on your front burner. There are a wide variety of personal and community-based networks available to you, depending on your interests and your willingness to become an active member of your local community.

Some are personal: family, friends, and service industry acquaintances; these tend to be the people you see on a regular basis.

Others are more formal and socially oriented: such as religious, community, local business, and volunteer groups. Some of these are professional in nature but not restricted to a specific profession (Kiwanis, etc.), while others are community-based groups that focus on a common interest (Big Brother, Big Sister). You don't necessarily know the people in these groups, but you do have a potential bond based on community involvement. You can find out about these groups in your local newspapers, at the library, through a local school or church, or by searching online.

Family and Friends, Good News/Bad News

The good news is that the people who know you best, your family and friends, will really try to help you. The bad news is that since most of them may have known you since you were a snot-nosed brat, you have been categorized, stereotyped, and pigeonholed. They might not really know—or might incorrectly guess—the nature of your career. Odds are they don't know what you are capable of doing or what you want to do. Case in point: after fourteen books and millions of copies sold, my immediate family is still genuinely surprised that I know to come in from the rain.

It is easy to squander this potentially valuable resource by tapping into it before you have thought through how you can best help your extended family help you.

These people aren't stupid, but unlike the contacts you make in your professional networks, they probably don't have a full grasp of what you do for a living. On the other hand, they are highly motivated to help you. Many job hunters make the mistake of confusing the members of this network by giving too much information about their professional life. With the right guidance, your immediate circle will cast a wide net and come up with leads for you, even if they have nothing to do with the professional world.

Here are the steps to help your loved ones help you:

1. Think carefully about what you do for a living and put it in a one- or two-sentence description that even Aunt Aggie can grasp: "I am a computer programmer; I write the instructions that help computers run."

2. Think carefully about the job you want, the kind of company you will work for, and the kind of people you need to talk to. Condense it into a one- or two-sentence explanation: "I'm looking for a job with another computer company. It would be great if you or your friends knew anyone I could talk to who works with computers." Keep it really simple.

3. Give them the information you need to get in touch with these people: "I am looking for the names, e-mail addresses, and telephone numbers of anyone in these areas (but maybe don't confuse Aunty Aggie with e-mail talk). I'm not looking for someone to hire me; I'm just looking for people in my field with whom I can network."

This process of breaking your networking needs into *just three* simple statements gives your immediate circle something they can really work with. You can do this with them one-on-one, or you can get everyone together for a barbecue and get the new program moving in one fell swoop.

Civic, Social, Volunteer, Religious, and Special Interest Networking Groups

It's good to be involved in your local community, both for your own emotional health and for the health of your community. Your involvement will provide you with a richer personal life, as well as a wide array of networking opportunities. You will find that effective networking with these groups is a little more time-consuming than with professional groups; after all, you have no prior professional relationships, and they don't have a familial obligation to help you out.

At the same time, you can't possibly join all the groups your community has to offer, so you will have to make some decisions about what is practical and which activities are going to be valuable to you in and of themselves; if the activity is personally fulfilling, you are more likely to stick with it over time and reap the personal fulfillment and networking rewards that come from your involvement. These might comprise:

- Service industry acquaintances. Electricians, plumbers, carpenters, accountants, lawyers, hairdressers—anyone whose services you retain is a potential networking resource.
- Religious/community/volunteer groups. These groups connect you with people who wish to make a difference by reaching out to others. Participation in spiritual and volunteer communities helps us achieve a sense of meaning and balance in our lives, and such groups are especially helpful in the emotionally troubled times of job and career change.
- Hobby or special interest groups. This could be a book club, a women's/men's group, a dance class, a jogging group, or any of the vast number of community-based special-interest

groups. It doesn't matter, so long as the activity is one that energizes the inner you by taking you away from the worries of your professional world. The people you meet will likely have professional careers and you can build a bond based on your shared interests.

• Business, professional, or civic groups. All communities have networks of professionals joined together in formal groups: Rotarians, Chamber of Commerce, Kiwanis, and many more. These community-based associations, societies, and clubs are professionally oriented in membership, but they aren't focused on one profession; they straddle the line between your professional and community-based networking activities. These groups were conceived as networking tools; they give you another angle of attack for your job search, and perhaps improve your social life.

In your local community networking, your need for job leads should take a back seat to being involved as a productive member. Soon enough, you'll learn what people do for a living, while they learn about you both as a professional and as a human being. As opportunities arise, you can talk about your job search needs.

Your Job Search Network

You will sometimes feel that companies are looking for everyone but you. This can get depressing at times, so you need to be aware of the emotion and manage it. One way is to join or create a support group and job search network with people in the same situation, whether these are online or local community-based networks.

A number of national organizations and many communities support job search networks through religious or other social organizations. Members meet, usually on a weekly basis, to exchange ideas and job leads and, just as important, to share and laugh with others in transition.

You can find groups in your area online at *www.careerjournal.com*, *www.jobbankinfo.org*, or *www.rileyguide.com*. Your local state employment office also maintains lists of job search support groups.

Gathering Leads and Referrals from Networking Conversations

You never know who you are going to meet at the grocery store, coffee shop, hairdresser, or gym. A "networking mindset" means you are always prepared to show an interest in others and speak to them in a friendly way, so that you won't let casual opportunities for expanding your networks slip away. With a networking mindset, you will be surprised at the range of useful people you will meet. Even if they know nothing about your profession, they might know someone involved in the same field as you. Everyone you meet has the potential to know someone who can be useful to your job search.

You can network with people you meet at conventions, association meetings, class reunions, fundraisers, the gym, the coffee shop, continuing-education classes, or at community, social, spiritual, and sporting events. You can talk to them over the telephone, by letter, or via e-mail, online chat, or message posting. While the information-gathering aspects of these conversations will remain fairly constant regardless of the communication medium, there are one or two unique considerations about networking in person.

KNOCK 'EM DEAD TIP
When networking, never talk about what you want in that ideal next job. It reduces the odds of someone telling you about an opening. Instead, talk about what you can do.

In-Person Networking

As you never know when you are going to make useful contacts, always maintain a well-put-together appearance in your local community. That doesn't mean that you always have to be dressed for a job interview, just that you should give consideration to your appearance.

Always grab a few of your business cards before leaving the house. Go to Google.com and type in "create business cards," and you will find suppliers and software for less than $20. When you attend social and professional events, keep those business cards handy. (See *Knock 'em Dead Resumes* for detailed instructions on how to create a "business card resume.") However, for networking in your community, leave your full resume at home: Thrusting one at every new acquaintance will come across as overanxious.

You have to make the effort to reach out to others, and that means working out how you will introduce yourself: at the tennis class: "Hello, I'd like to introduce myself. My name is Mark Germino. I just started playing tennis. How about you?" Always try to end with a question that encourages your contact to introduce and talk about himself. It doesn't really matter what the question is. Once there has been a conversational exchange, you can begin to move forward with your networking agenda, perhaps by saying what you do. Say, "I'm in accounting, how about you?" rather than plunging into a detailed description of your situation.

Keep It Short

Even though gatherings of associations, clubs, and societies provide excellent networking opportunities, they are not scheduled specifically for that activity. Try to keep your initial in-person networking conversations to less than five minutes. You don't want to be known as an overly solicitous bore. You can end a conversation gracefully with an offer of your business card, and you should recognize that a request for your card is a signal for you both to move on. If someone you meet isn't carrying a card, have her write her name and contact information on the back of one of yours, and always try to get a telephone number and an e-mail address.

Whenever you meet someone in person, send an e-mail to thank her for any helpful information you may have gathered from the conversation. It also serves to keep you on his radar.

The Secrets of Successful Networking Conversations

Your networks grow in proportion to the energy you put into them, expressed by the number of networking opportunities you create and how intelligently your networking conversations are structured. Networking opportunities can be created on the phone or through e-mail—and for professional networking these communication mediums are far more productive for all concerned—but with local networking, face time will always generate the best results.

Whatever your communication medium, your agenda remains the same. The following are ideas for the content of your networking conversations. Obviously, you will have to add the conversational context and take the essence of my words and make them your own. Show interest in your contacts first, and only then move on with your agenda.

The conversation happens in four stages, none of which should be rushed:

Introduction

Recall the last memorable interaction you had with your contact or mention someone you both know. Ask what is happening in your contact's personal and professional life. Listen to what is said and respond appropriately.

Statement of Your Situation

Prepare a statement that allows you to encapsulate your situation succinctly: "Malcolm, I just got laid off because of the downturn," or "We have a baby on the way, and _____ is a company where there just isn't room for me to grow professionally," or "My job just got sent to Mumbai, so I guess it's time for me to make a move."

Information Gathering

When common professional ground exists through an association or other social network, you can assume that your listener will be well disposed toward you. You can repay this good will by showing respect for that person's time and politely cutting to the chase. You could begin, "Brenda, I have been an accountant with Anderson for the last four years. I work in the small business area, and I'm looking to make a change." Rather than rambling, in fewer than ten seconds you have courteously provided a focus. Incidentally, it is at this point in the conversation that you have to be careful to avoid a common gaffe. Don't say something like, "My ideal job would be . . ." or "The next step I'd like to take is . . ."

By describing an ideal job or your desired next step up the professional ladder, you make things more difficult for the listener, who thinks, "This guy is looking for something very specific, and any introductions I can make will probably be a waste of everyone's time." It is more productive to talk in terms of what you do day-to-day, or even just tell the contact in general terms the profession in which you work ("I'm an accountant") and that you are looking for a new opportunity. If you handle yourself in a pleasant and professional manner, most people will try to be helpful.

Note that I'm assuming you are talking to professional colleagues and seeking leads on job openings, rather than talking to the managers, directors, vice presidents, and presidents who can make those hiring decisions. The conversations with anyone who has the potential to hire you are different because you are then making a marketing presentation.

Tell your contacts in general terms what you *do*, not what you *want*. Talking about your aspirations just reduces your chances of getting leads.

Ask for Assistance

You can ask for general guidance about your tactics: "If you were in my situation, Charlie, what would you do?" You can ask if he has heard about local companies hiring. These are good questions, and they typically comprise the content of 99 percent of all networking questions, but you can achieve much more with the right sequence of questions.

Great Networking Questions

We are now going to work through a sequence of networking questions that will lead you to jobs you would otherwise never hear about. These are the same question sequences asked every day by headhunters the world over, retooled to fulfill your needs.

These questions follow a logical sequence, but that order might not suit your needs, so as you examine them, figure out what you would ask if you had time for only one question, then if you had time for only two, and so on. The result will be a comfortably prioritized set of questions. Each question you ask should be specific, so avoid time-wasting questions like "How's business these days?" When you're satisfied with your list of questions, have a copy on your computer and/or smartphone, another by your phone (never at work), and a third that will go in your wallet or purse.

General Questions

You can ask if there are openings in the department or at the company, and with whom you should speak about them. *Don't* ask, "Can you or your company hire me?" *Do* ask:

- "What needs does your company have at present?"
- "Who in the company is most likely to need someone with my background?"
- "Who else in the company might need someone with my background?"
- "Is the company/department planning any expansion or new projects that might create an opening?"
- "When do you anticipate a change in company manpower needs?"
- "Does your company have any other divisions or subsidiaries? Where are they?"
- "I'd appreciate any e-mail addresses or telephone numbers of headhunters you hear from."

Profession-Specific Questions

You might wish to add some profession-specific questions. For instance, people in Information Technology might ask questions about operating systems, communication protocols, programs, and useful foreign languages. In this instance, after receiving an answer, add a similarly focused follow-up question—"Thanks, Gail. Who else do you know that uses these configurations?"—that will lead you to other companies likely to have similar needs. Be sure any question you add to your list is geared toward identifying names, titles, and companies in your areas of interest.

KNOCK 'EM DEAD TIP

Even when an offer of introduction is made—"Let me speak to Charlene Howarth for you"—don't rely on your contact to get you into that company. If the door hasn't opened in a few days, it might not. You should execute your own plan of attack, seeking other personal introductions within the company from your networking resources and making direct appeals by telephone, e-mail, and snail mail resume submissions.

Leads at Other Companies

When you are sure that no job openings exist within a particular department or company, move on to gathering leads in other companies. You can ask, "Do you know of anyone at other banks in town that I might speak to?" but you will get a better response if your question is more focused: "Who do you know at _____?"

If your contact can't think of a person, ask about other companies: "What companies have you heard about that are hiring now?" or "If you were going to make a move, which companies would you look at?" or "Which are the most rapidly growing companies in the area?"

Whenever you are offered a lead, even if it is an obvious one, say, "Hey, that's a great idea. I never thought of Google as hiring people." Your encouragement is positive reinforcement. Then, after a suitable pause, ask for another company name, as in, "I really appreciate your help, Sam. I never thought of _____. Who else comes to mind?" When people see that their advice is appreciated, they will often come up with more helpful information. When you have gathered two or three company names, you can backtrack with a request for contact names at each of the companies: "Do you know of anyone I could speak to at _____?"

You can also ask for leads at companies you plan to call, or even at those you have already called: "Jack, I was planning to contact_____, Inc. Would you happen to know anyone there who could give me a heads-up on hiring needs?"

When a conversation is going well, and if you are talking to someone in your profession, tacking on a last question that gives you job leads to trade with others can be a good idea: "Jane, I'm a member of a job search network. If you don't have a need for someone with my background right now, perhaps one of my colleagues could be just what you are looking for. What titles is your company looking for right now?"

If you are changing careers or considering a career change, your priorities might be different. In this case you can explain that you are considering a particular profession for a new career direction and ask what it is like working in the profession; what your contact likes least and most about the work; what education, experience, and professional behaviors help people succeed in the profession; who fails and why; and how one gets into and moves ahead in the profession.

The extent of your questioning depends on the willingness of your contact to continue the conversation; I've known these conversations to run for fifty minutes.

When You Get a Referral

When you get leads on companies and specific individuals to talk to, be sure to thank your benefactor and ask to use her name as an introduction. "Thank you, Linda. I didn't know _____was building a facility in town, and I appreciate getting Holly Barnes's name. May I use your name as an introduction?"

Every time you get a referral, be sure to ask whether you can use your contact's name as an introduction. The answer will invariably be "yes," but asking demonstrates professionalism and will encourage your contact to come up with more names and leads. For example, you can say, "That's very helpful, Bill. Does anyone else come to mind?"

When you get permission to use your contact's name, use it in an introduction: "Holly Barnes? My name is _____. I'm an (accounting) friend of Bill Smith who suggested I call, so before I go any further, Bill asked me to say hello." This is a bridge-building phrase and usually leads to a brief exchange about your mutual contact before you go into your information-gathering agenda.

When you do get help, say thank you. If you do it verbally, it's a nice touch to follow it up with a note (see the latest edition of *Knock 'em Dead Cover Letters* for networking letter examples). The positive impression you make might get you another lead, and it never hurts to include a copy of your resume with the thank-you letter.

Wrapping It Up

When your networking call or face-to-face conversation comes to its natural conclusion, offer your thanks and willingness to return the favor, and leave the door open for future calls: "Christine, thanks so much for your help. I do appreciate it. At times like this you realize how important your colleagues are, so I'd like to give you my telephone number and e-mail so that one day I might return the favor. Let's stay in touch. Might I call you again sometime?"

Other statements that you might use at the end of your conversation include:

- "I'll let you know how it works out with Holly Barnes."
- "Might I get in touch in a couple of months to see if the situation at _____, Inc. has changed?"

When talking to a management contact in your profession, you might suggest, "Would it be worthwhile e-mailing a copy of my resume for your personal talent database?" All smart managers keep such a database. After all, their job is to get work done through others, and being able to locate good talent is essential.

You are going to get some pleasant surprises when you network, but also a few disappointments. You will be surprised at how someone you always regarded as a real pal won't give you the time of day, and how someone you never thought of as a friend will go above and beyond the call of duty for you. Networking is a numbers game, so keep calling and e-mailing, and start every communication with an open mind. Stay in touch with your networking contacts, regardless of whether they were able to help you. Let them know when you get a job, and try to stay in contact at least once a year. A career lasts a long time, and next week or a decade from now, when a group of managers (including one from your personal network) talk about filling a new position, they will ask, "Who do we know?" That someone is more likely to be you when you are connected to networks in your profession and your local community.

CHAPTER 6
NETWORK-INTEGRATED JOB SEARCH TACTICS

IN A COMPETITIVE job market, you cannot rely exclusively on networking or any other single job-search tool. You need to use a number of different job search strategies and integrate networking into each of them.

A man who goes fishing and puts one hook in the water has only one chance of catching any of the millions of fish in the sea, and one fish is the best he can ever do. A man with two hooks in the water has double the chances of catching a fish and has also earned himself the opportunity to catch twice as many fish as the first guy.

The more hooks you have in the water, the better your chances of action. All the job search tools and approaches that we discuss in this section of the book—job banks, resume banks, headhunters, direct research and approach—have proven effective. No one alone is a guaranteed silver bullet, and any of them could deliver the ideal opportunity for you. Your plan of attack should embrace as many of these approaches as is practical in your situation. Intelligently pursuing all useful approaches will generate job leads. You can then leverage your networks for leads on and introductions to the hiring managers for the jobs you discover.

It's a Digital World

Corporate recruitment has moved online, so your job search must respond to these recruitment preferences.

With tens of thousands of job sites and resume banks out there, you could spend eternity strolling from one to the next. The danger is that this feels like productive work, and because it involves zero rejection it can be highly addictive. An Internet-based job search can seem magical because the media tells you it is magical, but *job banks and resume banks are not magical*. The Internet increases your ability to gather and disseminate information, but you need to understand, control, and leverage this power, not be controlled by it.

First Get Organized

If you've been through a job search before, you are groaning at starting all over again, but if you follow this plan of attack, apart from having a successful job search, you will be prepared for future job searches: You will have the mechanisms in place to track interesting opportunities; you will have a database of relevant employers and a wide range of networking contacts; plus you'll have a database of relevant job banks, resume banks, and headhunters. You will be more proactive in the management of your career and therefore more successful over the long haul.

If you don't organize properly, you will get buried in an avalanche of information and leads, but it doesn't have to be this way. Organization begins with setting up a career management base of operations for your professional life; this job search will be its first use, but the long-term success of your personal brand, MeInc, demands an organized place for your ongoing professional development and career management activities.

Security and Confidentiality

Online privacy is an issue for everyone today and is especially important during a job search.

Professional E-Mail Address

I recommend you set up a separate e-mail account devoted exclusively to job search and career management affairs. You need an e-mail address that reflects the *professional you*, and it's a good time to retire those addresses like *binkypoo@yahoo.com* or *bigboy@hotmail.com* that seemed such a good idea when your professional reputation wasn't an issue. If you have a family, a separate account can also prevent a rug rat destroying critical data.

It is easy to set up an additional e-mail account, as your ISP almost certainly allows multiple addresses. Create an account name that reveals something about your professional profile, such as *systemanalyst@hotmail.com* or *topaccountant@yahoo.com*. Addresses such as these help recipients focus on your communication from the start, because they act as headlines for the reader. Many names like *topaccountant@yahoo.com* are long gone, and you will be encouraged to accept *topaccountant1367@yahoo.com*; before you accept this, try some variations: *top10accountant@*, *greataccountant@*, *smartfinanceguy@*, *moneycounts@*, *PandL@*, etc.

> **KNOCK 'EM DEAD TIP**
> While you know better than to use your office e-mail for a job search, you should also never download your secure e-mail to your office e-mail box. Why? Companies can and do check Internet usage on your computer. Inappropriate activities can cost you a job.

Separate Telephone

Most telephone companies now allow you two or three alternate numbers at no extra charge with your basic service, and usually these come with a distinctive ring tone. This means you can have a dedicated and confidential number for all your job search and career management activities.

A Sanitized Resume

When you are employed—or if you want to create that impression—and involved in a job search, discretion is paramount. Consider sanitizing your resume by removing all "traceable-to-you" contact information (name, address, phone, fax), and replacing them with your career management e-mail.

By removing a current employer's name (all recruiters and employers understand the need for this), you can further protect your identity, replacing it with a generalized description of the company and location. For example, if you work for Pepsi-Cola in Chicago, you could describe this as a "Midwestern Beverage Company."

It usually isn't necessary to sanitize prior employer names. However, if you have a senior title associated with a particularly visible company, it could be a clue as to who you are. In this case replace it with a more generic but recognizable job title.

How to Organize Your Job Search and Career Management Database

It is important for your career that you build and *maintain* a career management database: Keep folders for target companies and your contacts within them, and the same for your contacts within recruitment firms. You might choose to add a Job Leads folder; into this you can put all the job postings you develop. You can add folders to contain contact info for both your on- and offline networking activities.

Additions to these groups can be made at any time; when you see recruiters who work in your industry, put them in the appropriate folder. You're creating a vehicle from which you can launch a massive career blitz tomorrow or four years from now. Organize yourself to capture information today that you can use throughout your work life.

We typically dump job postings or help wanted ads that don't turn into anything or for other reasons aren't suitable. I don't want you to do this for two reasons:

1. You can offer them to others in the course of your networking activities.
2. A company that hires accountants today is just as likely to be hiring them three years from today. Knowing about the company and its contact information gives you a head start next time. This job search and career management database is a tool you create for the benefit of *your entire career*. It is part of gaining control of your professional destiny.

Whenever you respond to a job posting, do exactly as requested, but also copy the job posting and all contact information for the company to a folder. You will need this if an interview occurs. Plus, you can cross-reference the job posting with people in your different networks and perhaps come up with a name and a title to which you can send the resume directly, thus doubling your chances of getting an interview.

On any job site it is a good idea to make your requirements broad to begin with; if a particular site drowns you with inappropriate jobs, gradually refine your target. Alternatively, you might not be getting enough responses from a particular site and might want to recast your needs in broader terms.

Job Sites and Resume Banks

There are so many thousands of job sites, you could never hope to visit them all, so you have to integrate the job site/resume bank aspect of your search intelligently. You start by identifying which sites are relevant to your search: At *www.knockemdead.com* you can find an extensive listing of jobs sites for many different professions, and hundreds of other useful job search links on the Internet Resources pages of the website; this would be a useful place to start.

So we'll assume you have sites to visit from the online resources and get right into what to do when visiting them.

- Does the site have job postings that are suitable for you? If it doesn't, you can move on to the next site. If it does, you will want to keep an eye on the site for relevant job postings as they come in. This means you will want to register with the site and receive job alerts in your e-mail inbox when new jobs matching your criteria get posted to the site.
- When you are asked to define the jobs that interest you, set your sights wide. You may get too many responses initially, but you can gradually narrow the parameters. It is better to plow through a little junk than miss a great opportunity.

> **KNOCK 'EM DEAD TIP**
> Remember, those jobs you hear about from the job site that aren't quite right for you are not a waste of your time. They are worth saving in a trading file to share with network contacts, for whom one of those jobs might be a perfect fit.

- If this is a good site for you, other sites it is linked to might also be useful; check the partners/links pages. These aren't always obvious; if they're not, look for a site map in those little links that always crowd the very bottom of the page.
- Because companies hire more people from smaller niche sites, you must check the specialty sites. You will find a good selection among the Internet resources at *www.knockemdead.com*.
- You will collect two types of job postings: those that are good for you and those that are suitable to offer to your network. Before you file any of these, go through them carefully looking for keywords that describe skill sets you have that are not captured as such in your existing resume. List these on a desktop document. You'll use this document to update your resume and to refresh it in the resume banks; more on this in the next section.
- Make a folder for each relevant site you visit, and as postings come in store them in the appropriate folder. You'll quickly see which sites are most productive.
- When you are asked to create a profile—and this is usually part of setting up your account on a site—you essentially cut and paste your resume, as this represents your most carefully considered packaging of the *professional you*. But this requires a little more explanation.

Most job sites are free for you to use. It's the employers who are paying to post their job openings and search the resume bank. The job sites work with employers to develop ever more efficient screening tools. Setting up your account and filling out a profile is part of this process: *Everything you do online is being tracked by someone for some reason.*

Whenever you are filling out a profile or questionnaire on a job site keep the following in mind.

Multiple Resumes/Profiles

Job sites recognize that many people can do more than one job, and so they frequently allow you to register as many as five separate resumes and/or profiles. It is also a tacit acknowledgment that one "general" resume won't cut the mustard. And yes, it is yet another benefit of the TJD exercises from Chapter 3 that it allows you to create relevant, intelligent, and deep profiles for each option.

Most job sites break up the registration/profile building/resume uploading process into a number of steps: often twelve or more specific dialogue boxes you have to work your way through. They typically include topics like: Target Job, Career Objective, Competencies, Relocation, Salary, Ideal Job, Education, and more.

These sites often offer examples to help you fill in the dialogue boxes—but remember that behind all this is the screening process.

Target Job Title

Copy and paste all the different job titles you collected in the first part of the TJD exercise. Putting in more than one title only serves to increase your visibility.

Career/Job Objective/Summary

No one wants to hear about your objectives, and putting them out there is only wasting space. This is where you will put your Performance Profile, weighted in accordance with employer needs as determined by the TJD process.

This dialogue box often has lots of space, so you can end it by inserting a header that says, "The opportunity to use these skills." Then paste in the entire collection of Core Competencies you identified in Chapter 3.

KNOCK 'EM DEAD TIP

You are not always limited to one answer—even in the case of check boxes. Always test and verify to see if you can select more than one answer. Never assume you are limited—not even if the directions on the screen indicate that you are. Similarly, you might not want to answer a supposedly mandatory question. Try leaving it blank; you'll find out if it really was mandatory when you click "submit."

Salary Requirements

It is always better to give a range rather than a single figure. I show you how to decide on this salary range in Chapter 22, where we discuss salary negotiation. Even though this box is always marked as mandatory, that isn't always the case. Sometimes you can leave it blank if you feel this will be helpful to your cause.

Ideal Job

No one is interested in your ideal job. The recruiter is searching a database and retrieving possible candidates from a list of keywords that they have put into the system. Copy and paste your Performance Profile and follow it with your Core Competencies. Test to see if there is more space by pasting in your Core Competencies again. No person will actually read the repetition (and if they did, they would regard it as a glitch) but the software will catch and reward you for it by increasing your ranking in the search results.

Core Competencies

If they have a separate section for this, paste in your Core Competencies . . . as often as space will allow.

Education

Education is the most questioned area of any candidacy. Much prone to exaggeration and outright lies, educational claims *do get checked*. Untruths can cause offers to be withdrawn and jobs to be terminated. Don't fake it.

If you are involved in the pursuit of any postsecondary education but haven't yet achieved it, you can use it if you state the school and the degree, and if you can, also state a projected graduation date . . . *because* you are enrolled in at least one course toward that degree. That you are pursuing education while you work is a plus in employers' eyes, and you have a right to show it to them.

Relocation

When completing questions about relocation, don't jump to make a selection; not all questions are mandatory; if the question is optional, leave it open. If you do answer, select the broadest option possible. Even if you have the ability to list many preferred locations, don't. Choose no preference, and you will get the same responses. Plus:

1. You can always say "no," but you can't say "yes" unless you've been asked.
2. For the right job, opportunity, and money, we would all move to Possum Trot, Kentucky.
3. Any job you interview for but reject will only improve your interviewing skills, which are probably your very weakest professional skill.
4. It gives you leads to trade in your networking initiatives.

Name Dropping

Recruiters often look for candidates who either are working for or have worked for certain companies or competitors. If you work for name companies and products, that is great. You can also drop corporate names and brand names if you have been a vendor or a client.

Resume Banks

If suitable jobs are posted to the job site, it probably means that recruiters are also visiting its resume bank. In that case you may well want to upload your resume. Some considerations to bear in mind:

1. Use the same considerations and values for filling out dialogue boxes as you would for any job site registration.
2. Some resume banks require that you upload your resume in something called ASCII format. This is not difficult to do, but it is a pain in the neck; you can find step-by-step directions in the latest edition of *Knock 'em Dead Resumes*.
3. Resume banks have purge dates, mostly so that the recruiters who pay for access can be assured that they are not looking at stale resumes. The purge usually happens every ninety days, and you will want to bear the dates in mind so that you can refresh your resume before then.
4. Of course, recruiters also have the ability to restrict their searches by the date a resume was uploaded; for example they might be able to restrict a search to resumes uploaded in the past ten days. This is important when a particular site has job postings suitable for you, because it also means that recruiters will be cruising its resume bank for candidates.
5. In instances when you want to maintain the highest visibility on a site like this, go in once a week and update your resume with new keywords you have identified in other job postings. Make any change to your resume and the database search engine will recognize it as a new document.

6. When there are no new words you can achieve the same effect quite simply: Log into your account, open your resume, replace a couple of words with a string of x's and log out. Take a couple of deep breaths, log in again, replace the x's with the original words, and log out again: To all intents and purposes you now have a brand new document.

Finding More Hidden Jobs

In addition to what we've talked about above, you can use job sites in other ways. Go to any job site and search their posted openings by putting in minimal keywords and restrictions. For example, if a medical insurance sales manager goes to *www.6figurejobs.com* and does a simple keyword search for "insurance," she may get hundreds of results, and the vast majority will be for jobs that do not interest her. At the same time, those results will reveal recruiters and companies in her profession and target location.

Visit these sites and see if there are suitable job openings posted. Companies all use their own websites as recruitment vehicles and usually have their open jobs posted there. Even if they do not have jobs for someone like you posted, upload your resume anyway. You don't really know what is going on at that company, and at the very least you will be in their database and therefore on their radar when a need arises.

If a company is looking for anyone even remotely connected with your area of professional expertise, they could also be looking for someone like you. Upload your resume and research the company to approach the appropriate hiring managers directly.

After visiting a company website, add the link to the appropriate folder in your career management database. Identify all the profession-specific employers at all the job sites you visit, then visit each of those employer websites and add them to a potential employers folder; your hit list of potential employers will grow exponentially.

KNOCK 'EM DEAD TIP
This list of companies will also help your social networking activities. You can use the company names in database searches on the social networking sites to find contacts to approach for leads and introductions at these target companies. Everything in a successful job search is geared toward getting into conversations with people who could make the decision to hire you; as we have noted, typically someone one to three title levels above your own. Always strive to identify and get into a conversation with anyone who holds any of these target titles at any and every company in your area.

Finding Names of Hiring Authorities for Direct Approach

Responding to job postings is a big part of most job searches, but you can double, triple, and quadruple your chances of getting interviews from job postings by making direct approaches to the people in a position to hire you.

Whenever you see a job you can do, respond to the posting in the requested way. Also, flag all contact information for the company: website, mailing address, etc. When you learn how to find the names and titles of managers one to three title levels above yours you can approach them directly in three different ways, each one much more likely to produce an interview:

1. E-mail your resume directly to that manager with a personalized cover letter, at least doubling your chances of a hit.
2. Send a resume and personalized cover letter to that manager, at least tripling your chances of a hit.
3. Make a follow-up telephone call to that manager first thing in the morning, at lunchtime, or at 5 P.M., at least quadrupling your chances of a hit.

A successful job search is all about *getting into conversations with people in a position to hire you, as quickly and as often as possible.*

The more frequently you get into conversations with managers whose job titles signify they have the authority to hire you, the faster you will land that new position. Because you have skipped right over needing to be pulled from the resume database, you have sidestepped the recruiter's evaluation process, and you have the opportunity to make a direct and personal pitch to the actual decision maker.

Your target for direct approach is always someone who can hire you (typically one to three title levels above yours) although any management title offers opportunity for referral. For example, while HR people won't have the authority to hire you, the pivotal nature of their work makes them aware of all areas within a company that could use your skills.

Getting a resume to someone by name with a personalized pitch gives you a distinct advantage, never more important than when the economy is down or in recovery. At such times your competition is fierce and employers recognize initiative and motivation as differentiating factors in your candidacy.

Who to Target in Your Job Search

The hiring titles to target during your job search are those titles most likely to be in a position to hire you. As indicated earlier, these people are usually one to three management titles above you.

Other titles likely to be involved in the selection process include management titles (again, one to three levels above you) in departments that have ongoing interaction with your department, and peers holding similar titles to that which you're applying for.

Titles most likely to know people involved in the selection process and be able to refer you include management titles one to three levels above you in any department, and internal recruiters and HR professionals.

In fact any name is better than no name, and with the Internet at your fingertips there is endless opportunity to identify the names of people who carry the appropriate hiring titles for your needs.

Sometimes sending a letter and resume to the levels of titles mentioned above can mean upward of half a dozen pitches to a desirable target company, just to assure that all the right people know you are available. For example, let's say you are a young engineer crazy for a job with Last Chance Electronics. It is well within the bounds of reason that you would submit a cover letter and resume to any or all of the following people, with each letter addressed by name to minimize its chances of going straight into the trash:

- Company President
- Vice President of Engineering
- Chief Engineer
- Engineering Design Manager
- Vice President of Human Resources
- Technical Engineering Recruitment Manager
- Technical Recruiter

Think through all the titles likely to be of use to you, based on the above criteria, and keep them in mind when you go looking for names to attach to them: The more options you have, the more results you will get.

Internet Research Tactics

Apart from cross-referencing target companies with the members of your expanded networks to get referrals and introductions, you can also use online search tactics and tools to locate the names of the people you need to reach.

Start with keyword searches on Google.com, Bing.com, Ask.com, and so forth. They are all likely to deliver names, and they'll all get different results. For example: A professional in pharmaceutical sales looking to make direct contact with hiring authorities for a job at a specific company in the Pittsburgh area could try all the following keyword searches and gather new usable information on each search.

Do each of these searches first as a standard Google search then as a Google News search, which looks for mentions of those keywords in media coverage:

Pharmaceutical sales (company name)

Pharmaceutical sales (company name) Pennsylvania

Pharmaceutical sales (company name) Pittsburgh

Pharmaceutical Mgr sales (company name) Pennsylvania

Pharmaceutical Mgr sales (company name) Pittsburgh

Pharmaceutical Director sales (company name) Pennsylvania

Pharmaceutical Director sales (company name) Pittsburgh

Pharmaceutical VP sales (company name) Pennsylvania

Now:

- Repeat all without "pharmaceutical"
- Repeat all without company name
- Repeat with just the job title
- Repeat with separate searches for target title plus: hired, resigned, deceased

Try these and other keyword phrases and, of course, you will come up with job openings and job sites. But look carefully and drill down beyond those first couple of pages and you will come up with names to go with your target hiring titles. Drill down five or ten pages, and you will come up with people holding these titles at this and other target companies in your area.

KNOCK 'EM DEAD TIP

When you find news information relevant to the subject of your search, use it as an opener for your letter or e-mail.

- In an e-mail, paste the article and attach it.
- With a traditional letter, enclose a copy of the article.

You can also:

1. Check out the company website. On the "about us" pages, you can sometimes find names and titles of management.
2. Call the company and ask for the name of the title-holder. This may sound old-fashioned, but it's very effective.

Online Research for Direct Approach

Online resources are a valuable supplement to the information you get from your personal and professional networks. Apart from reaching out through your networks to people who work or once worked at the target company, sites such as *www.vault.com* will tell you what past and current employees think about their employer. Other online resources such as *www.wetfeet.com* will give you great info about your target companies.

As you develop dossiers of information on potential employers, some companies will rise to the top as particularly desirable. This will provide useful background information for interviews and show that you have done your homework. It is also flattering to the interviewer, who sees you've paid attention to detail and shown effort and enthusiasm, each of which can end up being deciding factors in a tight job race.

This effort also has long-term value because you are building a personalized reference work of your industry/specialty/profession that will help you throughout your career.

Here are some other online resources for company research and identification of management title holders.

www.virtualpet.com/industry/howto/search.htm	*www.superpages.com*
www.standardandpoors.com	*www.jigsaw.com*
www.idexec.com	*www.zoominfo.com*
www.hoovers.com	*www.corporateinformation.com*
www.quintcareers.com	*www.ceoexpress.com*
www.vault.com	*www.infospace.com*
www.infousa.com	*www.search-it-all.com*
www.thomasnet.com	*www.searchbug.com*

Even More Resources for Finding Names of Hiring Authorities

The resources available reach to the horizon. Standard & Poor's has a database of executives by name and title with contact information called the "Biographical Directory/Database." Higher-level target hiring titles will be identifiable there or through one of the following options:

www.onesource.com
www.knowx.com
www.jigsaw.com
www.lead411.com/about.html
www.privateeye.com/?from=p31702&vw=background&Input=Name&piid=44
www.econtentmag.com/Articles/ArticleReader.aspx?ArticleID=4089
www.lambresearch.com/CorpsExecs.htm

KNOCK 'EM DEAD TIP

As you build these dossiers of information about individual companies, one of those folders will likely be for your dream company. Beware of applying for jobs at these "super desirable" employers right away. I'm sure you've heard about the latest Broadway hit, but you may not realize that hit shows don't start on Broadway; they go through months of rehearsals, previews with selected audiences, and even road trips to try out the show. They do this because they don't want to screw up when they hit the big time.

The same applies to you. Most likely your resume and interviewing skills (that is, your script and performance skills) are not up to speed at the beginning of your search. The last thing you need to do is fumble an opportunity to join the company of your dreams. It is better to hold off until you know that your resume is the best it can be for the target job on which it is focused. That way, it's also likely you will have had a couple of interviews, and you won't swallow your tongue in the first few minutes.

Employment Agencies and Headhunters

There are few clear-cut lines of demarcation in this area.

- *State employment agencies* are staffed by government employees. Their job is to help you find a job; they are almost the only people whose focus is entirely on helping you. They are funded by the state Labor Department and typically carry names like State Division of Employment Security, State Job Service, or Manpower Services. The names vary but the services remain the same. They will make efforts to line you up with appropriate jobs and otherwise help you as best they can. It is not mandatory for employers to list jobs with state agencies, but more and more companies are taking advantage of these free services. These public agencies now list positions that often exceed $100,000 a year, so they're a resource not to be ignored.

  If you are moving across the state or across the country, your local employment office can plug you into the national job bank, or you can connect yourself online at *www.nationjob.com*, which claims to be the largest job bank in the world.

- *Private employment agencies* are for profit, and their source of income derives from the company. They will search on behalf of employers, but typically only in their own databases, and they will market someone to employers only if that person is seen to be in high demand and can be used as a tool to develop other fee-paying assignments.

  When working with an employment agency, choose your agent with the same care and attention with which you would choose a spouse or a lawyer. The caliber of the individual and company you choose could well affect the kind of company you ultimately join.

Further, if you choose prudently, she can become a lifetime counselor who can guide you step-by-step up the ladder of success.

- *Career counselors and job search counselors.* Their money comes from you, but while there are charlatans in the business, there are also exemplary, talented, and dedicated professionals in this group. Typically, these people work alone or in very small companies, and they can help you with career choice, resume preparation, job search, and interview preparation.

  How do you choose whom to work with? Find out how many years they've been in business, what professional degrees they hold, their affiliations with professional associations, and their professional accreditations. Ideally, they should also have a background as contingency or retained recruiters.

- *Contingency recruiters* gain their income from employers and are largely involved with finding employed professionals for hard-to-fill positions. They do this on a contingency basis, the contingency being that they only collect a fee when they fill the position. Typically, contingency recruiters will search their databases and actively recruit for a percentage of the openings they have to fill. Most contingency recruiters and some contingency firms will market an "in-demand" professional to target companies for a day or two and as a tool to develop other fee-paying assignments. Contingency recruiters are a hybrid, doing search work but not working on a retainer basis, they are often more professionally sophisticated than local employment agency people.

- *Executive search firms* are also employer paid. They are the only group entirely focused on the employer's needs and have no interest in you unless you fit an existing requirement. This is because they receive cash up front, more when a candidate/recruit is hired, and the final payment when that person starts work. They are almost exclusively interested in people currently successful in their jobs because an employed person is less of a risk (the firms often guarantee their finds to the employer for up to a year) and is a more desirable commodity.

These people rarely deal with salary levels under $100,000 per year. They are more interested in obtaining your resume for their database than seeing you unless you match a specific job they are trying to fill for a client.

You may have heard the term *headhunter.* It is now applied to anyone who provides employment services, but in reality it only fits executive search consultants and a few contingency recruiters.

Whom to Work with, and How to Work with Them

What type of employment services company is best for you? Well, the answer is simple: the one that will get you the right job offer. The problem is, there are thousands of companies in each of these broad categories. How do you choose between the good, the bad, and the ugly?

Fortunately this is not as difficult as it sounds. A retained executive search firm is not necessarily better or more professional than a contingency search firm, which in turn is not necessarily better or more professional than a regular (EPF) employment agency. Each has its exemplary practitioners and its charlatans. Your goal is to avoid the charlatans and get representation by a company with experience placing professionals like you.

Involvement in professional associations is always a good sign, demonstrating commitment and an enhanced level of competence. In the employment services industry, the high-end employment agencies and contingency search firms—as well as some retained search firms—belong to the National Association of Personnel Services (NAPS), the premier professional organization with state associations in all fifty states. The Association for Executive Search Consultants (AESC) is the premier organization for the retained executive search firms. Career Management Institute (CMI) is the leading association for job search and career management counselors, and NATSS (National Association of Temporary and Staffing Services) is the leading association for temp firms.

Involvement in independent or franchise networks of firms can also be a powerful plus for a job search. For example, an independent headhunter network like NPA (*www.npaworldwide .com*) has hundreds of member firms around the world. Membership in one of the leading franchise groups, such as Management Recruiters, Robert Half, or Dunhill, likewise gives you access to a coordinated network of employment services professionals. These networks also have extensive training programs that ensure a high-caliber consultant. Franchise networks can be especially helpful if relocation is in your future, as they tend to have powerful symbiotic relationships with other franchise members around the country and the world.

It is prudent to ask whether your contact has professional accreditations. Most of the national professional associations have training programs that offer accreditation, so these can be another sign that the recruiter is a committed and connected member of his profession. The most widely recognized of all these is the CPC designation. CPC (or its international equivalent, CIPC) stands for Certified Personnel Consultant. The CPC and CIPC designations are recognized as a standard of excellence and commitment only achieved after rigorous training and study.

CIPC designation requires that the holder has already achieved CPC designation, and it requires adherence to an international code of ethics as designated by the International Personnel Association (IPA).

Although certification can be applied for after two years of experience in business, even the newest holders of a CPC usually have five years of experience. The average CPC probably has seven to ten years of experience, and with it comes excellent contacts on the corporate side.

Qualified CPCs (like holders of the other accreditations) can also be relied upon to have superior knowledge of the legalities and ethics of the recruitment and hiring process, along with the expertise and tricks of the trade that only come from years of hands-on experience. (I should note that while I hold a CPC accreditation, mine is an honorary one, in recognition of my contributions to the discussion of career management.)

Finally, when dealing with an agency or personnel professional, don't get intimidated. You are not obligated to sign anything, nor are you obligated to guarantee anyone that you will remain in any employment for any specific length of time.

> **KNOCK 'EM DEAD TIP**
> For a full list of the accreditations relevant to resume, recruitment, and career management professionals, go to *www.knockemdead.com* on the blog and advice pages.

It Comes Down to the Individual

You can develop mutually beneficial relationships with employment professionals in all these categories. Their livelihood depends on the people they know in the professional world. Look at how many years of experience they have in employment services and how well they understand your profession. Look for involvement with their professional communities and professional accreditations.

If a recruiter is interested in representing you, expect a detailed analysis of your background, and prepare to be honest. Do not overstate your job duties, accomplishments, or education. If there are employment gaps, explain them. Be circumspect, because an unethical headhunter can create further competition for you when you share information about companies you are talking to. The details of your communications with a company are nobody's business but your own. If the recruiter asks who you are talking with, say your job search is confidential and you'd like to know whom she plans to speak with. Explain that you will happily tell her if you are already in communication with that company.

Find out what the recruiter expects of you in the relationship, and explain what you expect. Reach commitments you both can live with, and stick with them. If you break those commitments, expect the representation to cease. Keep the recruiter informed about all changes in your status: salary increases, promotions, layoffs, or other offers of employment.

Don't consider yourself an employment expert. You get a job for yourself every three or four years. These people do it for a living. Ask for their objective input and seek their advice in developing interviewing strategies with their clients.

Temporary Services Companies

Such companies fill temporary assignments for employers and provide employment services to companies in all industries and at most professional levels, from unskilled and semiskilled labor (referred to as "light industrial") to administration, finance, technical, sales, and marketing professionals, as well as doctors, lawyers, and management up to the CEO and COO level.

KNOCK 'EM DEAD TIP
This latter part of the business is usually referred to as "interim management." To find companies and associations for the interim management sector, simply key "interim management jobs" into your browser.

Always useful for quickly getting skills up to speed and re-establishing credentials after an absence from the workforce, temp or interim management work can offer a valuable stopgap in a drawn-out job search.

If you are unemployed and need the cash flow for bills, working with a temp company can supply that and expose you to employers in the community that, if you really shine, could ask you to join the staff full-time. This "temp-to-perm" approach is increasingly popular with companies hiring at all levels, as it allows employers to try before they buy.

Here's some advice when considering interim and temp job agencies and services:

- Define the titles and the employment levels they represent, along with geographical areas they cover.
- Determine whether they are members of the National Association of Temporary and Staffing Services (NATSS).
- Select a handful of firms that work in your field; this will increase the odds of suitable assignments appearing quickly.
- Do not overstate your job duties, accomplishments, or education.
- Find out first what the temporary help professional expects of you in the relationship, then explain what you expect. Reach commitments you both can live with, and stick with them.
- Judge the assignments not solely on the paycheck (although that can be important), but also by the long-term benefits to your job search and career. For example, if you have been out of the world of work raising a family, temp work can help you get acclimated and develop some current experience.
- Keep the temporary help counselor informed about any and all changes in your status, such as offers of employment or acquisition of new skills.
- Resolve key issues ahead of time. Should an employer want to take you on full-time, will that employer have to pay a set amount, or will you just stay on as a temporary for a specific period and then go on the employer's payroll?

College Career Services

Career services can help recently graduated students, as well as those about to finish school, and an increasing number of these services also try to help alumni. These dedicated professionals are horrendously overworked. So take the time to stand out by having thought through your issues. Stress your willingness to listen to good advice. If you are then seen to act on that advice, when you come back for more you will have earned the department's respect and will garner yourself more personal attention and guidance.

For students, the best way into corporate America is through internships and on-campus recruiters, who can recommend interns and entry-level hires to the company. Career Services is the best way to learn about these recruiters. Treat your entire interaction with Career Services the same way you intend to treat the interview process. Make a real effort with your appearance and professional demeanor.

Campus recruiters go to society and association meetings on campus all year long to see who is engaged, enthusiastic, and professional in their approach to life and career. Most campus recruiters have already chosen the best before they officially arrive on campus for the job fairs. When you take an active part in campus affairs, you will get to know many of these recruiters. Career Services will usually know which recruiters are involved with which campus activities.

You will also start to build a powerful network of peers for your whole career, because these are likely to be the most successful people in the professional world, as they are already engaged and committed.

Job Fairs

Job fairs (sometimes called career days) are occasions where actively hiring companies get together, usually under the auspices of a job fair promoter, to attract large numbers of potential employees to a one-day-only event. They aren't of much value to senior-level professionals.

Job fairs aren't regular events, except in times of high employment, so they won't take much of your time, but you should become an active participant when they do occur.

They often charge a small entrance fee, in return for which you get direct access to all the employers and formal presentations by company representatives and local employment experts. When you organize yourself properly, take the right attitude, and work all the opportunities, job fairs make for a great job search opportunity.

When you attend job fairs, go prepared with:

- Proper business attire. You may be meeting your new boss, and you don't want the first impression to be less than professional.
- Business cards. If you are currently employed, remember to request discretion and confidentiality.
- Resumes. You should take as many copies of your resume as there are exhibitors, times two. You'll need one to leave at the exhibit booth and an additional copy for anyone you have a meaningful conversation with. If you have resumes targeted to different jobs, take copies of all of them.
- Laptop or notepad and pen, preferably in a folder.

Job fairs are an opportunity for networking with other job hunters as well. If you know other people going to a job fair (perhaps you are a member of a job search support group), you should go with a collaborative effort in mind. You may be in different professions, but if you all make the effort to speak to other attendees and to collect business cards from other attendees regardless of their profession, you can help one another find more leads.

If you are attending solo, still make the effort to network with other attendees. Ask them to meet you later in the day to exchange leads that might be mutually beneficial. I have witnessed this in action at job fairs and seen a group of twenty who were total strangers in the morning happily exchanging handfuls of business cards at the end of the day.

It's easy to walk into a job fair and be drawn like a moth to the biggest and most attractive booths, sponsored by the largest and most established companies, and ignore the lesser ones. Remember that *the majority of the jobs in America are generated by companies with less than 500 employees.* You should visit every booth, not just the ones with the flashing lights and all the moths fluttering around.

Attend with specific objectives in mind:

- **Talk to someone at every booth.** You can walk up and ask questions about company activities, and whom they are looking for, before you talk about yourself. This allows you to present yourself in the most relevant light.
- **Collect business cards from everyone you speak to** so you can follow up with an e-mail and a call when they are not so harried. Very few people actually get hired at job fairs; for most companies the exercise is one of collecting resumes so that meaningful meetings can take place in the ensuing days and weeks. Nevertheless, you should be "on" at all times, because serious interviews do sometimes occur on the spot.

  If you have a background and resume that are a match for a specific opportunity, make your pitch. If, on the other hand, there's a job you can do but your resume needs some adaptation to better position your candidacy, take a different approach. By all means pitch the company representative, but don't hand over a resume that will detract from your candidacy (you can come up with a harmless pretext, such as having run out of copies). Instead, get the contact's business card and promise to follow up with a resume, which you can then custom fit to the opportunity (see TJD process in Chapter 3).

- **Collect company brochures** and collateral materials.
- **Arrange times and dates to follow up** with as many employers as possible: "Ms. Jones, I realize you are very busy today, and I would like to speak to you further. Your opportunities in _____ sound exactly suited to my skills and interests. I would like to set up a time when we could talk."

In addition to the exhibit hall, there will probably be formal group presentations by employers. As all speakers love feedback, move in when the crush of presenter groupies has died down. You will have more knowledge of the company and the time to customize your pitch to the needs and interests of the employer, plus you'll get more time and closer attention.

Job fairs provide the best opportunities for administrative, professional, and technical people. However, this doesn't mean middle management and executive staff can't gather information, collect cards, and generate leads.

On leaving each booth, and at the end of the day, go through your notes while everything is still fresh in your mind. Review each company and what possibilities it may hold for you. Also review what you have learned about industry trends, new skill requirements, marketplace shifts, and long-term staffing needs. Plan to send e-mails and make follow-up calls within the week to everyone with whom you spoke.

E-Mail Subject Lines

When sending e-mails—not just job-related e-mails but all e-mails—it is a professional courtesy to provide a revealing and concise subject line. It should allow the receiver to immediately know who you are and what you want.

The use of a powerful subject line can mean the difference between getting your e-mail opened or not. The intent of a headline in a newspaper is to grab the reader and draw her into the story; in an e-mail, your subject line is your headline: It is what draws the reader into your e-mail and lets her know what she's going to be reading about. Your subject line needs to be intriguing and professional.

Do not use a subject line that states the obvious, like "Resume" or "Jim Smith's Resume." If you are responding to a job posting, the job title and job posting number are necessary, but just a start. Combine this factual information with a little intriguing information, such as:

Financial Analyst #MB450—CPA/MBA/8 yrs exp
Posting 2314—MIT Grad is interested

Job #6745—Top Sales Professional Here

Or if there is no job posting to refer to:

IT Manager—7 yrs IT Consulting
Benefits Consultant—Nonprofit Exp in NY
Referral from Tony Banks—Product Management Job

You can also try longer subject lines, for example:

Your next Reg HR Manager—EEOC, FLSA, & ADA exp

A message in your inbox will typically reveal a maximum of sixty characters (the previous example is just fifty-six characters), and an opened message will show up to 150 characters. To be safe, try to get your headline in the first thirty characters: "Your next Reg HR Manager—EEOC, FLSA." But feel free to use all the extra headline space for a subhead; for example: "Your next Reg HR Manager—EEOC, FLSA, ADA, OSHA. 10 years exp all HR includes arbitration, campus, executive recruitment, selection, compensation, T&D."

KNOCK 'EM DEAD TIP

All the social networking sites have special interest groups that are used by recruiters, and it is becoming increasingly common for job hunters to post pitches about themselves in the discussion groups; this helps them become visible to recruiters, Google searches, and the like. So it is common sense to create an extremely abbreviated resume that captures the *professional you* with the most important keywords as identified by your TJD exercises.

This same thinking for extended subject lines will apply to your discussion group posts. These aren't the place for "out-of-the-box thinker" warm-and-fuzzies, but hard-hitting, attention-grabbing statements like this: "HR Management - EEOC, FLSA, ADA, OSHA, T&D, arbitration, campus/executive recruitment, selection, compensation, restructuring."

Newspapers and Magazines

Almost all recruitment has now moved to the Internet, as have newspapers, so their role in your job search is not as it was in years gone by; however, there are still uses for a local or national newspaper in your job search campaign.

1. Companies that rely on the local community for both customers and employees still use the newspaper as a major recruitment vehicle.
2. The business news stories can tell you about company success stories, new contracts signed, new products and services introduced, and companies coming to town. They keep you informed and mention movers and shakers by name.

Reminding that person of the article ("I saw you quoted in the *Argus* last week . . .") is flattering and will get you a few minutes of that person's time to make a pitch, get an interview, or get some leads. (If you want to learn how to get yourself quoted in the press, examine the PR chapters in the e-book *Knock 'em Dead Professional Communication* available at *www.knockemdead.com*.)

3. Most local papers have a promotions/movers-and-shakers column. It will tell you about companies and give you the names of people you can contact. If someone gets promoted or leaves one company for another, that leaves a job to be filled.
4. Industry overviews and market development pieces can tip you off to subtle shifts in your local professional marketplace.

There are still some great job leads in newspapers and magazines, and the fact that most people aren't using them as a job search resource anymore is a good enough reason to at least check them out. A good place to start online is *www.onlinenewspapers.com,* which helps you identify and link to newspapers all over the world.

Passive Marketing with a Web Portfolio or Web-Based Resume

Almost all job search activities take time and effort, so use passive marketing tactics whenever you can to increase your professional visibility and credibility.

For some time now, artists and designers have been creating online portfolios for their work as a cost-effective marketing device. If audio/video/graphics/multimedia can help promote the professional you, it might be worth considering an e-resume or e-portfolio for yourself, or have it built for you. This can cost anywhere from $40 up to $3,000.

Think of your web resume as a miniature website (you'll need to update it to reflect current professional activities); it gives you a constant marketing presence and extends your professional visibility and credibility in a couple of other ways: Increased visibility increases your credibility. For example, recruiters are doing Google searches on people before meeting them as part of the selection screening process. A well-put-together web resume will enhance others' perception of you before those initial meetings.

For professionals in the creative arts, a web-based resume/e-portfolio allows you to provide a multimedia proof of your achievements and strengths. With a web-based resume on its own site, you have the opportunity to expand beyond the immediate page, offering access to examples and supporting documents in other media.

It will not replace your main resume (which can offer a link to your multimedia site), but it's a great opportunity to prove you have strong presentation skills—a claim supported by a video or audio clip of a presentation. Including articles, a list of awards, graphics, audio and video clips, blogs, and photos on your site are just some of the options you have to make your multimedia case. Prospective employers, headhunters, clients, and colleagues will get a far more comprehensive picture of the *professional you*, and because a properly delivered e-portfolio is more engaging (when the content is good), it speaks of a technologically adapted professional.

PART II
GET THE WORD OUT

IT IS ALWAYS a conversation that generates an interview, and the job offer follows from there. That's why the focus of your job search is always to get into conversations as quickly and as often as possible with the people who can hire you.

CHAPTER 7
MAKING CONTACT

LITTLE HAPPENS IN the professional world without conversations taking place; in job searches neither interviews get scheduled nor job offers made without them. That's why the focus of your job search is always to *get into conversations as quickly and as often as possible with the people who can hire you.*

Despite everything you've done up to now, nothing is going to happen without you getting into conversations with these people. You can wait for these conversations to happen or you can make them happen.

Sales and Marketing Strategies

You've posted your resume on resume banks and as your social networking profile on LinkedIn and other sites, and you've sent it in response to company and headhunter job postings. Every one of these resumes acts like a baited fish hook, but while positioning your resume where it can be seen is a sensible marketing tactic, just sitting back and waiting for a bite isn't the best way to land your next job.

Jobs in sales exist to generate revenue by getting into conversations with customers and selling them the product, because marketing alone is never enough for profitability.

MeInc too needs a sales operation to get into the conversations that lead to meetings, then negotiations, contracts, and the sale. Your successful job search, like any sales campaign, depends on *you getting into conversations as quickly and as often as possible with the people/job titles who can make the decision to hire you.*

Who to Approach Within Your Target Companies

Your identified target market should include every company within the geographic boundaries of your job search who could possibly hire someone like you. But companies aren't enough; you need to find people within those companies to talk to.

Getting into conversations with the people who have the authority to hire you is the central goal of all your job search strategies and tactics. It is the most effective way to get job offers and the activity that all job hunters most want to ignore, because talking to strangers on the telephone suddenly seems like a scary thing to do. It's not scary; you do it all the time.

Before you get into a conversation you have to identify whom you want to talk to and how to find them. The people you want to *reach as quickly, directly, and often as possible* are people holding those titles most likely to have the authority to offer you a job: Typically these high-value target hiring titles are one to three levels above your own and in the same department or functional area. The primary goal of your job search every day is to identify and get into a conversation with anyone who holds any of these target titles at any and every company in your target location:

- Corporate recruiters; because they are involved in the recruitment and selection cycle, they have a direct relationship with the hiring manager and a stake in completing searches in a timely and efficient manner.
- Titles one to three levels above your own in departments that have ongoing activities with your department. These people are the peers of the titles that will hire you and because of their continuing relations with your department are both likely to know of needs and able to make referrals.

- Titles similar to and one to three levels below your own, because these people either have jobs in the departments where you might like to work, or are looking for jobs in the same general area themselves.
- Titles of people in other departments or at other companies that had ongoing communication with you and your title.

Put these titles together and you have a hotlist of at least ten *high-value job titles* that represent the people who have the greatest odds of knowing about suitable jobs for you, being able to make the right introductions, and/or of hiring you. These are the people you want to *get into conversation with as quickly and as often as possible.*

The above titles represent the people you want to develop networking relationships with; they also represent the titles of job postings you'll stumble across and should snag.

Quick Review of Tools for Finding Names of Hiring Managers

Cross-reference target companies with the members of your social networks to get referrals and introductions. Look for these employers and for your identified high-value networking titles in the special interest groups you belong to on social networking sites and use the common interest shared by the group to make an initial connection.

You can find a wide array of online search tools to find people, by name, job title, company, industry, and location at *www.knockemdead.com*. Go to the Career Advice pages, then click on Secrets & Strategies, where you will find the Internet Resources link.

You can also use search engines to find job titles and names, as we discussed under the Internet Research Tactics heading in the last chapter.

While any name and conversation that gets you closer to an interview is valuable, the most valuable job titles to target in your networking are *one to three levels above your own.*

Doing searches of news media that involve the names of your target companies, you will find names and titles plus information that you can use as an icebreaker in your e-mails, letters, or conversations. Copy an interesting, relevant article and attach it in an e-mail. With a traditional letter, enclose a copy of the article. In both, your letter will open with mention of the media coverage, and this guarantees the rest of your message will be read. It is even more effective when you use it to open a telephone conversation: "I've been meaning to call you ever since I saw the article in . . . ."

When you know who you want to talk to and why, and you know the job and possess the skills that will contribute to the relationship, your irrational fears of talking to strangers on the phone should begin to evaporate.

Always Capture the Information

Capture the information you gather so that you can access and use it in this job search, and perhaps for other job searches down the road. If you stay in this profession and location, most of these companies are still going to be there, and many of the people you find will be too; and these companies and these people are still going to be hiring people like you. Capturing the information is another way in which you become knowledgeable about your profession and connected to the other players.

Beware of Approaching Dream Employers Too Soon

As you build these dossiers of information about individual companies in your target area, one or more of them will emerge as dream employers. Beware of applying for jobs at these "super desirable" employers right at the start of your search. Most likely your resume and interviewing skills are not up to speed at the beginning of your search. The last thing you need to do is fumble an opportunity to join the company of your dreams. It is better to hold off until you know that your resume is fine-tuned and that you won't swallow your tongue in the first few minutes of the interview. Do this and then, when you feel confident, use network contacts to get insider information and referrals, and your approach to that dream employer is likely to be a smoother experience.

Written Approaches with E-Mails and Letters

How many e-mails and letters to send out every week is a difficult question to answer. Two contacts a week is the behavior of the long-term unemployed. Mass e-mailing 700 employers with one resume isn't the smartest answer either, because you can't ID the right people to reach, personalize the pitches, or be able to follow up in a timely manner.

Every job search is unique; nevertheless, your campaign needs strategy. You should maintain a balance between the *number* of written pitches you send out on a weekly basis and the *types of people to whom they are sent*. Start off with a balanced e-mail and mailing campaign, and your phone follow-ups can maintain equilibrium, too.

The key is to organize and balance your job search activities so that you send as many resumes as possible directly to people by name in a volume that will allow you to make follow-up calls to those people. Start out with modest goals: Try to send between two and ten e-mails and letters each day addressed to someone by name and spread across each of the following areas:

- In response to job postings
- To the contacts you identify within target companies
- To headhunters
- To miscellaneous networking contacts

KNOCK 'EM DEAD TIP
Every name and contact you develop should go into a career management database with all relevant information. These contacts can be nurtured and developed over the years.

Will you need to create and use more than one type of letter in your search? Of course you will, because you will be approaching different types of people for different reasons. However, you don't have to craft every written communication entirely from scratch. You can create great letters quickly from the templates in *Knock 'em Dead Cover Letters*, where you will find letters for just about every job search scenario.

The key is to do each variation once and do it right, then save copies of these letters in folders within your career management database so you can access them at any time.

Multiple Submissions

You will sometimes find it valuable to make a number of contacts within a given company, especially the larger ones, to ensure that all the important players know of your existence. You'll remember the example from the last chapter of the engineer who wants to work for Last Chance Electronics, and the people such an engineer could send a resume to: the company president, the vice president of engineering, the chief engineer, the engineering manager, the vice president for human resources, the technical recruitment manager, and the technical recruiter, to name a few.

You wouldn't necessarily send all these communications out at once but might rather spread them over a period of time. Keep a log of your e-mail (and mail) contacts so you will know when to follow up with a phone call—usually about two days after an e-mail and five days after a traditional letter; exclude Monday mornings from this count, as everyone is busy getting up to speed for the week.

Keep track of these contacts beyond the initial follow-up period. Resumes do get misplaced, and employment needs change. You can comfortably resend e-mails and traditional mail to everyone on your list every couple of months; when you do this, it isn't necessary to remind them of earlier submissions. Most recipients won't register that they heard from you, and of those who do, most won't take offense. Any who might get upset are people who have no need for your professional skill set and whom you are therefore unlikely to run into anytime soon . . . so who cares?

An organized campaign will proceed on two fronts:

Front One: A carpet-bombing approach to every relevant management title within all the target companies in your area.

Front Two: A carefully targeted approach to a select group of companies. You may choose to hold back on contacting these special employers until comfortable with your developing job search skills—no point in getting into a conversation with a dream employer until you know how to handle that conversation.

You will continue to add to these lists of companies as you unearth fresh opportunities in your day-to-day research efforts, and as you identify new management titles within those companies.

In both these approaches you respond to job postings and upload your resume to their corporate databases in the standard way. Then as your direct research and networking identifies specific individuals within these companies, you begin e-mail/mailing one or two contacts within the company. Repeat the e-mails/traditional letters to other contacts when your follow-up calls to these people result in referrals or dead ends. Remember, just because Harry in engineering says there are no openings in the company, that doesn't make it so. Any one of the additional contacts you make within that company could be the person *who is the person or who knows the person* with the perfect job for you. Even when a company states it has a hiring freeze there are always, always exceptions.

How to Quadruple Your Chances of an Interview

The more ways you approach your target companies and hiring managers, the faster you will *get into conversations with the people who can and will hire you*. Let's say you respond to a job posting by uploading your resume; that gives you one chance of getting an interview.

You can quadruple your chances of an interview if you also:

- Identify a potential hiring manager and e-mail your resume directly to that manager by name with a personalized cover letter. This doubles your chances of an interview.
- Send a resume and personalized cover letter to that same manager by traditional mail, and you will triple your chances of an interview. Don't smirk at the idea of traditional mail. We all like a break from the computer screen, so delivering your sales message and resume this way can be very effective. When you do this, note in the cover letter that you sent the resume by e-mail and that this additional approach is because you are really interested in the company and "wanted to increase my chances of getting your attention." Doing this demonstrates that you are creative, and not just a technological Neanderthal.
- Make a follow-up telephone call to that manager, first thing in the morning, at lunchtime, or at 5 P.M. (when she is most likely to be available and picking up her own phone) and you will quadruple your chances of an interview.

Remember, a successful job search is all about *getting into conversations as quickly and as often as possible with people in a position to hire you*. The more frequently you approach and get into conversation with managers whose job titles signify that they have the authority to hire you, the faster you will land that new position, because you have skipped right over the hurdle of being pulled from the commercial resume database; you have sidestepped the corporate recruiter's evaluation process, and *as a result* you have the attention of the actual decision-maker and the chance to have a conversation, to make a direct and personal pitch.

Getting a resume to someone by name with a personalized pitch gives you a distinct advantage, which is never more important than when the economy is down or in recovery. At such times your competition is fierce and employers actually do recognize and appreciate the initiative and motivation you display by doing these things, especially picking up the phone and calling: All these approaches act as differentiating factors in your candidacy.

Avoid Wishful Thinking

Once your campaign starts to gain traction and you begin to schedule interviews from your calls, your emphasis will change, and you'll spend time preparing for interviews and following up after them.

This is the point at which most job searches stall. We get so excited about an interview and convince ourselves, "This will be the offer." As a result our job search activities slow to a halt. Here's an unsettling fact of life: The offer that can't fail usually does fail, and you are left depressed and without anything happening in your job search.

You *must* keep your job search pump primed with ongoing activity to generate interviews. Not only does this approach helping you get that next job most efficiently, it keeps your psychological pump primed too.

The more direct contacts you make through e-mail and regular mail, the more follow-up calls you can make to pitch your candidacy, schedule interviews, and get leads for more openings. Don't ignore sending letters through the mail; e-mail has drastically reduced the amount of business mail, so a resume sent this way is going to stand out.

Initiating Conversations with Hiring Managers

Phone conversations are more powerful than resumes, e-mails, and letters, and they are essential to getting you interviews. Talking with high-value titles who haven't seen your resume and following up on resumes you send out with a phone call are the best ways to get the interviews that lead to job offers.

At the same time as you are uploading to resume databases and e-mailing and traditional mailing your resume to high-value contacts and hiring managers you identified today, pick up the phone and introduce yourself to the ones you identified and approached with a resume a day or two ago. Make as many of these calls as you send e-mails and traditional letters pitching your resume. The more often these conversations happen, the quicker your search will end in success.

Don't deceive yourself by thinking this part of the search is not possible because you are terrified of picking up the phone to call strangers. We all talk on the phone every day—these are just calls with a distinct purpose. It is something you can learn to do successfully, and whatever small pain it causes is far outweighed by what you gain: a new job and a fresh start on managing your career more successfully.

In a past professional incarnation as a headhunter, I spent every day on the telephone talking to strangers. Even though I developed a global reputation I was also always absolutely terrified making calls, which of course no one at the time ever knew ;-). The adrenaline rush we associate with fear is usual for anyone engaged in a critical performance. In fact it is a very natural reaction; success comes from harnessing the adrenaline rush you feel at times like these.

I'd be surprised if you, too, weren't a little leery at the idea of actually calling prospective employers. Three pieces of advice helped me in my hour of abject terror:

- I knew that I would never meet these people unless they were interested in what I had to offer, in which case they'd be happy I called.
- Because I was on the phone, no one would know who I was or how scared I felt and looked.
- The third thing that helped was learning how to make almost every call successful. As outrageous as that sounds, it really is pretty easy.

If you have just a single goal when you pick up the phone—get an interview—you have just one chance of success but many more for failure. But if you have multiple goals for your call, you have multiple chances for success. When headhunters make sales/marketing calls, they usually have five goals in mind, so I have adapted the headhunter's goals to fit your needs:

1. I will arrange an interview date and time.
2. If my contact is busy, I will arrange another time to talk.
3. I will develop leads on promising job openings elsewhere in this and other companies.
4. I will leave the door open to talk with this person again in the future.
5. I will send a resume for subsequent follow-up.

Keep these goals in mind every time you talk with someone during your job search, because every conversation holds the potential to turn into an interview or lead you toward another conversation that will generate first a phone conversation and then a face-to-face meeting.

You might worry about calling people directly because you are concerned that they will be annoyed by the perceived intrusion. This is a misconception: The first job of any manager is to get work done through others, so every smart manager is always on the lookout for talent:

if not for today, then for tomorrow. If that isn't enough to allay your fears, keep in mind that the person on the other end of the line has very possibly been in your position and is sensitive to your situation. If you can be concise and professional, you'll find that the great majority of people you contact will try to be helpful.

Paint a Word Picture

The secret is being succinct. With an initial introduction and presentation that comes in at well under a minute, you won't be construed as wasting anybody's time.

Your aim is to paint a representation of your skills with the widest appeal, keeping it brief out of courtesy, while avoiding giving information that might rule you out.

KNOCK 'EM DEAD TIP
Writing out something you're going to say aloud is very different from writing something for someone else to read. Speech is more casually structured than the written word. You'll get the best results if you write down the bullet points you want to make rather than full sentences. Once you have written it out, speak it aloud a few times until it sounds conversational and relaxed. Then practice it with a friend or record yourself for critique until it sounds polished and professional.

Step #1

Give the employer a snapshot of who you are and what you do. The intent is to give that person a reason to stay on the phone. You may sometimes have an introduction from a colleague, in which case you will build a bridge with that:

"Miss Shepburn? Good morning, my name is Martin Yate, and our mutual friend Greg Spencer suggested I call . . . ."

Or you may have gotten the name and contact information from, for example, a professional association database, in which case you will use that as a bridge:

"Miss Shepburn? My name is Martin Yate. We haven't spoken before, but as we are both members of the _____ Association, I hoped I might get a couple of minutes of your time for some advice . . . ."

Never ask if you have caught someone at a bad time because that's offering your contact an excuse to say she is busy. On the other hand, asking whether you have caught someone at a good time will usually get you a positive response, or just pausing after stating the reason of your call, as I did above, will work. Then you can go into the rest of your presentation. If at any point your contact says or implies that he is harried, immediately ask when would be a good time to call back.

Now we come to the meat of your presentation. Grab the listener's attention now and you are off to a good start. You want to capture a complete picture of the *professional you* in less than one minute, ideally less than forty-five seconds. The good news is that you already have the text for what you need to say.

In creating your resume you completed TJD exercises that helped you prioritize employers' needs for your job title. When you wrote the Performance Profile for your resume, which introduced the professional you succinctly, you condensed the leading employer priorities into three to six short sentences. So you already know what aspects of your experience have widest and most relevant appeal, and we just have to retool them for speaking rather than reading; that's easy. After your introduction:

"Miss Shepburn? My name is Martin Yate. We haven't spoken before, but as we are both members of the _____ Association, I hoped I might get a couple of minutes of your time for some advice . . . ."

You pause for agreement, take your resume's Performance Profile—"Ten years' experience in office technology sales, including a successful track record selling B-to-B, including corporations, institutions, and small business."—and just make it a little less formal and less specific:

" . . . I'm in office technology sales, with a successful track record selling B-to-B: corporations, institutions, and small business . . . ."

Then complete the spoken version of your Performance Profile. To create a spoken version, take the sentences and turn them into bullet points so that you can't recite the sentences word for word and sound like you are reading a script.

Once you have your script down, practice speaking it aloud until it sounds conversational and relaxed. Then practice it with a friend or record yourself for critique. Do it in a normal speaking voice until you are comfortable with the content and the rhythm; you'll also know how long it takes. To keep it under the one-minute mark, remember that the idea is just to whet the listener's appetite to know more.

You might take out some information—for example describing yourself as experienced, rather than identifying a specific number of years in your field. This encourages the listener to qualify your statement with a question: "How much experience do you have?" Any question denotes a level of interest and might well mean a job exists or is about to exist.

Step #2

Keeping your presentation short and to the point makes Step #2 optional, depending on the time you have available and on whether you have something impressive to say about your achievements. If you can cover your Performance Profile points and still have a little time left over, add an example of what you can achieve:

"As the number three salesperson in my company, I increased sales in my territory fifteen percent, to over one million dollars. In the last six months, I won three major accounts from my competitors—a hospital, a bank, and a technology start-up."

Note that you always talk about what you can do, but never how you do it.

Step #3

Having introduced yourself professionally and succinctly, get to the reason for your call and move the conversation forward.

"The reason I'm calling is that I'm looking for a new challenge, and as I know a little about your company, I felt we might have some areas of common interest. Are these the types of skills and accomplishments you look for in your sales associates?"

Notice that your presentation finishes not with "Have you got a job? Can you hire me?" but with a question that encourages a positive response and opens the possibility of conversation.

When you make your presentation for real, there will likely be a silence on the other end of the line. Be patient, as the employer may need a few seconds to digest your words.

When the employer does respond, it will either be with a question, denoting interest, or with an objection.

Whatever the voice on the other end of the line says next, try to give short, reasonable answers and finish your reply, when it makes sense to do so, with a question. If a job exists, in answer to your questions the interviewer will tell you a little about that job. This will define what skills and qualities are important to this employer and help you customize your answers with your most relevant skills and experiences.

Conversation is a two-way street, and you are most likely to win an interview when you take responsibility for your half. Just as the employer's questions show interest in you, your questions should show your interest in the work done at the company. By asking questions of your own in the normal course of conversation—questions usually tagged on to the end of one of your answers—you will forward the conversation.

Here's an example of how such a conversation might proceed. Because you and I come from different backgrounds, we will never talk alike, so with the following sample questions and answers just capture the essence so that you can tailor them to your own speech patterns.

YOU: *". . . The reason I'm calling is that I'm looking for a new challenge, and as I know and respect your product line, I felt we might have areas for discussion. Are these the types of skills and accomplishments you look for in your staff?"*

[Pause]

MISS SHEPBURN: *"Yes, they are. What type of equipment have you been selling?"* [Buy signal!]

YOU: *"A comprehensive range from work stations, through routers, modems to printers and ink . . . and all the peripherals you would expect; I sell according to my customers' needs and the capabilities of the technology. I have been noticing a considerable interest in _____ recently. Has that been your experience?"*

MISS SHEPBURN: *"Yes, I have actually."* [Useful information for you.] *"Do you have a degree?"* [Buy signal!]

YOU: *"Yes, I do."* [Just enough information to keep the company interested.] *"I understand your company prefers degreed salespeople to deal with its more sophisticated clients."* [Your research is paying off.]

MISS SHEPBURN: *"Our customer base is very sophisticated, and they expect a certain professionalism and competence from us."* [An inkling of the kind of person the company wants to hire.] *"How much experience do you have?"* [Buy signal!]

YOU: *"Well, I've worked in both operations and sales, so I understand sales and fulfillment processes, and my customers benefit from not having to deal with false expectations because I understand how to work cooperatively with fulfillment."* [General but thorough.] *"How many years of experience are you looking for?"* [Turning it around, but furthering the conversation.]

MISS SHEPBURN: *"Ideally, four or five for the position I have in mind."* [More good information.] *"How many do you have?"* [Buy signal!]

YOU: *"I have two with this company, and one and a half before that, so I fit right in with your needs."*

MISS SHEPBURN: *"Uh-huh . . . What's your territory?"* [Buy signal!]

YOU: *"I cover the metropolitan area. Miss Shepburn, it sounds as if we might have something to talk about."* [Remember, your first goal is the face-to-face interview.] *"I am planning to take personal time off next Thursday or Friday. Can we meet then? Which would be best for you?"* [Encourage Miss Shepburn to decide *which* day she can see you, rather than *whether* she will see you.]

MISS SHEPBURN: *"How about Friday morning?"*

Your questions show interest, carry the conversation forward, and teach you more about the company's needs. By the end of the conversation you have an interview arranged and several key areas you should write down while they are fresh. You can do further research on these areas of interest prior to the interview:

- The company sees growth in _____, so be sure you research what is going on in this particular area.
- They want both professional and personal sophistication.
- They ideally want four or five years' experience.
- They are interested in your metropolitan contacts.

Let's look at the building blocks again before moving on to getting live leads from dead ends:

Step #1. Give the employer a succinct verbal snapshot of who you are and what you bring to the table (your Performance Profile).

Step #2. Finish your introduction off with an example of professional achievements.

Step #3. Move the conversation forward by explaining the reason for your call and finishing with a question that elicits a positive response.

At this point, the employer will either respond with a question or an objection. If it's a question, it shows that the listener is interested. Among the buy signals that often come up are the following:

Buy Signal: "How much experience do you have?"

Too much or too little experience could easily rule you out. Be careful how you answer this question and try to gain time. It is a vague question, and you have a right to ask for qualifications. Employers typically define jobs by years' experience. At the same time there is currently a major move away from simple chronological experience toward the more important concern about what you can deliver on the job. Managers and HR pros are now more open to thinking in terms of "performance requirements" and "deliverables" than ever before.

Here are a couple of ways to handle it:

"I have _____ years' chronological experience, but if you could you give me a brief outline of the performance requirements I can give you a more accurate answer." Then with the information you might be able to answer, *"I am comfortable with all aspects of the pre-sales, sales, and post-sales process and have considerable experience, comfort, and contacts throughout the B-to-B community here in Pittsburgh, including public corporations, institutions, and start-ups."*

Or:

"Could you help me with that question? If you give me a brief outline of the performance requirements, I can give you a more accurate answer." Or, *"I have _____ years' experience, but they aren't necessarily typical. If you'd give me a few details on the performance requirements I'd be able to give you a more accurate answer."*

The employer's response, while gaining you time, tells you what it takes to do the job and therefore what aspects of your experience are most relevant. Take mental notes as the employer talks—you can even write them down if you have time. Then give an appropriate response.

You can move the conversation forward by asking a follow-up question of your own. For example: "The areas of expertise you require sound like a match to my experience, and it sounds as if you have some exciting projects at hand. What projects would I be involved with in the first few months?"

Buy Signal: "Do you have a degree?"

An easy question if you have one. If not, qualify your answer and point the way forward: "My education was cut short by the necessity of earning a living. However, I'm currently enrolled in classes to complete my degree."

Buy Signal: "How much are you making/do you want?"

This is a direct question looking for a direct answer, yet it is a knockout question, so you should proceed warily. Earning either too little or too much could ruin your chances before you're given the opportunity to shine in person. There are a number of options that could serve you better than a direct answer. First, you must understand that questions about money at this point in the conversation are being used to screen you in or screen you out. The answers you give now should be geared toward getting you in the door and into a face-to-face meeting. (Handling the serious salary negotiations that are attached to a job offer are covered in Chapter 22, "Negotiating the Job Offer.") For now, your main options are as follows:

- **Direct answer:** If you know the salary range for the position and there is a fit, give a straightforward answer.
- **Indirect answer:** "In the 50s." Or "in the 120s."
- **Put yourself above the money:** "I'm looking for an opportunity that will give me the opportunity to make a difference with my efforts. If I am the right person for the job, I'm sure you'll make me a fair offer. By the way, what is the salary range for this position?"
- **Give a range:** Come up with two figures: a fair offer considering your experience and job location, and a great offer considering your experience and job location. "Hopefully between $x and $y. What's most important is an opportunity to make a difference. If I am the right person for the job, I'm sure you'll make me a fair offer. By the way, what is the salary range for this position?"

When you give a salary range rather than a single figure, you have more flexibility and have greater chance of "clicking" with the employer's approved range for the position.

When you are pressed a second time for an exact dollar figure, be as honest and forthright as circumstances permit. If you have the skills for the job and you are concerned that your current low salary will eliminate you before you have the chance to show your worth, you might add, "I realize this is well below industry norms, but it does not reflect on my expertise or experience in any way. It speaks of the need for me to make a strategic career move to where I can be compensated competitively and based on my skills."

If your current earnings are higher than the approved range, you could say, "Mr. Smith, my current employers feel I am well worth the money I earn due to my skills, dedication, and honesty. When we meet, I'm sure I can convince you of my ability to contribute to your department. A meeting would provide an opportunity to make that evaluation, wouldn't it?"

How to Deal with Objections

By no means will every presentation call you make be met with a few simple questions and then an invitation to interview. Sometimes the silence will be broken with an objection. This usually comes in the form of a statement, not a question: "Send me a resume," or "I don't have time to see you," or "You are earning too much," or "You'll have to talk to personnel," or "I don't need anyone like you right now." These seem like brush-off lines, but they can be turned into interviews, and when that isn't possible, they can almost always be parlayed into leads elsewhere.

Notice that all the following suggested response models end with a question, one that helps you learn more about the reason for the objection, perhaps to overcome it and lead the conversation toward a meeting.

In dealing with objections, nothing is gained by confrontation, while much can be gained by an appreciation of the other's viewpoint. Consequently, most objections you hear are best handled by first demonstrating your understanding of the other's viewpoint. Start your responses with phrases like "I understand," or "I can appreciate your position," or "I see your point," or "Of course." Follow up with statements like "However," or "Also consider," or a similar line that allows the opportunity for rebuttal and to gather further information.

It's not necessary to memorize these responses verbatim, only to understand the underlying concept and then put together responses in words that are natural to your character and style of speech.

Objection: "Why don't you send me a resume?"
The employer may be genuinely interested in seeing your resume as a first step in the interview cycle, or it may be a polite way of getting you off the phone. You should identify the real reason without causing antagonism, and at the same time open up the conversation. A good reply would be, "Of course, Mr. Grant. Would you give me your exact title and your e-mail address? Thank you. So that I can be sure that my qualifications fit your needs, what skills are you looking for in this position?" or "What specific job title and opening should I refer to when I send it?"

Notice the steps:

- Agreement with the prospective employer
- A demonstration of understanding
- A question to further the conversation (in this instance to confirm that an opening actually exists)

Answering in this fashion will open up the conversation. Mr. Grant will relay the aspects of the job that are important to him, and you can use the additional information to move the conversation forward again or to draw attention to relevant skills in:

- Your executive briefing or cover letter
- A customized resume
- Your face-to-face meeting

Following Mr. Grant's response, you can recap the match between his needs and your skills:

"Assuming my resume matches your needs, as I think we are both confident that it will, could we pencil in a date and time for an interview next week? I am available next Thursday and Friday; which would be preferable to you?"

A penciled-in date and time for an interview very rarely gets canceled, because they don't actually get "penciled in"—in this electronic age, they immediately take up a time slot in the schedule.

Objection: "I don't have time to see you."

If the employer is too busy to see you, it indicates that she has work pressures, and by recognizing that, you can show yourself as the one to alleviate some of those pressures through your problem-solving skills. You should avoid confrontation, however; it is important that you demonstrate empathy for the person with whom you are speaking. Agree, empathize, and ask a question that moves the conversation forward:

"I understand how busy you must be; it sounds like a competent, dedicated, and efficient professional [whatever your title is] could be of some assistance. Perhaps I could call you back at a better time to discuss how I might make a contribution in easing the pressure at peak times. When are you least busy, in the morning or afternoon?"

The company representative will either make time to talk now or will arrange a better time for the two of you to talk further.

You could also try, "Since you are so busy, what is the best time of day for you? First thing in the morning, or is the afternoon a quieter time?" Or you could suggest, "If you would like to see my resume you could study my background at your leisure. What's your e-mail address? Thanks, what would be a good time of day to follow up on this?"

Objection: "You are earning too much."

Don't give up immediately; follow the process through: "Oh, I'm sorry to hear that—what is the range for that position?" Depending on the degree of salary discrepancy, you might reiterate your interest. You can also refer to Chapter 22, "Negotiating the Job Offer," where you will find further advice on dealing with this issue.

If the job really doesn't pay enough—and there will be openings for which you are earning too much—you've gotten "close, but no cigar!" Just a bit further on, I'll tell you how to make a success of this seeming dead end by asking a couple of questions as you wrap up the conversation.

Objection: "We only promote from within."

Your response could be, "[smiling] Your development of employees is a major reason I want to get in! I am bright, conscientious, and motivated. When you do hire from the outside, and it must happen on occasion, what do you look for?" or "How do I get into consideration for such opportunities?"

The response finishes with a question designed to carry the conversation forward and to give you a new opportunity to sell yourself. Notice that the response logically presupposes that the company does hire from the outside, as all companies obviously do, despite your being told otherwise.

Objection: "You'll have to talk to Human Resources."

In this case, you reply, "Of course, Mr. Grant. Whom should I speak to in HR, and what specific position should I mention?"

You cover a good deal of ground with that response. You establish whether there is a job there or whether you are being fobbed off on HR to waste their time and your own. Also, you move the conversation forward again while modifying it to your advantage. Develop a specific job-related question to ask while the employer is answering the first question. It can open a fruitful line for you to pursue. If you receive a nonspecific reply, probe a little deeper. A simple phrase like, "That's interesting. Please tell me more," or "Why's that?" will usually do the trick.

Or you can ask, "When I speak to HR, will it be about a specific job you have, or is it to see whether I might fill a position elsewhere in the company?"

Armed with the resulting information, you can talk to HR about your conversation with Mr. Grant. Remember to get the name of a specific person in HR with whom to speak, and quote this prior contact by name in any e-mail or verbal contact.

"Good morning, Ms. Johnson. Cary Grant, over in marketing, suggested we should speak to arrange an interview for the open sales associate requisition."

This way you show HR that you are not a time waster, because you have already spoken to the person for whom the requisition is open.

Don't look at the HR department as a roadblock. It may contain a host of opportunities for you. In many companies different departments could use your talents, and HR is probably the only department that knows all the openings. With larger companies you might be able to arrange interviews for two or three different positions!

Objection: "I really wanted someone with a degree."

You should have learned the proper response to "Do you have a degree?" But in case you were abducted by aliens a few pages ago, you could respond by saying, "Mr. Smith, I appreciate your viewpoint. It was necessary that I start earning a living early in life. If we meet, I am certain you would recognize the value of my additional practical experience." If you have been smart enough to enroll in a course or two in order to pursue that always-important degree, you should add, "I am currently enrolled in courses to complete my degree, which should demonstrate my professional commitment, and perhaps that makes a difference?" In a world of ongoing education it usually will.

You might then ask what the company policy is for support and encouragement of employees continuing their education. Your response will end with, "If we were to meet, I am certain you would recognize the value of my practical experience, in addition to my ongoing professional commitment. I am going to be interviewing at the end of next week, and I know you will find the time to meet well spent. Is there a day and time that would be best for you?"

Objection: "I don't need anyone like you now."

Short of suggesting that the employer fire someone to make room for you (which, believe it or not, has been done successfully on a few occasions), the chances of getting an interview with this company are slim. With the right questions, however, your contact will give you a personal introduction to someone else who could use your talents.

Live Leads from Dead Ends

By no means will every hiring manager you call have a job opening that fits your skills, but you can still turn calls that don't result in interviews into successes. Just a couple of pages back we established that your calls have multiple goals: to arrange an interview, to arrange another time for a conversation, to send a resume for future follow-up, and to develop leads on job openings elsewhere. If there isn't a need for someone like you right now you can ask:

- "When do you anticipate new needs in your area?"
- "May I send you my resume and keep in touch for when the situation changes?"

- "Who else in the company might have a need for someone with my background and skills?"
- "What other companies might have a need for someone with my background?"

If the response is positive:

- "Thanks, I appreciate the help. Do you know whom I should speak to?"

If the response to *that* is positive:

- "May I mention your name?"

Mentioning a company you plan to call:

- "Do you know anyone I could speak to at _____?"

If you ask just this sequence of questions you will get leads and introductions, and this enables you to open that next call with:

"Hello, Mr. Jones? My name is Martin Yate, Chuck Harris gave me your name and said to tell you hello . . . ."

But if you don't ask you can never expect to receive. Your call has been entirely professional, and you haven't wasted anyone's time, because the person has either been in your situation or knows it could well happen. You will find the overwhelming majority of people will try to be helpful if you show them a way to do so.

By adding these questions and others in the same vein you will achieve a measure of success from the call, leaving you energized and with a feeling of achievement after every conversation.

Here are six categories of questions that can lead to job openings, interviews, and offers; read through them and then develop specific questions you can ask in each area:

1. Leads in department
2. Leads in company
3. Leads in other divisions of company
4. Leads to other companies
5. Contacts in other companies
6. Open door to keep in touch

Remember: Networking and marketing are continuous activities.

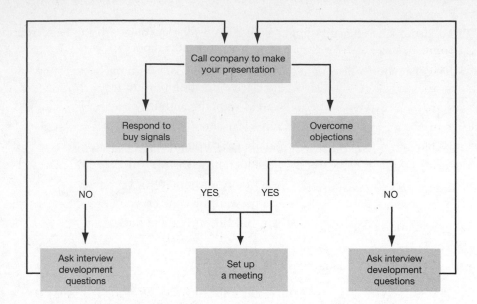

Corporate Gatekeepers

When you are making marketing and networking calls, an overly officious clerical assistant will sometimes try to thwart you in your efforts to present your credentials directly to a potential employer—at least it might appear that way.

In fact, it is very rare that these "corporate gatekeepers," as they are known, are directed to screen calls from professionals seeking employment, as to do so only increases employment costs to the company. What they are there to do is to screen nuisance calls from salespeople and the like.

However, to arm you for the occasional objectionable gatekeeper standing between you and making a living, you might try the following techniques used by investigative reporters, private eyes, and headhunters.

Preempting Questions

Most gatekeepers are trained at most to find out your name and the nature of your business. But when they are asking the questions, they control the conversation. You can remain in control by preempting their standard script: "Good morning. I'm Mr. Yate. I need to speak to Nikki Jones about an accounting matter. Is she there?" Should a truly obnoxious gatekeeper ask snidely, "Perhaps I can help you?" you can effectively use any of the following options: "Thank you, but I'd rather discuss it with Ms. Jones." "It's personal." "It's a professional matter." Or you can blind them with science: "Yes, if you can talk to me about the finer points of [*some esoteric aspect of your profession*] 10K reporting." They invariably can't, so you're in like Flynn.

Diction, tone of voice, confidence, and clarity are all-important when dealing with clerical staff. They are trained to respect and respond to polite authority, so always demonstrate self-confidence in your manner. When you are clear about whom you want to speak to and can predict possible screening devices, you usually get through. With such gatekeepers you should also avoid using your first name in your introduction, as in "Martin Carlucci"; instead, try "Mr. Carlucci" or "Ms. Carlucci," which is always more authoritative.

When you have been given a name by a networking contact, you can use that introduction to get past corporate gatekeepers: "Tell him Bill Edwards asked me to call."

Go Up the Ladder

If you can't get through to the person you want to speak to, say the accounting manager, instead of wasting the call you can go up the ladder to the controller or the vice president of finance; remember that one, two, and three management titles above you are all likely to be involved to some degree with selection of candidates like you.

Interestingly, the higher you go, the more accessible people are. In this instance, the senior manager may well not schedule an interview with you but instead refer you back down to the appropriate level. Sometimes that VP will switch you directly to the person with whom you want to speak; even if that doesn't happen, the next time you call you have a nice, hefty name to drop when dealing with the pesky gatekeeper: "Your divisional vice president of finance, Mr. Craig Wilde, asked me to call Mr. Jones. Is he there?" Even if you didn't speak directly to that VP up the corporate ladder, and the VP's secretary referred you back down the ladder, you can now say with all honesty, "Mr. (VP's) office recommended . . . ." Then the conversation with your target can begin with your standard introduction, but be sure to mention first the name of the person who referred you.

If you haven't yet gleaned any names from a particular company through your networking activities and are being thwarted by a gatekeeper, try these approaches:

- Over time you will develop a list of companies where you have no contacts. You can refer to this list when you run into a brick wall on either a networking or marketing call. "Jack, I was planning to contact _____, Inc. Would you happen to know anyone there who could give me a heads-up?" Or "Jack, do you know anyone at _____ or _____ that I could speak to? Any lead would be most appreciated."
- Check your association membership databases and your online networks and look for members who work or have worked at a target company. Regardless of their titles, these people can bring you one step closer to the right hiring authority contact.

- Visit the company's website and look for names there. Don't forget to read the media clippings that always get posted, since they invariably contain a quote or two from company representatives. You should also do Google News searches for media coverage of the company and its executives.
- For especially desirable companies, check back with those people who know you well and respect your work: your references. They might know or be able to find out the names of people working within your target.

When none of your research, networking, or marketing activities has presented you with a name, try these techniques:

- There is usually more than one person worth speaking to at any company, so whomever you speak to, ask for more than one name and title. For example, in the finance area (depending on your level), any or all of the following could provide useful contacts: accounting supervisor, accounting manager, assistant controller, controller, vice president of finance, chief financial officer, executive vice president, president, chief operating officer, chief executive officer, chairman. The last eight of these can usually be found on the company website or in reference databases and directories.
Anyone who gives you one name will invariably give you more than one. Some years ago in Colorado I sat with a job searcher who used these techniques to gather 142 names from receptionists in one hour!
- In some companies where security is at a premium, gatekeepers are expressly forbidden to give out names and titles. In this case, you can use some side-door techniques: There are certain people in every company who by the very nature of their jobs have contact with people at all levels of the company and who are not given the responsibility to screen calls. These include people in the mailroom, maintenance, shipping and receiving; second-, third-, and fourth-shift employees; new or temporary employees; advertising and public relations people; sales and marketing people; and travel center, Q/A, and customer service employees.

Another approach for getting by pesky gatekeepers is to vary the times when you call a target company. Try before 9 A.M., immediately after 5 P.M., and during lunch hours. Managers often pick up their own lines at these times.

Voice Mail

Voice mail is on the increase. Rather than treating it as a dead end, turn it into a useful means of getting through to your target contact.

When you have an introduction, you can use it to navigate voice mail systems and to leave as a teaser on your voice mail message: "Good morning, my name is William Powell. Ms. Loy suggested I give you a call. She thought we might have something to talk about. I'll try you later."

Don't leave long messages; be brief and get on with your job search and make another call. In cases where you don't get a response and need to call back again, do so, but if the person doesn't pick up and you get routed to the voice mail again, hang up and move on to your next call; if you leave countless voice mail messages, it will make you look needy.

When you lack a name, check to see if the system has a directory, and if it does, take note of as many names and extensions as you can. If there is no directory, and the voice mail system tells you to enter an extension key, keep keying until you hit one that results in a human voice. It doesn't matter who answers as long as someone does. The conversation goes something like this:

"Jack speaking."

"Jack, this is Martin Yate. I'm calling from outside and I'm lost on this darned telephone system." This usually gets a smile. *"I'm trying to get hold of [whatever the title is]. Could you check who that would be for me?"*

Develop a written list, and keep one on your desktop and one taped by your telephone.

Dealing with Abject Terror

The adrenaline rush you experience when picking up the phone to make the first of these calls is something we associate with fear, and *is normal for anyone engaged in a critical performance activity*. It is a very natural reaction, but because you:

- Know the product you are selling inside out
- Know (from your TJD exercises) exactly what you are going to say and how you are going to say it
- Know it will have the greatest relevance and therefore interest to the listener

You will be able to harness the adrenaline rush and channel it into peak performance. Nevertheless, I'd be surprised if you weren't still a little leery at the prospect of calling prospective employers. Three pieces of advice always helped me in my hours of abject terror and I know they will help you too:

- I knew I would never meet these people unless they were interested in what I had to offer, in which case they'd be happy I called.
- Because I was on the phone, no one would know who I was or how scared I felt and looked.
- I knew I had a plan and knew how to make almost every call successful.

It really is pretty easy once you start reaching out and making contact.

The Last Man Standing Wins

It is trite but true that you have never failed until you quit trying. Job searches will always take longer during economic downturns and will take longer the less professionally you approach them. Nevertheless, we have a huge economy, and even in the worst times people are landing new jobs. It's just that they're the ones who are working smarter and harder than everyone else.

If you are in the midst of a long job search, try to keep things in perspective. Although your 224th contact may not have an opening for you, ask questions and you may well discover that he has the good lead you need. Don't ask the questions and you'll never know.

In a job search there are only two "yeses": The employer's "we want you to work for us" and your "I can start on Monday." Every other conversation is, in reality, a "no" that brings you closer to the big "yes." Never take rejections of your resume or your phone call as rejections of you. There is a great opportunity right around the corner, so long as you keep turning that corner and maintaining your forward momentum.

Stacking the Odds in Your Favor

We all have 168 hours a week to become bagmen or billionaires and to make our lives as fulfilling as they can be. For some of us this means a better job; for others it means getting back to work to keep a roof over our heads. How we manage these hours will determine our success. These job search commandments will see you successfully through the job change and career transition process:

- **Start conversations.** It has been said that in order to gain that next job it takes on average twenty-five conversations with men or women who have the authority to hire you. What do we learn from this? Make every effort to get into conversations with decision makers with hiring authority and sooner or later you will get that job offer. It doesn't matter if it takes 25 or 125 such conversations, the essential truth still holds: Get into conversations with enough hiring authorities and you will get that desired job offer. To get into those critical conversations isn't easy; it might take you hundreds of contacts, but if you make the commitment every day of your job search, you will succeed, and you will succeed more quickly than your peers.
- **Work at getting a new job.** Work forty hours per week at it. Divide your time equally between all the intelligent job search approaches. No one knows which tactic is the one that will work for you, but this integrated approach gives you the shortest odds.

- **Research the companies you contact.** In a tightly run job race, the candidate who is most knowledgeable and intelligently enthusiastic about the employer has a distinct advantage.
- **Follow up on the resumes you send out with phone calls.** Resubmit your resume to identified openings after six or seven weeks. Change the format of your resume and submit it again. (See *Knock 'em Dead Resumes* for specific ideas on how to do this.)
- **Stay in telephone contact with your job leads.** Call them back on a regular basis to maintain top-of-the-mind awareness. If you find yourself needing to call existing contacts more than once every couple of months, you should be putting more emphasis on building your networks and doing direct research.
- **Develop examples of your professional profile that make you special**—and rehearse building these examples into your interview responses. More on this later.
- **Send follow-up notes** with relevant news clippings, cartoons, and so on to those in your networks. It's a light touch that helps people keep you in mind. You'll find lots of ideas for follow-up in Chapter 21.
- **Work on your self-image.** Use this time to get physically fit. Studies show that unfit, overweight people take longer to find suitable work.
- **Maintain a professional demeanor during the workweek** (clothing, posture, personal hygiene).
- **Use regular business hours for making contacts.** Use the early morning, lunchtime, after 5 P.M., and Saturday for doing the ongoing research and writing projects that maintain momentum.
- **Take off the blinders.** We all have two specific skills: our professional/technical skills—for example, computer programming; and our industry skills—for example, banking. Professional/technical skills can be transferable to other industries, and industry skills can open other opportunities in your industry. For example, that programmer, given decent communication skills, could become a technical trainer and/or writer for programmers or technophobes.
- **Don't feel guilty about taking time off from your job search.** Just do it responsibly. If you regularly spend Saturday morning in the library doing research, you can take Wednesday afternoon off to go to the driving range once in a while.
- **Maintain records of your contacts in the career management database.** They will benefit not only this job search but also those in the future.
- **Never stop the research and job search process** until you have a written job offer in hand and you have accepted that job in writing with an agreed-upon start date. Even then, continue with any ongoing interview cycles.
- **Remember: It's all up to you.** There are many excuses not to make calls or send resumes on any given day. There are many excuses to get up later or knock off earlier. There are many excuses to back off because this one's in the bag. But there are no real *reasons*. There

are no jobs out there for those who won't look, while there are plenty of opportunities for those who work at it.

• **The more you do today, the better you will feel about yourself.**

Follow-Up: The Key Ingredient

In theory, the perfect e-mails you send cold or as a result of phone calls will receive a response rate of 100 percent. Unfortunately, there is no perfect letter, e-mail, or call in this less-than-perfect world. If you sit waiting for the world to beat a path to your door, you may wait a long time.

An IT executive of my acquaintance once advertised for an analyst. By Wednesday of the following week he had over 100 responses. Ten days later he was still plowing through them when he received a follow-up call (the only one he received) from one of the respondents. The job hunter was in the office that afternoon, returned the following morning, and was hired before lunchtime.

What's the take-away? The candidate's resume was still sitting in the database, waiting to be discovered. The follow-up phone call got it discovered. The IT executive just wanted to get on with his work, and the job hunter in question made it possible by putting himself on the employer's radar. Follow-up calls do work.

Stay the Course

Make phone calls to initiate contact, and you'll get requests for resumes and requests to come right on over for an interview. Make follow-up calls on mailed and e-mailed resumes and you will generate further interviews.

No one is ever hired without passing through one or a series of formal interviews, and that is where *Knock 'em Dead* is headed next: how to turn interviews into job offers.

CHAPTER 8
ACE THE TELEPHONE INTERVIEW

INTERVIEWERS USE THE telephone to weed out applicants. Your goal is a face-to-face meeting, and these are the methods you must use to get it.

Some aspects of a job search are not clear-cut. For instance, a telephone interview for a job might be scheduled for a certain date and time, so you have plenty of time to prepare for it. Then again, a networking call can turn into a marketing presentation in a flash when you realize that the person on the other end of the phone is in a position to hire you. Likewise, when that marketing presentation progresses past the initial "buy signs" and objections, it can suddenly become a telephone interview. These things happen, but as you understand the steps to take in order to move each of these situations forward, you must be sensitive to the possibility that while telephone interviews can be scheduled in advance, they are just as likely to occur on the fly.

Employers use the telephone as a time-management tool. It is easier to cut to the chase and weed out candidates quickly on the telephone than in person. Your goal is a face-to-face meeting, so all you must do is convince the employer she will not be wasting time if she meets with you in person. Here are the techniques you should use to turn the phone conversation into a face-to-face meeting.

Organization for Marketing Calls and Telephone Interviews

Your first substantive contact with a potential employer will usually be by telephone; for entry-level professionals this first meeting will quite often take place at job fairs. For right now, let's concentrate on the telephone interview.

The phone interview happens in one of three ways:

- You are making a marketing or networking call, and the company representative goes into a screening process because you have aroused his interest.
- An employer calls unexpectedly as the result of a resume you have mailed or e-mailed.
- You have arranged a specific time for a telephone interview.

Odds are that you will experience plenty of telephone interviews during your job search. Whichever activities generate a telephone interview, you must think and act clearly to turn the opportunity into the real thing—a face-to-face meeting. The way you perform will determine whether you move ahead or bite the dust.

A few words about telephone services: Call waiting might be nice to have for social use, but responding to its demands during a job search will only annoy the person you have on the line at the time. If you have call waiting, disconnect it or ignore it. More and more telephone companies are also offering additional lines with distinctive rings for your basic service and at no extra charge. With this facility you can have a permanent job search/career management line and keep a constant eye on the job market without compromising day-to-day home life.

Perhaps the most important consideration about telephone interviews is that the employer has only her ears with which to judge you. If the call comes unexpectedly, and screaming kids or barking dogs surround you, stay calm and sound positive, friendly, and collected: "Thank you for calling, Mr. Wooster. Would you wait a moment while I close the door?" You can then take a minute to calm yourself, bring up the company website on your screen, and get your paperwork organized without causing offense. If you need to move to another phone, say so. Otherwise, put the caller on hold, take a few controlled, deep breaths to slow down your pounding heart, put a smile on your face (it improves the timbre of your voice), and pick up the phone again. Now you are in control of yourself and the situation.

If you are heading out the door for an interview, or if some other emergency makes this a bad time for an unexpected incoming call, say so straight away and reschedule: "I'm heading out the door for an appointment, Ms. Bassett. Can we schedule a time when I can call you back?" Beware of over-familiarity: You should always refer to the interviewer by his surname until invited to do otherwise.

Allow the company representative to guide the conversation and to ask most of the questions, but keep up your end. This is especially important when the interviewer does not give you the openings you need to sell yourself. Always have a few intelligent questions prepared to save the situation. The following questions will give you an excellent idea of why the position is open and exactly the kind of skilled professional the company will eventually hire:

- "What are the major responsibilities in this job?"
- "What will be the first project(s) I tackle?"
- "What are the biggest challenges the department faces this year and what will be my role as a team member in tackling them?"
- "Which projects will I be most involved with during the first six months?"
- "Who succeeds in this job and why?"
- "Who fails in this job and why?"

When you get a clear understanding of an employer's needs with questions like these, you can seize the opportunity to sell yourself appropriately: "Would it be of value if I described my experience in the area of office management?"; or "Then my experience in word processing should be a great help to you"; or "I recently completed an accounting project just like that. Would it be relevant to discuss it?"

When you identify an employer's imminent challenges and demonstrate how your skills can lessen the load, you portray yourself as a properly focused employee with a problem-solving mentality, and immediately move closer to a face-to-face interview. Everyone hires a problem solver.

You can also keep up your end of the conversation by giving verbal signals that you are engaged in it; you do this with occasional short interjections that don't interrupt the employer's flow but let her know you are paying attention. Comments like "uh-huh," "that's interesting," "okay," "great," and "yes, yes" are verbal equivalents of the body language techniques you'll use to show interest during a face-to-face meeting.

Always speak directly into the telephone, with the mouthpiece about one inch from your mouth. Numbered among the mystical properties of telephone technology is its excellence at picking up and amplifying background noise. This is excelled only by its power to transmit the sounds of food and gum being chewed, or smoke being inhaled and exhaled. Smokers take note: Nonsmokers instinctively discriminate, and they will assume that even if you don't actually light up at the interview, you'll have been chain-smoking beforehand and will carry the smell with you as long as you are around. They probably won't even give you a chance to get through the door once they hear you puffing away over the phone.

You should take notes when possible; they will be invaluable if the employer is interrupted. You can jot down the topic under discussion, then when he gets back on the line, helpfully recap: "We were just discussing . . . ." This will be appreciated and show that you are organized and pay attention. Your notes will also help you prepare for the face-to-face meeting.

The company representative may talk about the corporation, and from your research or the website on your screen you may also know something about the outfit. A little flattery goes a long way: Admire a company's achievements when you can, and by inference you admire the interviewer. Likewise, if any areas of common interest arise, comment on them, and agree with the interviewer when reasonably possible—people usually hire people like themselves.

On the 200 telephone interviews a year that I average (they are radio interviews, not job interviews, but I'm sure you can appreciate the similar level of nervous tension), I've found that standing for the interview calms the adrenaline a little, helps my breathing, and allows me to sound confident and relaxed. It might work for you, too, so give it a try.

Answering Questions

Beware of giving yes-or-no answers, as they give no real information about your abilities and do nothing to forward your agenda. At the same time, don't waffle; your answers need to be concise. Understanding someone over the telephone can sometimes be a challenge, so if you didn't hear or didn't understand a question, ask the speaker to repeat it. If you need time to think about your answer—and that is quite acceptable—say so: "Let me think about that for a moment."

Whenever possible, you should give real-world examples to illustrate your points: "That's interesting. I was involved in an audit like that a couple months back and it presented some interesting challenges."

There are some 200 questions you are likely to be asked during an interview, which we'll cover in detail in the coming pages. Meanwhile, there are a handful of questions often asked during telephone interviews in addition to the ones that will come right after you make a marketing presentation. Let's look at them in light of your probable lack of information about the company and the job.

- *"What are you looking for?"* With so little real knowledge about the company at this point, you need to be careful about specificity. Don't say, "I want to move into marketing," unless you know such opportunity exists. Otherwise keep your answer general and focused on (a) improving yourself professionally and (b) becoming a productive member of a respected team.

- *"What are your strengths?"* If you know about specific skill requirements, emphasize them; if not, stick to a brief outline of your key technical skills and a selection of the transferable skills and professional values that support them.
- *"What is your greatest weakness?"* Don't throw the opportunity away before you even get in the door and have a real understanding of the job. Mention a brand-new technology/skill you are developing and say you have been working on it and try to keep abreast of the latest approaches in all aspects of your profession.
- *"I don't think you'll be suitable because you lack _____ skill."* If the statement is true, acknowledge it, then follow with an example of a similar skill you picked up quickly and apply with consummate skill: "Yes, I understand. When I joined my current company I knew nothing about _____, but I studied on my own and with the help of a mentor within the department I was up to speed in a matter of weeks. Given my proven ability to learn quickly and my willingness to invest my own time, would you consider talking to me in more detail about this topic when we meet face-to-face?" With this type of response you are putting a positive spin on your shortcoming, which gives you a good shot at overcoming the objection. If you are successful in arranging a face-to-face interview, you'll now have time to bone up on the subject and identify a sensible development program before you meet with the employer.

Under no circumstances, though, should you ask about salary or benefits and vacation time; that comes much later. Your single objective at this point is to meet face-to-face; money is not an issue. If the interviewer brings up a direct question about how much you are earning, you can't get around it, so be honest. On the other hand, if you are asked how much you want, answer truthfully that at this point you don't know enough about the company or the job to answer that question. There is a whole chapter in this book on negotiation (Chapter 22) that covers the money issue in some detail.

The telephone interview has come to an end when you are asked whether you have any questions—perhaps, "What would you like to know about us?" This is a wind-down question, so it is a good opening to get some specific questions of your own answered that can advance your candidacy:

- "What are the most immediate challenges of the job?"
- "What are the most important projects of the first six months?"
- "What skills and behaviors are most important to success on the job?"
- "Why do some people succeed and others fail doing this work?"

By discovering answers to these questions now, you will have time before the face-to-face meeting to package your skills according to the needs at hand and to create an appropriate executive briefing for distribution with your resume to the different interviewers you meet.

If you have not already asked or been invited to meet the interviewer, now is the time to take the initiative.

"It sounds like a very interesting opportunity, Ms. Bassett, and a situation where I could definitely make a contribution. The most pressing question I have now is when can we get together?"

When an invitation for an interview is extended, there are practical matters that you need to clarify with a handful of simple questions that address the when (date and time) and where (don't assume the interview will take place at a facility that you associate with the company). You will also want to inquire about the interview procedure:

- "How many interviews typically occur before a decision is made?"
- "Who else will be part of the selection process, and what are their roles within the department or company?"
- "What is the time frame for filling this position, and how many other people are in consideration at this time?"

Follow with a casual inquiry as to what direction the meeting will take. You might ask, "Would you tell me some of the critical areas we will discuss on Thursday?" The knowledge gained will help you to package and present yourself, and it will allow you time to bone up on any weak or rusty areas. This is also a good time to establish how long the meeting is expected to last, which will give you some idea of how to pace yourself.

Once the details are confirmed, finish with this request: "If I need any additional information before the interview, may I feel free to get back to you?" The company representative will naturally agree. No matter how many questions you get answered in the initial conversation, there will always be something you forgot. This allows you to call again to satisfy any curiosity—it will also enable you to increase rapport. Don't take too much advantage of it, though: One well-placed phone call that contains two or three considered questions will be appreciated; four or five phone calls will not.

In closing your conversation, take care to ascertain the correct spelling and pronunciation of the interviewer's name. This shows your concern for the small but important things in life—and it will be noticed, particularly when the interviewer receives your follow-up thank-you note. (See the latest edition of *Knock 'em Dead Cover Letters* for a comprehensive selection of samples.)

It is difficult to evaluate an opportunity properly over the phone, so even if the job doesn't sound right, go to the interview; it will give you practice, and the job may look better when you have more facts. You might even discover a more suitable opening elsewhere within the company.

CHAPTER 9
DRESS FOR JOB INTERVIEW SUCCESS

WHEN YOU DRESS like a professional, you are likely to be treated as one, and that's a good head start before saying a word.

The moment you set eyes on someone, your mind makes evaluations and judgments with lightning speed. Potential employers also make the same lightning-speed evaluations when you first meet at the beginning of a job interview. It's a fair estimate that nine out of ten of today's employers will reject an unsuitably dressed applicant without a second thought.

See Is What You Get!"

you receive at the interview will be in direct proportion to the image you professional appearance won't get you the job offer—but it will lend every- much more credence and weight. Wearing a standard business uniform ates that you understand one of the paramount unwritten rules of professional life and that you have a confident self-image.

Employers rarely make overt statements about acceptable dress codes to their employees, much less to interviewees. Instead, there is a generally accepted but unspoken dictum that those who wish to succeed will dress appropriately, and those who don't, won't.

There are a few professions where on-the-job dress (as opposed to interview dress) is somewhat less conservative than in the mainstream: Fashion, entertainment, and advertising are three examples. In these and a few other fields, there is a good deal of leeway with regard to personal expression in workplace attire. But for 95 percent of us, jobs and employers require a certain level of traditional professionalism in our wardrobes. While you need not dress like the chairman of the board (although that probably wouldn't hurt), adopting "casual Friday" attire on the day of your interview is not in your best professional interests. For a job interview, it is generally accepted that you should dress one or two levels up from the job you are applying for, while remaining consistent with the type of occupation it is within. To maximize your career options over the long haul of a career you must aim to consistently meet or exceed these standards.

Your Interview Advantage

Your appearance tells people how you feel about yourself as an applicant, as well as how you feel about the interviewer, the company, and the interview process itself. By dressing professionally, you tell people that you understand the niceties of corporate life, and you send a subtle "reinforcing" message that you can, for example, be relied on to deal one-on-one with members of a company's prized client base.

How you dress sends signals about:

- How seriously you take the occasion, and, by extension, how much respect you feel for your interviewers and all others whom you meet at the interviews.
- How well you understand the confidence a look of traditional professionalism gives clients, customers, peers, and superiors.

Yet no matter how important these concerns might be, they pale in comparison to the impact a sharp appearance can have on your own sense of self. When you know you have taken care of your appearance and that you look the best you can, you feel pride and confidence: Your posture is better, you smile more, and you feel more "in control" of your destiny. In turn, others will respond positively to the image of professionalism and self-confidence that you present. Portraying the correct image at an interview will give you a real edge over your competition. You can expect what you say to be strongly influenced in the mind of your interviewer by the way you present yourself. Appearances count.

The Look

The safest look for both men and women at interviews is traditional and conservative. Look at investing in a good-fitting, well-made suit as your first step to a successful strategic career move. With your business clothes, quality matters far more than quantity; it's better to have one good outfit than two mediocre ones. Your professional wardrobe is a long-term career asset, so add quality items, and over time the quantity will come.

Up until recent years, this was fairly easy for men, as their professional fashions tended to remain constant. These days, men's fashions are experiencing a metamorphosis, with designers of high fashion offering affordable lines of updated, professionally acceptable looks. However, a man can always interview with confidence and poise in his six-year-old Brooks Brothers suit, provided it isn't worn to a shine.

For women, things are more complicated. Appropriate female attire for the interview should reflect current professional fashions if the applicant is to be taken seriously. Moreover, in selecting a current professional look, a woman must walk a fine line, combining elements of both conformity (to show she belongs) and panache (to show a measure of individuality and style).

The key for both sexes is to dress for the position you want, not the one you have. This means the upwardly mobile professional might need to invest in the clothes that project the desired image.

The correct appearance alone probably won't by itself get you a job offer, but it does go a long way toward winning the attention and respect you need to land the offer. When you know you look right, you can stop worrying about the impression your clothes are making and concentrate on communicating your message.

Every interview and every interviewer is different, so it isn't possible to set down rigid guidelines for exactly what to wear in any given situation. However, there are a handful of commonsense guidelines that will ensure you are perceived as someone savvy, practical, competent, reliable, and professional.

General Guidelines

The right look varies from industry to industry. A college professor can sport tweed jackets with elbow patches on the job, and an advertising executive may don the latest designer dress or wear wild ties as a badge of creativity (that is what they are being paid for). Nevertheless, that same college professor is likely to wear a suit to an important interview, and even professional men and women in advertising and the media are likely to dress more conservatively for a job interview.

Most of us are far more adept at recognizing the dress mistakes of others than at spotting our own image failings. When you look for a second opinion, you often make the mistake of asking only a loved one. Better candidates for evaluation of your interview attire are trusted professional friends who have proven their objectivity in such matters.

Whenever possible, find out the dress code of the company you are visiting. For example, if you are an engineer applying for a job at a high-tech company, a blue three-piece suit might be overpowering. It is perfectly acceptable to ask someone in Human Resources about the dress code (written or informal) of the company. You may even want to make an anonymous visit to get a sense of the corporate style of the company; if that isn't practical, you can always visit the website to see how the company likes to be perceived by its public.

I have been asked, "If everyone wears sweaters at the company where I am interviewing, shouldn't I wear the same if I want to be seen to fit in?" In fact, very few companies allow a very relaxed dress code for all their employees all the time. An increasing percentage allows a somewhat relaxed dress code on a particular day (often Friday), when "casual professional" attire is allowed, if not always encouraged. Sometimes, some younger professionals mistake this to mean they can dress for the beach at all times. Even if the company is casual all the time for all its employees, do not dress casually for a job interview. There are two big reasons to avoid casual interview attire:

1. The company is considering an investment that will probably run into hundreds of thousands of dollars if the hire works out, and potentially as much as tens of thousands of dollars if it doesn't—hardly a casual event.
2. Companies sometimes allow casual dress at times and in circumstances that will not jeopardize business. They are comfortable doing this because they already know everyone on the payroll knows how to dress appropriately. The interview is where the company needs to know you appreciate the niceties of business dress; they already have a fair idea that you own a sweater and a pair of khakis.

Tattoos and Piercings

If you are contemplating a professional career, recognize that visible body piercings and tattoos will forever close many doors to your entry, and most of the rest to your ascent. While tattoos and piercings are an individual expression and your right, corporations also have a right not to hire people who they feel are unable to represent company interests in the best light. Like it or not, *any and all body decoration is frowned upon by the vast majority of employers.*

In other words, if you sport tats or piercings, conceal them during the interview and at all times during your professional endeavors. If you are considering body decoration, ask yourself if in the history of humankind there has ever been one item in any man or woman's wardrobe that he or she has willingly worn every day for the rest of his or her life. Soberly weigh your personal interests against your professional success.

Men

The following are the best current dress guidelines for men preparing for a professional interview.

Men's Suits

A *Wall Street Journal* survey of CEOs showed a 53 percent preference for navy blue and dark blue, while 39 percent favored gray or charcoal gray. Brown can be acceptable for subsequent interviews at some companies. In summer months, a lightweight beige suit is fine at second or third interviews; you would never wear a light-colored suit except during the warmer months. Ideally, wear a 100 percent wool suit, as wool looks and wears better than any other material. The darker the suit, the more authority it carries. (Beware: A man should not wear a black suit to an interview unless applying for an undertaker's job.) Pinstripes and solids, in dark gray, navy, or medium blue, are equally acceptable, although many feel a dark solid suit is the best option because it gives authority to the wearer and is seen as less stuffy than a pinstripe suit. Somewhat less common but also acceptable are gray-colored glen plaid (also called "Prince of Wales") or hound's-tooth suits.

A well-cut two-piece suit is preferable (with the standard two-button suit jacket, although the older three-button, single-breasted jacket is quite acceptable) to a three-piece suit that includes a vest or waistcoat. The three-piece is seen as ultraconservative, which might be a useful tool in some situations, but the extra layer of clothing brings in the heat and sweat factor, which argues against it for more practical reasons. Double-breasted jackets are seen as more edgy, and you are more likely to wear them to an interview at an advertising agency than at the local bank.

Above all, it's the quality and fit of your suit that matters. Current fashions favor a slimmer cut, particularly in the trousers. However, the fit and cut must complement your own build. The leaner, tapered look elongates your appearance; the looser cuts add bulk. There should be no pull at the jacket shoulders and no gape at the back, and the jacket cuffs should break at your wrists. Your trousers should fit comfortably at the waist. A flat front is most flattering (unless you are enviably scrawny), and there should be only a slight break where the trouser hits the shoe. If your ankles are visible in the mirror, the pants are too damn short! Cuffed trousers add a very sophisticated and conservative look, but an important consideration might be that uncuffed trousers are seen to enhance your height.

Men's Shirts

The principles here are simple:

Rule One: Always wear a long-sleeved shirt, never wear a short-sleeved shirt.

Rule Two: Always wear a white, cream, or pale blue shirt.

By white, I do not mean to exclude, for instance, shirts with very thin red or blue pinstripes: Nevertheless, there is a presence about a solid white shirt that seems to convey honesty, intelligence, and stability; it should be your first choice. It is true that artists, writers, software engineers, and other creative types are sometimes known to object to white shirts because they feel that it makes it look like "the suit is wearing them." If this is you and you can't get over it, pale blue may be the best option. Remember—the paler and more subtle the shade, the better the impression you will make. Pale colors draw attention, and your collar is right next to your face, which is where you want the interviewer to stay focused.

While monograms are common enough, those who don't wear them may feel strongly about the implied ostentation of stylized initials on clothing; the great valet Jeeves once commented on the topic, saying, "I thought the practice was restricted to those in danger of forgetting their names."

Cotton shirts look better and hold up under perspiration more impressively than their synthetic counterparts. If at all possible, opt for a cotton shirt that has been professionally cleaned and starched. A cotton and polyester blend can be an acceptable alternative, but keep in mind that the higher the cotton content, the better the shirt will look. While these blend shirts wrinkle less easily, you are advised to ignore the "wash-and-wear" and "no need to iron" claims you'll read on the front of the package when you purchase them.

Make sure your shirt fits the neck properly; the sleeve cuff should end at the wrist. Details such as frayed fabric and loose buttons will not go unnoticed when you are under professional scrutiny. It's best to choose your interview clothes well in advance, make any minor repairs, have them cleaned, and keep them ready.

Ties

While a cheap-looking tie can ruin an expensive suit, the right tie can do a lot to pull the less-than-perfect suit together for a professional look. When you can't afford a new suit for the interview, you can upgrade your whole look with the right tie.

A pure silk tie makes the most powerful professional impact, has the best finish and feel, and is easiest to tie well. A pure silk tie or a 50 percent wool/50 percent silk blend (which is almost wrinkle-proof) should be your choice for the interview. Linen ties are too informal, can only be tied once or twice between cleanings because they wrinkle easily, and only look right during warmer weather anyway. A wool tie is casual in appearance and has knot problems. Most man-made fibers are too shiny, with harsh colors that may undercut your professional image.

The tie should complement your suit. This means that there should be a physical balance: The rule of thumb is that the width of your tie should approximate the width of your lapels. The prevailing standard, which has held for over a decade now, is that ties can range in width between 2¾ and 3½ inches. Wearing anything wider may mark you as someone still trapped in the disco era. Currently, ties are being worn narrower in the pages of the fashion magazines, but that really doesn't have to concern you.

While the tie should complement the suit, it should not match it. You would never, for instance, wear a navy blue tie with a navy blue suit. Choose an appropriate tie that neither vanishes into nor battles with your suit pattern. The most popular and safest styles are solids, foulards, stripes, and paisleys.

Do not wear ties with large polka dots, pictures of animals such as leaping trout or soaring mallards, or sporting symbols such as golf clubs or (God forbid) little men on polo ponies. Avoid wearing any piece of apparel that has a manufacturer's symbol emblazoned on the front as part of the decoration.

Other considerations include the length of the tie (it should, when tied, extend to your trouser belt), the size of the knot (smaller is better), and whether you should wear a bow tie to an interview (you shouldn't).

Men's Shoes

Shoes should be either black leather or brown leather. Stay away from all other materials and colors. Lace-up wingtips are the most universally acceptable. Slightly less conservative, but equally appropriate, are slip-on dress shoes—not to be confused with boating shoes. The slip-on, with its low, plain vamp or tassel is versatile enough to be used for both day and evening business wear. Those who are hyperconscious of fashion will say that a lace-up wingtip can look a bit cloddish at dinner. This may be true if you have a dinner interview with the senior law partner of a firm in Chicago, Los Angeles, or New York, but otherwise don't lose sleep over it.

In certain areas of the South, Southwest, and West, heeled cowboy boots are not at all unusual for business wear, and neither are those Grand Ole Opry versions of the business suit. But beware: Outside of Dallas, Nashville, Muskogee, and similar municipalities, you will attract only puzzled stares—so try to be aware of the regional variations in professional dress.

Men's Socks

Socks should complement the suit. Accordingly, they should be blue, black, gray, or brown. When they match the suit color, they extend the length of your leg, giving more height and authority. They should also be long enough for you to cross your legs without showing off bare skin, and should not fall in a bunch toward the ankle as you move. Elastic-reinforced, over-the-calf socks are your best bet.

Men's Accessories

The right accessories can enhance the professional image of any applicant, male or female, just as the wrong accessories can destroy it. The guiding principle here is to include nothing that could be misconstrued or leave a bad impression. For instance, you should not wear obvious religious or political insignias in the form of rings, ties, or pins, as they draw attention to matters that employers are forbidden to address by federal law. This does not necessarily apply when you are aware that a particular spiritual association will establish connectivity, such as wearing a cross when you interview with the Archdiocese.

The watch you wear should be simple and preferably plain, which means that funky Mickey Mouse is out. Sports- and Swatch-style watches, or digital monsters, are acceptable nowadays but aren't the best choice. Don't be afraid to wear a simple, slim analog watch with a leather strap; you will notice it is what the most successful and sophisticated business professionals wear.

A briefcase is always perceived as a symbol of authority and can make a strong professional statement. Leather makes the best impression, with brown and burgundy being the colors of choice. The case is best unadorned—embellishments can only detract from the effect of quiet confidence and authority.

It's a good idea to take a cotton or linen handkerchief on all interviews. Plain white is best because it looks crisp, but the color isn't really that important. You aren't taking a handkerchief to put in a breast pocket but for far more practical reasons. That handkerchief can be used to relieve the clammy-hands syndrome so common before an interview—anything to avoid the infamous "wet fish" handshake. Keep it in an inside pocket, avoiding the matching tie-and-pocket-square look of a dyed-in-the-wool doofus at all costs.

Belts should match or complement the shoes you select. Accordingly, a blue or gray suit will require a black belt and black shoes, while brown, tan, or beige suits call for brown. Wear a good-quality leather belt if you can. The most common mistake made with belts is the buckle; an interview is not the place for your favorite Harley Davidson, Grateful Dead, or Bart Simpson buckle. Select a small, simple buckle that doesn't overwhelm the rest of your look or make personal statements that you cannot be certain will resonate with an interviewer.

Men's Jewelry

Men may wear a wedding band, and cuff links are acceptable with French cuffs. Anything more in the way of jewelry can be dangerous. Necklaces, bracelets, neck chains, and earrings can send the wrong message, and tie tacks and clips are passé in most areas of the country.

Men's Raincoats

The safest and most utilitarian colors for raincoats are beige and blue; stick to these two exclusively. If you can avoid wearing a raincoat, do so (it's an encumbrance and adds to clutter), but it is better to have a raincoat than to have your suit drenched.

Women

Following are the best current dress guidelines for women preparing for a professional interview.

Women's Suits

You have more room for creativity in this area than men do, but also more room for mistakes. Until recent years, your professional fashion creativity had to remain within certain accepted guidelines dictated not by the fashion industry, but by the consensus of the business world—which trails far behind the pages of fashion magazines. And while there are still the limits of good taste and necessary conservatism for the interviewer, the fashion designers have worked hard to create workable professional alternatives for the ever-growing female workforce.

A woman's business wardrobe need no longer be simply a pseudo-male selection of drab gray skirts and blouses. With the right cuts, pinstripes and even ties can look both stylish and professional.

Wool and linen are both accepted as the right look for professional women's suits, but linen can present a problem. Linen wrinkles so quickly that you may feel as though you leave the house dressed for success and arrive at your destination looking like a bag lady. Cotton-polyester blends are great for warm climates; they look like linen but lack the wrinkle factor. Combinations of synthetics and natural fabrics have their advantages: Suits made of such material will certainly retain their shape better. The eye trained to pay attention to detail, however (read: the interviewer's), may detect the type of fabric—say, a cheap polyester blend—and draw unwarranted conclusions about your personality and taste. The choice is up to you. If you do opt for natural fabrics, you will probably want to stay with wool. It provides the smartest look of all and is the most versatile and rugged. There are wonderful, ultra-light wool gabardines available now that will take you through the toughest interview on the hottest summer day.

Like her male counterpart, the professional woman should stick to solids or pinstripes in gray, navy, and medium blues. The ubiquitous Prince of Wales plaid (glen plaid) or hound's-tooth check can both look very distinguished on a woman as well. At the same time, a much wider palette of colors is open for consideration by the professional woman, from lilac to fire engine red. While there are situations where you will want to choose one of the more powerful colors, it might be best at one of the subsequent interviews, rather than the first.

A solid skirt with a coordinating subtle plaid jacket is also acceptable, but make sure there is not too much contrast or it will detract from the focus of your meeting: the interview. Colors most suitable for interview suits include charcoal, medium gray, steel gray, black (whereas a man is advised against black, the color is open and acceptable for the professional woman), and navy blue. Of all these looks, the cleanest and most professional is the simple solid navy or gray suit with a white blouse.

Jackets should be simple, well tailored, and stylish, but not stylized. This is probably not the time to wear a peplum-style jacket—a standard length that falls just at the hips is preferable. The cut and style should flatter your build and reflect your personal style without detracting from what you have to say. Attention to details such as smooth seams, even hemlines, correctly hanging linings, and well-sewn buttons are essential.

How long a skirt should you wear? Any hard-and-fast rule I could offer here would be in danger of being outdated almost immediately, as the fashion industry demands dramatically different looks every season in order to fuel sales. (After all, keeping the same hemlines would mean that last season's clothes could last another season or two.) It should go without saying that you don't want to sport something that soars to the upper thigh if you want to be taken seriously as an applicant. Your best bet is to dress somewhat more conservatively than you would if you were simply showing up for work at the organization in question. Hemlines come and go, and while there is some leeway as to what is appropriate for everyday wear on the job, the safest bet is usually to select something that falls at or no more than two inches above the knee.

Increasingly popular is the one-piece business dress with a matching jacket. This outfit is particularly useful for the "business day into evening" crowd, but can be perfectly suitable for interviews if it is properly styled and fitted. It is particularly important to stick with subtle solid colors for this look.

Blouses

Blouses with long sleeves will project a responsible and professional look. Three-quarter-length sleeves are less desirable, followed in turn by short sleeves. Never wear a sleeveless blouse to an interview; you may be confident that there is absolutely no chance that you will be required to remove your jacket, but why take the risk of offending someone with unexpected glimpses of undergarments?

Solid colors and natural fabrics, particularly cotton and silk, are the best selections for blouses—although silk is warm and therefore raises perspiration concerns for a nervous interviewee. Combinations of natural and synthetic fabrics are wrinkle-resistant but do not absorb moisture well, so with these choices you will need to take perspiration countermeasures into account.

The acceptable color spectrum is wider for blouses than for men's shirts, but it is not limitless. The most prudent choices are still white or cream or gray; these offer a universal professional appeal. Pale pink or light blue can also work, but should be worn only if it fully blends into your overall look. Light colors are "friendly" and draw attention to your face, yet will not distract the interviewer from what you have to say. The blouse with a front-tie bow has become dated; a classic softened shirt collar works best with a suit. The button-down collar always looks great, particularly if you are interviewing with a conservative company or industry.

Women's Neckwear

While a woman might choose to wear a string of pearls instead of a scarf to an interview, the scarf can still serve as a powerful status symbol. Opting to wear a scarf says something dramatic about you; make sure it's something positive. A pure silk scarf will offer a conservative look, a good finish, and ease in tying. Some of the better synthetic blends achieve an overall effect that is almost as good. While some books on women's clothing will recommend buying blouses that have matching scarves attached to the collar, there is an increasingly vocal lobby of stylish businesswomen who feel this is the equivalent of mandating that a man wear a clip-on bow tie. As with men's ties, the objective is to complement the outfit, not match it. Avoid overly flamboyant styles, and stick with solids or basic prints (foulards, small polka dots, or paisleys) in subtle colors that will complement—not compete with—your outfit or your conversation.

Women's Shoes

The professional woman has a greater color selection in footwear than does her male counterpart. The shoes should preferably be leather, but in addition to brown and black, a woman is safe in wearing navy, burgundy, forest green, or even, if circumstances warrant—and it is not a first interview—red. The color of your shoes should always be the same or a darker tone than your skirt.

It is safest to stay away from faddish or multicolored shoes (even such classics as two-toned oxfords). First, all fashion is transitory, and even if you are up-to-date, you cannot assume that your interviewer is. Second, a good proportion of your interviewers might be men, who are less likely to appreciate vivid color combinations. As with the rest of your wardrobe, stay away from radical choices and opt for the easily comprehensible professional look.

Heel height is important, as well. Flats are fine; a shoe with a heel of up to about 2½ inches is perfectly acceptable. Stay away from high heels; at best you will wobble slightly, and at worst you will walk at an angle. The pump, or court shoe, with its closed toe and heel, is perhaps the safest and most conservative look. A closed heel with a slightly open toe is acceptable, too, as is the slingback shoe with a closed toe. The toe on any style should not be overly pointed. Just think moderation in all things; the goal is to get hired, not dated.

Pantyhose

These should not make their own statement. Neutral skin tones are the safest, most conservative choice, though you are perfectly within the realm of professional etiquette when wearing a sheer white or cream if it complements your blouse or dress. You may make an exception if you are interviewing for a job in the fashion industry, in which case you might coordinate colors with your outfit, but be very sure of the company dress code that is already in place. Even in such an instance, avoid loud or glitzy looks.

As you well know, pantyhose and stockings are prone to developing runs at the worst possible moment, so keep an extra pair in your purse or briefcase.

Women's Accessories

Because a briefcase is a symbol of authority, it is an excellent choice for the professional woman. Do not, however, bring both your purse and a briefcase to the interview. (You'll look awkward juggling them.) Instead, transfer essential items to a small clutch bag you can store in the case. In addition to brown and burgundy (recommended colors for the men), you may include navy and black as possible colors for your case, which should always be free of personal, expensive, or distracting embellishments.

Belts should match or complement the shoes you select. A black or gray suit will require a black belt and black shoes; brown, tan, or beige suits will call for brown; and navy looks best with navy or burgundy accessories. In addition, women may wear snakeskin, lizard, and the like (though beware of offending animal rights activists). Remember that the belt is a functional item; if it is instantly noticeable, it is wrong.

Women's Jewelry

As far as jewelry goes, less is more. A woman should restrict rings to engagement or wedding bands if these are applicable, but she can wear a necklace and earrings, as long as these are subdued and professional looking. I should note that some men are put off by earrings of any description in the workplace, so if you wear them keep them small, discreet, and in good taste. Avoid fake or strangely colored pearls, anything with your name or initials on it, and earrings that dangle or jangle. A single bracelet on a woman's wrist is acceptable; anything around the ankle is not. Remember, too much of the wrong kind of jewelry could cost you a job offer or inhibit your promotional opportunities once on the team.

Makeup

Take care never to appear overly made-up; "natural" is the key word. Eye makeup should be subtle, so as not to overwhelm the rest of the face. As a general rule, I advise very little lipstick at an interview because it can cause negative reactions in some interviewers, and because it can smudge and wear off as the hours wear on. (Who can say, going in, how long the meeting will last?) However, women tell me that as they advance into their thirties and beyond, the natural pinkness of the lips can fade; you might feel you look pale and washed-out without lipstick. So if you feel "undressed" without your lipstick, use some: But apply it sparingly and carefully, choose a neutral or subdued color, and, of course, never apply it in public.

For Men and Women: A Note on Personal Hygiene

Bad breath, dandruff, body odor, and dirty, un-manicured nails have the potential to undo all your efforts at putting across a good first impression. These and related problems all speak to an underlying professional slovenliness, which an interviewer may feel will manifest itself in your work. You want to present yourself as an appealing, self-respecting, and enjoyable professional to be around. You can't achieve this if the people you meet have to call on their powers of self-control in order to stay in the same room with you.

What was that old TV body odor commercial tag line: "What even your best friend won't tell you"? So don't ask yourself whether any friend or colleague has actually come out and suggested that you pay more attention to personal hygiene; it is such a touchy issue that most people will avoid you rather than discuss it. Ask yourself how you felt the last time you had to conduct business of any sort with someone who had a hygiene problem. Then resolve never to leave that kind of impression.

Personal grooming of hair, skin, teeth, and nails is easy and straightforward, but body odor is a different challenge. When it comes to body odor you are literally what you eat; onions, garlic, cilantro, and junk food can all give your bodily odors a distinctly unpleasant pungency. Because it takes time for your body to rid itself of such smells, the best advice is to start paying attention to diet as you begin to put your wardrobe together.

CHAPTER 10
BODY LANGUAGE

LEARN TO CONTROL negative body movements and encourage positive ones. Discover the seven guidelines for good body language during your interview.

As human beings, we rely to a remarkable degree on our ability to gather information visually. This really is not all that surprising, because while speech is a comparatively recent development, humans have been sending and receiving nonverbal signals since the dawn of the species. In fact, the language of the body is the first means of communication we develop after birth. We master the spoken word later in life, and, in so doing, we forget the importance of nonverbal cues—but the signals are still sent and received, usually at a subconscious level.

It is common to hear people say of the body language they use, "Take me or leave me as I am." This is all very well if you have no concern for what others think of you. For those seeking professional employment, however, it is important to recognize that your body is constantly sending messages, and you must make every effort to understand and control the information stream. If your mouth says, "Hire me," but your body says, "I'm not being truthful," you are likely to leave the interviewer confused. "Well," she will think, "the right answers all came out, but there was something about that candidate that just rubbed me the wrong way." Such misgivings are generally sufficient to keep a candidate from making the short list. The interviewer may or may not be aware of what causes the concern, but the messages will be sent, and your cause will suffer.

Of course, interviewers will listen carefully to what you say, too. When your body language complements your verbal statements, your message will gain a great deal of impact, but when your body language *contradicts* what you say, the interviewer will be skeptical. In short, learning to use positive body signals and control negative ones during an interview can have a significant impact on your job search and on the new job.

Under the Microscope

The challenge for the interviewer is to determine, using every means at his disposal, what kind of an employee you would make. Your task as a candidate is to provide the clues most likely to prompt a decision to hire. Let's begin at the beginning. When you are invited to an interview, you are probably safe in assuming that your interviewer believes you meet certain minimum standards and could conceivably be hired.

In this context, the adage that actions speak louder than words is something you should take quite literally. Studies done at the University of Chicago found that more than 50 percent of all effective communication relies on body language. Since you can expect interviewers to respond to the body language you employ at the interview, it is up to you to decide what messages you want them to receive.

There are also studies that suggest the impression you create in the first few minutes of the interview is the most lasting. Since the first few minutes after you meet the interviewer is a time when she is doing the vast majority of the talking, you have very little control over the impression you create with your words—you can't say much of anything! It is up to your body to do the job for you.

The Greeting
For a good handshake:

1. Your hands should be clean and adequately manicured.
2. Your hands should be free of perspiration.

It is professional protocol for the host (interviewer) to initiate the handshake. If, through nerves, you find yourself initiating the handshake, don't pull back, as you will appear indecisive. Instead, make the best of it, smile confidently, and make eye contact.

Your handshake should signal cooperation and friendliness. Match the pressure extended by the interviewer—never exceed it. A typical professional handshake lasts for between two and five seconds, just two or three reasonably firm up-and-down pumps accompanied by a smile. The parting handshake may last a little longer; smile and lean forward *very* slightly as you shake hands before departing.

Certain professional and cultural differences should also be considered as well. Many doctors, artists, and others who do delicate work with their hands can and do give less enthusiastic handshakes than other people. If you work in the media, you'll notice that quite frequently, on-air personalities don't want to shake hands at all; it's the easiest way to catch a cold, and they depend on their voices and appearance more than most. Similarly, the English handshake is considerably less firm than the American, while the German variety is typically firm.

Use only one hand and always shake vertically. Do not extend your hand parallel to the floor with the palm up, as this conveys submissiveness. By the same token, you may be seen as too aggressive if you extend your hand outward with the palm facing down.

While a confident and positive handshake helps break the ice and gets the interview moving in the right direction, proper use of the hands throughout the rest of the interview will help convey an above-board, "nothing-to-hide" message.

Watch out for hands and fingers that take on a life of their own, fidgeting with themselves or other objects such as pens, paper, your tie, or your hair. Pen-tapping is interpreted as the action of an impatient person; this is an example of an otherwise trivial habit that can take on immense significance in an interview situation. Rarely will an interviewer ask you to stop doing something annoying. Instead, she'll simply make a mental note that you are an annoying person and congratulate herself for picking this up before making the mistake of hiring you.

Other negative hand messages include:

- Clasping your hands behind your head. You'll expose perspiration marks, and you run the risk of appearing smug, superior, bored, and possibly withdrawn.
- Showing insecurity by constantly adjusting your tie. When interviewing with a woman, this gesture might be interpreted as displaying something beyond a businesslike interest in the interviewer.
- Slouching in your chair, with hands in pockets or thumbs in belt. This posture can brand you as insolent and aggressive (think of any teenage boy). When this error is made in the presence of an interviewer of the opposite sex, it can carry sexually aggressive overtones as well.

- Pulling your collar away from your neck. This may seem like an innocent enough reaction to the heat of the day, but the interviewer might assume that you are tense or masking an untruth. The same goes for scratching your neck during, before, or after your response to a question.
- Moving your hands toward a personal feature that you perceive as deficient. This is a common unconscious reaction to stress. A man with thinning hair, for example, may thoughtlessly put his hand to his forehead when pondering how to respond to the query ("Why aren't you earning more at your age?"). This habit may be extremely difficult for you to detect in the first place, much less reverse, but make the effort. Such protective movements are likely to be perceived—if only on a subliminal level—as an acknowledgment of low self-esteem.
- Picking at invisible bits of fluff on your suit. This gesture looks exactly like what it is, a nervous tic. Keep your focus on the interviewer. If you do have some bit of lint somewhere on your clothing, the best advice is usually to ignore it until you can remove it discreetly.

By contrast, employing the hands in a positive way can further your candidacy:

- Subtly exposing your palms now and then as you speak can help demonstrate that you are open, friendly, and have nothing to hide. You can see this technique used to great effect by politicians and television talk show hosts.
- It can, very occasionally, be beneficial to "steeple" your fingers for a few seconds as you consider a question or when you first start to talk. Unless you hold the gesture for long periods of time, it will be perceived as a neutral demonstration of your thoughtfulness. Of course, if you overuse or hold this position for too long, you may be taken as condescending. Steepling also gives you something constructive to do with your hands; it offers a change from holding your pad and pen.

Taking Your Seat
Some thirty inches from my nose
The frontier of my person goes.
Beware of rudely crossing it,
I have no gun, but I can spit.
—W. H. Auden

Encroaching on another's "personal zone" is a bad idea in any business situation, but it is particularly dangerous in an interview. The thirty-inch standard is a good one to follow: It is the distance that allows you to extend your hand comfortably for a handshake. Maintain this distance throughout the interview, and be particularly watchful of personal-space intrusions when you first meet, greet, and take a seat.

A person's office is an extension of her personal zone; this is why it is not only polite but also sound business sense to wait until the interviewer offers you a seat.

It is not uncommon to meet with an interviewer in a conference room or another supposedly "neutral" site. Again, wait for the interviewer to motion you to a spot, or, if you feel uncomfortable doing this, tactfully ask the interviewer to take the initiative: "Where would you like me to sit?"

The type of chair you sit in can affect the signals your body sends during an interview. If you have a choice, go with an upright chair with arms. Deep armchairs can restrict your ability to send certain positive signals and encourage the likelihood of slumping. They're best suited for watching television, not for projecting the image of a competent professional.

Always sit with your bottom well back in the chair and your back straight. Slouching, of course, is out, but a slight forward-leaning posture will show interest and friendliness toward the interviewer. Keep your hands on the arms of the chair; if there are no arms on the chair, keep your hands in your lap or on your pad of paper.

Crossed legs, in all their many forms, send a mixture of signals; most of them are negative:

- Crossing one ankle over the other knee can show a certain stubborn and recalcitrant outlook (as well as the bottom of your shoe, which is not always a pretty sight). The negative signal is intensified when you grasp the horizontally crossed leg or—worst of all—cross your arms across your chest.
- Some body language experts feel crossed ankles indicate that the person doing the crossing is withholding information. Of course, since the majority of interviews take place across a desk, crossed ankles will often be virtually unnoticeable. For women, some dress fashions encourage decorous ankle crossing. This posture is probably the most permissible body language faux pas, so if you must allow yourself one body language vice, this is the one to choose.
- When sitting in armchairs or on sofas, crossing the legs may be necessary to create some stability amid all the plush upholstery. In this instance, the signals you send by crossing your legs will be neutral, as long as your legs are not crossed ankle over knee.

The solution is to give a friend/loved one permission to call you on it every time you start drumming to the beat of your life. Learn to be conscious of when you are doing it, and don't do it at any point during a job interview. It is an indulgence that you can overcome . . . at least when you have to deal with the rhythm-less at job interviews.

Facial Signals

Once you take your seats, most often across a desk, and the conversation begins, the interviewer's attention will be focused on your face.

Our language is full of expressions testifying to the powerful influence of facial mannerisms. When you say that someone is shifty-eyed, tight-lipped, has a furrowed brow, flashes bedroom eyes, stares into space, or grins like a Cheshire cat, you are speaking in a kind of shorthand and using a set of archetypes that enable us to make judgments—consciously or unconsciously—about that person.

Tight smiles and tension in the facial muscles often bespeak an inability to handle stress; little eye contact can communicate a desire to hide something; pursed lips are often associated with a secretive nature; and frowning, looking sideways, or peering over one's glasses can send signals of haughtiness and arrogance. Hardly the stuff of which winning interviews are made!

The Eyes

Looking at someone means showing interest in that person, and showing interest is a giant step forward in making the right impression. Remember: We are all our own favorite subjects!

Looking away from the interviewer for long periods while she is talking, closing your eyes while being addressed, and repeatedly shifting focus from the subject to some other point are all likely to leave the wrong impression.

There is a difference between looking and staring at someone. Rather than looking at the speaker straight on at all times, create a mental triangle incorporating both of the eyes and the mouth; your eyes will follow a natural, continuous path along the three points. Maintain this approach for roughly three-quarters of the time; you can break your gaze to look at the interviewer's hands as points are emphasized or to refer to your notepad. This is the way we maintain eye contact in nonstressful situations, and it will allow you to appear attentive, sincere, and committed.

Be wary of breaking eye contact too abruptly and of shifting your focus in ways that will disrupt the atmosphere of professionalism. Examining the interviewer below the head and shoulders, for instance, is a sign of overfamiliarity. This is especially important when being interviewed by someone of the opposite sex.

The eyebrows send messages as well. Under stress, one's brows may wrinkle; this sends a negative signal about your ability to handle challenges in the business world. The best thing to do is take a deep breath and collect yourself. Most of the tension that people feel at interviews has to do with anxiety about how to respond to what the interviewer will ask.

The Head

Nodding your head slowly shows interest, validates your interviewer's comments, and subtly encourages him to continue. Tilting the head slightly, when combined with eye contact and a natural smile, demonstrates friendliness and approachability. The tilt should be momentary and not exaggerated, almost like a bob of the head to one side. (Do not overuse this technique unless you are applying for a job in a parrot shop!) Rapidly nodding your head can leave the impression that you are impatient and eager to add something to the conversation if only the interviewer would let you.

The Mouth

One guiding principle of good body language is to turn your mouth upward rather than downward. Look at two boxers after a fight: The victor's arms are raised high, his back is straight, and his shoulders are square. His smiling face is thrust upward and outward, and you see happiness, openness, warmth, and confidence. The loser, on the other hand, is slumped forward, brows knit and eyes downcast, and the signals you receive are those of anger, frustration, belligerence, and defeat.

Your smile is one of the most powerful positive body signals in your arsenal, and it exemplifies the up-is-best principle. Offer an unforced, confident smile as frequently as opportunity and circumstances dictate; avoid grinning idiotically, as this indicates that you may not be quite right in the head.

You should be aware that the mouth also provides a seemingly limitless supply of opportunities to convey weakness. This may be done by touching the mouth frequently, "faking" a cough when confronted with a difficult question, or gnawing on one's lips absentmindedly. Employing any of these "insincerity signs" when you are asked about, say, why you lost your last job, might instill or confirm suspicions about your honesty or openness.

Glasses

People who wear glasses sometimes leave them off when going on an interview in an attempt to project a more favorable image. There are difficulties with this approach. Farsighted people who don't wear their glasses will (unwittingly) seem to stare long and hard at the people they converse with, and this is a negative signal. Also, pulling out glasses for reading and peering over the top of your glasses—even if you have been handed something to read and subsequently asked a question—carries professorial connotations that can be interpreted as critical. If you wear glasses for reading, you should remove them when conversing, replacing them only when appropriate.

Wearing dark glasses to an interview will paint you as secretive, cold, and devious. Even if your prescription glasses are tinted, the effect will be the same. You might consider untinted glasses for your interview, or contacts. At the same time, glasses on a younger-looking person can add an air of seriousness and might be considered a plus.

Body Signal Barricades

Folding or crossing your arms, or holding things in front of the body, sends negative messages to the interviewer: "I know you're there, but you can't come in. I'm nervous and closed for business."

It is bad enough to feel this way, but worse to express it with blatant signals. Don't fold your arms or "protect" your chest with hands, clipboard, briefcase, or anything else during the interview. You can, however, keep a pad and pen on your lap. It makes you look organized and gives you something to do with your hands.

Feet

Some foot signals can have negative connotations. Women and men wearing slip-on shoes should beware of dangling the loose shoe from the toes; this can be distracting, and, as it is a gesture often used to signal physical attraction, it has no place in a job interview. Likewise, avoid compulsive jabbing of floor, desk, or chair with your foot; this can be perceived as a hostile and angry motion, and is likely to annoy the interviewer.

Some people (your author is included in the front ranks on this one) have an annoying habit of jiggling one leg up and down on the ball of the foot. Those of us who do this know it is a tic that says we are totally engaged and excited about some topic (and sometimes even the one under discussion), but those forced to endure it find it distracting and can interpret it as impatience. If you are a dreaded jiggler, you must get this under control for your job interviews!

Walking

Many interviews will require that you walk from one place to the next—on a guided tour of facilities, from one office to another, or to and from the table in a restaurant. (Of course, if you are interviewing in a restaurant, you will have to walk with your interviewer to and from the dining facility.) How long these walks last is not as important as how you use them to reinforce positive professional behaviors and impressions.

Posture is your main concern: Keep your shoulders back and stay erect. Smile and make eye contact as appropriate. Avoid fidgeting with your feet as you move, rubbing one shoe against the other, or kicking absentmindedly at the ground if you stand to talk; these signals will lead others to believe that you are anxious or insecure. Crossing your arms or legs while standing carries the same negative connotations as it does when you are sitting. Hands-in-pockets, hands-on-hips, or thumbs-in-belt postures are all to be avoided. These send messages that you are aggressive and dominating. It is better to hold a pad and pen or keep your arms on the arms of the chair, which will also help you avoid slouching. Remember to show one or both of your palms occasionally as you make points, but do not overuse this gesture.

Putting It All Together

Now you have the big picture, and you can begin to be more aware of the signals your body can unwittingly send. Let's reduce all this information into a handful of simple recommendations. Positive signals reinforce one another; employing them in combination yields an overwhelming positive message that is truly greater than the sum of its parts.

So far we have focused primarily on the pitfalls to avoid—but what messages *should* be sent, and how? Here are seven general suggestions on good body language for the interview:

1. Walk slowly and stand tall upon entering the room.
2. On greeting your interviewer, give a smile, make eye contact, and respond warmly to the interviewer's greeting and handshake.
3. As you sit, get your butt well back in the chair; this allows the chair back to help you sit upright. Increase the impression of openness ("I have nothing to hide!") by unbuttoning your jacket as you sit down. Keep your head up. Maintain eye contact a good portion of the time, especially when the interviewer begins to speak and when you reply. Smile naturally whenever the opportunity arises.
4. Use mirroring techniques to reproduce the positive signals your interviewer sends. Say the interviewer leans forward to make a point; a few moments later, you too lean forward slightly, demonstrating that you don't want to miss a word. Perhaps the interviewer leans back and laughs; you "laugh beneath" the interviewer's laughter, taking care not to overwhelm your partner by using an inappropriate volume level. This can seem contrived at first, but through observing those in your own social circle, you'll notice that this is natural behavior for good communicators.
5. Keep your head up and don't slouch in your seat.
6. Try to remain calm and do not hurry your movements; you'll look harried and are more likely to knock things over. Most people are more klutzy when they are nervous, and consciously slowing your body movements will lessen the chances of disaster and give you a more controlled persona.
7. Remember to breathe. When we are nervous we can forget to do this, which leads to oxygen deprivation and obviously screws up cognitive processes.

Open for Business

The more open your body movements during the interview, the more you will be perceived as open yourself. Understanding and directing your body language will give you added power to turn interviews into cooperative exchanges between two professionals.

Just as you interpret the body language of others, both positive and negative, your body language makes an indelible impression on those you meet. It tells them whether you like and have confidence in yourself, whether you are pleasant to be around, and whether you are more likely to be honest or deceitful. Like it or not, your body carries these messages for the world to see.

Job interviews are reliable in one way: They bring out insecurities. All the more reason to consciously manage the impressions your body sends. You will absorb the lessons in this chapter very quickly if you take the time to observe and interpret the body signals of friends and family. When you see and can understand body language in others, you'll be more aware of your own, and more capable of controlling it.

CHAPTER 11
THE CURTAIN RISES ON THE JOB INTERVIEW

FIRST IMPRESSIONS ARE the strongest. Here are the preparations to make before heading out to the interview.

Backstage in the theater, the announcement "Places, please" is made five minutes before the curtain rises. It's the performers' signal to psych themselves up, complete final costume adjustments, and make time to reach the stage. They are getting ready to go onstage and *knock 'em dead*. You should go through a similar process to get thoroughly prepared for your time in the spotlight.

Winning a job offer depends not only on the things you do well but also on the mistakes you avoid. As the interview approaches, settle down with your resume and the exercises you performed in building it. Immerse yourself in your past successes and the *transferable skills* and *professional values* that made them possible. Interview nerves are to be expected; the trick is to use them to your benefit by harnessing that nervous energy for your physical and mental preparation.

Here's what you should bring with you:

The company dossier: Always take copies of the resume you customized for this job and an executive briefing that clearly defines how you match the job's requirements: one for you and one for each of the interviewers you might meet. Your main interviewer will invariably have a copy of your resume, but you can't be certain of that with other people you meet. It is perfectly acceptable to have your resume in front of you at the interview; it shows you are organized, and it makes a great cheat sheet. It is not unusual to hear, "Mr. Jones wasn't hired because he didn't pay attention to detail and couldn't even remember his employment dates"—just the kind of thing you are likely to forget in the nervousness of the moment.

A decent folder with a pad of paper and writing instruments: These demonstrate your preparedness, and they give you something constructive to do with your hands during the interview; you can keep your resume in the folder.

Reference letters: If you have reference letters from past employers, take them along. Some employers don't put much stock in written references and prefer a one-on-one conversation with past employers. Nevertheless, having them with you and getting them placed in your candidate file can't do any harm.

A list of job-related questions: Asking questions that give you insight into the day-to-day realities of the job shows your engagement with the work. It also helps you advance your candidacy because our judgments about people are based, in part, on the questions they ask since those questions speak to the depth of their interest and understanding. Additionally, asking questions gives you insight into how you should best focus your answers to the interviewer's queries.

You can find more questions to ask at the end of Chapter 13.

(*Note*: In the early rounds of interviewing, stay away from questions about where the job can lead and what the pay and benefits are. It's not that these questions aren't important, just that the timing is wrong. It won't do you any good to know what a job pays when you aren't going to get a job offer. Instead, ask the questions that will lead to a job offer being extended, and then ask the questions you need answered to evaluate that offer. For questions to ask during the negotiation phase, see Chapter 22, "Negotiating the Job Offer.")

Any additional information you have about the company or the job: If time permits, visit the company website, review any company literature and research you might have, and do a Google search for news articles mentioning the company by name and for articles that relate to your profession.

Directions to the interview: Decide on your form of transportation and finalize your time of departure, leaving enough time to accommodate travel delays. Check the route, distance, and travel time. If you forget to verify date, time, and place (including floor and suite number), you might not even arrive at the right place, or on the right day, for your interview. Write it all down legibly and put it with the rest of your interview kit.

To arrive at an interview too early indicates over-anxiousness, and to arrive late is inconsiderate, so arrive at the interview on time, but at the location early. This allows you time to visit the restroom (usually your only private sanctuary at an interview) and make the necessary adjustments to your appearance, review any notes, and put on your game face. Remember to add contact numbers to your interview kit, so if you are delayed on the way to the interview, you can call and let the interviewer know.

Your dress should be clean-cut and conservative. As you could be asked to appear for an interview at a scant couple of hours' notice, keep your best outfit freshly cleaned, shirts or blouses wrinkle-free, shoes polished, and all readied for interviews at a moment's notice.

Visit the hairdresser once a month so that you always look groomed, and keep your nails clean and trimmed at all times (even if you work with your hands). When you get to the interview site, visit the restroom to check your appearance and take a couple of minutes to do the following:

- Review the company dossier.
- Recall your commitment to the profession and the team, and the professional behaviors that help you succeed.
- Breathe deeply and slowly for a minute to dispel your natural physical tension.
- Review the questions you will need to identify first projects and initial needs.
- Smile and head for the interview—you are as ready as you are ever going to be. Afterward you will review your performance to make sure the next one goes even better.

Under no circumstances should you back out because you do not like the receptionist or the look of the office—that would be allowing personal insecurities to triumph. You are here to improve one of your most critical professional skills—turning interviews into job offers; whatever happens, you can and must learn from this experience.

KNOCK 'EM DEAD TIP

It is inappropriate and distracting for you and for the interviewer to have a cell phone ring during an interview. If for any reason you forget and it does ring, just apologize and turn it off. *Never answer a personal call at a job interview.*

As you are shown into the office, you are on!

This potential new employer wants an aggressive and dynamic employee, but someone who is less aggressive and dynamic than he is, so take your lead from the interviewer.

Do:

- Give a firm handshake—respond to the interviewer's grip and duration.
- Make eye contact and smile. Say, "Hello, Ms. Larsen. I am John Jones. I've been looking forward to meeting you."

Do Not:

- Use first names (unless asked).
- Smoke (even if invited).
- Sit down (until invited).
- Show anxiety or boredom.
- Look at your watch.
- Discuss equal rights, sex, race, national origin, religion, politics, or age.
- Show samples of your work (unless requested).
- Ask about benefits, salary, or vacation.

Now you are ready for anything—except for the tough questions that are going to be thrown at you next. We'll handle those in the following pages.

PART III
GREAT ANSWERS TO TOUGH INTERVIEW QUESTIONS

IN THIS PART of the book you will learn why interviewers do the things they do. You'll also learn the formulas for answering tough interview questions in ways that are honest, unique to you, and advance your candidacy without making you sound like a snake oil salesman. Along the way you will also learn some useful strategies to make a greater success of your career.

"LIKE BEING ON TRIAL FOR YOUR LIFE" is how many people look at a job interview. With the interviewer as judge and jury, you are at least on trial for your livelihood, so you must have winning strategies. F. Lee Bailey, one of America's most celebrated defense attorneys, attributes his success in the courtroom to preparation. He likens himself to a magician going into court with fifty rabbits in his hat, not knowing which one he'll really need, but ready to pull out any single one. Bailey is successful because he is ready for any eventuality and because he takes the time to analyze every situation and every possible option. He never underestimates his opposition, he is always prepared, and he usually wins.

Another famous attorney, Louis Nizer, successfully defended all of his fifty-plus capital offense clients. When lauded as the greatest courtroom performer of his day, Nizer denied the accolade. He claimed for himself only the distinction of being the best prepared.

You won't win your day in court just based on your skills. As competition for the best jobs increases, employers are comparing more candidates for every opening and becoming more skilled in the art of selection. To consistently win against stiff competition, like Bailey and Nizer, you have to be prepared for the questions that can be thrown at you, and that requires understanding what is behind them.

During an interview, employers ask you dozens of searching questions—questions that test your knowledge, skills, confidence, poise, and professional behaviors (we'll address this in some detail in a few pages). There are questions that can trick you into contradicting yourself and questions that probe your analytical skills and integrity. They are all designed so the interviewer can make decisions in these critical areas:

- Can you do the job?
- Are you motivated to take the extra step?
- Are you manageable and a team player?
- Are you professional in all your behaviors?
- Are you a problem solver?

Being able to do the job is only a small part of getting an offer. Questions of whether you are motivated to make an extra effort, whether you are manageable and a team player, and whether you think of yourself as a problem-identifier and problem-solver, are just as important to the interviewer. In this era of high unemployment and deep specialization, companies look more actively at the way you behave in the workplace and your professional behavioral profile. Specific desirable professional behaviors cannot be ascertained by a single question or answer, so the interviewer will seek a pattern in your replies that shows your possession of such behaviors. You not only have to make a case for yourself in these five areas, you need to avoid these deadly traps that can damage your candidacy:

- Failing to listen to the question.
- Answering a question that was not asked.
- Providing superfluous, inappropriate, or irrelevant information.
- Being unprepared for the interview.

The effect of these blunders is cumulative, and each reduces your chance of receiving a job offer. The number of offers you win in your search for the ideal job depends on your ability to answer a staggering array of questions in terms that have value and relevance to the employer: "Why do you want to work here?" "What are your biggest accomplishments?" "How long will it take you to make a contribution?" "Why should I hire you?" "What can you do for us that someone else cannot do?" "What is your greatest weakness?" "Why aren't you earning more?" and "What interests you about this job?"

The questions and answers in the following chapters come from across the job spectrum. Though a particular sample answer might come from the mouth of an administrator (while you are a scientist or perhaps an executive in one of the service industries), we all have a common ground in the ways we contribute to our respective bottom lines; this overlap guarantees their relevance to your concerns. I'll give you the question, then explain its motivation and the types of information the employer will be looking for in your answers.

Notice that many of the sample answers teach a small lesson in professional survival—something you can use both to get the job and to help you climb the ladder of success. The answers provided in the following chapters should not be repeated word for word, exactly as they come off the page. You have to tailor them to your profession, illustrate them with examples from your own real-world experience, and, since you have your own style of speech, put the answers into your own words.

CHAPTER 12
THE FIVE SECRETS OF THE HIRE

UNDERSTANDING HOW AN interviewer thinks, and on what criteria hiring decisions are based, is an important career management skill.

No employer wakes up in the morning saying, "It's a wonderful day in the neighborhood; I think I'll hire an accountant." Staff is only ever added to the payroll in the belief that the additional costs inherent in a new hire will be exceeded by the contributions that hire makes to the bottom line, by earning or saving money, saving time, or otherwise increasing productivity.

An integral part of every employee's responsibility is the *identification, prevention, and solution of problems* within her area of responsibility: problems that throw a wrench into the moneymaking machinery. Because these responsibilities are integral to every job, they are part of your job too. You get hired to contribute to the bottom line in some small way, to prevent any problems within your area of expertise that get in the way of this, and, when prevention isn't an option, to solve these problems.

Whatever your job title, that job is a small but important cog in the complex moneymaking machinery of the corporation. Your cog has its own *problem identification, prevention, and solution* functions and must simultaneously mesh seamlessly with other cogs, working in harmony to execute tasks beyond the scope of individual effort.

There are five criteria that smart hiring managers apply to every hiring decision to help ensure a successful outcome; for you, these are the five secrets to turning a job interview into a job offer. These secrets are based on the logical evaluations that interviewers make when hiring for any job, at any level, and in every profession. Understanding the five secrets of the hire will revolutionize the way you perform at job interviews; and applying them every day in your work will propel your climb up the professional ladder on your next job and throughout your career.

The First Secret: Ability and Suitability

Saying, "Hey, I can do this job—give me a shot and I'll prove it to you" is not enough to land a job offer. You have to prove it by demonstrating a combination of all the skills that define your ability to do that job. You bring two sets of skills to a job:

1. You must demonstrate an *ability* to do the work, that you are in full possession of the *technical skills* required for execution of your responsibilities. And you have to show a clear grasp of the job and the role it plays in the department, as a small but important cog in the complex moneymaking machinery of the corporation.
2. You must also establish your *suitability* for the job. You possess a body of professional/industry knowledge that helps you understand "the way things get done in banking/agribusiness/pharmaceuticals." These ways differ from one industry to the next. It must be obvious that you speak the language and understand the protocols of your profession.

For example, a computer programmer working in a bank has *technical skills*. She shows *ability* to do the job by demonstrating possession of the skills and how to apply them in writing good code. She shows *suitability* for the job by demonstrating an understanding of how the program will be used in application and why it will be used that way. That comes from a *familiarity with the operations of the financial world and the terminology used to communicate within that professional community.*

Ability, Suitability, and Career Change

But wait, you say, a computer programmer doesn't have to know banking: He can pick that up fairly quickly. It's the programming skills that are important. I don't disagree, but if you were hiring and you had to pick between two programmers with equal technical skills, who would *you* hire, the one who knew your business or the one who didn't?

Given the transferability of certain *technical skills*, suitability is one of the biggest hurdles career-changers have to overcome in both their resumes and in the ensuing interviews.

If you are considering a career change, you can use understanding of this first secret of the hire as part of your preparation to make that career change. Take time to find people already doing this work in your target industry/profession who can explain the mechanics of the business and the reasons for those mechanics, the professional protocols that have been developed to deal with the realities and contingencies of that world, and the terminology professionals in the field use to discuss them, so that in turn you can make the connections between your credentials and the new world in which they will be applied.

The Second Secret: Every Job Is about Problem Anticipation, Identification, Prevention, and Solution

Regardless of profession or title, at some level we are all hired to do the same job: We are all problem solvers, paid to *anticipate, prevent, and solve problems* within our areas of expertise. This applies to any job, at any level, in any organization, anywhere in the world, and being aware of this is absolutely vital to job search and career success in any field.

Once you have identified the particular problem-solving business you are in, you've gone a long way toward isolating what the interviewer will want to talk about. The *TJD* exercises helped you identify the problems that are the meat and potatoes of your work and gave you plenty of examples of your use of *critical thinking* skills in the problem resolution process. When you can tell stories of problems you've dealt with efficiently, it helps interviewers visualize you solving their problems—on their payroll, as a member of the team.

Identify and list for yourself the typical problems you tackle on a daily basis. Come up with plenty of specific examples. Then move on to the biggest, dirtiest problems you've faced. Recall specifically how you solved them.

Here's a technique used by corporate outplacement professionals to help people develop examples of their problem-solving skills and the resulting achievements (you went through a similar exercise while developing your resume):

1. State the problem. What was the situation? Was it typical of your job, or had something gone wrong? If the latter, be leery of apportioning blame.

2. Isolate relevant background information. What special knowledge or education were you armed with to tackle this dilemma?
3. List your key qualities. What professional skills and professional behaviors did you bring into play to solve the problem?
4. Recall the solution. How did things turn out in the end?
5. Determine what the solution was worth. Quantify the solution in terms of money earned, money saved, or time saved. Specify your role as a team member or as a lone gun, as the facts demand.

Interviewers are impressed by candidates who ask intelligent questions about the job, because *those questions demonstrate the depth of that candidate's understanding*. You can definitely help your candidacy by asking questions about the problems that lie at the heart of your job; it turns a one-sided examination of skills into a two-way conversation between professionals with a common interest; very few candidates understand this. When you ask about the problems, challenges, projects, deadlines, and pressure points that will be tackled in the early months, you demonstrate the *critical thinking skills* that underlie your problem-solving abilities, which proves you will be able to hit the ground running on those first critical projects.

Show this in the way you answer questions, and in the questions you ask, and bells will ring for the interviewer; indeed, the poor old dear might drop dead and go to heaven on the spot.

The Third Secret: Professional Behavior

Professionals are seen to be professional because they *behave* in a certain way. Solid possession of the *transferable skills* and *professional values* informs your judgment, opinions, and conduct; it is your embodiment of them in everything you do that does most to convey quiet professional confidence. These are the *skills* and *values* that get you hired, get you noticed, land you top assignments, and lead to promotions and raises; they enable you to succeed in all your professional endeavors. Just to refresh your memory, here are those skills and values again. Keep referring back to them—they're one of the most valuable things you'll take away from this book.

▶ **Transferable Skills**
Technical
Critical Thinking
Communication
Multitasking
Teamwork
Leadership
Creativity

▶ **Professional Values**
Motivation and Energy
Commitment and Reliability
Determination
Pride and Integrity
Productivity
Systems and Procedures

Showing your possession of *transferable skills* and *professional values*, with illustrative examples you give in answers to interviewers' questions, is your passport to success at any interview. They give your answers substance and a ring of truth.

KNOCK 'EM DEAD TIP

There are seven *transferable skills*. Apart from the *technical skills* of the job, all these skills are transferable between all jobs in the same profession *and* all jobs in different professions. However, with *technical skills*, it is likely that only some of them will apply to jobs in different professions.

The Fourth Secret: Motivation and Intelligent Enthusiasm

Motivation is one of the *professional values* that all employers like to see in their employees. From the employer's side of the desk, the preference for motivated, *intelligently enthusiastic* candidates is roughly this:

- The motivated and *intelligently enthusiastic* candidate will work harder and will turn in a superior work product.
- Someone who really enjoys his work and is engaged in his profession will be easier to work with and get along with, and that will be a positive influence and a welcome, happy addition to the team.
- Someone who is enthusiastic and motivated by her work is likely to have a greater understanding of the job and therefore a greater commitment to taking the rough with the smooth.

In a tightly run job race, when there is really nothing to choose between two top contenders, the job offer will always go to the most *intelligently enthusiastic* candidate. However, interviews are stressful situations, and when you are stressed, your defenses are up and you retreat behind a wall of stiff professionalism: The natural enthusiasm and motivations that normally are part of your professional persona are restrained.

So, the fourth secret of the hire is an admonishment to allow your natural enthusiasm for your work and for this job opportunity to shine through, rather than hide it because of interview nerves or a misconstrued sense of professionalism.

I repeat: When it comes to a tightly run job race between equally qualified candidates, remember that *the offer will always go to the most intelligently enthusiastic candidate.* Show enthusiasm for your work, your profession, and the opportunity; it just might be the tiebreaker for your ideal job.

The Fifth Secret: Teamwork and Manageability

Teamwork relates to your ability to function productively as a member of a group focused on achieving large-scale goals. Working on a team takes patience, balance, tolerance, and an ability to assert your own personality without overpowering everyone else's. You don't have to *like* everyone on your team; but you have to be able to *work* with them, and that requires *emotional maturity*. Your willingness to be a team player and your ability to function as an integrated member of the team is critical because many of the contributions your department must make toward the smooth running of the corporate machine are beyond the scope of your individual contribution.

When you embrace and apply the five secrets, you will turn job interviews into job offers, and applying these secrets on your new job will steadily increase your credibility and visibility, and simultaneously deliver greater job security, forward momentum, and marketability.

Why You Go to Job Interviews

You need to have the right focus going into the interview. *You are not going to the interview to decide if you want the job*, because you have nothing to decide until an offer is on the table. You go to any job interview for one reason only: to get a job offer; nothing else matters. Turning interviews into job offers is a critical professional survival skill, and *of all the professional skills you possess, this one is almost certainly a weakness, and needs to be strengthened*. In the following chapter, I'll show you how to make it one of your most powerful tools.

CHAPTER 13

THE OTHER SIDE OF THE DESK: WHY INTERVIEWERS DO THE THINGS THEY DO, AND HOW TO RESPOND

SITTING IN FRONT of the interviewer, your mind racing with the possibilities of what could happen next as he looks over your resume, you are probably thinking, "This is crazy. Why am I here? I'd rather be abducted by aliens." What probably won't occur to you is that quite a lot of the time the interviewer feels the same way.

There are two terrible places to be during an interview—in front of the desk wondering what on earth is going to happen next and behind the desk asking the questions. The average interviewer dreads the meeting almost as much as the interviewee, but for opposite reasons.

Business frequently yields to the mistaken belief that any person, on being promoted to the ranks of management, becomes mystically endowed with all necessary managerial skills. That is a fallacy; perhaps only half of all managers have been taught how to interview. Most just bumble along and pick up a certain proficiency over time. Consequently, at any job interview you are quite likely to run into one of two types of interviewers.

1. The experienced interviewer knows what she is doing and has a plan for the interview.
2. The inexperienced interviewer doesn't know what he is doing, and worse, *doesn't know* he doesn't know what he is doing; he's what's known as an unconscious incompetent.

They both present challenges—and opportunities, when you know how to handle them. But first, let's take a look at the different strategies both types of interviewer are liable to use.

Interview Strategies

There are a number of interview strategies that interviewers can use to help gather information.

1. Behavioral
2. Stress
3. Situational

We'll look at them in order.

Behavioral Interview Strategies

Behavioral interviewing has become an integral part of almost every job interview today. It is based on the reasonable premise that your past behavior can predict your future performance: "If I know how you behaved in specific situations on someone else's payroll I'll know how you will behave on mine." To get this insight an interviewer asks a general question about a skill area and then asks you to talk about specific events. "Tell me about a time when . . . ."

Behavioral interviewing also looks for balance. If the interviewer is feeling impressed, he will try to temper a positive response with, "Great, now tell me about a time when things didn't work out so well." You prepared for this line of questioning when you did the TJD exercises for your resume, and came up with exactly these kinds of examples.

Stress Strategies

Any job interview is a stress interview. Beyond that, if the ability to function under stress is part of your job—for example, sales—then the interviewer might reasonably be expected to try to create a temporary environment that reveals how you perform under stress; she is most likely to do this with questions or demands, for example, "Sell me this pen"; "What would you say if I told you your presentation was lousy?"; "I'm not sure you're right for this job."

Whenever you feel stress rising in an interview, stay calm:

- Breathe evenly and calmly. Shortness of breath will inhibit your thinking process and make you sound nervous.
- If you've been offered a glass of water, take a sip. It buys you time and swallowing reduces the tension a little and gets the frog out of your throat (there are more techniques to gain time later in this chapter).
- Keep your body posture relaxed and open. Many people have a tendency, when under stress, to contract their bodies. This adds to the tension and sends the wrong message.
- Think through the question. Consciously remove any perceived intimidating verbal inflection. For example, depending on the tone of voice used, the question, "I'm not sure you are right for the job. What do you think?" can be heard as, "You just aren't right for this job." Or you could hear it as, "I'd like to hire you and you're one of my top candidates, but I'm not sure you're the one, so please convince me."

The stress interview is covered in more detail in Chapter 16.

Situational Strategies

Situational strategies give the interviewer an opportunity to see you in something close to a real work situation, with the goal of getting a better idea of how you perform your duties. The situational strategy will always relate to a frequently executed task, something at the very heart of your job, and it can happen as a formal part of the interview or very casually.

Customer service and sales jobs are prone to situational interviewing strategies more than most; if you face one of these, you'll panic a little, but the situational role-play is going to re-create a task or situation that is at the core of your work. Ask a few questions for clarification and to get nerves under control. If it's going to take more than a few minutes, you can ask for a restroom break. Then, as much as you can, relax, step up, and do your job. Remember, what is being sought is confirmation that you understand the building blocks of that task: You aren't expected to deliver an Oscar-worthy performance.

The Experienced Interviewer

A manager's job is to get work done through others, and the first step is to hire the right people. If you cannot hire effectively, you can never manage productively; and if you can't manage productively . . . you lose your job. Consequently, most managers learn how to interview effectively. You can also rely on just about all headhunters, corporate recruiters, and HR people to run competent interviews because it's what they do every day.

Competent interviewers have a plan: They know what they are going to ask, why they are asking it, when they are going to ask it, and what they hope to find. They follow a set format for the interview process to ensure objectivity in the selection process, and a set sequence of questions to ensure the facts are gathered logically and in the right areas. They have all been in many more interviews than you have. Three pointers we can gain from this:

- You don't need to exaggerate or fabricate: What you have to say is going to capture their full attention; besides, they can tell fact from fiction and truth from dreams.
- Interviewing can get boring if you do a lot of it. The majority of candidates make this worse. You don't need to be uptight or stiff; try to relax and become the friendly, competent, outgoing person you are on your best days. Just don't be a wiseass.
- This is a job: It needs to be completed so they can go on to the next one. Your interviewers are hoping, praying, that you will be the one.

Competent interviewers always have a plan for the interview, and this is what it looks like from the other side of the desk:

How interviews are organized

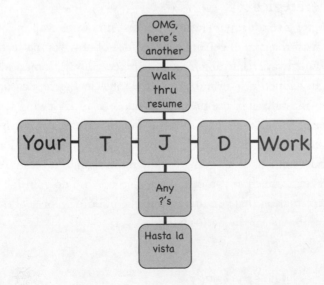

"OMG, Here's Another One"

Yes, that's the first thought in the interviewer's mind as you sit down to begin the interview. It continues, "I pray to the baby Jesus that this is the one. All I want is someone who 'gets' the job, can do it and wants to do it, comes to work on a regular basis, and gets on with people. I just need to hire someone and get on to the next project!"

Contrary to what you may think, *the interviewer wants you to relax*. That's because a more relaxed you is a more communicative you, and the interviewer needs information on which to base her decision. So at the beginning of an interview you'll move through some formulaic small talk and the offer of a beverage to prepare the way for the actual questioning to begin. Always accept the beverage, and ask for water. You *are* nervous, your throat is more prone to dryness, and water is the best remedy.

The interview gets underway with a statement from the interviewer, who will say something along the lines of "We're looking for a _____ , and I want to find out about your experience and the strengths you can bring to our team." He will then explain a bit about how the interview itself will go: whether you'll be talking to other people and if so, who they are. This is the time when you offer a nicely formatted version of your resume printed on decent paper, because next the interviewer is going to glance down at the resume, and say, "So tell me a little bit about yourself . . . ."

Walk Through Your Resume

Using your resume as a reference point, interviewers will often have you walk through your work history, asking you questions about different aspects of your experience. These early questions are designed to get you comfortable with talking, so they will mostly be straightforward, since a good interviewer wants to limit her contributions to about 20 percent of the interview, leaving you to talk the other 80 percent of the time—offering plenty of time to analyze your answers. Your answers should be similarly straightforward, and you'll make an effort here to show an understanding, in general terms, of your job's role within the department, and that in essence the job is about *problem identification, prevention, and solution*.

Some interviews end after this journey through the resume, either because the interviewer has enough information to rule you out, or because he doesn't know any better. Skilled interviewers use this walk through the resume as a qualifying round. If you pass, they'll take the interview to the next level.

Your TJD Work Pays Off

Now the interviewer wants to look at your qualifications and experience in each of the critical deliverables of the job. Fortunately, your resume is based on the focus you gained from the TJD of at least half a dozen similar jobs, your Performance Profile captured qualifications in exactly these critical deliverables, and the Core Competencies section backed this up with headlines on the relevant skills and experiences. You also invested time in working back and forth between this specific Job Description, your *Target Job Deconstruction* document, and your resume, connecting real-world experiences to the *problems anticipated, prevented, and solved* in each area by the intelligent application of the appropriate *technical* and *transferable skills*. The result of your earlier efforts to create a killer resume is that you can connect any topic the interviewer raises to the qualifications you bring to the table and illustrate them with real-world examples, explaining what you did and why you did it, the underlying *transferable skills* you used to get it done, the *professional values* that helped you make the right judgment calls, and finally what you learned and how you grew professionally from the experience.

Any Questions?

You know the interview is drawing to a close when you are asked if you have any questions. In Chapter 11 I suggested you make a list of such questions. Bringing the list out and checking off what hasn't been covered demonstrates the kind of *intelligent enthusiasm* that, again, helps set you apart from other candidates. The list you develop for your first interview can be the template for all subsequent interviews.

Hasta la Vista, Baby

The interviewer will thank you for your time and may give you some idea of next steps. If this information isn't offered, ask for it. If there is another round of interviews:

- Recap your understanding of the job
- What you bring to the table
- That you are qualified and very interested
- Ask to schedule the next interview

If there are no more interviews, ask when the decision will be made. Then repeat the steps above, but instead of asking for the next interview ask for the job. You have everything to gain and nothing to lose; showing *motivation* and *intelligent enthusiasm* for the job now could be the decisive factor.

KNOCK 'EM DEAD TIP
If you are entering the world of work for the first time, or making a substantial career shift, you might not have the knowledge to analyze the job's deliverables. In this case go back to your networks and call people already in the profession to identify the *transferable skills* and *professional values* necessary to succeed in the initial target job of your new career.

This is how competent interviewers are trained to develop structured interviews.

So much for the interviewer who knows what she's doing. Now for the hard part: dealing with the interviewer who doesn't know what he's doing and *doesn't even know* that he doesn't know.

The Unconscious Incompetent

Do you ever remember leaving an interview and feeling that you could do the job but that the interviewer didn't ask you the questions that would allow you to showcase your skills? You were probably facing an Unconscious Incompetent: an interviewer who doesn't know that he doesn't know how to interview, and who bases hiring decisions on "experience" and "knowing people" and "gut feeling."

As with the skilled interviewer, it is necessary to imagine how the unconscious incompetent thinks and feels to handle the situation to your advantage. There are many manifestations of the poor interviewer. Each of the following examples is followed by instructions for appropriate handling of the unique problems they pose for you.

Example One: The interviewer's desk is cluttered, and the resume or application that was handed to her a few minutes before cannot be found.

Response: Sit quietly through the bumbling and searching. Check out the surroundings. Breathe deeply and slowly to calm any lingering interview nerves. As you bring your adrenaline under control, you bring a calming tone to the interview and the interviewer.

Example Two: The interviewer experiences constant interruptions from the telephone or people walking into the office.

Response: This provides good opportunities for selling yourself. Make a note on your pad of where you were in the conversation and refresh the interviewer on the point when you start talking again. He will be impressed with your level head and good memory. The interruptions also give you time to think through a question or to add new information to a point made prior to the interruption.

Example Three: The interviewer starts with an explanation of why you are both sitting there, and then allows the conversation to degenerate into a lengthy diatribe about the company.

Response: Show interest in the company and the conversation. Sit straight, look attentive, make appreciative murmurs, and nod at the appropriate times until there is a pause. When that occurs, comment that you appreciate the background on the company, because you can now see more clearly how the job fits into the general scheme of things and that you see, for example, how valuable communication skills would be for the job. Could the interviewer please tell you some of the other job requirements?

When you want to make a point and the interviewer isn't asking questions that allow you to make it, ask questions like these: "Would it be of value if I described my experience with _____ ?" or "Then my experience in _____ should be a great help to you," or "I recently completed an accounting project just like that. Would it be relevant to discuss it?"

Example Four: The interviewer begins with, or quickly breaks into, the drawbacks of the job. The job may even be described in totally negative terms. That is often done without giving a balanced view of the duties and expectations of the position.

Response: An initial negative description often means that the interviewer has had bad experiences hiring for the position. Your course is to make it known that you recognize the importance of (for example) reliability, especially in this particular type of job. Illustrate your proficiency in that particular aspect of your profession with a short example from your work history. Finish by asking the interviewer why some people fail in this job. The interviewer's answers tell you exactly how to sell yourself for this position.

Example Five: The interviewer asks closed-ended questions, ones that demand no more than a yes-or-no answer (e.g., "Do you pay attention to detail?"). Such questions are hardly adequate to establish your skills, yet you must handle them effectively to secure the job offer.

Response: A yes-or-no answer to a closed-ended question will not get you that offer. The trick is to treat each closed-ended question as if the interviewer has added, "Please give me a brief yet thorough answer." Closed-ended questions are often mingled with statements followed by pauses. In those instances, agree with the statement in a way that demonstrates both a grasp of your job and the interviewer's statement. For example: "That's an excellent point, Mr. Smith. I couldn't agree more that the attention to detail you describe naturally affects cost containment. My track record in this area is . . . ."

Example Six: You can also run into "situationally incompetent interviewers," usually when a hiring manager arranges for you to meet with two or three other people. All too often, the other interviewers have not been told the details of the job for which you are interviewing or may not have been trained in appropriate interviewing skills.

Response: Always take additional copies of your executive briefing and resume with you to the interview to aid them in focusing on the appropriate job functions. Be ready to hold up your end of the conversation by asking intelligent questions, the answers to which will enable you to sell your candidacy.

Keeping Up Your End of the Conversation

There are a number of techniques you can use to keep up your end of the discussion.

1. You can show engagement with what the interviewer is saying by giving verbal signals; you do this with occasional short, quiet interjections that don't interrupt the employer's flow but let him know you are paying attention: "uh-huh," "that's interesting," "okay," "great," and "yes, yes" all work. But be careful not to overdo it.
2. If you don't fully understand a question or if you need time to think, ask, "Would you run that by me again?" The question is not only repeated, it is usually repeated with more detail, giving additional information and time to formulate an answer.
3. If a question stumps you, and having it repeated still doesn't help, it is better to say, "I'd like to come back to that later, I'm not used to interviewing and I'm nervous and drawing a blank right now." Odds are the interviewer will forget to ask again. If she remembers, at least your mind will have been working on it in the background and with the extra time will probably come up with an answer. If you have a great answer and the interviewer doesn't bring it up again, you can bring it up yourself.

Conversation Etiquette

Speak clearly and be careful not to mumble or shout, either of which can happen when you are nervous.

1. If you find your throat gets dry, stop and take a drink of water. The interviewer will be patient.
2. If for any reason you become flustered, stop for a moment and collect your thoughts before continuing. It's better to take a few seconds to calm down than to dig a hole deeper and deeper with babbling.
3. Keep in mind that the 80/20 rule applies to you as well. It's all right to talk a lot—that's what the interviewer expects—but don't dominate the conversation to the exclusion of anyone else. If the interviewer signals that he wants to communicate something, let him do so.

4. *Never* interrupt. You want all information possible before engaging your mouth, and often the most important part of a statement or question comes in the latter part of the sentence. Get in the habit of listening to what is being said all the way through, rather than just waiting your turn to talk.

Information-Gathering Questions

Demonstrate a good understanding of the job's deliverables and your possession of all the *technical* and *transferable skills* and *professional values* that help you do the job well, and you will be a top contender. If you want to turn a one-sided examination of skills into a two-way conversation between professionals with a common interest, you'll need to ask questions of your own, and the more they go to the heart of the job, the stronger the impression you will make.

Don't be afraid to ask questions. Your questions show interest, and we make our judgments of people based on both the statements they make and the questions they ask. The questions you ask show that you *get* the job and take it seriously. The interviewer's answers deliver insights into the job that you wouldn't otherwise have, giving you a better focus for your responses and the points you want to make.

This is especially important when the interviewer does not give you the openings you need to sell yourself. Always have a few intelligent questions prepared to save the situation. The following questions will give you an excellent idea of why the position is open and exactly the kind of skilled professional the company will eventually hire:

- "Who succeeds in this job and why?"
- "Who fails in this job and why?"
- "What do you consider the most important day-to-day responsibilities of this job?"
- "What is the hardest part of the job?"
- "What will be the first projects I tackle?"
- "What will you want me to have achieved in the first ninety days?"
- "What are the biggest challenges the department faces this year and what will be my role as a team member in tackling them?"
- "Which projects will I be most involved with during the first six months?"
- "What will you want me to have achieved in the first six months?"
- "What skills and values do you consider critical to success in this job?"

When you get a clear understanding of an employer's needs with questions like these, you can seize the opportunity to sell yourself appropriately, using the same techniques you would use when an interviewer talks but doesn't ask questions. Using that list as a starting point, make a list of your own to take to your job interviews.

The most important questions to ask at the end of an interview are the ones that determine whether:

- **There is another interview**—in which case you must ask for it, with an intelligent and enthusiastic explanation of why you are qualified and why you are interested in pursuing the opportunity.
- **This is the final interview**—in which case you must ask for the job with an intelligent and enthusiastic explanation of why you are qualified and why you are interested in pursuing the opportunity.

CHAPTER 14

HOW TO KNOCK 'EM DEAD: GREAT ANSWERS TO TOUGH INTERVIEW QUESTIONS

ONE OF THE two bad seats at a job interview is sitting in front of the interviewer wondering what she is going to ask next; the other is sitting across from a candidate wondering what kind of phony, canned platitudes you are going to be fed in response to a serious question.

All any interviewer really wants is to find someone who can do the job, wants to do the job, and can get along with others. All you need to do to win the job offer is show the interviewer you are this person.

Fortunately you have already done the lion's share of the work. You know exactly who gets hired for this job and why. Your TJD revealed how employers prioritize their requirements and how they express them. You determined the experience and skills you possess in each of the deliverable areas of the job, you developed examples of assignments that show you tackling that area's typical problems successfully, and you created a behavioral profile of the person everyone wants to work with and the person nobody wants as an employee. All this is supported by a clear understanding of how your *transferable skills* and *professional values* impact every aspect of your daily professional life. Showing these universally admired *skills* and *values* in action as you make passing reference to them in your answers gives those answers substance and a ring of truth.

Armed with this knowledge, you are already better prepared than the vast majority of other candidates. Apart from a healthy and perfectly natural case of pre-performance nerves, the only rational worry you have left is fear of the unknown: not knowing what questions you might be asked, what is behind them, and how to answer them. That will be our focus for the next few chapters.

I will help you understand what is behind each question—the kind of information an employer is likely to be seeking—and I'll give an example of the kind of points you might want to make in your answers. The idea is not to memorize my sample answers; they are meant to reveal the logic of the questions and to point the way toward answers that work for you.

Tell me a little about yourself.

This is often one of the first questions you will answer. There's logic behind the question: The interviewer knows you are nervous and that talking will help you relax; it is not an invitation to ramble. Simultaneously, she wants to know about your experience and qualifications for this job and if they warrant your being there. Answer the question well and you create a good first impression and set the tone for your candidacy; you also immediately feel more confident.

You already have the answer to this question prepared:

- Doing your TJD exercise helped you determine how employers prioritize the deliverables of this job.
- Your resume developed all the relevant experience you needed in each of these areas to tell the best story.
- The Performance Profile that kicks off your resume encapsulated all the most crucial experience in a few short sentences.

Your answer to this question takes the essence of your Performance Profile and turns it back into full sentences, giving you a condensed professional work history that focuses on the most important experience. Add chronology—"I spent _____ years at _____ , and this is where I learned . . ."—and you'll show the professional development that brought you to the point you are at today. This isn't a question that you can answer effectively without thought and preparation. Because this is such a common question, take some time in advance to think about your career to date and how it has prepared you for the position at hand. For example:

"I'm the area director of marketing for the _____ metropolitan area. I oversee all aspects of marketing to acquire and retain basic, digital, and online customers through tactics such as mass media and direct mail. In addition, I launch new products/services like VOD. I have a team of forty-six employees, which also includes twenty-six door-to-door sales reps.

"I rose to this position year by year, climbing through the ranks based on my performance, achievement, and an ever-growing frame of reference for my profession and our business. As we get into the nuts-and-bolts discussion of the job I hope to show you that I have a real understanding of the challenges faced by my direct reports, a steady hand, and the managerial skills required for a motivated and productive department."

What do you know about the company?

The interviewer spends the majority of his waking hours in the environment that the winning candidate will join. Your knowledge of the job and the company is a piece of the jigsaw puzzle that helps him evaluate your enthusiasm and *motivation* for your work. If you don't understand what the company does and is known for, you will lose out to candidates who do.

Use the Internet, company website, and networking contacts to gain insight into the company, its products, and why it is a good place to work. You need to visit the company website and read media coverage on the company and its key executives (Google News), as well as general news about the issues affecting your profession. Your research will raise as many questions as it answers, and you can use this in your answer: "I read that _____, and wonder how this is affecting you . . . ?" Such questions demonstrate engagement with your profession and get the interviewer talking, perhaps giving you useful information. It's okay to throw in some personal details as well, such as the fact that working for the company will bring you closer to family.

Walk me through your job changes.

This question comes early in an interview and helps the interviewer understand the chronology and reasoning behind your career moves and gaps in employment. Don't worry about gaps; everyone has to deal with them. You must be ready to walk through your resume without hesitation, making two statements about each employer:

1. What you learned from that job that applies to this one; in other words, the experience you gained from past jobs is an indicator of how you will perform in this one.
2. Why you left. You should have an acceptable reason for leaving every job you have held, such as:

- **C**hallenge: You weren't able to grow professionally in that position.
- **L**ocation: The commute was unreasonably long.
- **A**dvancement: There was nowhere for you to go. You had the talent, but there were too many people ahead of you.
- **M**oney: You were underpaid for your skills and contribution.
- **P**ride or prestige: You wanted to be with a better company.
- **S**ecurity: The company was not stable.

For example: "My last company was a family-owned affair. I had gone as far as I was able to go. It just seemed time for me to join a more prestigious company and accept greater challenges."

Under no circumstances should you badmouth a manager—even if she was a direct descendant of Attila the Hun. Doing so will only raise a red flag in the interviewer's mind: "Will he be complaining about me like this in a few months?"

Why did you leave _____ company?

This is a checkbox question—the interviewer wants to ask the question, check the box, and move on. You get into trouble with too much information. Any answer longer than fifteen words is too long; if the interviewer wants more, she will ask. Use a phrase from above.

Why have you changed jobs so frequently?

If you have jumped around, blame it on youth (even the interviewer was young once). Now you realize what a mistake your job hopping was, and with your added domestic responsibilities you are now much more settled. Or you may wish to impress on the interviewer that your job hopping was never as a result of poor performance and that you grew professionally as a result of each job change.

You could reply: "My first job had a long commute. I soon realized that, but I knew it would give me good experience in a very competitive field. Subsequently, I found a job much closer to home where the commute was only half an hour each way. I was very happy at my second job. However, I got an opportunity to really broaden my experience base with a new company that was just starting up. With the wisdom of hindsight, I realize that move was a mistake; it took me six months to realize I couldn't make a contribution there. I've been with my current company a reasonable length of time. So I have broad experience in different environments. I didn't just job-hop; I have been following a path to gain broad experience. So you see, I have more experience than the average person of my years, and a desire to settle down and make it pay off for me and my employer."

Or you can say: "Now I want to settle down and make my diverse background pay off in my contributions to my new employer. I have a strong desire to contribute and I am looking for an employer that will keep me challenged; I think this might be the company to do that. Am I right?"

Why were you fired?

If you were fired and you don't try to clean up the mess *and* change your ways, it can dog you for years.

Firing someone is unpleasant and never a decision any manager makes lightly, so in the majority of cases the employee bears a degree of responsibility. The first and most important thing is to take responsibility for the actions or behavior that led to your dismissal. If you do not take responsibility for your actions, you cannot change them.

If you take responsibility for your actions, you can clean up your act and clean up the past. Call the person who fired you; your aim is to clear the air, so whatever you do, don't be antagonistic. Reintroduce yourself and explain that you are looking (or, if you have been unemployed for a while, say you are "still looking") for a new job. Say that you appreciate that the manager had to do what was done, *that you want to apologize for being such a problem*, and that you learned from the experience.

Then address what you learned and ask, "If you were asked as part of a pre- or post-employment reference check, what would you say about me? How would you describe my leaving the company? Would you say that I was fired or that I simply resigned? You see, every time I tell someone about my termination, whoosh, there goes another chance of getting back to work!" Most managers will plump for the latter option. Taking responsibility and cleaning up the past really works and is the first step in putting yourself back on a track to success.

Have you ever been asked to resign?

When someone is asked to resign, it is a gesture on the part of the employer: "You can quit, or we will can you, so which do you want it to be?" Because you were given the option, that employer cannot later say, "I had to ask him to resign," since that is tantamount to firing and could lead to legal problems; that's the point of the gesture. If you answer "Yes," it's a mark against you and can derail your candidacy, so answer, "No."

Why does your resume have a gap? Or why were you out of work so long?

Whatever the reason for your hiatus, be honest. Discuss the decisions behind your absence from the workplace, whatever they were. *What's most important to the interviewer is how long it will take you to be productive if hired.*

Your answer should emphasize that while you may not have been in the corporate workplace, neither have you been idle. Talk about how you have kept current with classes or part-time work, and/or what you have been doing to keep the specific *technical skills* of the job honed. You can also talk about how you used other *transferable skills* and applied *professional values* in whatever work you were doing, noting that these skills are fresh, current, and needed in every job.

What aspects of your work do you consider most crucial?

Your answer begins with an explanation of why the job exists and what role it plays in achieving departmental and company goals. Then itemize the most important responsibilities of the job (you prioritized these in your TJD).

You then proceed to address:

- The *technical skills* you need to deliver on these responsibilities: "I need to be able to do _____ to execute my responsibilities."
- "Of course, crucial to the job is my ability to *identify, prevent, and solve* the problems that crop up in each of these areas every day . . . ."
- Selections of *transferable skills* that help you deliver on these crucial responsibilities: "So my *multitasking, communication*, and *critical thinking skills* help me do this every day . . . ."

How do you manage your work deadlines?

This examines the *time management* and *organization abilities* that enable you to *multitask* productively. You should address the Prioritize, Do, Review cycle: You set time at the end of every day to review that day's activities and plan tomorrow's. You prioritize all the planned activities and stick to those priorities to make sure the important work is attended to first.

Describe how your job contributes to the overall goals of your department and company.

Every company is in business to make a profit. Every company depends on individual initiative being harnessed to *teamwork* to achieve the complex tasks that result in corporate profitability. Describe how your job makes individual contributions and its role as an important cog in the machinery that is your department. Your cog needs to mesh with all the other cogs (your colleagues) for the gears of productivity to engage and move the department toward its goals.

Show that you are aware of the problems that crop up in your job every day and get in the way of company productivity. Identify how your job, at its core, is to *anticipate and prevent problems* from arising and to *solve them* when they do.

What is your greatest strength?

First talk about a must-have *technical skill*. Second, talk about one or more of the *transferable skills* that help you execute this critical part of your job; for example, you could talk about the roles that *communication*, *critical thinking*, and *multitasking skills* play in helping you execute your "greatest strength." This way you give a complete and believable answer that also speaks of skills you apply in other aspects of your work.

What is your greatest weakness?

The greatest-strength question is often followed by asking about your greatest weakness. While this question is handled at the start of Chapter 16, "How to Handle Stress and Illegal

Questions," you can start thinking about what might constitute an acceptable answer to this awful question now: What parts of your job are an ongoing challenge for everyone in your profession? This can help you position weakness as a challenge shared by all conscientious people in the profession.

What is your role as a team member?

Think for a moment about why the job exists: It is there to contribute to the bottom line in some way. Your department, in turn, has a similar but larger role in the company's bottom line. Your ability to link your job's role to that of the department's larger responsibilities, and then to the overall success of the company, will demonstrate your sense of the importance of *teamwork*. The department depends on *teamwork*, so describe yourself as a team player.

What kinds of decisions are most difficult for you?

The most difficult decisions always relate to the most crucial responsibilities of your work. The employer is looking for people who can make decisions and solve problems, not those who'll dither instead of do. You want to position yourself as someone who's decisive but not precipitate, who considers the implications of decisions, any side effects they might have on other activities, and whether the decision conflicts with existing *systems and procedures* or other company priorities. Emphasize that, having analyzed the situation and reached a logical conclusion, you act.

The question almost demands that you explain how you make these difficult decisions, and that you give an illustration, and if you don't give one, it might well come in a follow-up question. Your example should relate to one of the crucial responsibilities of your job, and itemize the logical steps you take in analyzing the problem to help you reach the right decision.

What bothers you most about your job?

Keep your answer focused on those aspects of your work that *everyone* agrees are annoying, and end your answer on a positive note about how you deal with them: You take the rough with the smooth, and take the time to do _____ well so you don't have to do the damn thing over. It is important that your answer show you remaining objective and calm.

Tell me about a time things went wrong.

You are asked to talk about something that went wrong, but that doesn't mean you can't do so with an example that turned out fine. Your TJD process identified a number of such examples you can use. Choose an example and paint it black, but don't point the finger of blame; crap happens.

End with how you solved the problem or contributed to its solution. Get in a subtle plug for *transferable skills*: ". . . so sticking with it and doing it by the book helped us put things right in the end."

You can go on to explain that the next time you faced the same kind of problem you had a better frame of reference, knew what to avoid, what to do more of, and what other new approaches you could try. Finish your answer with a statement about what you learned.

How have you benefited from your disappointments/mistakes?

You learn more from failures, mistakes, and errors than you do from successes, so this is an opportunity for you to demonstrate your *emotional maturity* (you stay calm) and *critical thinking skills* (you think things through objectively).

Your answer will explain how you treat setbacks as learning experiences: You look at what happened, why it happened, and how you can do things differently at each stage. Edison once explained his success as an inventor by claiming that he knew more ways *not* to do something than anyone else living; you can do worse than to quote him. In any event, sum up your answer with, "I treat disappointments as a learning experience. I look at what happened, why it happened, and how I would do things differently in each stage should the same set of circumstances appear again. That way, I put disappointment behind me and am ready with renewed vigor and understanding to face the new day's problems."

You don't need to be specific about your failures, but be prepared with an example in case of a follow-up question starting, "Tell me about a time when . . . ."

What are you looking for in your next job?

Ask not what your company can do for you; ask what you can do for your company. You are there to get a job offer, and you only want to address your needs when an offer is on the table and negotiation likely.

With so little real knowledge about the company—your research isn't the same as insights explained by a company representative—you need to be careful about specificity.

Keep your answer general and focus on the fulfillment you experience from a job well done, with a team similarly committed, working for a company with a solid reputation. If you're lower on the success ladder, add learned and earned professional growth to this—although if your future boss is the next step up . . . not such a good idea. You can add that you have observed that good people seem to move forward in groups and you'd like to earn a place within this inner circle and earn the opportunity to grow as circumstances allow by making a consistent difference with your presence.

What do you spent most of your time on, and why?

Your answer obviously needs to show that you focus your attention on top priorities, and you can make additional points by noting that you don't ignore the repetitive tasks that are also important and sometimes require considerable time. You can mention some small thing that has to be done frequently, because if it has to be done frequently, it is obviously critical to success. But don't do this at the expense of those top priorities, or you're likely to be pegged as someone who gets bogged down in minutiae.

Another tactic is to use an example of *multitasking* to emphasize how you manage the priorities of the job. For example, "Like a lot of businesspeople, I work on the telephone and meetings take up a great deal of time. What's important to me is prioritization of activities based on the deliverables of my job. I find more gets achieved in a shorter time if a meeting is scheduled, say, immediately before lunch or at the close of business. I try to block my time in the morning and the afternoon for main-thrust activities. At four o'clock, I review what I've achieved, what went right or wrong, and plan adjustments and my main thrust for tomorrow."

What are your qualifications for this job?

The interviewer is interested in your experience and your possession of the *technical skills* to do the job, your academic qualifications, and the *transferable skills* that enable you to do any task well. This is why you need a clear recall of which *transferable skills* help you execute which aspect of your job. If you are confident in your skills, you can learn more about the job and make points for your candidacy by asking a question of your own: "If you could tell me about specific work assignments I'll be involved with early on, I can show exactly how I can make real contributions in this job."

What can you do for us that someone else cannot do?

You cannot know other candidates' capabilities, so smilingly disarm your interviewer with this fact, then say, "But what I bring is . . . ." Your answer will then demonstrate your grasp of the job's responsibilities, the problems that occur in each area, and how you are prepared to deal with them.

You can finish your answer with reference to the *transferable skills* and *professional values* you also bring to the job: "I also bring to this job a *determination* to see projects through to a proper conclusion. I *listen* and take direction well. I am *analytical* and don't jump to conclusions. I understand we are in business to make a *profit*, so I keep an eye on cost and return." End with: "How do these qualifications fit your needs?" or "What else are you looking for?" If you haven't covered the interviewer's hot buttons, she will cover them now, and you can respond accordingly.

How do you stay current?

We live in an age of technological innovation, in which the nature of every job is changing as quickly as you turn these pages. This means you must look to professional education as the price of sustained employability. In your answer, talk about the importance of keeping abreast of changes in the profession. You can refer to:

- Courses you have taken or are planning to take
- Books you have read or are reading

- Membership in professional associations
- Subscriptions to professional journals or online groups you belong to

If you're not already doing some of these things, you need to start *now*.

What achievements are you most proud of?

Use an example of something that is at the core of your job and central to its success, where you were part of a team working on some larger project beyond the scope of individual contribution, or where you accepted responsibility for some dirty/ignored project that nevertheless also had importance to the success of your department. Don't exaggerate your contributions to major projects—share the success and be seen as a *team player*. Be honest, and to guarantee your illustrations are relevant, take them from your TJD. For example, you might say something like, "Although I feel my biggest achievements are still ahead of me, I am proud of my involvement with _____. I made my contribution as part of that team and learned a lot in the process."

Tell me about the most difficult project you've tackled.

When possible, discuss projects that parallel work you are likely to do at the new job. You will state the project, its challenges (in some detail), your *critical thinking* process to isolate causes and possible solutions, the story of your implementation of the solution, and the value it delivered to your employer. (This is the PSRV process discussed in Chapter 3 after the TJD.)

Tell me about an important goal you set recently.

Your answer should cite a goal that relates to productivity or another aspect related to the more important deliverables of your job in some way. You might use a skill-development goal, explaining why you chose it, how it helped you grow, and the benefits of completion. Or you can talk about a productivity/performance standard goal, why you chose it, and how it helped. You can add to this how you integrated achieving this goal into all your other activities, which allows you to talk about your *multitasking skills*.

What have you done to become more effective in your job?

Similarly to the prior question, behind this is an interest in your *motivation* to do the work being offered. The interviewer is looking for a fit between your dreams and her reality.

All worthwhile jobs require hard work and a desire to learn. Changes in technology mean your job skills must always be in development if you want to remain current and viable. The interviewer wants to know if you are *committed* to your profession and is looking for *at least* one example. You can also talk of the mentor relationships you have formed, the books and professional commentary you've read, the professional organizations you belong to, the certifications you're earning, courses you are enrolled in, and webinars you attend. If you aren't doing some of these things, wake up and start *now*.

How do you rank among your peers?

The interviewer is examining your self-esteem. In some cases (for instance in sales) it may be possible for you to quantify this: "I'm number two in the region." In other cases, you'll be more subjective, but you should strive to be realistic. You might slip in a real-life detail such as, "There are two groups in my department: those who make a difference, and those who watch. I'm in the first group."

How do you feel about your progress to date?

Your answer should illustrate a commitment to productivity and the effort you invest in professional development. Explain how you ensure that your work is executed effectively and, if you can, cite endorsements given you by managers. You see each day as an opportunity to learn and contribute, and you see the environment at this company as conducive to your best efforts. Perhaps say something like, "Given the parameters of my job, my progress has been excellent. I know the work, and I am just reaching that point in my career where I can make significant contributions."

You might finish by saying that being at this interview means you've gone as far as you can with your present employer and that this environment at _____ and its new ways will encourage a new spurt of growth.

Is it ever necessary to go above and beyond the call of duty in terms of effort or time to get your job done?

If you hope to get ahead in your professional life, any job you ever hold will every now and then deliver opportunities to reschedule your personal life and otherwise mess up your weekends ;-), but these invasions of personal time are nevertheless opportunities to show your *commitment* and *team spirit*, so you always step up when these sometimes unwelcome opportunities present themselves; doing so increases professional success . . . and that gives you better personal time. Answer "Yes," and then illustrate with a story of making extra and special efforts with good humor.

Tell me about a time when an emergency caused you to reschedule your workload/projects.

The question examines *multitasking skills* and how you handle emergency imperatives. You'll make points when you explain how your *planning* and *time management skills* help you stay on top of your regular responsibilities even when emergency priorities throw normal scheduling off.

The story you tell should illustrate your flexibility and willingness to work extra hours when necessary. Demonstrate that your *multitasking skills* allow you to change course without having a nervous breakdown.

How long will it take you to make a contribution?

It takes time to understand *systems and procedures*, who the power players are, and why things are done the way they are. Be sure to qualify the question: In what area does the interviewer need rapid contributions?

You might ask, "Where are your greatest areas of need right now?" You give yourself time to think while the interviewer explains priorities.

What is the most difficult situation you have faced?

You're really being asked two different questions: "What do you consider difficult?" and "How did you handle it?" This means the interviewer will be evaluating both your *critical thinking* and *technical skills*.

Don't talk about problems with coworkers in your answer. Instead, focus on a job-related problem. We have talked about the importance of problem-solving throughout the book and the steps a professional takes to identify the most appropriate approaches and solutions; you should have numerous examples from your TJD and the resume creation process with which to illustrate your answer. In ending your answer, be sure to identify the benefits of your solution.

What do you think determines progress in a good company?

The interviewer needs to see that you understand progress is earned over time, and does not come as a result of simply showing up to work on a regular basis. Begin with each of the technical skills required to do the job, briefly citing the transferable skills that allow you to do the job well. Finish with your willingness to take the rough with the smooth that goes with every job, and the good fortune of having a manager who wants you to succeed.

What are some of the problems you encounter in doing your job, and what do you do about them?

There's a trap in this question and two areas you need to cover in your response, so your answer has three steps.

1. First the trap: Note well the old saying, "A poor workman blames his tools," and don't find problems with the job itself or the tools you have to execute that job. Next, the two areas you need to cover:

2. Whatever your title, at its heart your job is about *problem identification, prevention, and solution*. Make this statement with details of the problems you are a specialist in preventing and solving. This part of your answer demonstrates your deep understanding of your work.

3. Your awareness that careless mistakes cost the company good money means you are always on the lookout for potential problems caused by oversight. For example: "Some parts of my job are fairly repetitive, so it's easy to overlook problems. Lots of people do. However, I always look for them; it helps keep me alert and motivated, so I do a better job. To give you an example, we make computer-memory disks. Each one has to be machined by hand, and, once completed, the slightest abrasion will turn one into a reject. I have a steady staff and little turnover, and everyone wears cotton gloves to

handle the disks. Yet about six months ago, the reject rate suddenly went through the roof. Is that the kind of problem you mean? Well, the cause was one that could have gone unnoticed for ages. Jill, the section head who inspects all the disks, had lost a lot of weight and her diamond engagement ring was slipping around her finger, scratching the disks as she passed them and stacked them to be shipped. Our main client was giving us a big problem over it, so my looking for problems and paying attention to detail really paid off."

In your last job, how did you plan to interview?

If you are a manager, getting work done through others is at the very heart of your job. Recruitment and selection are part of your job description, and you can expect this question. Your answer should give a description of how the skilled interviewer prepares, as we discussed in Chapter 13. You might also read *Hiring the Best* and the e-book *Knock 'em Dead Breaking Into Management: The Essentials of Survival & Success* (details at *www.knockemdead.com*).

If I hired you today, what would you accomplish first?

Gear your answer to first getting settled in the job, understanding how things are done, and becoming a member of the team. You would mention that of course this includes a clear priority on all your responsibilities. Then finish with a question, "What are the most critical projects/problems you'll want me to tackle?" The response to that becomes your final answer to what you will accomplish first.

What type of decisions do you make in your work?

This examines the extent of your authority and how *critical thinking* enters into your work. With the TJD, you will have a clear understanding of the job's deliverables and can determine the decision-making events that are integral to your job. The interviewer will certainly follow with a request for an example. Assume this will happen; your answer will address the types of decisions you make and include an example that shows how you approach making them.

How do you handle rejection?

This question is common if you are applying for a job in sales, including face-to-face sales, telemarketing, public relations, and customer service. If you are after a job in one of these areas and you really don't like the heavy doses of rejection that are any salesperson's lot, consider a new field. The anguish you will experience will not lead to a successful career or a happy life.

With that in mind, let's look behind the question. The interviewer simply wants to know whether you take rejection as rejection of yourself or whether you simply accept it as a temporary rejection of a service or product. Here is a sample answer that you can tailor to your particular needs and background: "I accept rejection as an integral part of the sales process. If everyone said 'yes' to a product, there would be no need for the sales function. As it is, I see every rejection as bringing me closer to the customer who *will* say 'yes.' Sales is a profession of communication, determination, and resiliency; rejection is just part of the process, it's nothing personal. I always try to leave the potential customer with a good feeling, as no sale today can well become a sale next month."

Tell me about a situation that frustrated you at work.

This question is about *emotional maturity*. The interviewer wants to know how you channel frustration into productivity. Give an example of a difficult situation in which you remained diplomatic and objective and found a solution that benefited all concerned. Show yourself to be someone who isn't managed by emotions: You acknowledge the frustration, then put it aside in favor of achieving the goals of the job you are paid to do.

What interests you least about this job?

The question is potentially explosive but easily defused. Regardless of your occupation, there is at least one repetitive, mindless duty that everyone groans about but that nevertheless goes with the territory. Use that as your example. "_____ is probably the least demanding part of my job. However, I know it is important for _____ , so I do it at the end of the day as part of my performance review and next-day planning." Notice how this response also shows that you are *organized* and possess *critical thinking* and *multitasking skills*; it also shows you understand that it is necessary to take the rough with the smooth.

I'm not sure you're suitable for the job (too inexperienced).

In a job search you quickly develop a feeling for whether a particular position is a close match, a job you've already done for so long that you might be perceived as too experienced (too heavy), or a job that might be a bit of a stretch (too light). If you can see a potential problem with an opportunity, the employer probably can too. Nevertheless, you were close enough to get the interview, so make every effort to land the offer.

It could also be used as a stress question (to see how you handle adverse situations on the job). The interviewer's "I'm not sure" could really mean, "I'd like to hire you, so here's a wide-open opportunity to sell me on you." Either way, remain calm and accept this as another opportunity to set you apart from other candidates.

Put the ball straight back into the interviewer's court, "Why do you say that?" You need more information and time to organize an appropriate reply, but it is also important to show that you are not intimidated.

When you might be too light, your answer itemizes all the experience and skills you bring, and offsets weaknesses with other strengths and examples of how efficiently you develop new skills.

You can also talk about the motivation you bring to the job, and that you will expect to be motivated for some considerable time because of the opportunity the job offers for your professional development, while someone with all the skills is going to need a quick promotion to keep him happy. You can finish your answer with a reflexive question that encourages a "yes" answer, "Wouldn't you agree?"

I'm not sure you're suitable for the job (too experienced).

If you are told you have too much experience, respond with the positives: how your skills help you deliver immediately, and why the position fits your needs; perhaps, "I really enjoy my work, so I won't get bored, and I'm not looking for a promotion, so I'm not after anyone's job. I'll be a reliable and trustworthy person to have at your back. I have excellent skills [itemize], so I can deliver quickly and consistently. My experience makes me a steadying member of the team, and when you think I'm ready I can help mentor." Finish with a smile, ". . . and let's not forget I've already made my mistakes on somebody else's payroll."

Do you have any questions?

A sign that the interview is drawing to a close. Take the opportunity to make a strong impression. Ask questions that help advance your candidacy by giving you information about the real-world experience of the job: "Yes I do have one or two questions." Go through the list of questions you developed after reading the interview preparation chapter and brought with you.

- Who succeeds in this job and why?
- Who fails in this job and why?
- What are the major projects of the first six months?
- What will my first assignment be?

Most candidates ask questions about money and benefits. These are nice-to-know questions that an interviewer is not really interested in discussing at this point. As your goal at every interview is to bring the interviewer to the point of offering you the job, such questions are really irrelevant because they don't bring you closer to the job offer. Better that you concentrate on gathering information that will help you further your candidacy.

Ask about next steps if there are more interviews. If there are, match your skills to the needs of the job, explain your interest in the job and desire to pursue it; then ask for the next interview.

If there's not another interview, cite your understanding of the job, how your skills match each of the deliverables, state that you want the job and want to join the team, and ask for the job.

CHAPTER 15

"WHAT ARE YOU LIKE TO WORK WITH, MR. JONES?": QUESTIONS OF MANAGEABILITY AND TEAM SPIRIT

LEARN THE TECHNIQUES an interviewer uses to find out whether you will fit into the company and department, and, most importantly, whether you are a good person to work with.

If you are offered the job and accept, you will be working with the other employees of the company, quite possibly including the interviewer, for fifty weeks of the year, so the interviewer really wants to know if you are going to reduce his life expectancy. Every employer wants to know whether you will fit in with the rest of the staff, whether you are a team player, and most of all, whether you are manageable.

A big part of your job as that small but important cog in the moneymaking machinery of the corporation is to mesh with the other cogs in your department (and beyond) to support those departmental deliverables that are beyond the scope of individual effort. Once your ability and suitability are considered up to scratch, the final and most significant overall consideration of hiring managers is your willingness to take direction and work for the common good of the group. Here are a number of questions your interviewers might use to examine this area.

How do you take direction?

The interviewer wants to know whether you are open-minded and can be a team player. Can you follow directions, or are you a difficult, high-maintenance employee? The employer hopes that you are a low-maintenance professional who is motivated to ask clarifying questions about a project before beginning and who then gets on with the job at hand, coming back with requests for direction as circumstances dictate.

This particular question can also be defined as "How do you accept criticism?" Your answer should cover both points: "I take direction well and recognize that it can come in two varieties, depending on the circumstances. There is carefully explained direction, when my boss has time to lay things out for me in detail; then there are those times when, as a result of deadlines and other pressures, the direction might be brief and to the point. While I have seen some people get upset with that, personally I've always understood that there are probably other considerations I am not aware of. As such, I take the direction and get on with the job without taking offense, so my boss can get on with her job."

Would you like to have your boss's job?

It is a rare boss who wants his livelihood taken away. On my own very first job interview, my future boss said, "Mr. Yate, it has been a pleasure to meet you. However, until you walked in my door, I wasn't out on the street looking for a new job." You see, I had this case of wanting to start at the top rather than actually work my way up.

The interviewer wants to know if you are the type of person who will be confrontational or undermining. She also seeks to determine how goal-oriented and motivated you are in your work life—so you may also want to comment on your sense of direction. But while ambition is admired, it is admired most by those far enough above the fray not to be threatened. Be cautiously optimistic; perhaps, "Well, if my boss were promoted over the coming years, I would hope to have made a consistent enough contribution to warrant his consideration. It's not that I am looking to take anyone's job; rather, I am looking for a manager who will help me develop my capabilities."

What do you think of your current/last boss?

Be short and sweet and shut up. People who complain about their employers are recognized as the people who cause the most disruption in a department. This question is the interviewer's way of finding out if you're going to cause trouble. "I liked her as a person, respected her professionally, and appreciated her guidance." The question is often followed by one that tries to validate your answer.

Describe a situation where your work or an idea of yours was criticized.

This is a doubly dangerous question because you are being asked to describe how you handle criticism, and to detail inadequacies. If you have the choice, describe a poor idea that was criticized, not poor work.

Put your example in the past, make it small, and show what you learned from the experience. Show that you go through these steps to become maximally productive:

- Listen to understand
- Confirm the understanding
- Ask for guidance
- Confirm the desired outcome
- Show a satisfactory resolution
- Address what you learned and how the experience helped you grow

You might end with something that captures the essence of your example: "I listened carefully and asked a couple of questions for clarification. Then I fed back what I heard to make sure the facts were straight. I asked for advice, we bounced some ideas around, then I came back later and represented the idea in a more viable format. My supervisor's input was invaluable." Those are steps you go through to become maximally productive in these situations. Listen for understanding (not just waiting for your turn to speak), confirm the understanding, ask guidance for the desired solution, confirm the path/outcome expected, show that a satisfactory resolution was ultimately reached, recognize the positive impact of the manager, then demonstrate what you learned and how your thinking/approach has changed as a result.

How do you get along with different kinds of people?

You don't have to talk about respect for others, the need for diversity, or how it took you ten years to realize Jane was a different sex and Charley a different color, because that is not what this question is about. If you respect others, you will demonstrate this by explaining to your interviewer how you work in a team environment (because this is, in reality, a "team player" question) and how you solicit and accept input, ideas, and viewpoints from a variety of sources. If you can give a quick, honest, illustration of learning from a coworker who is obviously different from you in some way, it won't hurt.

Rate yourself on a scale of one to ten.

This question is meant to plumb the depths of your self-esteem and self-awareness. If you answer ten, you run the risk of portraying yourself as insufferable. On the other hand, if you say less than seven, you might as well get up and leave. You are probably best claiming to be an eight, saying that you always give of your best, which includes ongoing personal and professional development, so that in doing so you always increase your skills and therefore always see room for improvement. It helps to give an example: "I just read a great book on time management called *How to Get Control of Your Time and Your Life*, and found that a daily plan/do/review cycle is a really useful tool for staying on top of and prioritizing multiple projects."

What kinds of things do you worry about?

Some questions, such as this one, can seem so off-the-wall that you might start treating the interviewer as a confessor in no time flat. Your private phobias have nothing to do with your job, and revealing them can get you labeled as unbalanced. It is best to confine your answer to the sensible worries of a conscientious professional. "I worry about deadlines, staff turnover, tardiness, back-up plans for when the computer crashes, or that one of my auditors will burn out or defect to the competition—just the normal stuff. It goes with the territory, so I don't let it get me down." Whatever you identify as a worry might then be the subject of a follow-up question, so think through what you identify as worrying and in turn what you do to eradicate the worry.

What have you done that shows initiative?

The question probes whether you are a doer, someone who will look for ways to increase revenue and/or productivity—the kind of person who makes a difference for good with her presence every day. Be sure, however, that your example of initiative does not show a disregard for company *systems and procedures*.

The story you tell shows you stepping up to do a job others didn't see as important or didn't want to do, but which nevertheless needed to be done. For example, "Every quarter, I sit down with my boss and find out the dates of all his meetings for the next six months. I immediately make the hotel and flight arrangements, and attend to all the Web-hosting details. I ask myself questions like, 'If the agenda for the July meeting is to reach the field at least six weeks before the meeting, when must it be finished by?' Then I come up with a deadline. I do that for all the major activities for all the meetings. I put the deadlines in his Outlook calendar and in mine two weeks earlier to ensure everything is done on time. My boss is the best-organized, most relaxed manager in the company."

If you could make one constructive suggestion to management, what would it be?

What matters here is less the specific content of your answer than the tone. Suggest what you know to be true and what your interviewer will appreciate as a breath of fresh air: Most people want to do a good job. Management should create an environment where striving for excellence is encouraged *and* where those retired on the job have the opportunity to change their ways or leave. Everyone would benefit.

Why do you feel you are a better _____ than some of your coworkers?

The trick is to answer the question without showing yourself in anything but a flattering light. "I don't spend my time thinking about how I am better than my colleagues, because that would be detrimental to our working together as a team. I believe, however, some of the qualities that make me an outstanding _____ are . . . ." From here, go on to itemize specific *technical skills* of your profession in which you are particularly strong, and a couple of the *transferable skills* that apply to doing these aspects of your work so well.

What are some of the things that bother you? Or, What are your pet peeves? Or, Tell me about the last time you felt anger on the job.

These questions are so similar they can be treated as one. It is tremendously important that you show you can remain calm. Most of us have seen a colleague lose his cool on occasion—not a pretty sight, and one that every sensible employer wants to avoid. This question comes up more and more often the higher up the corporate ladder you climb and the more frequent your contact with clients and the general public. To answer it, find something that angers conscientious workers. "I enjoy my work and believe in giving value to my employer. Dealing with clock-watchers and people who regularly get sick on Mondays and Fridays really bothers me, but it's not something that gets me angry." An answer of this nature will help you much more than the kind given by one engineer who went on for some minutes about how he hated the small-mindedness of people who don't like pet rabbits in the office.

What are some of the things about which you and your supervisor disagreed?

You did not disagree.

In what areas do you feel your supervisor could have done a better job?

The same goes for this one. No one admires a Monday-morning quarterback.

You could reply, though: "I have always had the highest respect for my supervisor. I have always been so busy learning from Mr. Jones that I don't think he could have done a better job. He has really brought me to the point where I am ready for greater challenges. That's why I'm here."

What are some of the things your supervisor did that you disliked?

If you and the interviewer are both nonsmokers, for example, and your boss isn't, use it. Apart from that: "You know, I've never thought of our relationship in terms of like or dislike. I've always thought our role was to get along together and get the job done."

How well do you feel your boss rated your job performance?

This is one very sound reason to ask for written evaluations of your work before leaving a company. Some performance-review procedures include a written evaluation of your performance—perhaps your company employs it. If you work for a company that asks you to sign your formal review, you are quite entitled to request a copy of it. You should also ask for a letter of recommendation whenever you leave a job: You have nothing to lose. If you don't have written references, perhaps say: "My supervisor always rated my job performance well. In fact, I was always rated as being capable of accepting further responsibilities. The problem was there was nothing available in the company—that's why I'm here."

If your research has been done properly you can quote verbal appraisals of your performance from prior jobs. "In fact, my boss recently said that I was the most organized engineer in the work group, because . . . ."

How do I get the best out of you/did your boss get the best out of you?

The interviewer could be envisioning you as an employee. Encourage the thought by describing a supportive manager who outlined projects and their expected results at the start, noted deadlines, shared her greater experience and perspectives, and told you about potential problems. She always shared the benefit of experience. You agreed on a plan of attack for the work, and how and when you needed to give status updates along the way. Your boss was always available for advice, preferred giving it early or late in the day, and taught you to take the work seriously but encouraged a collegial team atmosphere.

How interested are you in sports?

The interviewer is looking for your involvement in groups, as a signal that you know how to get along with others and pull together as a team.

"I really enjoy most team sports. I don't get a lot of time to indulge myself, but I am a regular member of my company's softball team." A recently completed survey of middle- and upper-management personnel found that the executives who listed group sports/activities among their extracurricular activities made an average of $3,000 per year more than their sedentary colleagues. Don't you just love baseball suddenly?

Apart from team sports, endurance sports are seen as a sign of determination: Swimming, running, and cycling are all okay. Games of skill (bridge, chess, and the like) demonstrate analytical skills; despite the recent popularity of poker and recognition of it as a game of analytical, math, communication, and negotiation skills, I feel that mentioning poker should be done carefully; you do not want to leave an image of yourself as a compulsive gambler.

What personal characteristics are necessary for success in your field?

You know the answer to this one: It's a brief recital of your *transferable skills* and *professional values*.

You might say: "To be successful in my field? Drive, motivation, energy, confidence, determination, good communication, and analytical skills. Combined, of course, with the ability to work with others."

Do you prefer working with others or alone?

This question is usually used to determine whether you are a team player. Before answering, however, be sure you know whether the job requires you to work alone. Then answer appropriately. Perhaps: "I'm quite happy working alone when necessary. I don't need much constant reassurance. But I prefer to work in a group—so much more gets achieved when people pull together."

Explain your role as a group/team member.

You are being asked to describe yourself as either a team player or a loner. Think for a moment about why the job exists in the first place: It is there to contribute to the bottom line in some way, and as such it has a specific role in the department to contribute toward that larger goal. Your department, in turn, has a similar, but larger, role in the company's bottom line. Your ability to link your small role to that of the department's larger responsibilities, and then to the overall success of the company, will demonstrate a developed professional awareness. Most departments depend on harmonious teamwork for their success, so describe yourself as a team player: "I perform my job in a way that helps others to do theirs in an efficient manner. Beyond the mechanics, we all have a responsibility to make the workplace a friendly and pleasant one, and that means everyone working for the common good and making the necessary personal sacrifices toward it."

How would you define a motivational work atmosphere?

This is a tricky question, especially because you probably have no idea what kind of work atmosphere exists in that particular office. The longer your answer, the greater your chances of saying the wrong thing, so keep it short and sweet. "One where the team has a genuine interest in its work and desire to turn out a good product/deliver a good service."

Do you make your opinions known when you disagree with the views of your supervisor?

If you can, state that you come from an environment where input is encouraged when it helps the team's ability to get the job done efficiently. "If opinions are sought in a meeting, I will give mine, although I am careful to be aware of others' feelings. I will never criticize a coworker or a superior in an open forum; besides, it is quite possible to disagree without being disagreeable. However, my last manager made it clear that she valued my opinion by asking for it. So, after a while, if there was something I felt strongly about, I would make an appointment to sit down and discuss it one-on-one."

What would you say about a supervisor who was unfair or difficult to work with?

"I would make an appointment to see the supervisor and diplomatically explain that I felt uncomfortable in our relationship, that I felt he was not treating me as a professional colleague, and therefore that I might not be performing up to standard in some way—that I wanted to right matters and ask for his input as to what I must do to create a professional relationship. I would enter into the discussion, taking responsibility for any communication problems that might exist and acknowledging that this wasn't just the manager's problem."

Do you consider yourself a natural leader or a born follower?

Ouch! The way you answer depends a lot on the job offer you are chasing. If you are a recent graduate, you are expected to have high aspirations, so go for it. If you are already on the corporate ladder with some practical experience in the school of hard knocks, you might want to be a little cagier. Assuming you are up for (and want) a leadership position, you might try something like this: "I would be reluctant to regard anyone as a natural leader. Hiring, motivating, and disciplining other adults and at the same time molding them into a cohesive team involves a number of delicately tuned skills that no honest person can say they were born with. Leadership requires first of all the desire; then it is a lifetime learning process. Anyone who reckons they have it all under control and have nothing more to learn isn't doing the employer any favors."

Of course, a little humility is also in order, because just about every leader in every company reports to someone, and there is a good chance that you are talking to such a someone right now. So you might consider including something like, "No matter how well developed any individual's leadership qualities, an integral part of leadership ability is to take direction from your immediate boss, and also to seek the input of the people being supervised. The wise leader will always follow good advice and sound business judgment wherever it comes from. I would say that given the desire to be a leader, the true leader in the modern business world must embrace both." How can anyone disagree with that kind of wisdom?

You have a doctor's appointment arranged for noon. You've waited two weeks to get in. An urgent meeting is scheduled at the last moment, though. What do you do?

What a crazy question, you mutter. It's not. It is even more than a question—it is what I call a question shell. The question within the shell—in this instance, "Will you sacrifice the appointment or sacrifice your job?"—can be changed at will. This is a situational-interviewing technique, which poses an on-the-job problem to see how the prospective employee will respond. A Chicago company asks this question as part of its initial screening, and if you give the wrong answer, you never even get a face-to-face interview. So what is the right answer to this or any similar shell question?

Fortunately, once you understand the interviewing technique, it is quite easy to handle—all you have to do is turn the question around. "If I were the manager who had to schedule a really important meeting at the last moment, and someone on my staff chose to go to the doctor instead, how would I feel?"

It is unlikely that you would be an understanding manager unless the visit was for a triple bypass. To answer, you start with an evaluation of the importance of the problem and the responsibility of everyone to make some sacrifices for the organization, and finish with: "The first thing I would do is reschedule the appointment and save the doctor's office inconvenience. Then I would immediately make sure I was properly prepared for the emergency meeting."

How do you manage to interview while still employed?

As long as you don't explain that you faked a dentist appointment to make the interview you should be all right. Beware of revealing anything that might make you appear at all underhanded. Best to make the answer short and sweet, and let the interviewer move on to richer areas of inquiry. Just explain that you had some vacation time due, or took a day off in lieu of overtime payments. "I had some vacation time, so I went to my boss and explained that I needed a couple of days off for some personal business and asked her what days would be most suitable. Although I plan to change jobs, I don't in any way want to hurt my current employer in the process by being absent during a crunch."

How have your career motivations changed over the years?

This question only crops up when you have enough years under your belt to be regarded as a tenured professional. The interviewer's agenda is to examine your *emotional maturity* and how realistic you are about future professional growth.

Your answer requires self-awareness. While the desire to rule the world can be seen as *motivation* in young professionals, it may not be interpreted so positively coming from a tenured corporate soldier from whom more realism is expected.

Your answer should reflect a growing maturity as well as a desire to do a good job for its own sake and to make a contribution as part of the greater whole. Here's an example you can use as a starting point in crafting your own:

"I guess in earlier years I was more ego-driven, with everything focused on becoming a star. Over the years I've come to realize that nothing happens with a team of one—we all have to function as part of a greater whole if we are to make meaningful contributions with our professional presence. Nowadays I take great pleasure in doing a job well, in seeing it come together as it should, and especially in seeing a group of professionals working together in their different roles to make it happen. I've discovered that the best way to stand out is to be a real team player and not worry about standing out."

How do you regroup when things haven't gone as planned?

In reality, we can all react to adversity in pretty much the same way we did as kids, but that isn't always productive. Here's a way you can deal with setbacks in your professional life and wow your interviewer in the process:

"I pause for breath and reflection for as long as the situation allows—this can be a couple of minutes or overnight. I do this to analyze what went wrong and why. I'm also careful to look for the things that went right, too. I'll examine alternate approaches and, time allowing,

I'll get together with a peer or my boss and review the whole situation and my proposed new approaches to get a second opinion."

You can go on to explain that the next time you face the same kind of problem you'll know what to avoid, what to do more of, and what other new approaches you can try.

You might consider finishing your answer with a statement about the beneficial effects of experiencing problems. "Over the years I've learned just as much from life's problems as from its successes."

Have you ever had to make unpopular decisions?

Inherent in the question is a request for an example, in which you'll demonstrate how *critical thinking* and *leadership skills* help you make the unpopular decisions, while *teamwork* and *communication skills* help make them palatable. Your answer needs to show that you're not afraid to make unpopular decisions when they are in the best interests of your job or the department's goals.

Simultaneously, stress your effort to make the decision workable for all parties and finish by explaining how everyone subsequently accepted its necessity and got on board.

What would your coworkers tell me about your attention to detail?

Say that you are shoddy and never pay attention to the details, and you'll hear a whoosh as your job offer flies out the window.

Your answer obviously lies in the question. You pay attention to detail, your analytical approach to projects helps you identify all the component parts of a given job, and your *multitasking* (time-management and organization) *skills* ensure that you get the job done in a timely manner without anything falling through the cracks.

What do you do when there is a decision to be made and no procedure exists?

You need to show that even though you're more than capable of taking initiative, you're not a rogue missile. Explain that the first thing you'll do will be to discuss the situation with your boss or—if time is tight and this isn't possible—with peers. That's exactly what the hiring manager wants to hear. Make clear that in developing any new approach/procedure/idea you'll stick to the company's established *systems and procedures.*

When do you expect a promotion?

Tread warily, show you believe in yourself, and have both feet firmly planted on the ground. "That depends on a few criteria. Of course, I cannot expect promotions without the performance that marks me as deserving of promotion. I also need to join a company that has the growth necessary to provide the opportunity. I hope that my manager believes in promoting from within and will help me grow so that I will have the skills necessary to be considered for promotion when the opportunity comes along."

If you are the only one doing a particular job in the company, or you are in management, you need to build another factor into your answer. "As a manager, I realize that part of my job is to have done my succession planning and that I must have someone trained and ready to step into my shoes before I can expect to step up. That way I play my part in preserving the chain of command." To avoid being caught off guard with queries about your having achieved that in your present job, you can finish with: "Just as I have done in my present job, where I have a couple of people capable of taking over the reins when I leave."

Tell me a story.

Wow. What on earth does the interviewer mean by that question? You don't know until you get her to elaborate. Ask, "What would you like me to tell you a story about?" To make any other response is to risk making a fool of yourself. Sometimes the question is asked to evaluate how analytical you are: People who answer the question without qualifying show they do not think things through carefully. It can also be asked to get a glimpse of the things you hold important. The answer you get to your request for clarification may give you direction, or it may not; but either way it demonstrates your *critical thinking skills*.

You need to have a story ready that portrays you in an appropriate light. If you speak of your personal life, tell a story that shows you like people, are engaged in life, and are determined. Do not discuss your love life. If the story you tell is about your professional life, make sure it shows you working productively as a member of a team on some worthwhile project that had problems but which came out okay in the end. Alternatively, tell stories that in some way show you employing *transferable skills* and *professional values* in some subtle way.

What have you learned from jobs you have held?

You've learned that little gets achieved without *teamwork* and that there's invariably sound thinking behind *systems and procedures*. To get to the root of problems it's better to talk less and listen more. Most of all, you've learned that you can either sit on the sidelines watching the hours go by or you can get involved and make a difference with your presence. You do the latter because you're goal-oriented, time goes quicker when you're engaged, and besides, the relationships you build are with better people. You might finish with: "There are two general things I have learned from past jobs. First, if you are confused, ask—it's better to ask a dumb question than make a dumb mistake. Second, it's better to promise less and produce more than to make unrealistic forecasts."

Define "cooperation."

The question examines *manageability* and asks you to explain how you see your responsibilities as a *team player*, both taking direction and working for the overall success of your department. Your answer will define "cooperation" as doing your job in a way that enables your colleagues to do theirs with a minimum of disruption. It's your desire to be part of something significant: through hard work and goodwill, to make the team something greater than the sum of its parts—and able to achieve goals beyond the scope of individual effort and contribution.

What difficulties do you have tolerating people with backgrounds and interests different from yours?

Another "team player" question with the awkward implication that you do have problems. Say, "I don't have any." But don't leave it there.

"I don't have any problems working with people from different backgrounds. In fact I find it energizing; with different backgrounds you get different life experiences and different ways of coming at problems. The opportunity to work with people different from yourself is a golden opportunity."

In hindsight, what have you done that was a little harebrained?

You are never harebrained in your business dealings, and you haven't been harebrained in your personal life since graduation, right? The only safe examples to use are ones from your deep past that ultimately turned out well. One of the best, if it applies to you, is: "Well, I guess the time I bought my house. I had no idea what I was letting myself in for and didn't pay enough attention to how much work the place would need. Still, there weren't any big structural problems, though I had to put a lot of work into fixing it up the way I wanted. Yes, my first house—that was a real learning experience." Not only can most people relate to this example, but it also gives you the opportunity to sell one or two of your very positive and endearing professional behaviors.

You have been given a project that requires you to interact with different levels within the company. How do you do this? What levels are you most comfortable with?

This is a two-part question that probes communication and self-confidence skills. The first part asks how you interact with superiors and motivate those working with and for you on the project. The second part is saying, "Tell me whom you regard as your peer group—help me categorize you." To cover those bases, include the essence of this: "There are two types of people I would interact with on a project of this nature. First, there are those I report to, who bear the ultimate responsibility for its success. With them, I determine deadlines and a method for evaluating the success of the project. I outline my approach, breaking the project down into component parts, getting approval on both the approach and the costs. I would keep my supervisors updated on a regular basis and seek input whenever needed. My supervisors would expect three things from me: the facts, an analysis of potential problems, and that I not be intimidated, as this would jeopardize the project's success. I would comfortably satisfy those expectations.

"The other people to interact with on a project like this are those who work with and for me. With those people, I would outline the project and explain how a successful outcome will benefit the company. I would assign the component parts to those best suited to each, and arrange follow-up times to assure completion by deadline. My role here would be to facilitate, motivate, and bring the different personalities together to form a team.

"As for comfort level, I find this type of approach enables me to interact comfortably with all levels and types of people."

Tell me about an event that really challenged you. How did you meet the challenge? In what way was your approach different from that of others?

This is a straightforward, two-part question. The first part probes your *critical thinking skills*. The second asks you to set yourself apart from the herd. Outline the root of the problem, its significance and negative impact on the department/company. The clearer you make the situation, the better. Having done so, explain your solution, its value to your employer, and how it was different from other approaches:

"My company has offices all around the country; I am responsible for seventy of them. My job is to visit each office on a regular basis and build market-penetration strategies with management, and to train and motivate the sales and customer service forces. When the recession hit, the need to service those offices was greater than ever, yet the traveling costs were getting prohibitive.

"Morale was an especially important factor: You can't let outlying offices feel defeated. I reapportioned my budget and did the following: I dramatically increased telephone contact with the offices and instituted weekly sales-technique e-mails and monthly training webinars—how to prospect for new clients, how to negotiate difficult sales, and so forth. I increased management training, again using webinars and concentrating on how to run sales meetings, early termination of low producers, and so forth.

"While my colleagues complained about the drop in sales, mine increased, albeit by a modest 6 percent. After two quarters, the new media/coaching approach was officially adopted by the company."

Give me an example of a method of working you have used. How did you feel about it?

You have a choice of giving an example of either good or bad work habits. Give a good example, one that demonstrates your understanding of corporate goals and your organizational or *critical thinking skills*. If you have taken the time to develop the time management and organization skills that underlie *multitasking* abilities, you have a great illustrative example to use.

You could say: "Maximum productivity requires focus and demands organization and time management. I do my paperwork at the end of each day, when I review the day's achievements; with this done, I plan for tomorrow, prioritizing all projected activities. When I come to work in the morning, I'm ready to get going without wasting time and sure that I will be spending my time and effort in the areas where it is most needed to deliver results. I try to schedule meetings right before lunch; people get to the point more quickly if it's on their time. I feel this is an efficient and organized method of working."

In working with new people, how do you go about getting an understanding of them?

Every new hire is expected to become a viable part of the group, which means getting an understanding of the group and its individual members. Understanding that everyone likes to give advice is the key to your answer. You have found that the best way to understand and become part of a new team is to be open, friendly, ask lots of questions, and be helpful whenever you can. The answers to your questions give you needed insights into the ways of the job, department, and company, and they help you get to know the person.

What would your references say about you?

You have nothing to lose by giving a positive answer. If you checked your references, as I recommended earlier, you can give details of what your best references will say. When you demonstrate how well you and your boss got along, the interviewer does not have to ask, "What do you dislike about your current manager?"

CHAPTER 16
How to Handle Stress and Illegal Questions

EVERY INTERVIEW IS a stress interview, but sometimes, with good reason, interviewers ratchet up the stress level. You need to be ready.

There is no greater fear than fear of the unknown, and that is exactly what you worry about going into a job interview; and worrying about the unknown in turn makes you more nervous and increases your stress level.

While interviewers categorically deny conducting stress interviews, they readily admit that if there is stress on the job, they need to know how a candidate will react to it and will try to recreate it by throwing in the occasional question to see how a candidate maintains her balance. These interviewers are using stress to simulate the unexpected and sometimes tense events of everyday business life. Seeing how you handle unexpected stress gives a fair indication of how you will react to the real thing.

The sophisticated interviewer talks very little, perhaps only 20 percent of the time, and that time is spent asking questions. Few comments, and no editorializing on your answers, means that you get no hint, verbal or otherwise, about your performance.

Interviewers are looking for the candidate who stays calm and continues to process incoming information during stressful events, and, having processed it, asks questions for clarification or responds professionally with actions and/or words suitable to the situation and capable of moving it toward a desirable conclusion.

If you are ill-prepared for an interview, no one will be able to put more pressure on you than you do on yourself. The only way to combat the stress you feel from fear of the unknown is to be prepared, to know what the stress questions might be, what the interviewer is trying to discover with the question, and to prepare your strategies for these situations. Remember: A stress interview is just a regular interview with the volume turned all the way up—the music is the same, just louder. Only preparedness will keep you cool and collected.

What is your greatest weakness?

This is one of the toughest of all interview questions and often comes right after you have been tossed that softball "What's your greatest strength?" question (see Chapter 14).

Every conceivable slick answer has already been used a hundred times, so saying you work too hard isn't going to impress anyone. The truth of the matter is that we all have weaknesses, even you and I, and this is one instance when any interviewer is going to relish an honest answer like a breath of fresh air. Your goal is to be honest and forthright without torpedoing your candidacy.

We all share a weakness: staying current with rapid changes in technology. Changes in technology give everyone an ongoing challenge: getting up to speed with the new skills demanded if you are to do your job well. Your answer can address this very issue and in the process still show that you are someone capable of staying on top of things in a rapidly changing workplace.

First talk about these constantly evolving challenges, then follow with examples that show how you *are* keeping up with technologies that affect your productivity. "I'm currently reading about . . ."; "I just attended a weekend workshop . . ."; or "I'm signed up for classes at . . . ."

With this type of answer you identify your weakness as *something that is only of concern to the most dedicated and forward-looking professionals in your field.*

You could also talk about the general difficulties in keeping up with all the deliverables of the job and use it to talk about what you are doing to develop your *multitasking skills*. You can also consider the following as effective alternatives or as additional illustrations if they are demanded:

- If there is a *minor* part of the target job where you lack knowledge—but knowledge you will pick up quickly and can prove that you will pick it up quickly—use that.
- Identify a weakness that has no possible relation to the needs of this job. Although if you do this, you might be asked for another example, which will bring you back to the first two options.

How do you go about solving problems in your work?

Every position, from CEO to fast-food server, has its problems and challenges. This question examines your grasp of *critical thinking*—one of the *transferable skills*—and asks you to explain your approach to problem solving. There is an established approach to problem solving that everyone who gets ahead in her professional life learns: When confronted with a problem, you take these steps:

- Define the problem.
- Identify why it's a problem and whom it's a problem for.
- Identify what's causing the problem.
- Seek input from everyone affected by the problem.
- Identify possible solutions.
- Identify the time, cost, and resources it will take to implement each option.
- Evaluate the consequences of each solution.
- Decide upon the best solution, based on these considerations.
- Identify and execute the steps necessary to solve the problem.

Your answer covers these steps. If asked for a real-world example, you'll have plenty in mind from your TJD exercises; remember to recall the results and benefits of your solution and the *transferable skills* that came into play.

With hindsight, how could you have improved your progress?

A question that asks you to discuss your commitment to success. As professional success affects so many other parts of your life, take time to think through the mistakes you have made and commit to getting better control of your career for the future. Whatever you do say, with questions asking for information detrimental to your candidacy, always put your answer in the past: You woke up, took responsibility, and corrected the situation. Show that, having learned from the experience, you are now committed to ongoing professional development.

What kinds of decisions are most difficult for you?

You are human—admit it, but be careful what you admit. The employer is looking for people who can make decisions and solve problems, not those who'll dither instead of do. You want to come off as someone who's decisive but not precipitate, who considers the implications of actions on outcomes, any side effects those actions might have on other activities, and whether they conflict with existing *systems and procedures* or other company priorities.

If you have ever had to fire someone, you are in luck, because no one likes to do that. Emphasize that, having reached a logical conclusion, you act. If you are not in management, tie your answer to transferable skills and professional values: "It's not that I have difficulty making decisions—some just require more consideration than others. A small example might be vacation time. Now, everyone is entitled to it, but I don't believe you should leave your boss in a bind at short notice. I think very carefully at the beginning of the year when I'd like to take my vacation, and then think of alternate dates. I go to my supervisor, tell him what I hope to do, and see whether there is any conflict. I wouldn't want to be out of the office for the two weeks prior to a project deadline, for instance. So by carefully considering things far enough in advance, I don't procrastinate, and I make sure my plans jibe with my boss and the department for the year."

Here you take a trick question and use it to demonstrate your consideration, analytical abilities, and concern for the department—and for the company's bottom line.

Tell me about the problems you have living within your means.

If you have experienced severe financial difficulties, you'll need to address them and how they have been handled. The answer needs to be carefully thought out and short, emphasizing that you are in control of the situation. Otherwise, you continually strive to improve your skills and your living standard: "I know few people who are satisfied with their current earnings. As a professional, I am continually striving to improve my skills and to improve my living standard. But my problems are no different from those of this or any other company—making sure all the bills get paid on time and recognizing that every month and year there are some things that are prudent to do and others that are best deferred."

What area of your skills/professional development do you want to improve at this time?

Another "tell me all your weaknesses" question. Don't damage your candidacy with careless admissions of weakness. Choose a skill where you are competent but that everyone, including the interviewer, knows demands constant personal attention. *Technology skills* as they apply to your job could be a good example of a "weakness" that every committed professional shares. Cite the importance and challenge of staying current in this area and finish with saying, "_____ is so important, I don't think I will ever stop paying attention to this area." Be prepared to explain how you are working on this skill development right now.

One effective answer to this is to say, "Well, from what you told me about the job, I seem to have all the necessary skills and background. What I would really find exciting is the opportunity to work on a job where . . . ." At this point, you replay the skill-development area you cited. This approach allows you to emphasize what you find exciting about the job and that you have all the required *technical skills* and are proactively committed to professional skill development. It works admirably.

You can finish with saying, "These areas are so important that I don't think anyone can be too good or should ever stop trying to polish their skills."

Your application shows you have been with one company a long time without any appreciable increase in rank or salary. Tell me about this.

Analyze why this state of affairs exists. It may be that you like your professional life exactly as it is. You take *pride* in your work and haven't pushed for promotions. If so, tell it like it is, because most people are eager for promotion—someone who isn't could make for a good hire; it could be your ace.

Here are some tactics you can use. First of all, try to avoid putting your salary history on application forms. No one is going to deny you an interview for lack of a salary history if your skills match those the job requires. And of course, you should never put such unnecessary information on your resume.

Now, we'll address the delicate matter of "Hey, wait a minute; why no promotions?" The interviewer has posed a truly negative inquiry. The more time either of you spend on it, the more time the interviewer gets to devote to concentrating on negative aspects of your candidacy. Make your answer short and sweet, then shut up. For instance, "My current employer is a stable company with a good working environment, but there's minimal growth there in my area—in fact, there hasn't been any promotion in my area since _____. Your question is the reason I am meeting here with you; I have the skills and ability to take on more responsibility, and I'm looking for a place to do that."

In your current job, what should you spend more time on and why?

Without a little self-control you could easily blurt out what you consider to be your greatest weaknesses. Tricky question, but with a little forethought your answer will shine.

Enlightened self-interest dictates that your ongoing career management strategies identify and develop the skills demanded in a constantly changing work environment that make you desirable to employers, and that each of your job changes should occur within the context of an overall career management strategy.

So your answer might address that existing skills always need to be improved and new skills acquired, citing an example of some skill development initiative you are working on now. Unless you are in sales/marketing, you could add that with networking seen as so important by everyone today, you should probably be investing more time in that; in sales and marketing of course this is your very lifeblood.

Your answer might include, "With the fast pace of change in our profession, existing skills always need to be improved and new skills learned. For instance, in this job I think the organizational software now available can have a major impact on personal productivity. If I stayed with my current employer this would be a priority, just as it will be when I make the move to my next job; it's in my own best interests to have good skills." With an answer along these lines you show foresight instead of a weakness. You can then end with:

- Courses you have taken and are planning to take
- Books you have read or book clubs you belong to
- Memberships in professional associations
- Subscriptions to professional journals

Such an answer will identify you as an aware, connected, and dedicated professional.

Are you willing to take calculated risks when necessary?

Confirm your understanding of the question by qualifying it: "How do you define calculated risks? Can you give me an example?" or "Would you run that by me again?" This will give you more information as well as more time to think while the interviewer repeats the question in more detail. You can use this "qualifying the question" technique with tough questions when you want a little recovery time.

Once you understand the question, you'll probably answer "yes" if you want the job offer. Be prepared with an example for the possible follow-up question showing how your calculations and preparation minimize potential risk. Whatever your answer, the risk taken must be within the normal bounds of the execution of your duties and in no way jeopardize colleagues or company.

See this pen I'm holding? Sell it to me.

This question often comes up for sales professionals, but every employee needs to know how to *communicate* effectively and sell appropriately. This is what the interviewer is getting at with this apparently out-of-the-blue request.

As such, you are being examined about your understanding of constitutive/needs-based/features and benefits sales, how quickly you think on your feet, and how effectively you use verbal communication. For example, the interviewer holds up a yellow highlighter. First you will want to establish the customer's needs with a few questions like, "What sort of pens do you currently use? Do you use a highlighter? Do you read reports and need to recall important points? Is comfort important to you?" Then you will proceed calmly, "Let me tell you about the special features of this pen and show you how they will satisfy your needs. First of all it is tailor-made for highlighting reports, and that will save you time in recalling the most important points. The case is wide for comfort and the base is flat so it will stand up and be visible on a cluttered work area. It's disposable—and affordable enough to have a handful for desk, briefcase, car, and home. And the bright yellow means you'll never lose it." Then close with a smile and a question of your own that will bring a smile to the interviewer's face: "How many gross shall we deliver?" Everyone is required to communicate effectively and sell appropriately—sometimes products, but more often ideas, approaches, and concepts.

How will you be able to cope with a change in environment after _____ years with your current company?

Another chance to take an implied negative and turn it into a positive: "That's one of the reasons I want to make a change. After five years with my current employer, I felt I was about to get stale. I have exemplary skills in _____, _____, and _____. It's just time for me to take these skills to a new and more challenging environment and experience some new thinking and approaches. Hopefully, I'll have the chance to contribute from my experience."

Why aren't you earning more at your age?

Accept this as a compliment to your skills and accomplishments. "I have always felt that solid experience would stand me in good stead in the long run and that earnings would come in due course. Also, I am not the type of person to change jobs just for the money. At this point, I have a set of desirable skills [*itemize them as they relate to the job's priorities*] and the time has come for me to join a team that needs and values these skills. How much *should* I be earning now?" The figure could be your offer.

What is the worst thing you have heard about our company?

This question can come as something of a shock. As with all stress questions, your poise under stress is vital: If you can carry off a halfway decent answer as well, you are a winner. The best response to this question is simple. Just say with a smile and a laugh: "You are a tough company to get an interview with, and you demand a lot of your employees. But I actually like that about you, because I'm looking to gain the sort of expertise that will facilitate my professional growth." This way you keep the compliment and allow for the negativity by implying that while all those *other* jerks think hard work is a bad thing, you thrive on it.

Why should I hire an outsider when I could fill the job with someone inside the company?

The question isn't as stupid as it sounds. Obviously, the interviewer has examined existing employees with an eye toward their promotion or reassignment. Just as obviously, the job cannot be filled from within the company. If it could be, it would be, and for two very good reasons: It is cheaper for the company to promote from within, and it is better for employee morale.

Hiding behind this intimidating question is a pleasant invitation: "Tell me why I should hire you." Your answer should include two steps. The first is a recitation of your *technical* and *transferable skills*, tailored to the job's needs.

For the second step, realize first that whenever a manager is filling a position, he is looking not only for someone who can do the job, but also for someone who can benefit the department in a larger sense. No department is as good as it could be—each has weaknesses that need strengthening. So in the second part of your answer, include a question of your own: "Those are my general attributes. However, if no one is promotable from inside the company, you must be looking to add strength to your team in a special way. How do you hope the final candidate will be able to benefit your department?" The answer to this is your cue to sell your applicable qualities.

Have you ever had any financial difficulties?

A common question, especially if you deal with money. Tell the truth because when references are checked, salary and credit are at the top of the list. Your answer succinctly gives the circumstances, the facts of your difficulties, and where you stand today in resolving those issues. Do not bring up financial problems until this question is asked or an offer is on the table and references are to be checked.

For someone to check your credit history, she must have your written consent. This is required under the 1972 Fair Credit and Reporting Act. Invariably, when you fill out a job application form, sign it, and date it, you've also signed a release permitting the employer to check your credit history.

If you have had to file for bankruptcy, it will show up in a credit check, so be honest, professional, and as brief as possible. Don't give any information about the circumstances: It isn't necessary and no one wants to know. What an employer does want to hear is that you have turned the corner and everything is under control now. They also want to know, very briefly, what you learned and have done to rebuild your credit and get back on your feet.

Financial difficulties aren't the deal-breaker they used to be, unless they affect the employer's insurance obligations, and in light of the corporate and personal financial crises of recent years, many corporations are re-evaluating and taking a more realistic stance on these matters. Once it's behind you, get it expunged from your record.

How should I handle a DWI?

Find out if it will show up, as this differs from state to state. If the application asks, answer and leave it be; if not, don't offer this information until background checks are close. Then be brief—"It happened, I was young, etc."—and stress what you learned from it. Try to get it expunged: Google "DWI expunge."

How should I handle a felony?

First determine if it's on your record, if it will show up in a background check, and what employers in your state can take into consideration. States handle felony records differently from one another, as they do the information an employer may inquire about. Learn what you have to disclose to an employer and don't disclose more than you have to. Briefly, tell the employer what you've learned and that it is behind you. Discrepancies between your application and convictions can cause problems.

There's no need to discuss issues that didn't result in conviction or anything that has been expunged.

Why were you out of work for so long?

Losing your job has happened to so many others and no longer carries the stigma it once used to, but nevertheless you must have a sound explanation for all gaps in your employment history. Your answer can start with noting that you lost your job in the worst economic recession in eighty years. You might then add that it wasn't a matter of getting job interviews but not offers, you were not just looking for another paycheck—you were looking for relevant work in a profession you love and with a company with which to settle and make a long-term contribution:

"I decided that I enjoy my work too much just to accept another paycheck. I determined that the next job I took would be one where I could do my best to make a solid contribution. From everything I have heard about this company, you are a group that expects people to pull their weight, and make extra effort for the sake of doing the best you can do rather than the least you can get away with. I like that, and I would like to be part of the team. What do I have to do to get the job?"

You answer the question, compliment the interviewer, and shift the emphasis from your unemployment to how you can get the job offer.

Tell me about a time things didn't work out well.

There are two techniques that every skilled interviewer will use, especially if you are giving good answers. In this question, the interviewer looks for negative balance; in the follow-up, the person will look for negative confirmation. Here, you are required to give an example of an inadequacy. The trick is to pull something from the past, not the present, and to finish with what you learned from the experience. For example: "That's easy. When I first joined the workforce, I didn't really understand the importance of systems and procedures. There was one time when I was too anxious to contribute and didn't have the full picture. There was a sales visit report everyone had to fill out after visiting a customer. I always put a lot of effort into it until I realized it was never read; it just went in the files. So I stopped doing it for a few days to see if it made any difference. I thought I was gaining time to make more sales for the company. I was so proud of my extra sales calls, I told the boss at the end of the week. My boss explained that the records were for the long term, so that should my job change, the next salesperson would have the benefit of a full client history. It was a long time ago, but I have never forgotten the lesson: There's always a reason for systems and procedures. I've had the best-kept records in the company ever since."

To look for negative confirmation, the interviewer may then say something like, "Thank you. Now can you give me another example?" He is trying to confirm a weakness. If you help, you could cost yourself the job. Here's your reaction: You sit deep in thought for a good ten seconds, then look up and say firmly, "No, that's the only occasion when anything like that happened." Shut up and refuse to be enticed further.

Tell me about a time when you put your foot in your mouth.

Answer this question with caution. The interviewer is examining your ability and willingness to interact pleasantly with others. The question is tricky because it asks you to show yourself in a poor light. Downplay the negative impact of your action and end with positive information about your candidacy. The best thing to do is to start with an example outside of the workplace and show how the experience improved your performance at work.

"About five years ago, I let the cat out of the bag about a surprise birthday party for a friend, a terrific faux pas. It was a mortifying experience, and I promised myself not to let anything like that happen again." Then, after this fairly innocuous statement, you can talk about communications in the workplace: "As far as work is concerned, I always regard employer-employee communications on any matter as confidential unless expressly stated otherwise. So, putting my foot in my mouth doesn't happen to me at work."

What was there about your last company that you didn't particularly like or agree with?

Be careful not to criticize a manager, or you might be seen as a potential management problem. It is safest to say that you didn't have any of these problems. If there was an unhappy work environment and this opinion was shared by many, you can mention it, but remain nonspecific, although you might discuss that some people didn't seem to care about anything they did, and you found this difficult.

Another option: "I didn't like the way some people gave lip service to 'the customer comes first,' but really didn't go out of their way to keep the customer satisfied. I don't think it was a fault of management, just a general malaise that seemed to affect a lot of people."

What do you feel is a satisfactory attendance record?

There are two answers to this question—one if you are in management, and one if you are not. As a manager: "I believe attendance is a matter of management, motivation, and psychology. Letting the employees know you expect their best efforts and won't accept half-baked excuses is one thing. The other is to keep your employees motivated by a congenial work environment and the challenge to stretch themselves. Giving people pride in their work and letting them know you respect them as individuals have a lot to do with it, too."

If you are not in management, the answer is even easier: "I've never really considered it. I work for a living, I enjoy my job, and I'm rarely sick."

What is your general impression of your last company?

Always answer positively. There is a strong belief in management ranks that people who complain about past employers will cause problems for their new ones. Your answer is, "A good department and company to work for." Then smile and wait for the next question. If pressed for more, add, "I had gone as far as I could and could see no opportunities opening up, so I determined it was time to make a strategic career move."

What are some of the things you find difficult to do? Why do you feel that way?

This is a variation on a couple of earlier questions. Remember, anything that goes against the best interests of your employer is difficult to do. Your answer should share a difficulty common to the job and everyone who does that job, and at the same time advance your candidacy; difficult, but not impossible:

"That's a tough question. There are so many things that are difficult to stay current with, considering the pace of business today and pace of change technology brings to our profession. One of my problems has been staying on top of the customer base in a productive and responsible fashion. I built my territory and had 140 clients to sell to every month, and I was so busy touching base with all of them that I never got a chance to sell to any of them. So I graded them into three groups. I called on the top 20 percent of my clients every three weeks. The balance of my clients I called on once a month, but with a difference—each month, I marked ten of them to spend time with and really get to know. I still have difficulty reaching all my clients in a month, but with time management, prioritization, and organization, my sales have tripled and are still climbing."

Jobs have pluses and minuses. What were some of the minuses on your last job?

A variation on the question, "What interests you least about this job?" which was handled earlier. Potentially explosive but easily defused. Regardless of your occupation, there is at least one repetitive, mindless duty that everyone groans about but has to be done. You just need to show that you recognize its importance despite the boredom factor and take care of business responsibly. For example, "Client visit reports are probably the least exciting part of my job. However, I know they are important for reference and continuity, so I do them at the end of the day as part of my daily performance review and next day planning." This response answers the question without shooting yourself in the foot, and shows that you possess *critical thinking* and *multitasking* (time management and organization) *skills*. You can finish with a nod toward your *professional values* and *teamwork skills*, "Besides, if I don't do the paperwork, that holds up other people in the company."

Or perhaps, "In accounts receivable, it's my job to get the money in to make payroll and good things like that. Half the time, the goods get shipped before I get the paperwork because sales says, 'It's a rush order.' That's a real minus to me. It was so bad at my last company that we tried a new approach. We met with sales and explained our problem. The result was that incremental commissions were based on cash in, not on bill date. They saw the connection, and things are much better now."

What kinds of people do you like to work with?

This is the easy part of what can be a tricky three-part question. Obviously, you like to work with people who are fully engaged in their work and who come to work with a smile and to make a difference with their presence, with people who are there to get results, not just mark time till the end of the day. You like to work with people who have *pride*, *honesty*, *integrity*, and *commitment* to their work.

What kinds of people do you find it difficult to work with?

This question can stand alone or can be the second part of a three-part question. Your answer comes from understanding why your job exists: It's a small cog in the complex machinery of making a company profitable, so you might say, "People who don't care about their work and don't care about being part of something larger than themselves, people who have the time to find fault but never to find solutions." End by noting that while they aren't the best coworkers, you don't let them interfere with your *motivation*.

Or, "People who don't follow procedures, or slackers—the occasional rotten apples who don't really care about the quality of their work. They're long on complaints, but short on solutions."

How have you successfully worked with this difficult type of person?

Sometimes this question is on its own or it's the third part of a three-part question. First, you don't let such people affect your *motivation* or quality of work. Second, you don't buy into their negativism by encouraging them. You are polite and professional but prefer to ally yourself with the people who come to work to make a difference. You maintain cordial relations but don't go out of your way to seek close acquaintance. Life is too short to be de-motivated by people who think their cup is half empty and it's someone else's fault.

Or you might reply with something like: "I stick to my guns, stay enthusiastic, and hope some of it will rub off. I had a big problem with one guy—all he did was complain, and always in my area. Eventually, I told him how I felt. I said if I were a millionaire, I'd clearly have all the answers and wouldn't have to work, but as it was, I wasn't, and had to work for a living. I told him that I really enjoyed his company but I didn't want to hear it anymore. Every time I saw him after that, I presented him with a work problem and asked his advice. In other words I challenged him to come up with positives, not negatives."

You might even end by noting that sometimes you've noticed that such people simply lack enthusiasm and confidence, and that energetic and cheerful coworkers can often change that.

How did you get your last job?

The interviewer is looking for initiative. Show that you went about your search with planning, *organization*, and intelligence, the same way you'd approach a work project. At least show *determination*. For example: "I was turned down for my last job for having too little experience. I asked the manager to give me a trial for the afternoon, then and there. I was given a list of companies they'd never sold to. I picked up the phone and didn't get close to a sale all afternoon, but she could see I had guts."

How would you evaluate me as an interviewer?

The question is dangerous, maybe more so than the one asking you to criticize your boss. If you think the interviewer is a congenital imbecile whom you wouldn't work for on a bet, don't tell the truth. This is an instance where honesty is not the best policy: Remember, you are there to get a job offer. It is best to say, "This is one of the toughest interviews I have ever been through, and I don't relish the prospect of going through another. I have great professional skills, but interviewing is not one of them; it's not something I have had much experience doing. Yet I do realize that you are just trying to determine if I have the skills you need." Then go on to explain how your skills match the job. You may choose to finish the answer with a question of your own: "I think I can do this job, and I think I would like it. What do you think?"

Wouldn't you feel better off at another company?

Relax, things aren't as bad as you might assume. This question is usually asked if you are really doing quite well or if the job involves a certain amount of stress. A lawyer, for example, might well be expected to face this one. The trick is not to be intimidated. Your first step is to qualify the question. Relax, take a breath, sit back, smile, and say, "You surprise me. Why do you say that?" The interviewer must then talk, giving you precious time to collect your wits and come back with a rebuttal.

Then answer "no," and explain why. All the interviewer wants to see is how much you know about the company and how determined you are to join its ranks. Overcome the objection with an example showing how you will contribute to the company. You could reply: "Not at all. My whole experience has been with small companies. I am good at my job and in time could become a big fish in a little pond. But that is not what I want. This corporation is a leader in its business. You have a strong reputation for encouraging skills development in your employees. This is the type of environment I want to work in. Coming from a small company, I have done a little bit of everything. That means that no matter what you throw at me, I will learn it quickly."

Then end with a question of your own. In this instance, the question has a twofold purpose: first, to identify a critical area to sell yourself; and second, to encourage the interviewer to imagine you working at the company: "For example, what would be the first project you'll need me to tackle?"

You end with a question of your own that gets the interviewer focusing on those immediate problems. You can then move the conversation forward with an explanation of how your background and experience can help.

What would you say if I told you your presentation this afternoon was lousy?

"If" is the key word here. The question tests your poise, *critical thinking*, and *communication skills*. Don't assume you are being criticized. An appropriate response would be: "First of all, I would ask which aspects of my presentation were lousy. My next step would be to find out where you felt the problem was. If there was miscommunication, I'd clear it up. If the problem was elsewhere, I would seek your advice and be sure that the problem did not recur." This would show that when it is a manager's duty to criticize performance, you will respond to criticism in a professional and *emotionally mature* way.

The Illegal Question

Of course, one of the most stressful—and negative—questions is the illegal one, a question that delves into your private life or personal background. Such a question will make you uncomfortable if it is blatant, and could also make you angry.

Your aim, however, is to overcome your discomfort and avoid getting angry: You want to get the job offer, and any self-righteous or defensive reaction on your part will ensure you don't get it. You may feel angry enough to get up and walk out, or say things like, "These are unfair practices; you'll hear from my lawyer in the morning." But the result will be that you won't get the offer, and therefore won't have the leverage you need. Remember, no one is saying you can't refuse the job once it's offered to you.

So what is an illegal question? Title VII is a federal law that forbids employers from discriminating against any person on the basis of sex, age, race, national origin, or religion. More recently, the Americans with Disabilities Act was passed to protect this important minority.

- **An interviewer may not ask** about your religion, church, synagogue, or parish, the religious holidays you observe, or your political beliefs or affiliations. He may not ask, for instance, "Does your religion allow you to work on Saturdays?" But he *may* ask something like, "This job requires work on Saturdays. Is that a problem?"
- **An interviewer may not ask** about your ancestry, national origin, or parentage; in addition, you cannot be asked about the naturalization status of your parents, spouse, or children. The interviewer cannot ask about your birthplace. But she may ask (and probably will, considering the current immigration laws) whether you are a U.S. citizen or a resident alien with the right to work in the United States.

- **An interviewer may not ask** about your native language, the language you speak at home, or how you acquired the ability to read, write, or speak a foreign language. But he may ask about the languages in which you are fluent if knowledge of those languages is pertinent to the job.
- **An interviewer may not ask** about your age, your date of birth, whether you are married or pregnant, or the ages of your children. But she may ask you whether you are over eighteen years old.
- **An interviewer may not ask** about maiden names or whether you have changed your name; your marital status, number of children or dependents, or your spouse's occupation; or whether (if you are a woman) you wish to be addressed as "Miss," "Mrs.," or "Ms." But the interviewer may ask about how you like to be addressed (a common courtesy) and whether you have ever worked for the company before under a different name. (If you have worked for this company or other companies under a different name, you may want to mention that, in light of the fact that this prospective manager may check your references and additional background information.)

As you consider a question that seems to verge on illegality, take into account that the interviewer may be asking it innocently and may be unaware of the laws on the matter. Even more likely is that the interviewer really likes you, and is interested in you as a person. When we meet someone new, often some of the first questions will be: Where are you from? Are you married? Have kids? What church do you go to? Bear this in mind so that you don't overreact.

Your best bet is to be polite and straightforward, just as you would be in any other social situation. You also want to move the conversation to an examination of your skills and abilities, and away from personal issues. Here are some common illegal questions—and possible responses. Remember as you frame your answers to the odd illegal question that your objective is to get job offers; if you later decide that this company is not for you, you are under no obligation to accept the position.

What religion do you practice?

In most instances, an interviewer may not ask about religious beliefs. However, as with most illegal questions, it's sometimes in your interest to answer.

You might say, "I attend my church/synagogue/mosque regularly, but I make it my practice not to involve my personal beliefs in my work." Or, "I have a set of beliefs that are important to me, but I do not mix those beliefs with my work and understand this is something employers don't want their people discussing."

If you do not practice a religion, you may want to say something like, "I have a set of personal beliefs that are important to me, but I do not attend organized services at present. And I do not mix those beliefs with my work, if that's what you mean."

Are you married?

If you are, the company is concerned about the impact your family duties and future plans will have on your tenure there. Although illegal if it is asked, it's best to answer this question and remove any doubts the interviewer might otherwise have. Your answer could be, "Yes, I am. Of course, I make a separation between my work life and my family life that allows me to give my all to a job. I have no problem with travel or late hours; those things are part of my work and family obligations have never interfered. My references will confirm this for you."

Do you have/plan to have children?

Most often asked of single women in their childbearing years. This isn't any of the interviewer's business, but he may be concerned about whether you will leave the company early to raise a family. Behind the question is the impact of absences on departmental deliverables. You could always answer "no." If you answer "yes," you might qualify it, "but those plans are for way in the future, and they depend on the success of my career. Certainly, I want to do the best, most complete job for this company I can. I consider that my skills are right for the job and that I can make a long-range contribution. I certainly have no plans to leave the company just as I begin to make meaningful contributions."

If the questions become too pointed, you may want to ask—innocently—"Could you explain the relevance of that issue to the position?" That response, however, can seem confrontational; you should only use it if you are extremely uncomfortable, or are quite certain you can get away with it. Sometimes, the interviewer will drop the line of questioning.

Illegal questions tend to arise not out of brazen insensitivity but rather out of an interest in you. The employer is familiar with your skills and background, feels you can do the job, and wants to get to know you as a person. Outright discrimination these days is really quite rare. With illegal questions, your response must be positive—that's the only way you're going to get the job offer.

Building Stress Into a Sequence of Questions

Sometimes an interviewer will build stress into a sequence of questions. Starting off innocently enough, the questions are layered and sequenced to dig deeper and deeper. If you are adopting the *Knock 'em Dead* philosophy and investing yourself in your professional life, these stress question sequences will hold few worries for you. Let's take the simple example of "Can you work under pressure?"

This example will use a reporter's technique of asking why, when, who, what, how, and where. The technique can be applied to any question you are asked and is frequently used to probe those success stories that sound too good to be true. You'll find them suddenly tagged on to the simple closed-ended questions as well as to the open-ended ones. They can often start with phrases like: "Share with me," "Tell me about a time when," or "I'm interested in finding out about," followed by a request for specific examples from your work history.

Can you work under pressure?

A simple, closed-ended question that requires just a yes-or-no answer, but you won't get off so easy.

Good, I'd be interested to hear about a time when you experienced pressure on your job.

An open-ended request to tell a story about a pressure situation. After this, you will be subjected to the layering technique—six layers in the following instance.

Why do you think this situation arose?

It's best if the situation you describe is not a peer's or manager's fault. Remember, you must be seen as a team player.

When exactly did it happen?

Asking when an event happened can often lead to further questions. This is why the process of self-discovery in the earlier part of the book pays dividends throughout the entire interview cycle.

How do you feel others involved could have acted more responsibly?

An open invitation to criticize peers and superiors, which you should diplomatically decline.

Who holds the responsibility for the situation?

Another invitation to point the finger of blame, which should be avoided.

Where in the chain of command could steps be taken to avoid that sort of thing happening again?

This question probes your analytical skills and asks whether you are the type of person who takes the time to revisit the scene of the crime to learn for the next time.

After you've survived that barrage, a friendly tone may conceal another zinger: "What did you learn from the experience?" This question is geared to probe your judgment and *emotional maturity*. Your answer should emphasize whichever of the key professional behaviors your story was illustrating.

When an interviewer feels you were on the edge of revealing something unusual in an answer, you may well encounter "mirror statements." Here, the last key phrase of your answer will be repeated or paraphrased, and followed by a steady gaze and silence. For example, "So, you learned that organization is the key to management." The idea is that the silence and an expectant look will work together to keep you talking. It can be disconcerting to find yourself rambling on without quite knowing why. The trick is knowing when to stop. When the interviewer gives you an expectant look in this context, expand your answer (you have to), but by no more than a couple of sentences. Otherwise, you will get that creepy feeling that you're digging yourself into a hole.

Facing an Interview Panel

There will be situations where you face more than one interviewer at a time. When these occur, remember the example of an attorney who had five law partners all asking questions at the same time. As the poor interviewee got halfway through one answer, another question would be shot at her. Pausing for breath, she smiled and said, "Hold on, ladies and gentlemen. These are all excellent questions, and, given time, I'll answer them all. Now I believe the managing partner has a question?" In so doing, she showed the interviewers exactly what they wanted to see—and what is behind every stress interview and every negatively phrased question—a desire to find poise and calm under fire, combined with a refusal to be intimidated.

You never know when an interview, or series of interviews can take a more stressful turn. It might appear that way because you are tense and tired (remember, it is okay to ask for a restroom break, to recharge yourself, at any time during a day of interviews); or it can be that rubber-stamp meeting with the senior vice president at the end of a series of grueling meetings. That is not surprising. While other interviewers are concerned with determining whether you are able, willing, and a good fit for the job in question, the senior executive who eventually throws you for a loop may be looking at your promotion potential.

CHAPTER 17
WELCOME TO THE REAL WORLD

AS A RECENT graduate, most likely entering the professional world for the first time, you can expect questions designed to determine your potential.

Corporate recruiters liken the gamble of hiring recent graduates to laying down wines for the future: Some will develop into full-bodied, excellent vintages, but others will be disappointments. When hiring professionals with work experience, there is a track record to evaluate; with recent graduates, there is little or nothing. Often, the only solid things an interviewer has to go on are the degree, SAT scores, and that ubiquitous burger-flipping job. That's not much on which to base a hiring decision.

Of all the steps a recent graduate will take up the ladder of success over the years, none is more important or more difficult than getting a foot on that first rung. You have no idea how the professional game is played and you are up against thousands of other grads with pretty much the same to offer. Differentiating yourself by demonstrating your understanding of the professional world, as well as your motivation and potential, will be important tools in helping get your career off to a good start.

Interviewers will look at what you have done to show initiative and how willing you are to learn, grow, and get the job done.

Your goal is to stand out from all the other entry-level candidates as someone altogether different: You are more engaged in the success of your professional life, more knowledgeable about the job and the world in which it functions, and more prepared to listen, learn, and do whatever it takes to earn your place on a professional team. Don't be like thousands of others who, in answer to questions about their greatest strength, reply lamely, "I'm good with people," or, "I like working with others." Answers like this brand you as average. To stand out, a recent graduate must recount a past situation that illustrates *how* she is good with people, or one that demonstrates an ability to be a team player.

Fortunately, the *transferable skills* and *professional values* discussed throughout the book are just as helpful for getting your foot on the ladder as they are for increasing your employability and aiding your climb to the top.

It isn't necessary to have snap answers ready for every question, and you never will. It is more important for you to pause after a question and collect your thoughts before answering: That pause shows that you think before you speak, an admired trait in the professional world. Remember that critical thinking is one of the transferable skills.

Asking for a question to be repeated is useful to gain time and is quite acceptable, as long as you don't do it with every question. And if a question stumps you, as sometimes happens, do not stutter incoherently. It is sometimes best to say, "I don't know" or, "I'd like to come back to that later." Odds are the interviewer will forget to ask again; if he does come back to it, at least your mind, processing in the background, has had some time to come up with an answer.

The following questions are commonly asked of entry-level professionals, but these are not the only questions you will be asked, so you will still need to study the other chapters on turning interviews into offers. For example, the first two questions you are likely to face at most of the job interviews you go to over your entire career are likely to be "Tell me a little about yourself" and "What do you know about our company?" The questions in this chapter are just those aimed exclusively at entry-level professionals.

How did you get your summer jobs?

Employers look favorably on recent graduates who have any work experience, no matter what it is. "It is far easier to get a fix on someone who has worked while at school," says Dan O'Brien, head of employment at Grumman. "They manage their time better, are more realistic, and more mature. Any work experience gives us much more in common." So, as you think about some of those crummy jobs you held, take the time to think, in hindsight, about what you actually learned about the professional world from that experience. At the very least you learned that business is about making a profit, doing things more efficiently, adhering to *systems and procedures* (which are always there for good reason), and putting in whatever effort it takes to get the job done. In short, treat your summer jobs, no matter how humble, as a launch pad for greater things. Someone wisely said that it's not the job that defines you, it's what you bring to the job.

In this particular question, the interviewer is looking for something that shows initiative, creativity, and flexibility. Here's an example: "In my town, summer jobs were hard to come by, but I applied to each local restaurant for a position waiting tables, called the manager at each one to arrange an interview, and finally landed a job at one of the most prestigious. I was assigned to the afternoon shift, but because of my quick work, accurate billing, and ability to keep customers happy, they soon moved me to the evening shift. I worked there for three summers, and by the time I left, I was responsible for the training and management of the night-shift waiters, the allotment of tips, and the evening's final closing and accounting. All in all, my experience showed me the mechanics of a small business and of business in general."

Which of the jobs you have held have you liked least?

It is likely that your work experience contained a certain amount of repetition and drudgery, as all early jobs in the business world do. So beware of saying that you hated a particular job "because it was boring." You'll also be knocked out of the running if your "least liked" match up with the job's "most critical."

The job you liked least or what you liked least about a job, and how you express it, speaks of your willingness to take the ups and the downs that go with every job. Put your answer in the past; perhaps, "Burger King—hated smelling of french fries . . . ." Then show that you learned, too. "When you get involved, there's always something to learn. I learned that . . . ." End by moving the conversation forward, "Every job I've held has given me new insights into my profession. All of my jobs had their good and bad points, but I've always found that if you want to learn, there's plenty to pick up every day. Each experience was valuable."

What are your future vocational plans?

This is a fancy way of asking, "Where do you want to be five years from now?" The mistake all entry-level professionals make is to say, "In management," because they think that shows drive and ambition. It has become such a trite answer, though, that it immediately generates a string of questions most recent graduates can't answer: What is a manager's job? What is a manager's prime responsibility? A manager in what area? Your safest answer identifies you with the profession you are trying to break into and shows you have your feet on the ground: "I want to get ahead, and to do that I must be able to channel my energies and expertise into those areas that my industry and employer need. So in a couple of years I hope to have become a thorough professional with a clear understanding of the company, the industry, and where the biggest challenges and opportunities lie within my area of expertise. By that time, my goals for the future should be more sharply defined." An answer like that will set you far apart from your contemporaries.

What college did you attend, and why did you choose it?

The college you attended isn't as important as your reasons for choosing it—the question is trying to examine your reasoning processes. Emphasize that it was your choice, and that you didn't go there as a result of your parents' desires or because generations of your family have always attended the Acme School of Welding. Focus on the practical: "I went to Greenbriar State—it was a choice based on practicality. I wanted a school that would give me a good education and prepare me for the real world. State has a good record for turning out students fully prepared to take on responsibilities in the real world. It is [or isn't] a big school, and [or but] it has certainly taught me some big lessons about the value of [*transferable skills* and *professional values*] in the real world of business."

Are you looking for a permanent or temporary job?

This question is often asked of young candidates. The interviewer wants reassurance that you are genuinely interested in the position and won't disappear in a few months. Go beyond saying, "Permanent." Explain why you want the job: "Of course, I am looking for a permanent job. I intend to make my career in this field, and I want the opportunity to learn the business, face new challenges, and learn from experienced professionals like you." You will also want to qualify the question with one of your own: "Is this a permanent or a temporary position you are trying to fill?" Don't be scared to ask. The occasional unscrupulous employer will hire someone fresh out of school for a short period of time—say, for one particular project—then lay him off.

How did you pay for college?

Avoid saying, "Oh, Daddy handled all of that." Your parents may have helped you out, but if you can, emphasize that you worked part-time as much as you could. People who paid for their own education make big points with employers, because it shows *motivation*, and the experience always delivers a better grasp of the professional world. If this isn't you, find and listen to someone who can tell you what working in the professional world teaches you, and use the knowledge.

We have tried to hire people from your school/your major before, and they never seem to work out. What makes you different?

This question examines your poise under pressure and *critical thinking skills*. It's often asked of candidates for sales jobs, where pressure situations have you thinking on your feet. However, you can't answer this question without more information. Respond this way: "First, may I ask you exactly what problems you've had with people from this school/background?" Once you know what the problem is (if one really exists at all—it may just be a curve ball to test your poise), you can illustrate how you are different—but only then. Otherwise, you run the risk of your answer being interrupted with, "Well, that's what everyone else said before I hired them. You haven't shown me you are different."

I'd be interested to hear about some things you learned in school that could be used on the job.

This question is most likely for entry-level candidates. The interviewer wants to hear about "real-world" skills, so explain what the experience of college taught you about your profession and the professional world, rather than specific courses. You can use internships and any work experience to illustrate your points.

If you look back at college you can find examples in every activity that gave you the opportunity to develop *transferable skills* and *professional values*. Your answer might say, in part, "Within academic and other on-campus activities I always looked for the opportunity to apply and develop some of the practical skills demanded in the professional world, such as _____."

Do you like routine tasks/regular hours?

The interviewer knows from bitter experience that most recent graduates hate routine and are hopeless as employees until they come to an acceptance of such facts of life. Explain that, yes, you appreciate the need for routine, you expect a fair amount of routine assignments before you are entrusted with the more responsible ones, and that the routine and the repetitive always have a role in even the most creative of jobs. As far as regular hours go you could say, "No, there's no problem there. A company expects to make a profit, so the doors have to be open for business on a regular basis."

What have you done that shows initiative and willingness to work?

You can tell a story about how you landed or created a job for yourself, or got involved in some volunteer work. Your answer should show that you both handled unexpected problems calmly and anticipated others. Your motivation is demonstrated by the ways you overcame obstacles. For example: "I worked for a summer in a small warehouse. I found out that a large shipment was due in a couple of weeks, and I knew that room had to be made. The inventory system was outdated, and the rear of the warehouse was disorganized, so I came in on a Saturday, figured out how much room I needed, cleaned up the mess in the rear, and cataloged it all on the new inventory forms. When the shipment arrived, the truck just backed in. There was even room to spare."

After your illustration, recap with something similar to, "I stick with my *commitments*. I am invested in doing good work and commit whatever time and effort is necessary to finish tasks properly, because I know other people's productivity depends on all aspects of my work being done properly."

Often after an effort above and beyond the call of duty, a manager might congratulate you, and if it happened to you in this instance, you might conclude your answer with the verbal endorsement: "The divisional manager happened along just when I was finishing the job and said she wished she had more people who took such pride in their work."

Can you take instructions without feeling upset or hurt?

This is a manageability question. If you take offense easily or bristle when your mistakes are pointed out, you won't last long with any company. Competition is fierce at the entry level, so take this as another chance to set yourself apart: "Yes, I can take instruction—and more important, I can take constructive criticism without feeling hurt. Even with the best intent, I will still make mistakes, and at times someone will have to put me back on the right track. I know that if I'm ever to rise in the company, I must first prove myself to be manageable."

Have you ever had difficulties getting along with others?

This question examines your people skills and manageability. Are you a *team player*, or are you going to disrupt the department and make the manager's life miserable?

You can give a yes-or-no answer and shut up, but if you think through what you are going to say, your answer can also say something about your *professional values*. In this case, you say that that there are two types in every department: the type that is engaged and committed to peak performance every day, and the type that does his job but without the same level of *commitment*. You can and do get on with everyone, but tend to bond more with the people who take a genuine *pride* in becoming their best.

What type of position are you interested in?

Another entry-level question that tempts you to mention management. Tell the interviewer you are interested in an entry-level job, which is what you will be offered anyway. "I am interested in an entry-level position that will enable me to learn this business from the ground up and will give me the opportunity to grow professionally when and as I prove myself."

What qualifications do you have that will make you successful in this field?

There is more to answering this question than reeling off your academic qualifications. In addition you will want to stress relevant work experience and address the *transferable skills* and *professional values* you are developing as they relate to the target job. It's a wide-open question that says, "Hey, we're looking for an excuse to hire you. Give us some help."

Why do you think you would like this type of work?

This is a deceptive question because there is no pat answer. It is usually asked to see whether you really understand what the specific job entails on a day-to-day basis. To answer it requires you to have researched the company and job functions carefully, as suggested earlier in the book. One of those suggestions was to network with people already in the profession engaged in exactly this target job. Ask what the job is like and what that person does day to day. How does the job fit into the department? What contribution does it make to the overall efforts of the company? Why does she like that type of work? Armed with that information, you will show that you understand what you are getting into; most recent graduates do not.

What's your idea of how this industry works?

The interviewer does not want a dissertation, just the reassurance that you don't think this company and the business world in general work along the same lines as a registered charity. Your understanding should be something like this: "The role of any company is to make as much money as possible, as quickly and efficiently as possible, and in a manner that will encourage repeat business from the existing client base and new business from word of mouth and reputation." Finish with the observation that it is every employee's role as a team member to help achieve those goals: "I am a small but important cog within this moneymaking machinery. I need to mesh well with the other cogs in my department so that we can collectively deliver on the department's responsibilities. On an individual basis my job is to enhance productivity and profitability by the timely identification, anticipation, prevention, and solution of the problems that arise within my areas of professional expertise."

Why do you think this industry will sustain your interest over the long haul? Or, Why do you think you will shine in this profession?

Your answer should speak both to your pragmatism and to your motivation. "At this point in my career, I am looking at the industry because I believe it offers stability and professional growth potential over the years [*explain why*]. Also, I'll be using skills [*itemize strong skill sets that are relevant to the job*] that are areas of strength, from which I derive great personal satisfaction."

What do you think determines progress in a good company?

Your answer will include a selection of *transferable skills* and *professional values* that are relevant to success in every company and profession. Begin with each of the technical skills you know are required to do the job, then follow with each of the other *transferable skills* that help you to do the job well. Finish with reference to the *professional values* of integrity, commitment, a willingness to play by the rules, the ability to take the rough with the smooth, and the good fortune to have a manager who wants you to succeed.

Do you think grades should be considered by first employers?

If your grades were good, the answer is obviously "yes." If they weren't, your answer needs a little more thought: "Of course, an employer should take everything into consideration. Along with grades there should be an evaluation of real *motivation* and manageability, an understanding of how business works, and actual work experience; plus, the best academics don't always make the most productive professionals. Einstein and Edison, two of the most intellectually and economically productive minds of modern times, had terrible academic records."

Many candidates are called for entry-level interviews, but only those who prepare themselves with an understanding of their target jobs will be chosen. Preparation takes time, so don't leave preparing for them until the last minute. You are taking a new product to market. Accordingly, you've got to analyze what it can do, who is likely to be interested, and how you are going to sell it to them. Start now and hone your skills to get a head start on your peers; you'll get more interviews, and the more you interview, the better you'll get.

CHAPTER 18
STRANGE VENUES FOR JOB INTERVIEWS

LEARN THE TIPS that will help you master interviews in noisy, distracting hotel lobbies, restaurants, at poolside, and in other unusual settings.

Why are some interviews conducted in strange places? Are meetings in noisy, distracting hotel lobbies designed as a form of torture? What are the real reasons that an interviewer invites you to eat at a fancy restaurant?

For the most part, these tough-on-the-nerves situations happen because the interviewer is a busy person, fitting you into a busy schedule. A woman I know had heard stories about tough interview situations but never expected to face one herself. It happened at a retail convention in Arizona, to which she had been asked for a final interview. The interview was conducted by the pool. The interviewer was there, taking a short break between meetings, in his bathing suit. The first thing the interviewer did was suggest that my friend slip into something comfortable.

That scenario may not lurk in your future, but the chances are you will face many tough interview situations in your career. They call for a clear head and a little gamesmanship if you want to stay ahead of the competition. The interviewee at the pool used both. She removed her jacket, folded it over the arm of the chair, and seated herself, saying pleasantly, "That's much better. Where shall we begin?"

It isn't easy to remain calm at such times. On top of interview nerves, you're worried about being overheard in a public place, or (worse) surprised by the appearance of your current boss. That last item isn't too far-fetched. It actually happened to a reader from San Francisco. He was being interviewed in the departure lounge at the airport when his boss walked through the arrivals door. Oops—he had asked for the day off "to go to the doctor."

Could he have avoided the situation? Certainly, if he had asked about privacy when the meeting was arranged. That would have reminded the interviewer of the need for discretion. The point is to do all you can in advance to make such a meeting as private as possible. Once that's done, you can ignore the rest of the world and concentrate on the interviewer's questions.

Hotel Lobbies and Other Strange Places

Strange interview situations provide other wonderful opportunities to embarrass yourself. You come to a hotel lobby in full corporate battle dress: coat, briefcase, perhaps an umbrella. You sit down to wait for the interviewer. "Aha," you think to yourself, opening your briefcase, "I'll show him my excellent work habits by delving into this computer printout."

That's not such a great idea. Have you ever tried rising with your lap covered with business papers, then juggling the briefcase from right hand to left to accommodate the ritual handshake? It's quite difficult. Besides, while you are sitting in nervous anticipation, pre-interview tension has no way of dissipating. Your mouth will become dry, and your "Good morning, I'm pleased to meet you" will come out sounding like a cat being strangled.

To avoid such catastrophes in places like hotel lobbies, first remove your coat on arrival. Instead of sitting, walk around a little while you wait. Even in a small lobby, a few steps back and forth will help you reduce tension to a manageable level. Keep your briefcase in your left hand (unless you are a leftie) at all times—it makes you look purposeful, and you won't trip over it when you meet the interviewer.

If for any reason you must sit, breathe deeply and slowly. This will help control the adrenaline that makes you feel jumpy.

A strange setting can actually put you on an equal footing with the interviewer. Neither of you is on home turf, so in many cases the interviewer will feel just as awkward as you do. A little gamesmanship can turn the occasion to your advantage.

To gain the upper hand, get to the meeting site early to scout the territory. By knowing your surroundings, you will feel more relaxed. Early arrival also allows you to control the outcome of the meeting in other subtle ways. You will have time to stake out the most private spot in an otherwise public place. Corners are best. They tend to be quieter, and you can choose the seat that puts your back to the wall (in a physical sense, that is). In this position, you have a clear view of your surroundings and will feel more secure. The fear of being overheard will evaporate.

The situation is now somewhat in your favor. You know the locale, and the meeting place is as much yours as the interviewer's. You will have a clear view of your surroundings, and odds are that you will be more relaxed than the interviewer. When she arrives, say, "I arrived a little early to make sure we had some privacy. I think over here is the best spot." With that positive demonstration of your organizational abilities, you give yourself a head start over the competition.

The Meal Meeting

Breakfast, lunch, and dinner are the prime choices for interviewers who want to catch the seasoned professional off guard. In fact, the meal is arguably the toughest of all tough interview situations. The setting offers the interviewer the chance to see you in a nonoffice (and therefore more natural) setting, to observe your social graces, and to consider you as a whole person. Here, topics that would be impossible to address in the traditional office setting will surface, often with virtually no effort on the part of the interviewer. The slightest slip in front of that wily old pirate—thinly disguised in a Brooks Brothers suit—could get your candidacy deep-sixed in a hurry.

Usually you will not be invited to a "meal meeting" until you have already demonstrated that you are capable of doing the job. An invitation to a meal means that you are under strong consideration, and therefore intense scrutiny.

This meeting is often the final hurdle and could lead directly to the job offer—assuming that you properly handle the occasional surprises that arise. The interviewer's concern is not whether you can do the job but whether you have the growth potential that will allow you to fill more senior slots as they become available.

But be careful. Many have fallen at the final hurdle in a close-run race. Being interviewed in front of others is bad enough; eating and drinking in front of them at the same time only makes it worse. If you knock over a glass or dribble spaghetti sauce down your chin, the interviewer will be so busy smirking that he won't hear what you have to say.

To be sure that he remains as attentive to the positive points of your candidacy as possible, let's discuss table manners.

Your social graces and general demeanor at the table can tell as much about you as your answer to a question. For instance, over-ordering food or drink can signal poor self-discipline. At the very least, it will call into question your judgment and maturity. High-handed behavior toward waiters and busboys could reflect negatively on your ability to get along with subordinates and on your *leadership skills*. Those concerns are amplified when you return food or complain about the service, actions which, at the very least, find fault with the interviewer's choice of restaurant.

By the same token, you will want to observe how your potential employer behaves. After all, you are likely to become an employee, and the interviewer's behavior to servers in a restaurant can tell you a lot about what it will be like on the job.

- **Alcohol:** Soon after being seated, you will be offered a drink—if not by your host, then by the waiter. There are many reasons to avoid alcohol at interview meals. The most important reason is that alcohol fuzzes your mind, and research proves that stress increases the intoxicating effect of alcohol. So, if you order something to drink, stick with something nonalcoholic, such as a club soda, Coke, or Pepsi, or simply a glass of water.
  If you do have a drink, never have more than one. If there is a bottle of wine on the table, and the waiter offers you another glass, place your hand over the top of your glass. It is a polite way of signifying no.
  You may be offered alcohol at the end of the meal. The rule still holds true—turn it down. You need your wits about you even if the interview seems to be drawing to a close. Some interviewers will try to use those moments, when your defenses are at their lowest, to throw in a couple of zingers.
- **Smoking:** Don't smoke unless encouraged. If both of you are smokers, and you are encouraged to smoke, never smoke between courses, only at the end of a meal. Even most confirmed nicotine addicts, like the rest of the population, hate smoke while they are eating.
- **Utensils:** Keep all your cups and glasses at the top of your place setting and well away from you. Glasses are knocked over at a cluttered table most often when one stretches for the condiments or gesticulates to make a point.

Here are some other helpful hints:

- Never speak with your mouth full.
- To be on the safe side, order something that is easy to eat, as you are there for talking, not eating. Of course, while this rule makes sense in theory, you probably will be asked to order first, so ordering the same thing can become problematic. Solve the problem before

you order by complimenting the restaurant during your small talk and then, when the menus arrive, asking, "What do you think you will have today?"

- Do not change your order once it is made, and never send the food back.
- Be polite to your waiters, even when they spill soup in your lap.
- Don't order expensive food. Naturally, in our heart of hearts, we all like to eat well, especially on someone else's tab. But don't be tempted. When you come right down to it, you are there to talk and be seen at your best, not to eat.
- Eat what you know. Stay away from awkward, messy, or exotic foods (e.g., artichokes, long pasta, and escargot, respectively). Ignore finger foods, such as lobster or spare ribs. In fact, you should avoid eating with your fingers altogether, unless you are in a sandwich joint, in which case you should make a point of avoiding the leaky, overstuffed menu items.
- Don't order salad. The dressing can often get messy. If a salad comes with the meal, request that the dressing be on the side. Then, before pouring it on, cut up the lettuce.
- Don't order anything with bones. Stick with fillets; there are few simple, gracious ways to deal with any type of bone.
- Checks and Goodbyes: I know an interviewer whose favorite test of composure is to have the waiter, by arrangement, put the bill on the interviewee's side of the table. She then chats on, waiting for something interesting to happen. If you ever find yourself in a similar situation, never pick up the check, however long it is left by your plate. When ready, your host will pick it up, because that's the protocol of the occasion. By the same token, you should never offer to share payment.

When parting company, always thank the host for her hospitality and the wonderful meal. Of course, you should be sure to leave on a positive note by asking good-naturedly what you have to do to get the job.

Strange interview situations can arise at any time during the interview cycle, and in any public place. Wherever you are asked to go, keep your guard up. Your table manners, listening skills, and overall social graces are being judged. The question on the interviewer's mind is: Can you be trusted to represent the company gracefully and with a professional demeanor?

CHAPTER 19
HOW TO ACE THE PSYCHOLOGICAL TESTS

CAREFUL! ANSWERING THESE questions casually can be hazardous to your professional health.

In late 1989, Congress banned most private-sector applications of the polygraph test, voice-stress analysis, and other electronic screening methods. While many government personnel (for instance, those involved in drug interdiction activities) are still subject to these tests, many private employers have had to change their ways, and are increasingly turning to psychological testing to weed out what they consider to be undesirable job applicants. These tests may be known as aptitude tests; personality profiles; personnel selection tests; or skills, aptitude, and integrity tests, but in the end they are all the same thing: an attempt to find out if you show signs of being a "risky" hire.

Although the 1989 legislation led to new popularity for psychological tests, they have been around for decades. Psychological exams come in two flavors. One is a face-to-face meeting with a psychologist, and the other (far more common) is a written test, often multiple choice.

In any discussion of this issue, we should bear in mind that psychology is, by the admission of its own practitioners, an inexact science, and that few of the tests used in employee selection were designed for that purpose. While these tests cannot be regarded as a definitive litmus test of your potential employability, many companies are grafting the imprecise discipline of psychological testing onto the equally imprecise one of employment selection. The result is cheap and easy to administer. Those seeking employment are often asked to answer "a few routine questions" that end up being anything but routine. The tests, which should not be used as the sole basis for a hiring decision, are nevertheless often used in a pass-or-fail way and have a huge effect on people's livelihoods. In your case, let's do everything we can to make sure they don't have a negative effect on your job prospects.

It isn't surprising that many of the companies using the tests are concerned about the honesty of prospective employees. Each year, American industry loses an estimated $40 billion from employee theft. While honesty is often one of the behavioral profiles examined, the tests can also examine aptitude and suitability for a position. Often, the exams are geared toward evaluating the amount of energy a person might bring to the job; how he or she would handle stress; and what his or her attitudes toward job, peers, and management would be.

Unfortunately, answering a psychological test with complete personal honesty may very well threaten your chance of being offered employment. That's the bad news. Here's the good news: You can ace the tests without having to compromise your personal integrity.

Not long ago, I did an in-house employee selection and motivation seminar for a large corporation. When asked for my opinion on the subject of psychological testing, I replied the tests were often used inappropriately as a pass-or-fail criterion for hiring, and anyone with half a brain could come up with the desired or correct answers. "The question is," I concluded, "how many people who could have served you well will you miss out on because of a test?"

The managers assured me they had a test that was "virtually infallible" in helping to identify strong hires and certainly not subject to the machinations of the average applicant. They asked if I would be prepared to take it. I not only agreed but also promised to prove my point. "Let me take the test twice," I said. "The first profile you get will tell you to hire me; the second will say I'm a bad risk."

I took the test twice that day. "Applicant #1" came back with a strong recommendation for hire. "Applicant #2" came back with a warning to exercise caution. How was this possible? Well, none of us is the same person in the workplace as in our personal life. Over a period of time at work, we come to understand the need for different behavioral patterns and different ways of interacting with people.

Sometimes our more considered, analytical, and logical approaches pass over from our "professional self" into the personal realm. However, in the world of work, we are not expected to override the "corporate way" to do things according to our personal preferences. When this happens, and personal preferences take precedence over existing corporate theories of behavior, we get warnings and terminations. In other words, as professionals, we are inculcated with a set of behavioral patterns that enable us to be successful and productive for our employers.

Did I really "fool" the test? No. I was completely honest both times. The "winning" test was the one in which I viewed myself—and, thus, described myself—as a thoroughly professional white-collar worker in the job for which I was applying. The "losing" test was the one I used to describe myself as the kind of person I see myself as in my personal life.

This was not a hoax perpetrated by a smart aleck. I am that person they would have hired, and I possess a strong track record to back up my claim. I simply learned the behaviors necessary to succeed, adopted them, and made them my own—just as you have undoubtedly done, or are in the process of doing.

Many of the tests lack an awareness of the complexity of the human mind. They seem to miss the point when they ask us to speak honestly about our feelings and beliefs. They do not take into account that our learned behaviors in our professional lives are, invariably, distinct from the behaviors we display in our personal lives.

If you understand what you are likely to face, you can prepare and present yourself in the most effective way, and you can do it without compromising your integrity.

How to Prepare for, Read, and Answer the Tests

There are five different types of tests designed to plumb different aspects of your doubtless troubled psyche:

- Personality
- Personnel selection
- Aptitude
- Skills
- Integrity

Let's take a look at each of these.

Personality Tests

Are you a people person? Do you get upset easily? Are you quick to anger? Employers are using tests of general personality more frequently these days to screen job candidates. They use these tests because they believe that certain personality traits are required for success in a particular position.

There are two basic kinds of personality tests: projective and objective.

Projective Personality Tests. The projective tests ask you to tell a story, finish a sentence, or describe what you see in a blob of ink. These tests, in some form or other, have been around for decades, and psychologists use them a great deal to help understand how we deal with tough issues.

One popular test shows you pictures of a scene and asks you to describe what's going on. The psychologist may ask you to "tell me more about it." These areas of your mind are also accessed through the use of incomplete sentences, where you are given the beginning of a sentence and have to fill in the rest of it on your own. So, for instance, you may be asked to complete a sentence such as "When I am at work, I . . . ."

In an employment-selection context, these tests are generally looking for leaders, achievers, and winners. They search for analytical and system thinking skills, and look at decision-making and consensus-building styles.

Objective Personality Tests. Objective personality tests ask dozens, sometimes hundreds, of questions using some sort of rating scale, like strongly agree to strongly disagree, true-or-false, or yes-or-no. These tests usually have good reliability and validity. They were not designed to be used for employee screening, although they often are.

Knowing the names of the most common tests can tip you off to the type of screening being done. Tests you might run into that screen personality include:

- *NEO Personality Inventory*: measures adjustment, extroversion, openness, agreeability, and conscientiousness
- *16 PF*: measures sixteen personality factors, including a lie scale
- *California Psychological Inventory*: measures twenty personality scales such as empathy, tolerance, responsibility, and dominance. (This is a good personality test, but it can be expensive for an employer, so it isn't used as often as some others.)
- *Minnesota Multiphasic Personality Inventory*: a very long, heavy-duty test of major psychological problems, often (wrongly) used in employee selection

Personnel Selection Tests

Personnel selection tests are personality tests designed specifically to screen job candidates. These tests measure psychological behaviors such as trustworthiness, reliability, and conscientiousness. Some of them also psychologically screen you for potential alcohol or substance abuse. Tests you might run into that examine these areas include:

- Hogan Personality Inventory
- Employee Reliability Inventory
- PDI Employment Inventory

Aptitude Tests

If you don't have the skills it takes to do the job, do you have the aptitude to learn? In a work world where the learning curve for new skill development becomes increasingly interesting to potential employers, we can expect to see the use of aptitude tests on the upswing. Judging your ability to develop skills in general or skills in a particular area is the premise behind these aptitude tests.

- Wechsler Adult Intelligence Scale—Revised
- Raven's Progressive Matrices
- Comprehensive Ability Battery
- Differential Aptitude Tests

Skills Tests

If the job calls for typing seventy-five words per minute, you may be given a typing test. If you are a programmer, you may be asked to take an objective test of programming skills or asked to debug a program. There are tests to measure every possible skill: filing, bookkeeping, mechanical comprehension, specific computer programs, math, credit rating, and so on. Some of them are typical paper-and-pencil written tests. Newer tests present the information using a software program.

It's hard to argue against some of these tests. After all, if the job calls for you to type letters and reports all day, the employer wants to hire the best typist. If you're supposed to use Microsoft Word on the PC all day, the employer will look for the person with the best knowledge of that program. As long as the employer is measuring an important skill, testing skills makes sense.

Integrity Tests

Integrity tests are increasingly popular. Some companies are leery of personality tests, so they turn to integrity tests to screen out liars, cheats, and thieves. Some tests measure honesty, or integrity, whereas others measure other psychological traits.

The problem with these integrity tests is that they don't work. A psychologist wrote that in one case using an integrity test would eliminate 2,721 honest applicants so that 101 potentially dishonest applicants would be denied employment. I should point out that the integrity test itself actually is okay; it's just that so few people actually steal that the use of the test eliminates a heck of a lot of good applicants. Another major study found that 95.6 percent of people who take these tests and get a failing score are actually incorrectly classified!

Here are a couple of integrity tests in consistent use today:

- Personnel Selection Inventory
- Personnel Reaction Bank

So listen carefully and apply what you learn in this chapter so that you don't become an incorrectly classified statistic.

Getting to Know Yourself and Acing the Mind Readers

Born independently wealthy, very few of us would be doing the jobs we do. But we are doing them, and we have learned certain sets of skills and behavioral traits that are critical to our ability to survive and succeed professionally. The first thing you must do, then, is identify and separate the professional you from the personal you.

✎ **Step One:** Never answer a test question from the viewpoint of your innermost beliefs. Instead, use your learned and developed professional behavior traits and modus operandi. Ask yourself, "How has my experience as a professional taught me to think and respond to this?" To do this effectively (and to understand ourselves a little better in the process), we need some further insights into the three critical skill sets that every professional relies on to succeed:

- Professional/technical skills (whether you're a secretary or a senior vice president)
- Industry skills (such as—if you happen to be in banking—your overall knowledge of the world of banking: how things work, how things get done, what is accepted within the industry, and so on)
- Professional behavior traits (the traits, discussed in Chapter 2 of this book, that all employers look for and that will get you ahead once you are on the job)

✎ **Step Two:** Look at yourself from the employer's point of view. Review "The Five Secrets of the Hire" and "The Other Side of the Desk" for some helpful ideas. Evaluate the traits that enable you to discharge your duties effectively. Examine the typical crises/emergencies likely to arise: What supportive behavioral traits are necessary to overcome them? As you do this, you will almost certainly relive some episodes that seemed to put you at a disadvantage for a time. When it was tough to do things the right way, you had to buckle down and see the problem through, even though doing so did not necessarily "come naturally." The fact is, though, you overcame the obstacle. Remember how you did so, and keep that in mind as you answer the questions.

Conversely, you will want to look at those instances where a crisis had a less-than-successful outcome. What traits did you swear you would develop and use for next time?

Highlighting such traits constitutes your acknowledgment of the supremacy of learned behavior in the workplace. It does *not* constitute lying. (Why do you think so many professionals strive to keep their business lives separate from their personal lives? What is the point of such a separation if the two lives are identical?)

✎ **Step Three:** Think of people you've known who have failed on the job. Why did they fail? What have you learned from their mistakes and made a part of the "professional you"?

✎ **Step Four:** Think of people you've known who have succeeded on the job. Why did they succeed? What have you learned from their success and made a part of the "professional you"?

Once you have completed this exercise in detail, you will have determined how a professional would react in a wide range of circumstances and identified the ways in which you have, over time, developed a "professional self" to match that profile.

Getting Ready for the Test

Any test can be nerve-wracking, but when it comes to these tests your livelihood is in the balance, so tip the odds in your favor with these tried and proven techniques:

- The tests instruct you to answer quickly, offering the first response that comes to mind. Don't. Following this path may cost you a job. Instead, look at the test in terms of the exercises outlined above; provide reasoned responses from the viewpoint of the "professional you."
- Time limits are usually not imposed. On the contrary, those administering the test will often begin the proceedings with a soothing "take your time, there's no pressure." (Except, of course, the minor pressure of knowing a job offer is on the line!)
- If there is a time limit, find out how much time you have. Figure out about how much time per question or section you have. Pacing yourself helps, because you won't panic when you realize you've only got five minutes to complete the second half of a fifteen-minute test. Of course, you'll bring your watch.
- When in doubt, guess. Some of the really sophisticated tests you may have taken to get into college nailed you if you guessed wrong, but skill tests usually work differently. They

add up all your right answers to get your test score. So, when in doubt, eliminate any of the obviously wrong answers, and take your best shot.

- With skill tests, ask for a warm-up or practice section. One computer-typing test has an optional practice session. Ask about it. If the test is on a computer, adjust your chair, keyboard, and monitor before the timer starts.
- For paper and pencil tests, make sure you have enough desk space and sharp pencils.
- If the test is going to be done with other applicants in a group situation, stay focused on what you are doing. If you have to sit in the front of the room so no one else distracts you, do it. If the test will be long and there's no break, make sure you won't get hungry (take a power bar) or have to use the bathroom.
- No matter what, use all your allotted time! Check your answers, and make sure they are written in the right places. Depending on your remaining time, review every other, or every fourth, question. Of course, if you can recall at the end which questions you were unsure about, review those first.
- You may not even realize you're taking an integrity test until the direction of the questions gives it away: "Have you ever stolen anything?" "Have you ever felt guilty?" "Have you ever told a lie?" Avoid the temptation to respond impulsively with something like "Lies? No, I prefer to chop down the damned cherry tree." The truth is, we have all done these things in our lives. When you are asked, for instance, whether there is anything you would ever change about yourself, or whether you think everyone is dishonest to some degree, the overwhelming likelihood is that your own honesty is being tested: The best answer is probably "yes."

In fact, if you never admit to these behaviors, you could be pegged as a faker. While fakers may be kept in the running, they've earned a question mark. Fakers are sometimes viewed as being eager to please or simply a bit out of touch with their true feelings.

Many of the better tests in use today also use lie scales that can detect when someone is faking. How do they do this? One way is to include questions like "I always tell the truth" or "I never have a negative thought about a coworker." When the test is developed, hundreds or thousands of people take it, and the researchers figure out what the typical response is to these questions. Anyone who deviates from the average response on enough of these faking questions is also flagged as a faker.

If you must answer questions about ethics in a face-to-face encounter, explain your answer, placing it far in the past where appropriate, and explain what you have learned from any negative experience. If such questions must be answered on paper, the best approach is to follow the dictates of your own conscience and try to bring the issue up after the test. You might say something like this:

"Gee, that question about lying was a tough one. I guess everyone has told a lie at some time in the past, and I wanted to be truthful, so I said 'yes.' But I'd be lying if I didn't tell you it made me nervous. You know, I saw a show on television recently about these tests. It told the story of someone

who lost a job because of answering a question just like that; the profile came back with an untrustworthy rating."

This may reduce the odds of your being denied the job in the same way. If the test does come back with a question about your honesty, you will at least have sown seeds of doubt about the validity of such a rating in the interviewer's mind. That doubt, and your disarming honesty, might just turn the tables in your favor.

Be careful, and take a balanced approach as you answer integrity test questions. Honesty is the best policy:

- In a face-to-face meeting with a psychologist, use the same techniques we have discussed throughout *Knock 'em Dead* to qualify the questions before answering them; when you suspect a trap, employ the tricks that will help you clarify things and buy time.
- The written tests may contain "double blinds," where you are asked a question on page 1, and then asked a virtually identical one thirty or forty questions later. The technique is based on the belief that most of us can tell a lie, but few of us can remember that lie under stress, and are therefore likely to answer differently later. This is held to show the potential for untruthfulness. The problem isn't that one answer is likely to deny you employment; the questions are asked in patterns to evaluate your behavior and attitudes on different topics.
- Read the test through before you start answering questions! (There's "plenty of time" and "no pressure," remember?) Review the material at least three times, mentally flagging the questions that seem similar. This way you will be able to answer consistently.
- Resist any temptation to project an image of yourself as an interesting person. These tests are not designed to reward eccentricity; think sliced white bread. You are happy at work and home. You enjoy being around people. You don't spend all your evenings watching movies. You don't spend your weekends with a computer or pursuing other solitary pastimes (unless you are a programmer or an aspiring Trappist monk). You have beliefs, but not too strong. You respect the beliefs of all others, regardless of their age, sex, race, or religion.
- Relax. One part of the Wechsler test (a developmental aptitude test) asks you to repeat back a string of numbers to the psychologist. If you're too hyped up, you'll get flustered and blow it. These tests measure intelligence plus your test-taking behavior. And you can certainly improve your test-taking behavior!
- Learn to visualize success in advance. Picture yourself at the test. Go through each step: You hear the instructions, the examiner says to begin. You read the test questions and realize you will do well. You get to a really tough part of the test. Visualize your success, and visualize your setbacks. Realize that you can and you will pull through okay because you have a clear vision of the professional you. When you finish the test, read through your answers a few times. If you don't like any answers, change them.
- Remember to use your professional, working mindset when you take these tests. Answer as you would if you were on the job and your boss were asking the questions.

◆ ◆ ◆

Everything I have said here takes for granted that the overriding goal of the employer is to determine whether or not you are suitable for the job. If you can give an accurate, affirmative answer to that question, the approach you take in doing so is—to my way of thinking—of little consequence. If you have learned and applied what it takes to prosper in your profession, it is your right to provide an honest profile of your professional self, in whatever forum you are to be evaluated.

CHAPTER 20
THE GRACEFUL EXIT

TO PARAPHRASE SHAKESPEARE, all the working world's a stage. Curtains rise and fall, and your powerful performance must be capped with a professional and memorable exit. To ensure that you leave the right impression, this chapter will review the dos and don'ts of leaving an interview.

A signal that the interview is drawing to a close comes when you are asked whether you have any questions. Ask questions, and by doing so, highlight your strengths and show your enthusiasm. Remember, your goal at the interview is to generate a job offer. Make sure your exit is as graceful as your entrance.

Dos:

1. *Ask appropriate job-related questions.* When the opportunity comes to ask any final questions, review your notes. Bring up any relevant strengths that haven't been addressed.

2. *Show decisiveness.* If you are offered the job, react with enthusiasm. Then sleep on it. If it's possible to do so without making a formal acceptance, lock the job up now and put yourself in control; you can always change your mind later. Before making any commitment with regard to compensation, see Chapter 22, "Negotiating the Job Offer."

3. *When more than one person interviews you, be sure you have the correct spellings of their names.* "I enjoyed meeting your colleagues, Ms. Smith. Could you give me the correct spellings of their names, please?" This question will give you the names you forgot in the heat of battle and will demonstrate your consideration.

4. *Review the job's requirements with the interviewer.* Match them point-by-point with your skills and attributes.

5. *Find out whether this is the only interview.* If so, you must ask for the job in a positive and enthusiastic manner. Find out the time frame for a decision and finish with, "I am very enthusiastic about the job and the contributions I can make. If your decision will be made by the fifteenth, what must I do in the meantime to ensure I get the job?"

6. *Ask for the next interview.* When there are subsequent interviews in the hiring procedure, ask for the next interview in the same honest and forthright manner: "Is now a good time to schedule our next meeting?"

7. *Keep yourself in contention.* A good leading question to ask is, "Until I hear from you again, what particular aspects of the job and this interview should I be considering?"

8. *Always depart in the same polite and assured manner in which you entered.* Look the interviewer in the eye, put on a smile (there's no need to grin), give a firm handshake, and say, "This has been an exciting meeting for me. This is a job I can do, and I feel I can contribute to your goals, because the atmosphere here seems conducive to doing my very best work. When will we speak again?"

Don'ts:

1. *Don't discuss salary, vacation, or benefits.* It is not that the questions are invalid, just that the timing is wrong. Bringing up such topics before you have an offer is asking what the company can do for you—instead, you should be saying what you can do for the company. Those topics are part of the negotiation (handled in Chapter 22, "Negotiating the Job Offer"); remember, without an offer you have nothing to negotiate.

2. *Don't press for an early decision.* Of course, you should ask, "When will I know your decision?" But don't press it. Don't try to use the "other opportunities I have to con-

sider" gambit as leverage when no such offers exist—that annoys the interviewer, makes you look foolish, and may even force you to negotiate from a position of weakness. Timing is everything; the issue of how to handle other opportunities as leverage is explored in detail later.

3. *Don't show discouragement.* Sometimes a job offer can occur on the spot. Usually it does not. So don't show discouragement if you are not offered the job at the interview, because discouragement shows a lack of self-esteem and determination. Avoiding a bad impression is the foundation of leaving a good one, and the right image to leave is one of enthusiasm, guts, and openness—just the professional behaviors you have been projecting throughout the interview.

4. *Don't ask for an evaluation of your interview performance.* That forces the issue and puts the interviewer in an awkward position. You can say that you want the job, and ask what you have to do to get it.

PART IV
FINISHING TOUCHES

ONCE THE JOB interview is over, you move on to the next step in the process for securing job offers. You are never the only qualified candidate for a job, and the better the job, the stiffer your competition is likely to be. On top of this, interviewers expect that a candidate who is interested in the job will make an effort to follow up on the interview in a professional manner.

THE SUCCESSFUL COMPLETION of every interview is a big stride toward getting job offers, yet it is not the end of your job search. Following up after your interviews isn't being needy, it is being professional.

A company rarely hires the first competent person it sees. A hiring manager will sometimes interview as many as fifteen people for a particular job, but the strain and pace of conducting interviews naturally dim the memory of each applicant. Unless you are the last person to be interviewed, the impression you make will fade with each subsequent interview the interviewer undertakes. And if you are not remembered, you will not be offered the job. You must develop a strategy to keep your name and skills constantly in the forefront of the interviewer's mind. These finishing touches often make all the difference.

Some of the suggestions here may not seem earth-shattering: just simple, sensible demonstrations of your manners, enthusiasm, and determination. But remember that today all employers are looking for people with that extra little something. You can avoid a negative or merely indifferent impression, and be certain of creating a positive one, by following these guidelines.

CHAPTER 21
OUT OF SIGHT CAN MEAN OUT OF MIND

YOU LEAVE YOUR interviewers with a strong, positive image and don't want that memory to slip with the passage of time and a busy schedule. But out of sight means out of mind, and out of mind means out of the job offer race, so following up with your interviewers shows that you pay attention to detail and are enthusiastic about the job. The longer the decision-making period, the less distinct candidates become from each other in the hiring manager's memory.

The first thing you do on leaving the interview is breathe a sigh of relief. The second is make sure that "out of sight, out of mind" will not apply to you. You do this by starting a follow-up procedure immediately after the interview: Sitting in your car, on the bus, train, or plane, write a recap of the interview while it's still fresh in your mind.

This information will help with your follow-up with this company, and reviewing all your follow-up notes after two or three interviews may alert you to a weakness you hadn't noticed. Make notes on these categories:

- Who did you meet? What were their titles and e-mail addresses?
- What did you find out about the job?
- What are its first projects/challenges?
- Why can you do the job? What are the problems?
- What did the interviewer say on any topic related to the job, company, competition, industry, or profession that might give you a unique follow-up were you to Google something interesting?
- What aspects of the interview went well? Why?
- What aspects of the interview went poorly? Why?
- What did the interviewer say was the next step?
- Are there other candidates in contention?
- When will a decision be made?
- What did the interviewer say in concluding the interview?

KNOCK 'EM DEAD TIP
Identify aspects of your interview that went poorly. A person does not get offered a job based solely on strengths; those questions will be easy enough for you to answer. On the other hand, you may get that job offer based on your lack of negatives compared to the other candidates. It is important to identify any negatives from your performance so that you can overcome them in your follow-up and during subsequent interviews.

Using the information gathered from this exercise, you can begin a follow-up campaign. Knowing if there is another round of interviews or if the decision is going to be made tomorrow afternoon or next week has a significant impact on how and when you will follow up.

Follow-Up Steps and Pacing

Knowing where you are in the selection cycle will help you execute a well-paced follow-up campaign. We'll start with a follow-up after the first interview in a series.

After the First Interview in a Series

Informal First Follow-Up Within Twenty-Four Hours

If you can find something interesting related to the job, company, competition, industry, or profession, your first follow-up will be professional-casual, reinforcing the tone of an ongoing conversation between two professionals with a common interest. You'll send an e-mail that opens with a salutation: "Hi John/Jane," if you are close enough in years and experience to use first names. If you are younger and have been encouraged to use first names, that's okay too, but reverting to the formalities of Mr./Ms. in written communication (until after the second meeting), will usually be received as respectful and flattering. If use of first names hasn't been encouraged, don't presume: It won't win you points, while showing professional courtesies always does.

Note the short, punchy, conversational tone of this sample follow-up e-mail; it is considerably more casual and direct than traditional follow-up letters:

"It was great to meet you this afternoon. I really enjoyed talking about the _____ position. Your comments/our conversation on _____ [*the topic of your attachment, or what you paste into the body copy*] has been buzzing in the back of my mind all day. I just ran across this and knew you'd enjoy it. On a deadline, so I'll follow up properly as soon as my schedule permits."

Send the e-mail between 7 P.M. and 10 P.M. that evening or early the next morning when you first get up, whichever is closer to the limits of the twenty-four-hour mark. Do not send an e-mail during business hours.

Your first meeting will have tagged you as someone different. This initial follow-up aims to continue the differentiation. The tone is respectful, and shows a committed professional working late (you can't write fully because you are working on a deadline) and being *intelligently enthusiastic* (you are actively engaged in thinking about this job and your profession outside of business hours).

Formal First Follow-Up

Your formal first follow-up should arrive two to no later than three days after the first interview, *or* after your first *informal* follow-up; adjusting your timing to the needs of each separate selection cycle. This formal follow-up letter should make the following points:

- The date and time you met with the interviewer and the title of the target job
- You paid attention to what was said in the interview
- Why you can do the job
- You are excited about the job and want it
- You have the experience to contribute to those first major projects as discussed in the interview

Here are some ideas and phrases you'll find useful:

- Appreciation: "I enjoyed meeting you to discuss . . . ." Professional etiquette requires you express appreciation for the interview; remember to identify the date and time you met and the job you interviewed for.
- Recognition: "I recognize the importance of . . . ."
- Observation: "Listening to the points you made . . . ."
- Motivation: "I am excited about the job . . . ." Let the interviewer catch your enthusiasm and see that you are motivated by the opportunity. This is very effective, especially as your communication may well arrive while other, less prepared applicants are stumbling their way through the interview.
- Enthusiasm: "I was impressed . . . ." Let the interviewer know that you were impressed with the people/product/service/facility/market/position. "It was energizing to meet a group of people who really cared about their work."
- Confidence: Draw attention to one of the topics that was of special interest: "I feel confident I can handle the challenge of . . . ." There is a job to be done and a challenge to be met; let the interviewer know you are confident of doing both well.
- Interest: "I want this job, and you can rely on me to do a good job for you." If you want the job (or next interview), say so. At this stage, the company is buying and you are selling. Ask for the job in a positive and enthusiastic manner.
- If interview nerves caused you to forget something, you can introduce it with "On reflection . . ."; "Interview nerves got the better of me . . ."; "When we were talking about . . ."; "I should have mentioned my work with . . ."; "Having thought about our meeting, I thought I'd mention . . ."; or "I should have mentioned that . . . ."

Keep the note short (less than one page) and address it to the hiring manager or main interviewer if you haven't met your new boss yet. If you interviewed with other people and the meeting was more than cursory, you can send separate e-mails to each. Remember:

1. Whenever possible and appropriate, mention the names of the people you met at the interview.
2. Address the follow-up e-mail/letter to the main interviewer. You can send separate e-mails/letters to others in the selection cycle. Each makes a positive impression and shows extra effort and attention to detail.
3. Don't write too much. Keep it short—less than one page—and don't make claims that will not withstand scrutiny.
4. Depending on the time constraints, send an e-mail within forty-eight hours and a letter within twenty-four hours; this gives you time to write, edit, and polish. If the

decision is going to be made in the next couple of days, e-mail and/or hand-deliver a traditional letter. This way your follow-up will refresh your image in the mind of the interviewer just when it would normally be starting to dim.

E-mail is the way almost all business communication is done today; the average executive gets 90 percent less traditional mail than she did ten years ago, but this doesn't mean you should ignore traditional mail. Incoming mail used to provide a pleasant short break from the affairs of the day. With so little mail arriving, the break it offers is even more appreciated; a large and neatly hand-addressed envelope will always get opened, something you can no longer say about an e-mail. Sending letters by traditional mail is contrarian thinking and the more effective because of it.

5. When a hiring decision is imminent, follow up with an e-mail, then a telephone call as the decision timeline dictates. A phone call might begin, "Mr. Massie? Martin Yate. We met for an interview on Wednesday afternoon at 2 P.M. about the _____ position. I know you are making a decision by close of business tomorrow and I wanted to catch up with you personally to say . . . . "

Cover the following points in this phone conversation:

- Thanks for your time.
- I can do the job and this is why.
- I am excited about the job and this is why.
- I will make a good hire and this is why.
- I want this job; will you make me a fair offer?

If you are making a call, it is best not to write everything out in full sentences: You'll sound like one of those telemarketers. Instead, write down the bullet point you want to make: You'll sound more natural.

Additional Interviews

If the selection cycle is normal, three interviews for each of a handful of short-list candidates can take three or four weeks, so with the second and subsequent interviews (excepting the final interview), your follow-up pattern should replicate that of the initial interview.

1. An informal follow-up within twenty-four hours, essentially saying:
"Good to see you again Jack and to meet the guys. Thanks for your time. Preparing for a client meeting. I'll get back to you properly in the next couple of days."

You might replace this with an equally brief phone call, when there is something to warrant a brief conversation. If the manager doesn't pick up, leave a complete but brief message. You don't need to call back.

2. A formal follow-up, following the same principles and timing as before. As the interview cycle progresses, you want to maintain awareness of your candidacy, but you don't want to be seen as doing anything by rote.

Although the bulk of business correspondence these days is done via e-mail, remember that a traditional letter can make you stand out.

Extended Interview Cycles

You don't want to make a pest of yourself by calling or e-mailing every day, but neither do you want to drop out of sight. If the process stretches out into a month or months, make contact every couple of weeks, but keep it very low-volume. You don't want to seem overly anxious, just interested. Google.com has a nice feature that allows you to track news on any topic you choose. Taking advantage of this allows you to keep up to speed on your profession and factors affecting it, and this knowledge-gathering can be put to additional good use.

As you did before, you might send profession-relevant information:

"Harry, being so busy you may not have seen the article I've attached. It's about new legislation that's bound to affect us.

Regards,

Martin

P.S. I'm still determined to be your next _____."

You can do this in an e-mail and/or by traditional mail.

Funny E-mails

Getting a funny e-mail always brightens the day, and giving the interviewer a smile is a great way to be remembered, but this requires judgment. Don't send anything of a sexual, political, or religious nature, as it constitutes a breach of *professional values*.

The same considerations apply when sending a cartoon via traditional mail. This works because it's a different delivery medium and the cartoon causes a smile; plus, if you're lucky, it gets stuck on the wall or passed on.

KNOCK 'EM DEAD TIP

Check out the *follow-up letter templates* at www.knockemdead.com. Here you'll find four different categories of cover letters, plus advice on networking, follow-up (telephone and face-to-face), candidacy resurrection, negotiation, rejection, acceptance, resignation, and after-hire thank-you letters.

Reposted Jobs

Sometimes jobs remain open for a long time, or they may be frozen because of budgetary constraints and reposted under a different job title. Here's what you do:

1. Match the needs of the new job description with your resume and what was addressed at the interviews. Refocus a customized copy of the resume using as many keywords from the job posting as you reasonably can.
2. If you are out of touch with the decision makers, apply again in the requested manner.
3. If you are in touch with the decision makers, approach them again with the newly customized resume, reiterating your continued interest and qualifications.
4. Make a follow-up call to the recruiter and the hiring manager.
5. After a couple of follow-up letters to decision makers, you need to change the tone and might try the article approach mentioned earlier; something that is of relevance to your profession and therefore by extension to your target decision makers.

Not sure this will work? As I was updating *Knock 'em Dead*, I heard from Michael, who wrote to me through the website; he said, in part, "I have been tracking jobs since last spring that are now reappearing and I'm wondering what to do."

Not long after I sent him the above ideas I heard from him again. "Thanks Martin, I spoke with the recruiter a couple of times, then last Thursday, called the hiring manager directly. We spoke for almost ten minutes, so it was a well-received call. *She admired my guts in calling her directly because she had recently been out of work herself, and hated making those calls*" (my italics). It is this kind of extra effort that pays off in job offers.

KNOCK 'EM DEAD TIP

The longer the hiring process drags on, the less likely it is that you will get the offer. It can happen, but the odds get longer as time goes by. Don't let your job search stand still while you're waiting for a response from one company. Remember: *You don't have the job until you have a written offer in hand.*

When the Hiring Decision Is Imminent

Based on many years' experience, I can tell you that a decision next Friday means that an offer will be extended on that date, while the actual decision will be made *at least* seventy-two hours to five days prior (allowing HR the time to shepherd the paperwork through the authorization process). Of course this isn't the case if you are interviewing for a job today and they tell you the decision will be made at the end of the week, and as always you adapt the follow-up strategy to reflect the demands of the hiring cycle.

If you know in advance that a decision is coming, say, Friday of the following week, you can aim to get an e-mail on the hiring manager's desk this Friday/Monday; a slight variation of that message might arrive via traditional mail on the same or following day; and you can make a telephone call no later than Wednesday morning. This leaves seventy-two hours before decision time.

Final Written Communications

The content of these communications should cover:

- "We last met on _____ and have been talking about _____ job."
- "I can do the job and this is why: [talk about the *technical skills* you bring]."
- "I am excited about the job and this is why: [talk about how you can contribute to first projects and your desire to join a great group of people]."
- "I will make a good hire and this is why: [talk about the *transferable skills* and *professional values* you bring to the job]."
- "I want the job. What do I have to do to get it?"

Making That Final Call

If a hiring decision is imminent, succinctly following up on your e-mails and letters within seventy-two hours of decision time might help seal the deal. Work out what you want to say, write it down in bullet points, and make practice calls to a friend, keeping it brief and to the point. Then, when you are ready, make the call; you have nothing to lose and a job offer to gain.

CHAPTER 22
NEGOTIATING THE JOB OFFER

THE JOB OFFERS finally begin to arrive and you're never going to have this much leverage with this employer again. In this chapter you will learn the essentials of salary and benefits negotiations: handling good job offers and poor job offers, negotiating future salary, and how to evaluate the salary and the offer.

When you negotiate salary, you shouldn't be thinking of a magic number that you'd love to make, but a reasonable and acceptable range. All jobs have salary ranges attached to them. Your approach is to come up with a salary range that *puts you in the running, but doesn't nail you down to a specific figure*. You need to come up with three different figures:

1. First, given your skills, experience, and location, determine the least you would accept for a suitable job with a stable company.

2. Second, given the same considerations, what would constitute a fair offer for a suitable job with a stable company? There are three ways to figure out what would constitute a fair offer.
   - A salary calculator, such as the one at *www.salary.com*
   - Job postings
   - Headhunters with whom you have a relationship

3. Third, given the same considerations of skills, experience, and location, come up with the figure that would make you drop dead and go to heaven on the spot.

At the end of this process, you've got three figures: a minimum, a midpoint, and a dream salary. Kick out the lowest because you can always negotiate downward. This leaves you with a salary range—your midpoint to your high point—that you can give with confidence.

When to Bring Up Salary

Unless by some cosmic coincidence you and the interviewer spontaneously start talking salary at the exact same moment, one of two situations will occur.

They're Ready to Talk Salary, But You Aren't

What do you do when the question of money is brought up before you have enough details about the job to negotiate from a position of knowledge and strength? Postpone money talk until you have the facts in hand. Do that by asking something like: "I still have one or two questions about my responsibilities, and it will be easier for me to talk about money when I have cleared them up. Could I first ask you about _____?"

Proceed to clarify duties and responsibilities, being careful to weigh the relative importance of the position and its individual duties to the success of the department you may join.

You're Ready to Talk Salary, But They Aren't

If you are sure of your ability to deliver on the job and you want it, but the employer isn't rushing to put an offer on the table, you can encourage him with some carefully phrased questions of your own. Here are a few questions that will make the interviewer face the fact that you certainly are able to do the job and that the time has therefore come to talk turkey:

- "How do you think I would fit in with the group?"
- "I feel my background and experience would definitely complement the work group, don't you?"
- "I have what it takes to do this job. What questions are lingering in your mind?"
- "I think I could make a real contribution here. What do you think?"

You Want Each Other, But Are Both Being Coy

They want you, but they don't have you. This is the first time you really have decisions to make: Do you want this job, and on what terms? The issues for your consideration are the job and its potential, the company and its stability, the money and the benefits. *This is probably the only time in your relationship with your new employer when you'll have even a slim negotiating edge.* If you under-negotiate your salary, that has an impact, not only today, but on your future earnings, because all raises will be based on a lower salary. Employers are also more inclined to respect and honor a person who has a clear understanding of her worth in the marketplace—they want a savvy and businesslike professional. Armed with this knowledge, you can move the conversation forward.

The interviewer will generally initiate salary discussions with one or more of the following questions. Her goal is to make you name a figure; your goal is to avoid naming a figure: Otherwise you'll be trapped.

Why should I hire you?

Keep your answer short and to the point. Demonstrate your grasp of the job's responsibilities, the problems typically occurring in each area, the *transferable skills* that allow you to consistently deliver on them, and then a brief review of what you are like as a professional colleague, personalizing the behavioral profile for success you identified in your TJD.

What are you earning currently? Or, What were you making on your last job?

Ideally the offer you negotiate should be based on salary norms and on the value you bring to the job, not your salary history. However, it can be difficult to make that statement clear to the interviewer without appearing objectionable. A short answer might include: "I am earning $xx,ooo, but I want you to know that a major reason for making a job change right now is to significantly increase my salary. I am currently underpaid for my skills, experience, and contributions, and my capabilities are under-utilized."

Education and salary are factors that very often get checked, and untruths in either of these areas are grounds for termination with cause. The interviewer could ask to see a payroll stub or W2 form at the time you start work, or could make the offer dependent on verification of salary. A new employer may request verbal or written confirmation from previous employers or might use an outside verification agency.

In any instance where an employer checks references, credit, or other matters of verification, he is obliged by law to get your written permission. The impossibly small print on the bottom of the job application form—followed by a request for your signature—usually authorizes him to do just that.

It is important to understand the "areas of allowable fudge." For instance, if you are considerably underpaid, you may want to weigh the dollar value of such perks as medical and dental plans, pay in lieu of vacation, profit sharing and pension plans, bonuses, stock options, and other incentives. For many people, those can add between 20 to 35 percent to their base salary—you might honestly be able to mention a higher figure than you at first thought possible. Also, if you are due for a raise imminently, you are justified in adding it in.

What is an adequate reward for your efforts?

A glaring manageability question and money probe all in one. The interviewer probably already has a typist on staff who expects a Nobel Prize each time he gets out a faultless letter. Your answer should be honest and cover all bases. "My primary satisfaction and reward comes from a job well done and completed on time. The occasional good word from my boss is always welcome. Last but not least, I think everyone looks forward to a salary review."

What is your salary history? Or, What was your salary progress on your last job?

The interviewer is looking for a couple of things. First, she is looking for the frequency, percentage, and dollar value of your raises, which in turn tell her about your performance and the relative value of the offer that is about to be made. What you want to avoid is tying the potential offer to your salary history—the offer you negotiate should be based solely on the value of the job in hand.

Your answer needs to be specifically vague. Perhaps: "My salary history has followed a steady upward path, and I have never failed to receive merit increases. I would be glad to give you the specific numbers if needed, but I'll have to sit down with my records and give it some thought." The odds are that the interviewer will not ask you to do that; if he does, nod in agreement and say you'll get right to it when you get home. Don't begin the task until you are requested a second time, which is unlikely.

If for any reason you do get your back against the wall with this one, be sure to include in the specifics of your answer that "one of the reasons I am leaving my current job is that raises were standard for all levels of employees, so that despite my superior contributions, I got the same percentage raise as the tardy employee. I want to work in an environment where I will be recognized and rewarded for my contributions." Then end with a question: "Is this the sort of company where I can expect that?"

Have you ever been refused a salary increase?

This implies that you asked for one. An example of your justifiable request might parallel the following true story. An accountant in a tire distributorship made changes to an accounting system that saved $65,000 a year, plus thirty staff hours a week. Six months after the methods were obviously working smoothly, he requested a salary review; he was refused but was told he would receive a year-end bonus. He did: $75. If you can tell a story like that, by all means tell how you were turned down for a raise. If not, it is best to explain that your work and salary history showed a steady and marked improvement over the years.

How much do you need to support your family?

This question is sometimes asked of people who will be working in a sales job, where remuneration is based upon a draw against forthcoming commissions. If this scenario describes your income patterns, be sure you have a firm handle on your basic needs before you accept the position.

For salaried positions, this question is of dubious relevance. It implies the employer will try to get you at a subsistence salary, which is not why you are there. In this instance, give a range from your desired high-end salary down to your desired midpoint salary.

How much will it take to get you? Or, How much are you looking for? Or, What are your salary expectations? Or, What are your salary requirements?

You are being asked to name a figure here. Give the wrong answer and you could be eliminated. It is always a temptation to ask for the moon, knowing you can come down later, but there are better approaches. It is wise to confirm your understanding of the job and its importance before you start throwing numbers around, because you will have to live with the consequences. You need the best possible offer without pricing yourself out of the market, so it's time to dance with one of the following responses.

"Well, let's see if I understand the responsibilities fully . . . ." You then proceed to itemize exactly what you will be doing on a daily basis and the parameters of your responsibilities and authority. Once that is done, you will seek agreement: "Is this the job as you see it or have I missed anything?" Remember to describe the job in its most flattering and challenging light, paying special attention to the way you see it fitting into the overall picture and contributing to the success of the department, work group, and company. You can then finish your response with a question of your own: "What figure did you have in mind for someone with my track record?" or "What range has been authorized for this position?"

You could also ask, "What would be the salary range for someone with my experience and skills?" or "I naturally want to make as much as my background and skills will allow. If I am right for the job, and I think my credentials demonstrate that I am, I am sure you will make me a fair offer. What figure do you have in mind?"

Another good response is: "I would expect a salary appropriate to my experience and ability to do the job successfully. What range do you have in mind?"

Such questions will get the interviewer to reveal the salary range and concentrate her attention on the challenges of the job and your ability to accept and work with those challenges.

When you are given a range, you can adjust your money requirements appropriately, latching on to the upper part of the range. For example, if the range is $40,000 to $50,000 a year, you can come back with a range of $45,000 to $55,000.

Consequently, your response will include: "That certainly means we have something to talk about. While your range is $40,000 to $50,000, I am looking for a minimum of $45,000 with an ideal of $55,000. Tell me, what flexibility is there at the top of your salary range?" You need to know this to put yourself in the strongest negotiating position, and this is the perfect time and opportunity to gain the information and the advantage.

All this fencing is aimed at getting the interviewer to show his hand first. Ask for too much, and it's "Oh dear, I'm afraid you're overqualified"—to which you can reply, "So overpay me." (This actually works when you can carry it off with an ingratiating smile.) Ask for too little, and you'll be kicking yourself for years, because all future pay raises will be based on this lower amount.

When you have tried to get the interviewer to name a range and failed, you must come up with specific dollars and cents. The key is to understand that all jobs have salary ranges attached to them. Consequently, the last thing you will ever do is come back with a specific dollar figure— that traps you. Instead, you will mention your own range, which will be from your midpoint to your maximum. Remember, you can always negotiate down but can rarely negotiate up.

What do you hope to be earning two to five years from now?

A difficult question. The interviewer is probing your desired career and earning path and is trying to see whether you have your sights set high enough—or too high. A jocular tone might not hurt here: "I'd like to be earning just about as much as I can work out with my boss!" Then, throw the ball back with your own question: "How much is it possible to make here?"

If you give a specific figure, the interviewer is going to want justification. If you come up with a salary range, you are advised also to have a justified career path to go along with it.

You could also say, "In two years, I will have finished my CPA requirements, so with that plus my additional experience, industry norms say I should be earning between *$xx,000* and *$yyy,000*. I would hope to be earning at least within that range, but hopefully with a proven track record of contributions, I would be making above the norm." The trick is to use industry statistics as the backbone of your argument, express confidence in doing better than the norm, and, whenever possible, stay away from specific job titles unless pressed.

Do you think people in your occupation should be paid more?

This one can be used prior to serious salary negotiation to probe your awareness of how your job really contributes to the bottom line. Or it can occur in the middle of salary negotiations to throw you off balance. The safe and correct answer is to straddle the fence. "Most jobs have salary ranges that reflect the job's relative importance and contribution to a company. Those salary ranges reflect the norm for the great majority of people within that profession. That does not mean, however, that the extraordinary people in such a group are not recognized for their extra performance and skills. There are always exceptions to the rule."

Once an Offer Is on the Table

You don't have to accept or reject the first offer, whatever it is. In most instances you can improve the initial offer in a number of ways, but you have to know something about the existing market conditions for people in your line of work. If you are female, bear in mind that simply settling for a few points above your current rate of pay is bad advice for anyone and downright crazy for you.

The Women's Bureau of the U.S. Department of Labor tells us that men out-earn women in nearly every field. (For what it's worth, my research could not turn up a single industry in which this was not the case.) Even if a woman's responsibilities, background, and accomplishments are exactly the same as those of her male colleague, she is statistically unlikely to take home a paycheck equal to his. According to the Women's Bureau, male engineers make 14.3 percent more than their female counterparts. Male mathematicians make 16.3 percent more. Male advertising and public relations professionals make 28 percent more. Male lawyers and judges make 28 percent more. And male editors and reporters make a whopping 43 percent more than women performing the same or comparable work. No offense intended, but I think that this salary-parity gap will only be closed when every professional woman knows her true worth and has the ability to succinctly communicate what she brings to the table, plus the knowledge and willingness to use negotiating skills and determination to her own benefit.

Man or woman, there is no guarantee you are being paid what you are worth. The simple facts are these: If you don't get it while they want you and don't have you, you sure can't count on getting it once they do have you. When a thirty-year-old under-negotiates his salary by just $4,000 on a new job, it will cost him a minimum of $140,000 over the course of a career. Remember, every subsequent raise will come from a proportionately lower base; factor in inflation, and real dollars lost over an entire career span could actually be double this figure.

Salaries are fairly standardized, so the majority of offers will come within your negotiating range. But even if the offer is fair or even exceptional, you can still negotiate.

The state of the job market can impact negotiations too: When supply exceeds demand negotiating upward is harder. Nevertheless, with an offer on the table, the hiring manager has made the decision that she can hire you and get back to work; she and everyone else want to be done with this project; negotiate in good faith and your negotiations will be accepted in the same way.

The formal offer can fall into one of two categories.

306   Knock 'em Dead

- **It sounds fair and equitable:** In this case, you still want to negotiate for a little more—employers almost expect it of you, so don't disappoint them. Mention a salary range again, the low end of which comes at about the level of their offer and the high end somewhat above it. You can say, "Well it certainly seems that we are close. I was hoping for something more in the range of *$xx,000* to *$yyy,000*. How much room do we have for negotiation here?"

  No one will withdraw an offer because you say you feel you are worth more. After all, the interviewer thinks you are the best person for the job and has extended a formal offer, and the last thing he needs now is to start from square one again. The employer has a vested interest in bringing the negotiation to a satisfactory conclusion. At worst, she can stick to the original offer.

- **It isn't quite what you expected:** Even if the offer isn't what you thought it would be, you still have options other than accepting or rejecting the offer as it stands. Your strategy for now is to run the money topic as far as you can in a calm and businesslike way. Once you have gone that far, you can back off and examine the other potential benefits of the job. That way you will leave yourself with an opening, if you need it, to hit the money topic once more at the close of negotiations.

If you feel the salary could do with a boost, say so. "I like the job, and I know I have what it takes to be successful in it. I would also be prepared to give you a start date of [e.g.] March 1 to show my sincerity. But quite honestly, I couldn't justify it with your initial salary offer. I hope we have some room for negotiation here."

Or you can say, "I could start on March 1, and I do feel I could make a contribution here and become an integral part of the team. The only thing standing in the way is my inability to make ends meet based on your initial offer. I am very interested in the opportunity and flattered by your interest in me. If we could just solve this money problem, I'm sure we could come to terms. What do you think can be done about it?"

The interviewer will probably come back with a question asking how much you want. "What is the minimum you would be prepared to work for?" she might ask. You can reply, "I'd really like to make at least [now respond with your midpoint]. Is something in this range going to be a stumbling block?"

Depending on the interviewer's response, this is the time to be noncommittal but encouraging and move on to the benefits included with the position: "Well, yes, that is a little better. Perhaps we should talk about the benefits."

Alternatively, the interviewer may come back with another question: "That's beyond our salary range for this job title. How far can you reduce your salary needs to fit our range?"

This question shows good faith and a desire to close the deal, but don't give in too easily—the interviewer is never going to want you as much as he does now. Your first response might be: "I appreciate that, but if it is the job title and its accompanying range that is causing the problem, couldn't we upgrade the title, thereby putting me near the bottom of the next range?" Try it—sometimes it works. If it doesn't, it is probably time to move to other negotiable aspects of the job offer.

Evaluating Nonsalary Factors

Money is important, but your career trajectory more so. New jobs are pivotal points in your life that affect not just this job and the next couple of years, but your whole life going forward. They shouldn't represent decisions made without thought or purely on salary.

The Job and Its Potential

- How long has the job been open?
- Why is it open? Who held the job last?
- What is she doing now? Promoted, fired, or quit?
- How long was she in that job?
- How many people have held this job in the last three years? Where are they now?
- How often have people been promoted from this position—and how many, and where to?
- Who in the company was in this position the shortest length of time? Why? Who has remained in this position the longest? Why?

Other questions that might follow include:

- What does it take to succeed in this job?
- Who fails in this job and why?
- What personality traits do you consider critical to success in this job?
- What kind of training does the company provide/encourage/support?
- How long have you held this position?
- Why did you choose to work here?
- Tell me about your management style.
- How often will we meet?
- How frequent are performance and salary reviews? Are they weighted toward merit and performance, and if so, how?
- How does the performance appraisal and reward system work? Exactly how are outstanding employees recognized, judged, and rewarded?
- To what extent are the functions of the department recognized as important and worthy of review by upper management?

- Where and how does my department fit into the food chain?
- What does the department hope to achieve in the next two to three years? How will that help the company?
- What do you see as the strengths of the department? What do you see as weaknesses?
- What role do you see me playing in the department?
- What informal and formal benchmarks will you use to measure my effectiveness and contributions?
- Based on my effectiveness, how long would you anticipate me holding this position? When my position and responsibilities change, what are the possible titles and responsibilities I might grow into?
- What is the official corporate policy on internal promotion? How many people in this department have been promoted from their original positions since joining the company?
- How do I pursue promotion and how do you determine my suitability?
- What training and professional development programs are available?
- How does the company support independent skill development initiatives?
- Does the company sponsor all or part of any costs?
- What are the potential career paths within the company for someone with my job title?
- To what jobs have people with my title risen in the company?

Corporate Culture

All companies have their own way of doing things—that's corporate culture. Not every corporate culture is for you.

- What is the company's mission? What are the company's goals?
- What approach does this company take to its marketplace?
- What is unique about the way this company operates?
- What is the best thing you know about this company? What is the worst thing you know about this company?
- How does the reporting structure work? What are the accepted channels of communication and how do they work?
- What kinds of checks and balances, reports, or other work-measurement tools are used in the department and company?
- What advice would you give me about fitting into the corporate culture—about understanding the way you do things here?
- Will I be encouraged or discouraged from learning about the company beyond my own department?

Company Growth and Direction

For those concerned about employment stability and career growth, a healthy company is mandatory.

- What expansion is planned for this department, division, or facility?
- What is your value proposition to a prospective customer?
- When you lose a deal, to whom do you lose it?
- What markets does the company anticipate developing?
- Does the company have plans for mergers or acquisitions?
- Currently, what new endeavors is the company actively pursuing?
- How do market trends affect company growth and progress? What is being done about them?
- What production and employee layoffs and cutbacks have you experienced in the last three years?
- What production and employee layoffs and cutbacks do you anticipate? How are they likely to affect this department, division, or facility?
- When was the last corporate reorganization? How did it affect this department? When will the next corporate reorganization occur? How will it affect this department?
- Is this department a profit center? How does that affect remuneration?

Benefits

Below is a listing of commonly available benefits. Although many of these benefits are available to all employees at some companies, you should know that, as a rule of thumb, the higher up the ladder you climb, the more benefits you can expect. Because the corporate world and its methods of creating a motivated and committed workforce are constantly in flux, never assume that a particular benefit will be available to you.

The basic rule is to ask—if you don't ask, there is no way you will get. A few years ago, it would have been unthinkable that anyone but an executive could expect something as glamorous as an athletic club membership in a benefits package. Today, however, more companies have a membership as a standard benefit, and an increasing number are even building their own health club facilities. Benefits that may be available to you, if you ask, include:

- 401(k) and other investment matching programs
- Accidental death insurance
- "Cafeteria" insurance plans—you pick the insurance benefits you want
- Car or car allowance
- Car insurance, maintenance, and/or gas

- Compensation days—for unpaid overtime/business travel time
- Country club or health club membership
- Deferred compensation
- Dental insurance—note deductibles and the percentage that is employer-paid
- Employment contract and/or termination contract
- Expense account
- Financial planning and tax assistance
- Life insurance
- Medical insurance—note deductibles and percentage that is employer-paid
- Optical insurance—note deductibles and percentage that is employer-paid
- Paid sick leave
- Pension plans
- Performance review after a specified number of days (90/120), followed by a raise
- Personal days off
- Profit sharing
- Short- or long-term disability compensation plans
- Signing bonus
- Stock options
- Title promotion after a specified period
- Vacation
- Year-end bonus

You can ask these questions over the phone, or request another meeting to review these points. I prefer the latter because you get to meet everyone as the new member of the team and the boss is buoyant because he can at last get back to work. These factors encourage agreement with reasonable requests, as might a *tiny* worry that you might walk and leave them back at square one.

You may get nothing more than the standard package, but you have nothing to lose by asking and everything to gain. Once the package is straightened out, *come back to the base salary one last time*: "I want the job, Charlie. I'm excited by the opportunity and working for you and joining the company, but is there anything we can do about the starting salary?" *The answer to this question is going to determine what the final offer will be.*

Negotiating Stock Options

Stock options, while typically handled in a separate document, will be offered at the same time as your other benefits. It is usually best to address the stock issue once all the others have been settled.

In good economic times, employers turn to stock options as an effective recruitment and retention incentive. Options give you the right to purchase a set amount of stock in the company at a predetermined price (usually attractive) and over a fixed period of time. In exercising your options (buying the stock), you need to remember that stocks can and do decrease in value, sometimes dramatically.

There are several types of stock options, each with its own specific tax ramifications. However, as an employee, you are most likely to be offered "incentive stock options." Fortunately, with this type of option, you only have to pay taxes on your gains when you sell the stock; if you keep the stock for at least a year after purchase, you will not have to pay capital gains tax.

When negotiating stock options, always bear in mind that they are a gamble. The employer is going to talk about the offered stock options as if they were money in the bank, but they are not. Don't get bamboozled by rosy descriptions of the company's future; stay focused instead on the current market value of the stock. This is especially important if you are being asked to accept options as part of your overall compensation package. In some instances, you can be asked to accept options in lieu of cash. If the options you are offered are in any way meant to replace salary, think carefully, as you can't eat stock options.

If you are accepting a job with a publicly traded company, learn the value and performance of that stock by obtaining public records. On the other hand, if the company is privately held, you'll have to rely on the information that is provided to you by the employer. In this instance, consider market segment, business strategy, operations, liquidity, and senior management track record. In effect, you are evaluating your faith in the company, the imminence of their going public, and whether or not the company is a start-up or a well-established entity.

Of course, if the stock options do not impact your take-home pay, it can't hurt to get as many as you can. There is a big difference between getting the options and actually exercising your right to buy and sell them. Your considerations will include: what the purchase price will be, when you can exercise your options, and the restrictions on when you can buy the stock and when you can sell it. These matters will all be laid out in the separate options agreement furnished by the employer at the same time as the employment agreement, so read it carefully before you start negotiations in this area.

Everything to do with stock is negotiable, so you don't have to accept whatever you are offered without question and negotiation. Naturally, you will ask for more options than you are initially offered. You may not exercise those options, but having them available is in your best interests.

Your stock options will have a vesting period—the length of time you must work for the company before you can exercise your options. The employer, who is using the options as a retention tool, wants the vesting period to be as long as possible, thus tying you to the company with the lure of the stock. You, on the other hand, want to shorten the vesting period and, if possible, get an "incremental vesting schedule."

An incremental vesting schedule allows you to buy a few shares every month or quarter, probably getting you fully vested in the same period of time, but in smaller, more frequent steps along the way. Another reasonable request is to ask for "accelerated vesting" in the event of the employer merging or being bought by another company. This way, you become fully vested at the time of the acquisition.

Your agreement will also limit the time period in which you can exercise your options—not only when you can first exercise them, but also the point at which your option ends. For your financial flexibility, you will want to negotiate to extend this period as far as you can, even after you leave the company. For example, if you have a noncompete clause, you are essentially still tied to the company for a specific period of time, so it is reasonable to ask if you can exercise your options through the same period of time covered by your noncompete and nondisclosure clauses.

If you are not offered a "cashless exercise provision" you should certainly negotiate for it. A cashless exercise provision allows you to buy stock without spending any of your hard-earned money. The way it works is that when you buy a block of stock, you are simultaneously allowed to sell as many shares as are required to cover the costs of buying the stock; hence it becomes a cashless exercise, leaving you with the stock but not out of pocket.

Getting the stock options is one thing. Exercising them is another step, which you will not want to take without professional financial counsel.

Raises, Bonuses, Promotions, and Other Goodies

Here are a few arrangements corporate headhunters frequently negotiate for their recruits.

- **A single, lump-sum signing bonus**—nice to have, but it is money here today and gone tomorrow. Don't make the mistake of adding it onto the base. If you get a $2,500 signing bonus, that money won't be figured in for your year-end review—your raise will be based on your actual salary, so the bonus is less meaningful than it appears.
- **A 60-, 90-, or 120-day performance review** with raise attached. You can frequently negotiate a minimum percentage increase here if you have confidence in your abilities.
- **A title promotion and raise** after two, three, or four months.
- **A year-end bonus.** When you hear talk about a year-end bonus, don't rely on "what it's going to be this year" or "what it was last year," because the actual bonus will never bear any resemblance to either figure. Base your estimate of any bonus on a five-year performance history.
- **Things other than cash.** Also in the realm of real disposable income are things like a company car, gas, maintenance, and insurance. They represent hard dollars you would not have to spend. It's not unusual to hear of employers paying car and/or insurance allowances, picking up servicing bills for your personal automobile, or paying gas up to a certain amount each month. But if you don't ask, you can never expect an employer to offer. What have you got to lose? The worst that can happen is that the employer declines. Remember to get any of those unusual goodies in writing—even respectable managers in respected companies can suffer amnesia.

Employment Obligations and Restrictions

Any verbal offer you accept is dependent on the offer being in writing and your being comfortable with what's in the employment agreement. Pay careful attention to what the company will ask of you in signing the agreement. Employment contracts are legal documents designed to obfuscate and intimidate the neophyte. You can and should take the time to have it explained and then take it home and see if you agree with that interpretation; if in doubt, take it to any employment lawyer.

Your employment contract may include:

Assignment of Inventions

If you create anything during the period of your employment, the company may require you to turn it over. This may include work you do on your own time if it relates to your duties at the company.

Nondisclosure Clauses

Companies will likely require that you not discuss company business with any outside source to prevent the competition from learning company secrets. The language is likely to be general and thus unfavorable to you. If you're concerned about this, try to get the language more specific.

Noncompete Clauses

The company may want to restrict you from working for competitors after you leave the company. This can have a negative impact on your future career, since it restricts your employability. Try to make the language more specific.

Severance

Negotiate for as extensive a severance package as you can—say, a month's salary for every year of employment or every $10,000 of salary, with outplacement/job search assistance. Since outplacement is only as good as the person giving it, it is preferable to negotiate a dollar amount so that you can spend the money in the way you think most suitable to your needs and with the consultant of your choice.

If you sign a noncompete clause, request that your severance extend through the entire period of your noncompete restrictions. This is a perfectly reasonable request that should be accommodated without trouble.

Relocation

When job-related relocation comes around, we all find ourselves in an ocean of unexpected expenses. So once the overall offer is acceptable to you, key in on relocation issues. Many companies expect to pay all or part of your relocation costs unless you live within fifty miles of your new workplace, in which case you are usually on your own. Since the employer regularly addresses these issues, you should not be reticent about negotiating them.

Relocation packages vary enormously from person to person and company to company. However, if they want you badly enough, employers will usually try to accommodate reasonable requests.

The higher up the corporate ladder you climb, the more relocation services you are likely to receive. On the low end, you may get offered reimbursement for a moving truck and a few hundred dollars for incidental expenses. While the employer expects to bear the cost of your relocation, every dollar spent affects the bottom line of the HR department. So no matter where you stand on the corporate ladder, getting above and beyond the standard offer will require your asking for it.

For example, companies know your relocation costs will be treated as taxable income, but they won't say anything about it unless you do. Explain that the taxes you expect to pay can amount to 30 percent of the monies spent, and that this would place a heavy burden on you financially. With a typical executive relocation running around $50,000, the tax implications of relocating to accept a new job could come as a nasty shock. Ask that the company pick up the personal income tax burdens you incur as a result of your move.

Only some aspects of your relocation are tax deductible. For example, the costs of moving your personal belongings and one trip to the new location are deductible, but house-hunting trips and the costs of temporary accommodation are not.

Other things you can ask the company to help or reimburse you for include:

- House-hunting trips before you start. After all, it is in the best interests of the company to have you settled as quickly as possible.
- Temporary housing costs while you find a suitable permanent residence. Again, most companies will comply with at least thirty days, sometimes as many as 90 to 120 days.
- Shipping of autos, boats, and so on.
- Costs of a professional moving company packing, shipping, and delivering your household goods.
- Costs of selling and buying a house if you are a homeowner.
- Job search assistance for a working spouse. Try to get a dollar amount so that you can choose your service provider. Come to *www.knockemdead.com* for advice on coaching services.
- Help in finding schools for the kids.
- Orientation programs for the new community.

It will help your negotiating position to estimate these costs in advance. You can pick up the phone and request estimates, or you can visit websites like *www.homefair.com* and *www.homestore.com*, which have electronic calculation tools and cost-of-living comparisons. The latter will help you evaluate how far a dollar will go in the new town in comparison with where you live today.

When it comes to offer letters and employment agreements, the employer naturally hopes that you will accept them as they are presented, but you are under no obligation to do so. Every aspect of the offer is negotiable, and as these are largely issues that have not arisen in the interview cycle, the employer will expect a savvy professional to address them. Remember: *This is probably the only time in your relationship with your new employer when you'll have even a slim negotiating edge.*

Handling References When a Job Offer Arrives

A few words here on handling your references when an offer is imminent. When references get checked, employment dates and leaving salary are always verified; don't think of fudging, as it is cause for a dismissal that could dog your footsteps for years. Beyond that, your immediate past manager is the one most likely to be checked. Depending on the company and your level, coworkers and other past managers can also be contacted.

Call potential references, describe the job you have been (or are about to be) offered, explain why you think it is a good opportunity and why you believe you can be successful (omit these details when talking to exact peers unless the offer is already in the bag). Ask if they think it would be a good fit, and why.

You can then, if it's appropriate and time allows, tell the reference some of the questions he might be asked. These might include the time you have known each other; your relationship to each other; the title you worked under (be sure to remind your reference of promotions and title changes); your five or six most important duties; the key projects you worked on; your greatest strengths; your greatest weaknesses; your attitudes toward your job, your peers, and management; the timeliness, quality, and quantity of your work; your willingness to achieve above and beyond the call of duty (remind him of all those weekends you worked); whether he would rehire you (if company policy forbids rehiring, make sure your reference will mention this); your earnings; and any additional comments the reference would like to make. This whole list may be an overwhelming amount of information to unload on a colleague, so pass on questions tailored to your situation.

If you have any doubt about the quality of a pivotal reference, take the precaution of having a friend do a dummy check on all references just to confirm what they will say when the occasion arises. Of course, this only works if that friend is a consummate professional capable of carrying it off! This way you can distinguish the excellent references from the merely good.

Better yet, go to *www.allisontaylor.com*, the leader in the reference-checking business. For a modest fee (about $80 for a basic reference check), they verify references on your behalf. That way you'll know in advance just who will be your best spokespeople.

Offer Letters and Employment Agreements

Never resign an existing job until you have an acceptable written offer in hand. The rule is: if you don't have an offer in writing, you don't have an offer. When that offer letter or employment agreement does arrive, you are in the final stages of negotiation. This is the time when you'll see if the written offer reflects your understanding of previous conversations, and you'll see if there are some things still to negotiate.

An offer letter should include specifics about your compensation package, start date, benefits, policies and procedures, and relocation issues; an employee handbook detailing everything you are entitled to as an employee may well accompany the offer letter.

Employment agreements become more common the higher up the corporate ladder you climb and the more critical your work becomes to the success of the corporation. An employment agreement is a more restrictive document that goes into greater detail about what you can and cannot do as a result of employment with the company.

In the employment agreement, you'll find everything you would in an offer letter, plus issues such as assignment of inventions, nondisclosure, noncompete, severance, and relocation, all of which are likely to be addressed in detail. Any stock option agreement will probably be in a separate document but presented to you at the same time as the formal offer. As these contracts can be extremely limiting and even affect your employability after you leave the company, you may wish to consult with counsel. An employment lawyer can review and advise you on the specific implications of each clause and help you with revised and less restrictive wording. As you will have a solid understanding of the issues, you will be able to phrase your questions succinctly and control the costs of any such legal consultation.

Once you have a clear understanding of the complete offer, review it with the employer: "I understand the offer is . . ." and after itemizing the components of the offer, finish by asking, "Is this your best and final offer?" With this question, you must look the interviewer directly in the eye, and maintain eye contact. Remember that the *tone* in which such a question is delivered is important: With the wrong intonation this can be interpreted as combative.

Evaluating the Offer

Once the offer has been negotiated to the best of your ability, you need to evaluate it—and that doesn't have to be done on the spot. Some of your requests and questions will take time to get answered, and very often the final parts of negotiation—"Yes, Mr. Jones, we can give you the extra $10,000 and six months of vacation you requested"—will take place over the telephone. Regardless of where the final negotiations are completed, *never accept or reject the offer on the spot*.

Be positive, say how excited you are about the prospect and that you would like a little time (overnight, a day, two days) to think it over, discuss it with your spouse, whatever. Not only is this delay standard practice, but it will also give you the opportunity to leverage other offers, as discussed in the next chapter.

Use the time you gain to speak to your mentors or advisors. First, a word of caution: In asking advice from those close to you, be sure you know exactly where that advice is coming from—you need clear-headed objectivity at this time.

Once the advice is in, and not before, weigh it along with your own observations—no one knows your needs and aspirations better than you do. While there are many ways of doing that, a simple line down the middle of a sheet of paper, with the reasons to take the job written on one side and the reasons to turn it down on the other, is about as straightforward and objective as you can get.

You will weigh salary, future earnings and career prospects, benefits, commute, lifestyle, and stability of the company, along with all those intangibles that are summed up in the term "gut feelings." Make sure you answer these questions for yourself:

- Do you like the work?
- Can you be trained in a reasonable period of time, thus having a realistic chance of success on the job?
- Are the title and responsibilities likely to provide you with a challenge?
- Is the opportunity for growth in the job compatible with your needs and desires?
- Are the company's location, stability, and reputation in line with your needs?
- Is the atmosphere/culture of the company conducive to your enjoying working at the company?
- Can you get along with your new manager and immediate work group?
- Is the money offer and total compensation package the best you can get?

Notice that money is but one aspect of the evaluation process. There are many other factors to take into account as well. Even a high-paying job can be less advantageous than you think. For instance, you should be careful not to be foxed by the gross figure. It really is important that you get a firm handle on those actual, spendable, after-tax dollars—the ones with which you pay the rent. Always look at an offer in the light of how many more spendable dollars a week it will put in your pocket.

Accepting New Jobs, Resigning from Others

Once your decision is made, you should accept the job verbally. Spell out exactly what you are accepting: "Mr. Smith, I'd like to accept the position of engineer at a starting salary of $82,000. I will be able to start work on March 1. And I understand my package will include life, health, and dental insurance, a 401(k) plan, and a company car." Then you finish with: "I will be glad to start on the above date pending a written offer received in time to give my present employer adequate notice of my departure. I'm sure that's acceptable to you."

Notify your current employer in the same fashion. Quitting is difficult for almost everyone, so you can write a pleasant resignation letter, walk into your boss's office, hand it to her, then discuss things calmly and pleasantly once she has read it. A career spans upward of half a century, so you don't want to burn bridges today that you may need to cross again tomorrow. Take the time to craft professional documents. One of the companion volumes to this work, *Knock 'em Dead Cover Letters*, will help you create powerful, professional letters for all occasions. The book is full of examples and has specific sections on acceptance, rejection, and resignation letters.

Notify any other companies that have been in negotiation with you that you are no longer on the market but that you were most impressed with meeting them and would like to keep communications open for the future. (See Chapter 24, "Multiple Job Interviews, Multiple Job Offers" for more on this topic.)

It bears repeating that your resignation is not the time to air your grievances; you have simply been presented with a great opportunity and are thankful for the skills this job gave you. This same person may be checked for a reference down the line, and you want the recollections to be positive.

CHAPTER 23
SNATCHING VICTORY FROM THE JAWS OF DEFEAT

REJECTION? IMPOSSIBLE! THEN again, you won't be right for every job. Here are some techniques that help you to create opportunities in the face of rejection.

During the interviewing process, there are bound to be interviewers who come to the erroneous conclusion that you are not the right person for the job they need to fill. When that happens, you will be turned down. Such an absurd travesty of justice can occur in different ways:

- At the interview
- In a letter of rejection
- During your follow-up telephone call

Whenever the turndown comes, you must be emotionally and intellectually prepared to take advantage of the opportunity being offered to you.

When you get turned down for the only prospect you have going, the rejection can be devastating to your ego. That is why I have stressed the wisdom of having at least a few interviews in process at the same time.

You will get turned down. No one can be right for every job. The right person for a job doesn't always get it; however, the best prepared and most determined often does. While you may be responsible in part for the initial rejection, you still have the power to correct the situation and win the job offer. What you do with the claimed victory is a different matter—you will then be in a seller's market with choice and control of your situation.

Almost every job you desire is obtainable once you understand the hiring process from the interviewer's side of the desk. Your initial—and temporary—rejection is attributable to one of these reasons:

- The interviewer does not feel you can do the job.
- The interviewer feels you lack a successful profile.
- The interviewer did not feel your personality would contribute to the smooth functioning of the department—perhaps you didn't portray yourself as either a team player or as someone willing to take the extra step.

With belief in yourself, you can still succeed. Repeat to yourself constantly through the interview cycle: "I will get this job, because no one else can give as much to this company as I can!" Do that and implement the following plan immediately when you hear of rejection, whether in person, via mail, or over the telephone.

- **Step One:** Thank the interviewer for the time and consideration. Then ask politely: "To help my future job search, why wasn't I chosen for the position?" Assure the interviewer that you would truly appreciate an honest, objective analysis. Listen to the reply and do not interrupt. Use your time constructively and take notes. When the company representative finishes speaking, show that you understood the comments. (Remember, understanding and agreeing are different animals.)

    "Thank you, Mr. Smith, now I can understand the way you feel. Because I don't interview that often I'm afraid my nerves got in the way. I'm very interested in working for your company [*use an enthusiastic tone*] and am determined to get the job. Let me meet with you once again. This time, when I'm not so nervous, I am confident you will see I really do have the skills you require [*then provide an example of a skill you have in the questionable area*]. You name the time and the place, and I will be there. What's best for you, Mr. Smith?"

End with a question, of course, and note here that you're asking *when* you can meet again, and not *if*. An enthusiastic request like that is very difficult to refuse and will usually get you another interview—an interview, of course, at which you must shine.

- **Step Two:** Check your notes and accept the company representative's concerns. Their validity is irrelevant; the important point is that the negative points represent the problem areas in the interviewer's perception of you. List the negative perceptions, and using the techniques, exercises, and value keys discussed throughout the book, develop different ways to overcome or compensate for every negative perception.
- **Step Three:** Reread Part III of this book.
- **Step Four:** Practice aloud the statements and responses you will use at the interview. If you can practice with someone who plays the part of the interviewer, that's even better. This will create a real interview atmosphere and increase your chances of success. Lacking a role-play partner, you can create that live answer by putting the anticipated objections and questions on a tape and responding to them.
- **Step Five:** Study all available information on the company.
- **Step Six:** Congratulate yourself continually for getting another interview after initial rejection. This is proof of your self-worth, ability, and tenacity. You have nothing to lose and everything to gain, having already risen phoenix-like from the ashes of defeat.
- **Step Seven:** During the interview, ask for the job in a positive and enthusiastic manner. Your drive and staying power will impress the interviewer. All you must do to win the job is overcome the perceived negatives, and you have been given the time and information to prepare. Go for it.
- **Step Eight:** Even when all has failed at the subsequent interview, do not leave without a final request for the job. Play your trump card: "Mr. Smith, I respect the fact that you allowed me the opportunity to prove myself here today. I am convinced I am the best person for the job. I want you to give me a trial, and I will prove on the job that I am the best hiring decision you have made this year. Will you give us both the opportunity?"

A reader once wrote to me as I was revising *Knock 'em Dead*, "I read the chapter entitled 'Snatching Victory from the Jaws of Defeat' and did everything you said to salvage what appeared to be a losing interview. My efforts did make a very good impression on the interviewer, but as it was finally explained to me, I really did not have equal qualifications for the job, and finally came in a close second. I really want to work for this growing company, and they say they have another position coming up in six months. What should I do?"

I also know of someone who wanted a job working for a major airline. He had been recently laid off and had high hopes for a successful interview. As it happened, he too came in second for the position. He was told that the firm would speak to him again in the near future. So he waited—for eight months. Finally, he realized that waiting for the job would only leave him unemployed. The moral of the story is that you must be brutally objective when you come out second-best, and, whatever the interviewer says, you must sometimes assume that you are getting the polite brush-off.

With that in mind, let's see what can be done on the positive side. First of all, send a thank-you note to the interviewer, acknowledging your understanding of the state of affairs and reaffirming your desire to work for the company. Conclude with a polite request to bear you in mind for the future.

Keep an eye out for any news item about the company in the press. Whenever you see something, cut it out and mail it to the interviewer with a very brief note that says something like: "I came across this in *Forbes* and thought you might find it interesting. I am still determined to be your next account manager, so please keep me in mind when the next opening occurs."

You can also call the interviewer once every couple of months, just to check in. Remember, of course, to keep the phone call brief and polite—you simply want to keep your name at the top of the interviewer's mind.

And maybe something will come of it. Ultimately, however, your only choice is to move on. There is nothing to gain waiting on an interviewer's word. Go out and keep looking, because chances are that you will come up with an even better job. Then, if you still want to work for that company that gave you the brush-off, you will have some leverage.

Most people fail in their endeavors by quitting just before the dawn of success. Follow these directions and you can win the job. You have proven yourself to be a fighter, and that is universally admired. The company representative will want you to succeed because you are made of stuff that is rarely seen today. You are a person of guts, drive, and endurance—the hallmarks of a winner. Job turn-downs are opportunities to exercise and build on your strengths, and, by persisting, you may well add to your growing number of job offers, now and in the future.

CHAPTER 24
MULTIPLE JOB INTERVIEWS, MULTIPLE JOB OFFERS

RELYING ON ONE interview at a time can only lead to anxiety, so you must create and foster an ever-growing network of interviews and, consequently, job offers.

False optimism and laziness lead many job hunters to be content with only one interview in process at any given time. That severely reduces the odds of landing the best job in town within your chosen time frame. Complacency guarantees that you will continue to operate in a buyer's market.

The recommended approach is to generate as many interviews as possible in a two- to three-week period. Interviewing skills are learned and consequently improve with practice. With the improved skills comes a greater confidence, and those natural interview nerves disperse. Your confidence shows through to potential employers, and you are perceived in a positive light.

Because other companies are interested in you, everyone will move more quickly to secure your services. This is especially important if you are unfortunate enough to be unemployed. Being out of work is when you need money the most and is the time when the salary you can command on the open market is substantially reduced. The interview activity you generate will help offset this.

By generating multiple interviews, you bring the time of the first job offer closer and closer. That one job offer can be quickly parlayed into a number of others. And with a single job offer, your unemployed status has, to all intents and purposes, passed.

Immediately, you can call every company with whom you've met, and explain the situation. "Mr. Johnson, I'm calling because while still under consideration with your company I have received a job offer from one of your competitors. I would hate to make a decision without the chance of speaking with you again. I was very impressed by my meeting with you. Can we get together in the next couple of days?" End, of course, with a question that carries the conversation forward.

If you were in the running at all, your call will usually generate another interview; Mr. Johnson does not want to miss out on a suddenly prized commodity. Remember: It is human nature to want the very things one is about to lose. Your simple offer can be multiplied almost by the number of interviews you have in process at the time.

A single job offer can also be used to generate interviews with new firms. It is as simple as making your usual telephone networking presentation, but it ends differently. You would be very interested in meeting with them because of your knowledge of the company/product/service, but also because you have just received a job offer—would it be possible to get together in the next couple of days?

Relying on one interview at a time can only lead to prolonged anxiety, disappointment, and, possibly, unemployment. That reliance is due to the combination of false optimism, laziness, and fear of rejection. Those are traits that cannot be tolerated except by confirmed defeatists, for defeat is the inevitable result of those traits. As Heraclitus said, "A man's character is his fate." Headhunters say, "The job offer that cannot fail will."

Self-esteem, on the other hand, is vital to your success, and happiness is found with it. With it you will awake each day with previously unknown vitality. Your vigor will increase, your enthusiasm will rise, and a desire to achieve will burn within. The more you do today, the better you will feel tomorrow.

Even when you follow this plan to the letter, not every interview will result in an offer. But with many irons in the fire, an occasional firm "no" should not affect your morale. It won't be the first or last time you face rejection. Be persistent and, above all, close your mind to all negative and discouraging influences. The success you experience from implementing this plan will increase your store of willpower and determination, effect a successful outcome of your job search, and enrich your whole life. Start today.

The key to your success is preparation. Failing is easy—it requires no effort. It is the achievement of success that requires effort, and that means effort today, not tomorrow, for tomorrow never comes. So start building that well-stocked briefcase today.

PART V
WHERE THE JOBS ARE

THIS SECTION TELLS you where today's top job markets are and gives you tips on how to break into them.

WHERE CAN I FIND A JOB? In a bad economy it's easy to believe there are no jobs left out there. However, nothing could be further from the truth.

While job hunting in these troubled times is not easy, it's by no means impossible. The trick is to know in what fields there's a demand for skilled workers. Effective job search today simply needs to be more efficient and organized than in the past, more focused and informed.

In this section, we'll look at the top fields for job growth and I'll give you some important information on how to land employment and grow your career.

CHAPTER 25
THIRTY FAST-GROWING OCCUPATIONS

EVEN IF YOU are currently employed, you should still pay attention to the changing job market and economic climate.

Now, as you are the one person who truly cares about your long-term economic survival, you are noting that one major result of a global economy, apart from cheap goods at Wally World and higher wages overseas, is the increasing instability of the professional workplace here at home. So the strategies for making informed career choices about professions, the credentials professions require for entry, and the industries in which you pursue employment are issues of importance to anyone who hopes to achieve stability and success in life.

The changing nature of our society impacts where the jobs are *now* and where they are likely to be in the *future*. You need to gain focus for and then keep an eye on the big picture—not only which jobs are in greater demand, but also why they're growing and how they're changing. When you understand the trends that are changing the world of work, you have a foundation on which to base the career decisions that impact your life for years into the future.

With deeper knowledge, you will be more able to withstand the hysterics of the media news cycle. In mid-2011, while writing this new edition, I was doing countless radio appearances talking about the economy and where the jobs are and will be. I wanted to talk about the jobs that are out there for everyone, but all the media wanted to talk about was the "green" jobs that were going to change our world. Very topical, very newsworthy, but when it's your life you have to be practical about these things. Pursuing "green jobs" in the midst of a recession might not *always* be the smartest thing to do.

If you are looking for a job in your profession that carries a "green" tag, that's fair enough, but if you are changing careers on the basis of jobs you hope will come in this area, that's not so smart.

Here's a simple test I did, using the job aggregator *www.indeed.com*. I performed a national search of more than 4,000 job banks, looking for "green jobs." I got 31,000 hits for all job postings that had the word "green" somewhere in the job description. I then dropped the "green" designation and did a national search for just one title from this list, "pharmacist." I got 31,500 jobs.

That isn't to say you shouldn't pursue jobs and careers in the green sector of the economy. If you want to be true to your ideals and feel you're making a difference in your workplace, that's great—but do it with your eyes open.

By the same token, I haven't included some of the widely touted high-growth jobs like "blogger," because although its growth percentage is phenomenal, the overall *number* of advertised jobs for this job title I could find on over 4,000 job sites was just 3,200. It is more prudent to anchor your search in jobs that are large in numbers now and projected for steady growth into the future. This leads to greater stability and more.

In this chapter, we'll focus on jobs whose history and growth projections are based on significant demographic changes in society, jobs that exist in lots of companies spread across every city in the country. Such positions mean more potential for job security, greater opportunity for professional growth, and more choice when you want to or must change jobs.

This list is meant as a starting point. There are many other jobs that have high growth potential in real numbers. Each job listing offers a brief overview of an occupation that the U.S. Bureau of Labor Statistics expects to grow at a minimum rate of 21 percent or more through the year 2016, and is categorized as "much faster than average." This growth will largely be fueled by our aging population and the globalization of the workplace. These "hot" occupations fall into the fields of **health care** (we live in an aging society), **science and technologies** (computers, information systems, and the environment), **business services** (occupations in a variety of industries that reflect trends in our culture), as well as segments of **education and**

social services (which are impacted by population changes and societal challenges). These are the growing sectors in America for the predictable future.

THE TOP THIRTY	
OCCUPATION	**ANTICIPATED GROWTH PERCENTAGE**
Sector: Health Care	
1. Veterinary Technician/Technologist	41%
2. Veterinarian	33%
3. Medical Assistant	34%
4. Pharmacy Technician	32%
5. Dental Hygienist	30%
6. Physical Therapist	27%
7. Physician Assistant	39%
8. Radiation Therapist	25%
9. Surgical Technician	24%
10. Athletic Trainer	37%
11. Registered Nurse	22.2%
12. Pharmacist	22%
Sector: Science and Technology	
13. Computer Software Engineer	36%
14. Computer Scientist and Database Administrator	37%
15. Computer Systems Analyst	29%
16. Environmental Scientist and Hydrologist	25%
17. Environmental Engineer	25%
18. Biomedical Engineer	21% to 72%
Sector: Business Services	
19. Financial Analyst and Personal Financial Advisor	41%
20. Gaming and Surveillance Officer	34%
21. Court Reporter	25%
22. Actuary	24%
23. Interpreter and Translator	24%
24. Paralegal and Legal Assistant	22%
Sector: Educational and Social Services	
25. Personal and Home Care Aide	50%
26. Social and Human Services Assistant	34%
27. Health Educator	26%
28. Postsecondary Teacher	23%
29. Instructional Coordinator	22%
30. Social Worker	22%

Source: U.S. Bureau of Labor Statistics (www.bls.gov).

For each occupation listed, you'll find six key components explained in detail:

- **Day-to-Day:** daily nature of the work; general job description
- **The Big Picture:** the employment outlook through 2018 as projected by the U.S. Department of Labor
- **Training Track:** the education or training needed to succeed
- **The Bottom Line:** pros and cons of this career choice
- **The Paycheck:** average earnings and the highs and lows for the category
- **Web Links:** websites for national organizations and/or career opportunities in that field

At the end of the chapter you will also find links to:

- The Bureau of Labor Statistics (bls.gov), which creates more high-growth jobs using different criteria; you will find some of the jobs mentioned here in each of those lists
- Useful links to investigate the projected high-growth green jobs and the explosive growth jobs in new technology

KNOCK 'EM DEAD TIP

If you are wondering what to do with that degree you already have or are thinking of pursuing, check out the new "What can I do with this degree?" database at *www.knockemdead.com.*

Health Care Professions

Employment in health care will continue to grow through 2016 for many reasons:

1. The number of people in older age groups, who have much-greater-than-average health care needs, will grow. As a result, the demand for health care will increase.
2. Employment in home health care and residential care should increase rapidly as life expectancies rise and as baby boomers rely more on long-term care facilities.
3. Advances in medical technology will increase the number of people who survive severe illness and injury. Those patients will then need extensive therapy and care.
4. New technology and medical breakthroughs will make it possible to identify and treat conditions that were previously unknown or untreatable.
5. Medical group practices and integrated health systems will become larger and more complex, increasing the need for administrative help.
6. Industry growth will also occur as a result of the shift from inpatient to less expensive outpatient and home health care because of improvements in diagnostic tests and surgical procedures. In addition, many patients would rather be treated and/or recover at home.

Jobs within the typical inpatient hospital scenario are expected to grow the least, while occupations outside that realm, such as pharmacy technicians and home care aides, are expected to grow rapidly. Hospitals will be the slowest growing segment within the health care industry because of efforts to control costs and the increasing popularity of outpatient clinics and other alternative care sites. Because of cost pressures, many health care facilities will lower staffing levels to reduce labor costs. Where patient care demands and regulations allow, health care facilities will substitute lower-paid providers instead and will cross-train their workforces.

Luckily, traditional inpatient hospital positions are no longer the only option for health care workers, so opportunities still abound. If you're seeking a career in the field, you must be willing to work in various settings.

Veterinary Technician/ Technologist

Day-to-Day

Veterinarians use the skills of veterinary technologists and technicians to provide state-of-the-art care to all kinds of animals. Vet technicians and technologists perform many of the same duties for a veterinarian that a nurse would for a physician, such as laboratory tests and clinical procedures. Although specific job duties vary by employer, technicians and technologists often perform the same tasks, despite some differences in formal education and training. Most workers in this occupation are called technicians.

Veterinary techs typically work in a private practice under the supervision of a licensed veterinarian. They conduct various tests and treat and diagnose medical conditions and diseases in animals. Veterinary technicians assisting small-animal practitioners usually care for companion animals, such as cats and dogs, but can also work with mice, sheep, cattle, monkeys, birds, fish, and frogs. Very few technicians work in mixed animal practices, where vets care for both small companion animals and larger, non-domestic animals.

Veterinary technicians may also work in research facilities, where they conduct experiments; record an animal's vital stats; analyze data; and attempt to make improvements in food safety, animal health, and comparative medicine (the field of study concentrating on similarities and differences between veterinary and human medicine).

The Big Picture
Expected to grow 41 percent through 2016.

Excellent job opportunities will likely stem from the limited output of qualified veterinary technicians from two-year programs. The current enrollment rates indicate that there will not be enough technicians to meet anticipated demand.

In addition, pet owners are more affluent and more willing to pay for advanced veterinary care because many consider their pet to be a family member. In addition, the number of pet owners who use veterinary services for their pets is expected to grow through 2016, substantially increasing employment opportunities.

Training Track
Most entry-level veterinary technicians have a two-year associate degree from a community college accredited by the American Veterinary Medical Association (AVMA; *www.avma.org*). Courses are taught in both clinical and laboratory settings using live animals. About twenty colleges, including Purdue University, State University of New York (SUNY)–Canton, Michigan State University, and California Polytechnic University, offer four-year veterinary technology programs that culminate in a bachelor's degree in veterinary technology. (For a full list, visit *www.avma.org*.) These four-year

colleges, in addition to some vocational schools, also offer two-year programs in laboratory animal science.

In 2009, 160 veterinary technology programs in forty-four states were accredited by the AVMA. Nine offered long-distance learning opportunities. Graduation from an AVMA-accredited veterinary technology program allows students to take the credentialing exam in any state in the country.

The Bottom Line

People who love animals find both career and personal satisfaction working with and helping them. However, the work can be physically and emotionally demanding. Vet techs must lift, hold, and restrain animals at times, and may be bitten or scratched as a result. In addition, the work setting can be noisy and cleaning cages can be unpleasant. Veterinary techs who work with abused animals or who euthanize animals may experience emotional stress.

THE PAYCHECK

Median annual earnings	$29,850
Highest 10 percent earned	>$41,490
Lowest 10 percent earned	<$19,770
Best-paying states	New York, Illinois, California, Connecticut, District of Columbia

KNOCK 'EM DEAD TIP

A weak economy has not hurt the pet industry. According to the American Pet Products Association, Americans will spend approximately $50.8 billion on their pets in 2011. That's a $5.4 billion increase over 2009.

Web Links

www.avma.org
www.veterinarytechnicianschools.com
www.vet.com
www.veterinarytechjobs.com
www.wheretechsconnect.com

Veterinarian

Day-to-Day

Most veterinarians care for the health of pets, livestock, and animals in animal hospitals, zoos, racetracks, and laboratories. They diagnose animal medical conditions; vaccinate; prescribe medication to animals; treat and dress wounds; set fractures; perform surgery; and advise owners about proper feeding, behavior, and breeding.

Other veterinarians are researchers, studying all facets of human and animal health problems in both clinical and laboratory settings.

The Big Picture

Expected to grow 33 percent through 2016.

Pet owners are now more aware of the availability of veterinary care and are more willing to pay for extensive procedures than owners in the past. Veterinary science has caught up to human medicine, so procedures such as hip replacements, kidney transplants, and blood transfusions are now available for animals as well.

Furthermore, pet insurance is rising in popularity, which means that more money will be spent on care.

The majority of veterinarians practice in animal hospitals or clinics and care primarily for companion animals. Faster growth of pet cats is expected to increase the demand for feline veterinary services, while demand for veterinary care for dogs is projected to grow at a more modest pace.

The number of jobs for large-animal veterinarians will not grow as dramatically as jobs for companion-animal vets. Vets may find more job openings in rural areas, because many people do not want to work in isolated areas—however, they are likely to earn less money there.

In addition, more pet owners are likely to take advantage of nontraditional veterinary services where a veterinarian may be on staff, such as "doggy day care centers," and pet spas and hotels.

Training Track

Veterinarians need a doctor of veterinary medicine (DVM or VMD) degree from a four-year program at an accredited college of veterinary medicine. There are currently twenty-eight colleges in twenty-six states that meet the accreditation standards set by the Council on Education of the American Veterinary Medical Association (AVMA; *www.avma.org*).

All states and the District of Columbia require that veterinarians be licensed before they can practice, and that they pass a national exam, the North American Veterinary Licensing Exam (*www.nbvme.org*). This eight-hour examination consists of multiple-choice questions and visual materials designed to test diagnostic skills. Beyond those requirements, specific licensing demands differ from state to state.

The Bottom Line

As with vet techs, many people find personal and career satisfaction in caring for animals. However, veterinarians in private or clinical practice often work long hours in a noisy, indoor environment. In addition, they sometimes have to interact with pet owners who are emotionally distressed or demanding. When working with animals that are frightened or in pain, veterinarians risk being bitten, kicked, or scratched. Solo practitioners may work extended and weekend hours, usually responding to emergencies.

KNOCK 'EM DEAD TIP

There is currently a shortage of food supply veterinarians—those who protect the country's food supply from farm to table. These individuals treat local livestock populations. The supply of vets in this specialized area is expected to fall short by 4 to 5 percent annually through 2016, which makes this choice within the veterinary career category a hot prospect for people entering the field.

THE PAYCHECK

Median annual earnings	$71,990
Highest 10 percent earned	>$133,150
Lowest 10 percent earned	<$43,530
Best-paying states	District of Columbia, Connecticut, New Jersey, California, New York

Web Links

www.avma.org
www.thevetrecruiter.com
www.ihireveterinary.com
www.talktothevet.com

Medical Assistant

Day-to-Day

Medical assistants are responsible for administrative and clinical tasks that help manage the offices of physicians and other health practitioners. (They are not the same as physician assistants, who examine, diagnose, and treat patients under the direct supervision of a physician.) The duties of medical assistants vary depending on the location, the size of the practice, and the practitioner's specialty. In small practices, medical assistants usually handle both administrative (e.g., answering phones, filing) and clinical duties (e.g., taking vital signs) and report to an office manager, physician, or other health practitioner. Those in large practices tend to specialize in a particular area, under the supervision of department administrators.

Typical administrative tasks include updating and filing patients' medical records, filling out insurance paperwork, and arranging for hospital admissions and lab tests. They also perform general tasks such as answering phones, greeting patients, scheduling appointments, handling billing and bookkeeping, purchasing supplies and equipment, and keeping waiting and examining rooms neat and clean.

Medical assistants' simple medical responsibilities vary according to what is allowed by state law, but might include taking medical histories, recording vital signs, explaining procedures to patients, preparing patients for examinations, sterilizing medical instruments, and assisting physicians during examinations. Medical assistants may also collect and prepare laboratory specimens and sometimes even perform basic laboratory tests on the premises. They might instruct patients about medications and special diets, prepare and administer medications as directed by a physician, authorize drug refills as directed, send prescriptions to a pharmacy, draw blood, prepare patients for X-rays, take electrocardiograms, remove sutures, and change dressings.

The Big Picture
Expected to grow 34 percent through 2016.

Most medical assistants (62 percent) work in doctors' offices; 12 percent work in hospitals, including inpatient and outpatient facilities; and 11 percent work in offices of other health practitioners. As the health care industry expands because of medical advances and the aging of the baby boomer generation, there will be an increased need for all health care workers. Helping to drive job growth is the increasing number of group practices, clinics, and other health care facilities that need support personnel, particularly medical assistants who can handle both administrative and clinical duties. In addition, medical assistants work primarily in outpatient settings, a rapidly growing sector of the health care industry. Job opportunities should be excellent, particularly for those with formal training or experience and certification.

Training Track

Some medical assistants get on-the-job training, but they are expected to at least have a high school diploma or the equivalent. To be more employable, however, many complete one-year or two-year programs. Postsecondary medical assisting programs are offered in vocational-technical high schools, postsecondary vocational schools, and community and junior colleges. One-year programs yield a certificate or diploma, and two-year programs end in an associate's degree. Courses include anatomy, physiology, medical terminology, accounting, and insurance processing. Students also learn hands-on medical skills: laboratory techniques, clinical and diagnostic procedures, pharmaceutical principles, the administration of medications, and first aid. Studying patient relations, medical law, and ethics is a plus.

Employers prefer to hire experienced workers or those who are certified. Although not required, certification indicates that a medical assistant meets certain standards of competence. There are various associations that award certification credentials to medical assistants, such as the American Association of Medical Assistants (*www.aama-ntl.org*). Some medical assistants become certified in a clinical specialty of interest to them.

The Bottom Line

Although medical assistants are dependent on practitioners and work under a physician who is responsible for their actions, they are still subject to individual liability for providing medical care. Medical assistants should consider obtaining an insurance rider (either through their employer or on their own) to protect them in the event of a lawsuit.

THE PAYCHECK

Median annual earnings	$26,290
Highest 10 percent earned	>$36,840
Lowest 10 percent earned	<$18,860
Best-paying states	District of Columbia, Alaska, Massachusetts, Connecticut, Washington

Web Links

www.aama-ntl.org
www.amt1.com
www.medicalassistant.net
www.medicalassistantjobsnow.com

Pharmacy Technician

Day-to-Day

Pharmacy technicians help licensed pharmacists provide medication and other health care products to patients. Technicians usually help by counting tablets and labeling bottles, as well as by answering phones, stocking shelves, and operating cash registers.

Pharmacy technicians who work in retail or mail-order pharmacies have varying responsibilities, depending on state rules and regulations. They usually receive written or electronic prescriptions from patients, or from a doctor's office. First, they verify that information on the prescription is complete and accurate. Next, they prepare the prescription by retrieving, counting, pouring/weighing, and sometimes mixing the medication.

In hospitals, nursing homes, and assisted-living facilities, technicians often have added responsibilities, including reading patients' charts and preparing the appropriate medication from the directions given. After the pharmacist checks the prescription for accuracy, the pharmacy technician may deliver it to the patient.

The Big Picture

Expected to grow 32 percent through 2016.

The increased number of middle-aged and elderly people—who use more prescription drugs than younger people due to health problems associating with aging—will spur demand for technicians in the near future. In addition, more and more drugs will appear on the market as doctors and scientists discover new treatments—and more pharmacy techs will be needed to administer those drugs. Many local pharmacies are doubling as patient-care centers, so pharmacy technicians will likely assume responsibility for some of the more routine tasks previously performed by pharmacists, including interacting with customers.

Training Track

Although most pharmacy technicians receive informal on-the-job training, employers prefer candidates who have completed formal training and certification. However, there are currently few state and no federal requirements for formal training or certification of pharmacy technicians. Two organizations, the Pharmacy Technician Certification Board (*www.ptcb.org*) and the Institute for the Certification of Pharmacy Technicians (*www.nationaltechexam.org*), administer national certification examinations. Certification is voluntary in most states, but is required by some states and employers. (Some technicians are hired without formal training, but under the condition that they will obtain certification by an agreed-upon deadline.) To be eligible for either exam, candidates must have a high school diploma or GED, no felony convictions of any kind within five years of applying, and no drug- or pharmacy-related felony convictions at any point.

Under both programs, technicians must be recertified every two years. Recertification requires twenty hours of continuing education (with at least one hour in pharmacy law) within the two-year certification period.

The Bottom Line

Drug dispensing machines may change the nature of the pharmacy tech's job. These machines increase productivity and attempt to ensure accuracy by counting pills and placing them into prescription containers. These machines currently are only used for the most common medications, however, and their effect on employment should be minimal.

Mathematics, spelling, and reading skills are important to this occupation. Pharmacy techs must be precise; details are sometimes a matter of life and death, and may result in job stress.

THE PAYCHECK

Median annual earnings	$28,500
Highest 10 percent earned	>$39,480
Lowest 10 percent earned	<$19,270
Best-paying states	Alaska, California, Washington, Hawaii, District of Columbia

Web Links

www.ptch.org
www.nationaltechexam.org
www.pharmacytechnician.org
www.pharmacytech.org

Dental Hygienist

Day-to-Day

Dental hygienists clean teeth, examine gums, and record the possible presence of diseases or abnormalities for a dentist to investigate. They also teach patients how to practice good oral hygiene and provide other preventive dental care, possibly including taking X-rays.

In some states, hygienists are allowed to administer general anesthetics; in other states, they can only administer local anesthetics using syringes. Some states also allow hygienists to place and carve filling materials, temporary fillings, and periodontal dressings; remove sutures; and smooth and polish metal restorations.

The Big Picture

Expected to grow 30 percent through 2016.

Job prospects are expected to remain excellent in this field because of population growth, older people increasingly retaining more teeth, and the continued focus on preventive dental care. To meet this demand, facilities will employ more hygienists per office. In addition, as dentists' workloads increase, they are expected to have hygienists perform preventive dental care, such as cleaning, so that they may devote their own time to more complex procedures.

More than half of dental hygienists work part-time; flexible scheduling is an attractive feature of this job.

Training Track

Dental hygienists need a minimum of an associate's degree or certificate in dental hygiene in order to practice in a private dental office. A bachelor's or master's degree is usually required for research, teaching, or clinical practice in public or school health programs. In order to get into a degree program, candidates need a high school diploma and college entrance test scores. Some dental hygiene programs also require applicants to have completed at least one year of college courses. Specific entrance requirements vary from one school to another. Most dental hygiene programs grant an associate's degree, although some also offer a certificate, a bachelor's degree, or a master's degree.

Dental hygienists must be licensed by the state in which they practice. Nearly all states require candidates to graduate from an accredited dental hygiene school and pass both a written and clinical examination. The American Dental Association's Joint Commission on National Dental Examinations (*www.ada.org*) administers the written examination, which is accepted by all states and the District of Columbia, while state or regional testing agencies administer the clinical examination. In addition, most states require candidates to pass an examination on the legal aspects of dental hygiene practice.

The Bottom Line

Dental hygienists must have good manual dexterity because they need to move sharp dental instruments within a patient's mouth. In addition, hygienists can be exposed to infectious diseases, and may suffer backache from leaning forward to look inside patients' mouths.

THE PAYCHECK

Median annual earnings	$66,950
Highest 10 percent earned	>$91,470
Lowest 10 percent earned	<$44,180
Best-paying states	Alaska, Washington, California, Oregon, Nevada

Web Links

www.adha.org
www.dhed.net
www.dentalassistantjobs.com
www.dentalhygienistjobs.com
www.dentalhygienists.com

KNOCK 'EM DEAD TIP
According to the American Dental Hygienists' Association's website (*www.adha.org*), two states—Colorado and Washington—have independent practice laws that allow registered dental hygienists to practice without the supervision of a dentist. These states acknowledge that dental hygienists, by virtue of their comprehensive education and clinical preparation, are capable of providing safe and effective preventive oral health care services to the public without dental supervision.

Physical Therapist

Day-to-Day

Physical therapists (PTs) help patients restore a variety of physical functions, improve their range of mobility, relieve pain, and prevent or limit permanent physical disabilities. They work with accident victims and individuals with disabling conditions such as lower-back pain, arthritis, heart disease, fractures, and head injuries.

When they begin working with a patient, PTs examine his medical history and then measure his range of motion, balance, posture, muscle strength, respiration, and motor function. When they have assessed the patient's condition, they develop a treatment plan and outline its projected result.

The treatment plan often includes daily exercises, especially for patients who have been immobilized or who lack flexibility, strength, or endurance. PTs encourage patients to use their muscles in various ways to improve their conditions. The goal is to improve how an individual functions at work and at home.

The Big Picture

Expected to grow 27 percent through 2016.

The increasing number of elderly people in the population will drive the demand for physical therapy services because older people are more vulnerable to chronic and debilitating conditions that require therapeutic services. Also, members of the baby boom generation are entering the prime age for heart attacks and strokes, which usually require cardiac and physical rehabilitation.

In addition, more children than ever will use physical therapy as scientific advances save the lives of newborns who have a variety of serious conditions. Job opportunities will be good, especially in acute hospital, rehabilitation, and orthopedic settings.

Training Track

In order to practice, a PT usually needs a master's degree from an accredited physical therapy program and a state license, which is awarded after the candidate passes national and state examinations. The Commission on Accreditation in Physical Therapy Education (*www.apta.org*) is the only agency that grants accreditation, and it only accredits master's degree and doctoral degree programs. In the future, a doctoral degree might be the required entry-level degree. Master's degree programs typically last two years, and doctoral degree programs last three years. Specific eligibility requirements for licensure vary by state.

The Bottom Line

PTs work in hospitals, clinics, and private offices that have special equipment. They also treat patients in hospital rooms, homes, or schools. Therapists often have to stoop, kneel, crouch, lift, and stand for long periods of time—making the job quite physically demanding. In addition, PTs often must manage heavy equipment and lift patients or help them move.

According to the U.S. Bureau of Labor Statistics, the number of physical therapy positions is greater than the number of practicing PTs because some of them work part-time for two or more jobs. For example, a therapist may work in a private practice and in another health care facility.

THE PAYCHECK

Median annual earnings	$66,200
Highest 10 percent earned	>$94,810
Lowest 10 percent earned	<$46,510
Best-paying states	Nevada, California, New Jersey, Rhode Island, Illinois

KNOCK 'EM DEAD TIP

Confused about the difference between a physical therapist (PT) and an occupational therapist (OT)? A PT helps a patient rehabilitate his body from surgery or a specific injury, working to rebuild muscle groups. An OT focuses on helping a patient regain daily life skills, such as dressing, feeding, and living independently.

Web Links

www.apta.org
www.fsbpt.org
www.physical-therapy-jobs.net
www.ptjobs.com
www.physicaltherapy.com

Physician Assistant

Day-to-Day

Physician assistants (PAs) practice medicine under the supervision of physicians and surgeons. (They should not be confused with medical assistants, who perform routine clinical and clerical tasks; see earlier for more about that occupation.) Physicians delegate certain work to PAs, such as diagnostic, therapeutic, and preventive health care services. PAs conduct medical histories, examine and treat patients, order and analyze lab tests and X-rays, and make diagnoses. They also suture, splint, and cast patients' minor injuries. PAs also record progress notes, teach patients about conditions or behaviors, and answer patients' questions. PAs may prescribe some medications in all states, the District of Columbia, Guam, and the Commonwealth of the Northern Mariana Islands.

In some cases (such as in rural areas or inner city clinics, where the supervising physician may only be in the office one or two days a week), PAs may be the principal care providers in the practice. In those cases, the PA confers with the supervising physician and other medical professionals as needed and as required by law. Some PAs even make house calls or go to hospitals and nursing care facilities to check on patients, after which they report back to the physician about the patient's condition or progress. The supervising physician and state laws dictate exactly what a PA's duties will be at a certain practice.

The Big Picture

Expected to grow 39 percent through 2016.

Both private practice physicians and health care facilities are expected to employ more PAs to provide primary care and to assist with medical and surgical procedures because PAs are cost-effective. They earn less than full physicians, yet can effectively diagnose and treat a wide variety of common ailments and conditions. Job prospects are projected to be promising, especially in rural and inner-city clinics, because those settings have difficulty attracting physicians. Opportunities will be best in states that allow PAs a wider scope of practice. States' laws change frequently; visit *www.aapa.org/news_and_publications* to view recent information.

Training Track

All states and the District of Columbia require PAs to complete an accredited, formal education program and pass a national licensure exam. PA programs usually last at least two years. Admission requirements vary by program, but many require at least two years of college and some health care experience. Most programs are in schools of allied health, academic health centers, medical schools, or four-year colleges; a few are offered by community colleges, the military, or large hospitals. Many accredited PA programs have clinical teaching affiliations with medical schools.

All states and the District of Columbia have legislation governing the qualifications or practice of PAs, who must pass the Physician Assistant National Certifying Examination. This test is administered by the National Commission on Certification of Physician Assistants (NCCPA; *www.nccpa.net*) and is open only to graduates of accredited PA programs. Only those who pass the examination may use the credential "Physician Assistant-Certified." To remain certified, PAs must complete 100 hours of continuing medical education every two years and pass a recertification exam every six years.

The Bottom Line

PAs can take on added responsibilities and earn higher paychecks as their knowledge base and experience grows. However, by the very nature of the profession, PAs always are supervised by physicians and while they often function as a fill-in to a physician, they will never have the same earning power or the prestige of the position.

Besides working in traditional doctors' offices, PAs should also find opportunities in institutional settings such as hospitals, academic medical centers, public clinics, and prisons. PAs may find open positions at inpatient teaching hospitals. This trend may take hold as facilities reduce the number of hours physician residents are permitted to work and instead use PAs to supply some of the medical services those residents would have offered.

THE PAYCHECK

Median annual earnings	$74,980
Highest 10 percent earned	>$102,230
Lowest 10 percent earned	<$43,000
Best-paying states	Alaska, Nevada, Connecticut, Washington, New Jersey

Web Links

www.aapa.org
www.nccpa.net
www.physicianassistantjobs.com
www.paworld.net
www.physicianassistant.com

Radiation Therapist

Day-to-Day

Radiation therapy is primarily used to treat cancer in the human body. Radiation therapists use machines called linear accelerators to administer radiation treatment to patients. These machines project intense X-rays at cancer cells. As the X-rays collide with human tissue, they produce highly energized ions that can shrink and sometimes eliminate cancerous tumors. This type of therapy is sometimes used as the sole treatment for cancer, but is usually used in conjunction with chemotherapy or surgery. For that reason, radiation therapists often work as part of a patient's oncology team.

As they administer the treatments, radiation therapists keep detailed patient records, which include the dose used per treatment, the total amount of radiation used to date, the area treated, and the patient's reactions. Radiation oncologists and dosimetrists (who calculate and manage radiation doses for each patient) review these records to measure the effectiveness of the treatment plan, to monitor the total amount of radiation exposure that the patient has received, and to minimize side effects.

The Big Picture

Expected to grow 25 percent through 2016.

Current statistics for the prevalence of cancer in the United States are striking. The American Cancer Society (ACS; *www.cancer.org*) estimates that men in the United States have approximately a 1-in-2 lifetime risk of developing cancer; women's lifetime risk is approximately 1 in 3. The ACS also notes that about 77 percent of all cancers are diagnosed in people aged fifty-five and older. Because an increasing percentage of the U.S. population is in this older age group, the number of people needing cancer treatment is expected to increase and thus spur demand for radiation therapists. In addition, as radiation technology advances and is able to treat more types of cancer, radiation therapy will be prescribed more often.

Training Track

Radiation therapists need a bachelor's degree, associate's degree, or certificate in radiation therapy. Many states also require radiation therapists to be licensed. Some states, as well as many employers, require that radiation therapists be certified by the American Registry of Radiologic Technologists (ARRT, *www.arrt.org*). To become ARRT-certified, an applicant must complete an accredited radiation therapy program, adhere to ARRT ethical standards, and pass the ARRT certification examination. The examination and accredited academic programs teach radiation protection and quality assurance, clinical concepts in radiation oncology, treatment planning and delivery, and patient care and education.

The Bottom Line

Though being a radiation therapist can be very rewarding when patients' health improves, it can also be stressful. Also, radiation therapists are obviously exposed to radioactive materials regularly; they must ensure that they are not exposed to dangerous levels of radiation. Following standard safety procedures can prevent overexposure.

THE PAYCHECK

Median annual earnings	$66,170
Highest 10 percent earned	>$92,110
Lowest 10 percent earned	<$44,840
Best-paying states	New Jersey, California, Montana, Washington, Oregon

Web Links

www.arrt.org
www.asrt.org
www.radworking.com
www.ihireradiology.com

Surgical Technician

Day-to-Day

Surgical technologists, who are also referred to as scrubs, surgical technicians, or operating room technicians, assist with surgeries under the supervision of surgeons, registered nurses, or other medical personnel. Surgical technologists are members of operating room teams, and work alongside surgeons, anesthesiologists, and nurses.

Before an operation, surgical techs prepare the operating room by compiling and arranging surgical instruments and equipment and sterile solutions. Techs also prep patients by cleaning and disinfecting incision sites. They also transport patients to the operating room, help position them on the operating table, and then cover them with sterile surgical drapes.

During surgeries, techs pass instruments and other supplies to surgeons and surgeon assistants, operate lights and suction machines, and observe patients' vital signs. They may hold retractors; cut sutures; and help count sponges, needles, supplies, and instruments. After the surgery, they arrange for specimens to be tested in labs and help apply dressings to the incision site.

The Big Picture

Expected to grow 24 percent through 2016.

The number of surgical procedures is expected to rise as the population grows and ages. In addition, technological advances, such as fiber optics and laser technology, will pave the way for new surgical procedures to be performed. More surgical techs will be needed to assist with this increase in volume.

Training Track

Surgical technologists must enroll in programs offered by community and junior colleges, vocational schools, universities, hospitals, and the military. Programs last from nine to twenty-four months and lead to a certificate, diploma, or associate's degree.

Most employers prefer to hire certified technologists. Technologists may obtain voluntary professional certification from the Liaison Council on Certification for the Surgical Technologist by graduating from a Commission on Accreditation of Allied Health Education Programs–accredited program (*www.caahep .org*) and passing a national certification examination. Once requirements are met, they can use the Certified Surgical Technologist (CST) designation. To maintain certification, surgical techs must participate in continuing education or re-examinations.

Certification may also be granted by the National Center for Competency Testing (NCCT; *www.ncctinc.com*). To qualify to take the exam, candidates must have completed an accredited training program; a two-year hospital on-the-job training program; or seven years of experience working in the field. After passing the exam, individuals may use the designation Tech in Surgery-Certified, TS-C (NCCT). This certification must be renewed every five years through either continuing education or re-examination.

The Bottom Line

Surgical techs must stand for long periods of time and remain alert during surgery. At times, they may be exposed to communicable diseases as well as unpleasant sights, odors, and materials.

Surgical technologists need manual dexterity to handle instruments quickly. They also must be conscientious, orderly, and emotionally stable in order to handle the demands of the stressful operating room environment.

KNOCK 'EM DEAD TIP

"Scrubs" got their start in the military because nurses were not permitted on the battlefield or on combat ships during wartime. After the Korean War, the shortage of operating room nurses led army medics and navy corpsmen to careers as operating room technicians. In 1973, the official title of the position was changed to surgical technologist.

THE PAYCHECK

Median annual earnings	$36,080
Highest 10 percent earned	>$51,140
Lowest 10 percent earned	<$25,490
Best-paying states	District of Columbia, California, Maryland, Nevada, Minnesota

Web Links

www.nsaa.net
www.surgicaltechsuccess.com
www.getsurgicaljobs.com
www.ast.org

Athletic Trainer

Day-to-Day

Athletic trainers help people prevent, treat, and rehab musculoskeletal injuries. They work with everyone from professional athletes to industrial workers. Because these trainers are sometimes "first responders" when injuries occur (such as during a sports game), they must be able to recognize, evaluate, and assess injuries and provide immediate care when needed. Athletic trainers are not the same as fitness trainers or personal trainers, who are not health care workers, but rather train people to become physically fit.

Aside from treating injuries, athletic trainers often help people prevent injuries by advising the use of protective gear such as tape, bandages, and braces. They also educate people on what they should do to avoid putting themselves at risk for injuries, such as proper stretching routines.

Athletic trainers work under the supervision of a licensed physician and in a team with other health care providers. The level of medical supervision varies, depending on the setting.

The Big Picture

Expected to grow 37 percent through 2016.

Job growth will be concentrated in the health care industry, including hospitals and private practices. The demand for health care in general should grow dramatically because of medical breakthroughs, an increased emphasis on preventive care, and an aging population. Athletic trainers will benefit because they are a cost-effective way to expand the services offered at a particular practice. Athletic trainers are now more widely accepted as health professionals thanks to more standardized licensing and regulation.

Fitness and recreational sports centers will also provide many new jobs, as these establishments become more popular and increase their client bases. The number of opportunities with sports teams—though perhaps the most famous of athletic trainer jobs—will not change much, however. Most professional sports teams and colleges and universities already have complete athletic training staffs.

Training Track

According to the National Athletic Trainers Association (*www.nata.org*), 68 percent of athletic trainers have a master's or doctoral degree. Athletic trainers may need a master's or higher degree to be eligible for some positions (especially those in colleges and universities), and to increase their advancement opportunities. Because some positions in schools involve teaching academic classes along with traditional athletic trainer duties, candidates may need a teaching certificate or license as well.

Nearly all states require athletic trainers to be certified by the Board of Certification, Inc. (BOC; *www.bocatc.org*). For certification, athletic trainers need a bachelor's degree from an accredited athletic training program and must pass a rigorous examination. To maintain their certification, trainers must participate in continuing education courses. In states where licensure is not required, certification is voluntary but will probably be helpful for job seekers and those in the field who want career advancement.

The Bottom Line

Athletic trainers in nonsport settings generally have an established schedule—usually about forty to fifty hours per week—with nights and weekends off. Athletic trainers who work for sports teams or facilities, however, have more varied schedules and work more hours per week. These athletic trainers must be present for team practices and games, which often take place on evenings and weekends, and their schedules can change on short notice when events have to be rescheduled due to bad weather. As a result, athletic trainers in sports settings may regularly work six or seven days per week, including late hours.

In high schools, athletic trainers who also teach may work sixty to seventy hours a week, or more. In National Collegiate Athletic Association Division I colleges and universities, athletic trainers generally work with one particular sports team; when that team's sport is in season, they work at least fifty to sixty hours a week.

Some athletic trainers may find the position stressful and be affected by the pressure to win that is associated with competitive sports.

THE PAYCHECK

Median annual earnings	$36,560
Highest 10 percent earned	>$57,580
Lowest 10 percent earned	<$21,940
Best-paying states	District of Columbia, Rhode Island, Illinois, Hawaii, Tennessee

Web Links

www.nata.org
www.bocatc.org
www.athletictrainer.com
www.collegeathletictrainer.org
www.nasm.org

Registered Nurse

Day-to-Day

Registered nurses (RNs) treat patients, educate them about medical conditions, and provide advice and emotional support to patients' family members. They work in all medical specialties and in a variety of settings (hospitals, clinics, nursing care facilities, private practices, and so on). RNs are responsible for a wide range of duties, including recording patients' medical histories and symptoms, helping perform diagnostic tests and analyzing the results, giving treatment and medications, and following up with patients' rehabilitation.

RNs can specialize in one or more areas of patient care or the medical field, including these four most common ways: work setting or type of treatment (such as operating room nurses), specific health conditions (such as oncology nurses), working with one or more organs or body system types (such as cardiac nurses), or working with a specific type of patient (such as geriatric nurses). Some RNs may combine specialties, such as pediatric oncology nurses, who deal with children and adolescents who have cancer.

The Big Picture

Expected to grow 22.2 percent through 2016.

Job opportunities for registered nurses are expected to be excellent through 2016, but may vary by type of employer and location. Still, registered nurses are projected to generate 587,000 new jobs, among the largest number of new jobs for any occupation. Additionally, hundreds of thousands of job openings will result from the need to replace experienced nurses who leave the occupation. Some experts predict that by 2025, there could be a vacancy rate of 40 percent or higher. Also, an aging baby boom population with longer life spans will require nursing care as they age.

Training Track

Registered nurses usually enter the field by obtaining a bachelor's degree, an associate's degree, or a diploma from an approved nursing program. Nurses most commonly complete an associate's degree or bachelor's degree program and then must complete a national licensing examination (the NCLEX-RN) in order to work in any state or territory or the District of Columbia. Nurses may be licensed in more than one state, either by taking that state's exam or by one state endorsing another state's license. Further training or education can qualify nurses to work in specialty areas and may improve career advancement.

The Bottom Line

Many nurses find the career immensely rewarding. However, the nursing field is rife with challenges. Nurses are likely to come into close contact with patients with infectious diseases and with toxic, harmful, or potentially hazardous materials and medications. They are also susceptible to back injury when moving patients, shocks from electrical equipment, and hazards posed by compressed gases and accidental needle pricks. RNs also may suffer emotional stress from caring for patients (and their families) who are suffering, the need to make critical decisions, and ethical dilemmas.

THE PAYCHECK

Median annual earnings	$57,280
Highest 10 percent earned	>$83,440
Lowest 10 percent earned	<$40,250
Best-paying states	California, Massachusetts, Hawaii, Maryland, New York

Web Links

www.nursingworld.com
www.nsna.org
www.aacn.nche.edu
www.nurse.com

KNOCK 'EM DEAD TIP
The U.S. Bureau of Labor Statistics published in the November 2007 *Monthly Labor Review* that more than 1 million new and replacement nurses will be needed by 2016. Government analysts project that more than 587,000 new nursing positions will be created through 2016, making nursing the nation's top profession in terms of projected job growth.

Pharmacist

Day-to-Day

Pharmacists distribute prescription drugs to patients and advise their patients, as well as physicians and other health practitioners, on the selection, dosages, interactions, and side effects of medications. Compounding—the actual mixing of ingredients to form medications—is nowadays a small part of a pharmacist's practice, because most medicines are produced by pharmaceutical companies in a standard dosage and drug delivery form. The majority of pharmacists work in a retail drugstore or in a health care facility, such as a hospital, nursing home, mental health institution, or clinic.

Pharmacists in retail pharmacies dispense medications, give patients information about their prescriptions and about over-the-counter medications, and advise physicians about patients' treatments. They also provide information on durable medical equipment or home health care supplies. In addition, they may fill out insurance paperwork.

The Big Picture

Expected to grow 22 percent through 2016.

The increasing numbers of middle-aged and elderly people—who use more prescription drugs than younger people—will continue to spur demand for pharmacists. In addition, pharmaceutical companies are likely to bring more drug products to market, and insurance plans will begin covering more and more types of prescription drugs.

As the use of prescription drugs increases, demand for pharmacists will grow in most settings. Demand will also increase as cost-conscious insurers, in an attempt to improve preventive care, use pharmacists in areas such as patient education and vaccination.

Demand is also increasing in managed care organizations, where pharmacists analyze trends and patterns in medication use, and in pharmacoeconomics, which is the financial analysis of different drug therapies. New jobs also are being created in disease management—the development of new methods for curing and controlling diseases—and in sales and marketing. Rapid growth is also expected in pharmacy informatics—the use of information technology to improve patient care.

Training Track

Pharmacists need a Pharm.D. degree from an accredited college or school of pharmacy. The Pharm.D. degree has replaced the bachelor of pharmacy degree, which is no longer offered. To be admitted to a Pharm.D. program, an applicant must have completed at least two years of undergraduate study, although most have completed three or more years. About 70 percent of Pharm.D. programs require applicants to take the Pharmacy College Admissions Test (PCAT; *www.pcatweb.info*).

Besides graduating from an accredited school, a pharmacist also needs a license to practice pharmacy in all states and territories and the District of Columbia. All states, U.S. territories, and the District of Columbia require the North American Pharmacist Licensure Exam (NAPLEX; *www.nabp.net*), which tests pharmacy skills and knowledge.

The Bottom Line

The American Federation for Pharmaceutical Education reports that more than 8,000 vacancies exist in retail pharmacies, hospitals, and clinics. Demand is currently outpacing supply, which means that pharmacist job candidates should be well positioned for employment. The job can be stressful because of the detail-orientation required.

THE PAYCHECK

Median annual earnings	$94,520
Highest 10 percent earned	>$119,480
Lowest 10 percent earned	<$67,860
Best-paying states	California, Maine, New Hampshire, Alaska, Minnesota

Web Links

www.aacp.org
www.ashp.org
www.rxcareercenter.com
www.pharmacistjobs.com

KNOCK 'EM DEAD TIP

Gallup's 2008 Annual Survey of the Honesty and Ethics of Professions ranked how the American public feels about the integrity of certain members of the workforce. For the seventh consecutive year, nurses earned the highest accolades. A full 84 percent of Americans feel their ethical standards are high or very high. In the number two spot were pharmacists/druggists, with 70 percent of the public ranking their ethical standards as high or very high.

Science and Technology Professions

Four types of technologies have invaded and impacted every corner of academia, industry, and commerce. They have ushered in a new era, and revolutionized the way we communicate and interact with each other.

- Biotechnology is changing the way we take care of our health and our food sources.
- Environmental technology is changing the way we take care of our environment and nurture our resources.
- Engineering technology is changing the way we build our manufacturing and supply systems.

- Information technology is changing the ways we increase our knowledge, communications, and competitiveness.

These technologies often work hand in hand with each other to achieve new breakthroughs, so it has become more and more difficult to define exactly where one technology stops and another begins. The same applies to job titles in these fields. Job titles such as "engineer," "scientist," and "analyst" are gradually becoming interchangeable, depending largely on the employer, context, and application of the work.

There's never been a better time to be a computer specialist. While computer technology continues to increase in sophistication, so have the population's needs. Significant growth is still expected in this industry as organizations look for more efficient communications systems, improved Internet and wireless technologies, and tighter data security.

Almost 1 million new jobs are expected to be created over the next decade, making information technology the fastest growing profession of all career disciplines. In the corporate environment, the focus for the next decade will be on designing and adopting more sophisticated technologies, such as the expansion of client/server networking environments to facilitate the sharing of information; enhancement of communication systems, electronic commerce and data storage systems to make them more efficient and secure; and "cybersecurity" to protect intellectual property and sensitive information, such as customer data.

The development of personal mobile devices and falling prices of computer hardware and software have made technology more accessible than ever before. These factors will drive a need for specialists and analysts who can integrate wireless/mobile technologies into existing networks.

Almost all industries will see an increase in employment of computer professionals over the next decade. Opportunities in the information sector will mainly be in computer systems design and related services, primarily for software publishers and data processing and related industries. Self-employment opportunities for computer professionals have never been better. Entrepreneurial network systems and data communications analysts especially may find success in self-employment.

As was the case a decade ago, if you plan a career in information technology, you cannot be someone who likes the status quo; change and volatility are still very much a part of this industry. Your goal will probably not be to find a lifetime employer, but to maintain your employability. This will require constant upgrading of your skills on your own time and an awareness of industry trends. Interpersonal skills applied with nontechnical people will be paramount to your success, and, because of the increasing influence of overseas markets, languages and multicultural awareness will put anyone's career in good stead.

Computer Software Engineer

Day-to-Day

Computer software engineers apply the principles of computer science and mathematics to the design, development, testing, and evaluation of the software that make computers run. The exact job specifications of computer software engineers change rapidly due to constant improvements in technology.

Software engineers can be involved in the design and development of many types of software, including computer games; word processing and business programs; operating systems and network configuration; and compilers, which convert programs to machine language for execution on a computer.

Their job begins by analyzing users' needs, and then designing, testing, and developing software to meet those needs. In order to execute their plan, they create the detailed sets of instructions that tell the computer exactly what to do. They also may be responsible for converting these instructions into a computer language (coding), but programmers usually handle this task. Computer software engineers must be experts in operating systems to ensure that all facets of their plan will work and interact properly.

Computer *systems* software engineers coordinate the construction, maintenance, and expansion of an organization's computer systems. Based on the organization's needs, they coordinate each department's priorities—ordering, inventory, billing, and payroll for example—and make suggestions based on their expertise. They also might set up the organization's intranets—the networks that link computers within the organization and ease communication among various departments.

The Big Picture

Expected to grow 36 percent through 2016.

About 324,000 new computer software engineers jobs are expected to be generated by 2016, one of the largest employment increases of any occupation. Businesses will continue to compete against each other to boast the most advanced, secure, and user-friendly computer systems, so computer software engineers will be in demand. Demand will also increase as computer networking continues to grow, especially for Internet, intranet, and web applications. Likewise, electronic data-processing systems in business, telecommunications, and government will become more sophisticated and complex and will therefore need oversight by a computer software engineer.

Increased Internet usage, the proliferation of websites, and wireless technology also spawn new products and create worker demand. As individuals and businesses rely more on hand-held computers and wireless networks, computer software engineers will need to integrate current computer systems with this new technology. Additionally, concerns over "cybersecurity" should result in businesses and government investing heavily in software that protects their networks and vital electronic infrastructure from attack. The expansion of cybersecurity will lead to an increased need for computer engineers to design and develop software and systems that will integrate with already existing older systems.

Training Track

Most employers prefer applicants who have at least a bachelor's degree (usually in computer science or software engineering) and experience with a variety of computer systems and technologies. Systems software engineers often study computer science or computer information systems. Those pursuing more complex or higher-level jobs will probably need a graduate degree. Some software vendors offer certification and training programs in their particular system, but most experts say that program certification alone is not sufficient for the majority of software engineering jobs.

The Bottom Line

Like other workers who spend long hours in front of a computer, software engineers are susceptible to eyestrain, back discomfort, and hand and wrist problems such as carpal tunnel syndrome.

Outsourcing is a concern in this industry. Firms may cut costs by shifting operations to foreign countries with lower wages and highly educated workers. However, jobs in software engineering are less prone to being off-shored than are jobs in other computer specialties, because software engineering requires constant communication, knowledge of the company's valuable intellectual property, and intense research and development.

THE PAYCHECK

Median annual earnings	$92,430
Highest 10 percent earned	>$135,780
Lowest 10 percent earned	<$57,810
Best-paying states	Massachusetts, California, Maryland, Virginia, Colorado

Web Links

www.acm.org
www.computer.org
www.Dice.com

KNOCK 'EM DEAD TIP

According to the Entertainment Software Association, computer and video game companies directly and indirectly employ more than 80,000 people in thirty-one states. Projected growth for 2009 is 250,000 jobs. The average salary is $92,300.

Computer Scientist and Database Administrator

Day-to-Day

Computer scientists are distinguished from other employees in computer technologies by the higher level of theoretical expertise and innovation they apply to complex problems and the creation or application of new technology. Computer scientists may research new theories, programming languages, or hardware. Some researchers work on multidisciplinary projects, such as virtual reality, human-computer interaction, or robots. They may work on a team with electrical engineers and other specialists.

Database administrators work with database software and determine ways to organize and store data. They may create new databases or update existing ones by integrating data from outdated systems into a new system. They also test and coordinate modifications to the system when needed and troubleshoot problems. Because many databases are connected to the Internet, database administrators also plan and coordinate security measures with network administrators. With the growing volume of sensitive data and the increasing interconnectedness of computer networks, data integrity, backup systems, and database security have become increasingly important aspects of the job.

The Big Picture

Expected to grow 37 percent through 2016.

Overall, job increases will be driven by very rapid growth in computer systems design and related services, which is projected to be one of the fastest-growing industries in the U.S. economy through 2016. Demand for database administrators will grow as companies' data becomes more complex and sophisticated, and as cybersecurity becomes increasingly important. Expansion of electronic commerce—doing business on the Internet—and the continuing need to build and maintain databases that store companies' critical proprietary information are fueling demand for database administrators.

Training Track

Jobs in these fields usually require at least a bachelor's degree; however, some jobs may require only a two-year degree. Relevant work experience also is very important. For more complex jobs, employers prefer candidates with graduate degrees. Most computer scientist positions require a PhD, as their main job function is research.

For database administrator positions, most employers seek applicants who have bachelor's degrees in computer science, information science, or management information systems (MIS).

Job seekers can better their chances by getting certified in relevant areas. Most certifications are offered through private companies, with many related to specific products. Many employers regard these certifications as the industry standard.

The Bottom Line

Due to spending long periods in front of a computer, computer scientists and database administrators are susceptible to eyestrain, back discomfort, and hand and wrist problems such as carpal tunnel syndrome or cumulative trauma disorder.

THE PAYCHECK

Median annual earnings of computer scientists	$93,950
Highest 10 percent earned	>$144,880
Lowest 10 percent earned	<$53,590
Median annual earnings of database administrators	$64,670
Highest 10 percent earned	>$103,010
Lowest 10 percent earned	<$37,350
Best-paying states for both positions	Maryland, California, New York, New Jersey, Virginia

Web Links

www.acm.org
www.computer.org
www.aitp.org
www.itjobs.net
www.tech-centric.net

Computer Systems Analyst

Day-to-Day

Computer systems analysts help organizations use technology effectively and incorporate new aspects of technology into their existing systems. They may design and develop new computer systems to fill a company's needs by configuring new hardware and software, or they may upgrade an existing system. Computer systems analysts also fix problems with an organization's computers.

Most systems analysts work with a specific genre of computer systems—for example, business/accounting/financial systems or scientific/engineering systems—and become an expert in that particular system. Analysts who specialize in helping an organization select the proper system software and infrastructure are called *system architects*. Analysts who specialize in developing and fine-tuning systems often are known as *systems designers*.

When starting a project, systems analysts consult various members of the organization to define the system's goals. Next, they devise a plan based on structured analysis, data modeling, information engineering, and mathematical model building to make sure their plans are efficient and complete. They also may prepare cost-benefit and return-on-investment analyses to help management decide whether the project would be cost-effective.

If a system is approved, systems analysts then narrow down what computer hardware and software is needed to set it up. Before the system goes "live," they coordinate tests and try out different aspects of the system to troubleshoot initial problems. Next, they prepare specifications, flow charts, and process diagrams for computer programmers to follow; then they work with programmers to "debug," or eliminate errors, from the system. Systems analysts who do more in-depth testing may be called *software quality assurance analysts*. In addition to running tests, these workers diagnose problems, suggest solutions, and determine whether program goals have been met.

The Big Picture
Expected to grow 29 percent through 2016.

Virtually every company needs to have some presence on the Internet—some merely have information available to consumers, but others have vast ordering systems. The explosion in technology in this area has helped fuel the need for computer systems analysts to develop and integrate these applications. In addition, the introduction of the wireless Internet and of handheld computers, have created a need for experts who can integrate these technologies into existing networks. Analysts who are knowledgeable about systems integration and security should be in particularly high demand.

Most systems analysts work for companies who specialize in computer systems design. However, they are also employed by governments, insurance companies, financial institutions, hospitals, consulting firms, data processing services firms, universities, and managers of companies and enterprises.

Training Track

At the very least, a computer systems analyst must have a bachelor's degree in a technical field, such as computer science, information science, applied mathematics, engineering, or the physical sciences. Some employers seek applicants with at least a bachelor's degree in a business-related field such as management information systems (MIS). For higher level or more complex positions, companies will look for a candidate with a master's degree in business administration (MBA) with a concentration in information systems.

Employers generally look for people with expertise relevant to the job. For example, systems analysts who wish to work for a bank should have some expertise in finance, and systems analysts who wish to work for a hospital should have some knowledge of the health care industry.

The Bottom Line

Like other technology jobs, off-shoring will temper growth possibilities. Routine work may be sent to foreign countries to save money, although the Bureau of Labor Statistics anticipates 149,000 added to the workforce through 2016.

Many systems analysts work on a temporary or contract basis (approximately 29,000); usually on one specific project for a company or organization. Many of these analysts run their own contracting or consulting business. This arrangement is fine for some analysts, but others may prefer the stability of a full-time position.

THE PAYCHECK

Median annual earnings	$69,760
Highest 10 percent earned	>$106,820
Lowest 10 percent earned	<$42,780
Best-paying states	Virginia, New Jersey, Massachusetts, Rhode Island, Arizona

Web Links

www.acm.org
www.computer.org
www.iasahome.org
www.Dice.com
www.getcomputersystemsanalystjobs.com

Environmental Scientist and Hydrologist

Day-to-Day

In general, environmental scientists and hydrologists use their knowledge of the physical makeup and history of the Earth to protect the environment, study the properties of water (both above and below ground), locate water and energy resources, predict water-related hazards, and provide environmental site assessments and advice on air quality and hazardous-waste-site remediation.

More specifically, environmental scientists conduct research that helps them identify, lessen, and/or eliminate hazards that affect people, wildlife, and the environment. These workers measure and observe aspects of air, water, and soil to determine the way to clean and preserve the environment. Environmental engineers must understand the main ways that humans can protect the environment—conservation, recycling, and replenishment. They use this understanding to design and monitor waste disposal sites, preserve water supplies, and reclaim contaminated land and water to comply with federal regulations. They also write risk assessments, describing the likely effect of construction and other environmental changes; write technical proposals; and give presentations to necessary parties.

Hydrologists study the quantity, distribution, circulation, and physical properties of bodies of water. They usually focus their research on either underground water or surface water. They also examine precipitation, its rate of infiltration into the soil, its movement through the Earth, and its return to the ocean and atmosphere.

Consulting firms that help organizations comply with government regulations employ many environmental scientists and hydrologists. Environmental scientists who help create local, state, and federal governments' environmental policies may help identify ways that human behavior can be modified in the future to avoid such problems as groundwater contamination and depletion of the ozone layer. Some environmental scientists work in managerial positions, usually after spending some time performing field research or learning about environmental laws and regulations.

Some environmental scientists specialize in subfields such as environmental ecology and conservation, environmental chemistry, environmental biology, or fisheries science.

The Big Picture

Employment of environmental scientists and hydrologists is expected to grow 25 percent through 2016.

Engineers develop new technology, design software, and rebuild the infrastructure. They are the professionals who make new ideas come to life. The Bureau of Labor Statistics projects the addition of about 315,000 new engineering jobs through 2016, and considers this to be average growth based on the sheer number of people employed in these occupations. Out of the various engineering specialties, environmental engineers, hydrologists, and biomedical engineers are expected to grow the fastest.

A main reason for this growth is the increasing focus on compliance with environmental regulations and on cleaning up existing hazards. In addition, environmental scientists will be needed to help planners develop and construct eco-friendly buildings, transportation systems, and utilities that protect water resources and reflect efficient and beneficial land use.

Demand for hydrologists should also be strong, as the population increases and more people need to live in environmentally sensitive locations. As people increasingly migrate toward coastal regions, for example, hydrologists will assess building sites for potential hazards and to mitigate the effects of natural hazards such as floods, landslides, and hurricanes. Hydrologists also will be needed to study hazardous-waste sites and determine the effect of pollutants on soil and groundwater so that engineers can design remediation systems. Increased government regulations on water use and contamination, conservation, deteriorating coastal environments, and rising sea levels also will stimulate employment for these workers.

Consulting firms will likely continue to hire these scientists to help businesses and government address issues related to underground tanks, land disposal areas, and other hazardous-waste-management facilities. Currently, environmental consulting is focused on creating remediation and engineering solutions. New federal and state initiatives that integrate environmental activities into the business process itself will result in a greater focus on waste minimization, resource recovery, pollution prevention, and the consideration of environmental effects during product development. This shift in focus to preventive management will provide many new opportunities for environmental scientists and hydrologists.

Training Track

Entry-level positions may only require a bachelor's degree in an earth science, but environmental scientists increasingly need a master's degree in environmental science, hydrology, or a related natural science in order to practice at higher levels. A master's degree also is the minimum educational requirement for most applied research positions in private industry, in state and federal agencies, and at state geological surveys. Environmental scientists or hydrologists who plan to teach at the college level, or who want to do research, will need a doctoral degree.

The Bottom Line

Most entry-level environmental scientists and hydrologists spend the majority of their time in the field, while more experienced workers generally devote more time to office or laboratory work. Many beginning hydrologists and some environmental scientists, such as environmental ecologists and environmental chemists, often take trips that involve physical activity to examine sites and collect materials or data. When on these site visits, they will likely encounter warm or cold climates, and all kinds of weather. In their research, they may dig or chip with a hammer, scoop with a net, come in contact with water, and carry equipment. Travel is usually required to meet with prospective clients or investors or to visit sites. Researchers and consultants might face stress when looking for funding.

Demand for hydrologists who understand both the scientific and engineering aspects of waste remediation should be strong. Because few colleges and universities offer specific programs in hydrology, the number of qualified workers ready to work in that career will likely be small. Job prospects for environmental scientists also will be good, but less favorable than for hydrologists because of the larger number of people already poised to enter the field.

Funding for federal and state geological surveys depends largely on the political climate and budget situation. Thus, job security for environmental scientists and hydrologists may vary. During periods of economic recession, consulting firms may lay off environmental scientists and hydrologists; layoffs are much less likely in government.

THE PAYCHECK

Median annual earnings of environmental scientists	$56,100
Highest 10 percent earned	>$94,670
Lowest 10 percent earned	<$34,590
Best-paying states for environmental scientists	District of Columbia, Massachusetts, Colorado, Wisconsin, California
Median annual earnings of hydrologists	$66,260
Highest 10 percent earned	>$98,320
Lowest 10 percent earned	<$42,080
Best-paying states for hydrologists	Tennessee, New Hampshire, Massachusetts, Pennsylvania, Nevada

Web Links

www.agiweb.org
www.hydroweb.com
www.earthworks-jobs.com
www.newscientistjobs.com
www.ecoemploy.com

KNOCK 'EM DEAD TIP

Which American president first voiced his concern for the environment? It was Theodore Roosevelt. In a speech before the Colorado Livestock Association in Denver, Colorado, on August 29, 1910, he said, "The nation behaves well if it treats the natural resources as assets which it must turn over to the next generation increased, and not impaired, in value."

Environmental Engineer

Day-to-Day

Environmental engineers use their knowledge of biology and chemistry to find solutions to environmental problems. They study water and air pollution, recycling, waste disposal, and public health issues. Many environmental engineers specialize in hazardous-waste management—they determine how serious and pervasive the hazard is, suggest how to contain and/or clean it up, and may develop regulations to prevent the same problem from happening again. Some are involved in planning major projects from the outset; for example, designing municipal water supply and industrial wastewater treatment systems.

Environmental engineers are concerned with local and worldwide environmental issues. They study and attempt to minimize the effects of acid rain, global warming, emissions, and ozone depletion. They may also be involved in the protection of wildlife. Many environmental engineers work as consultants, helping their clients comply with governmental or industry regulations, prevent damage to the environment, and clean up hazardous sites.

The Big Picture

Expected to grow 25 percent through 2016.

Companies and organizations that must comply with environmental regulations will need the expertise of environmental engineers to do so. A shift in emphasis toward preventing new environmental harms in addition to controlling those that already exist, as well as increasing public health concerns about environmental hazards, also are expected to spur demand for environmental engineers. Job opportunities should be good even as more students earn degrees in this field.

Training Track

An advanced degree is a necessity for an environmental engineer. To stay current in their field, which is always evolving, engineers obtain a master's degree and take continuing education courses throughout their career. Online environmental engineering degrees, found primarily at the master's level, have become popular with working professionals who want to boost their careers but can't take the time off from work for a traditional degree.

The Bottom Line

A downturned economy will likely reduce the amount of money spent on environmental protection, thus reducing job opportunities. However, environmental engineers are less likely to be affected than other engineers due to the current emphasis on the importance of environmental responsibility.

THE PAYCHECK

Median annual earnings	$77,970
Highest 10 percent earned	>$115,430
Lowest 10 percent earned	<$45,310
Best-paying states	District of Columbia, New Mexico, Maryland, Hawaii, California

Web Links

www.aaee.net
www.environmentalengineer.com
www.greenjobs.com

Biomedical Engineer

Day-to-Day

Biomedical engineering is a specialized field that is responsible for developing devices and procedures that solve medical problems. For example, biomedical engineers are in large part the creators of artificial organs and prostheses, as well as certain instrumentation, medical information systems, and health management and care delivery systems. Biomedical engineers also design devices used in medical procedures, such as magnetic resonance imaging (MRI) machines and devices for automating insulin injections. Most engineers in this specialty need a solid educational background in another engineering specialty, such as mechanical or electronics engineering, in addition to specialized biomedical training. Some specialties within biomedical engineering include biomaterials, biomechanics, medical imaging, rehabilitation engineering, and orthopedic engineering.

The Big Picture

Expected to grow between 21 percent and 72 percent through 2016.

The BLS estimates that 3,000 new jobs will be created in the industry through 2016. The demand for increasingly sophisticated medical devices is propelling this increase. The fact that a higher percentage of the population will be older will also drive demand for better medical devices and equipment, much of which is designed by biomedical engineers. Pharmaceutical manufacturing and related industries will also use biomedical engineers to develop cost-effective equipment and procedures.

According to the Bureau of Labor Statistics, approximately 14,000 biomedical engineers are currently employed nationwide. The majority of them work for companies that make medical equipment and supplies. Other employers include pharmaceutical and drug companies, scientific and research development services, and health care facilities.

Training Track

Biomedical engineers need quite a bit of higher education—many entry-level people in this field have a master's degree. They often combine formal training in mechanical and electronics engineering with focused biomedical training. Some universities offer undergraduate degrees in biomedical engineering; courses may include neuroengineering; biofluid mechanics; engineering electrophysiology; diagnostic imaging physics; and drug design, development, and delivery.

All fifty states and the District of Columbia require licensure for engineers who offer their services directly to the public. Engineers who are licensed are called professional engineers (PE). This licensure generally requires a degree from a program accredited by the Accreditation Board for Engineering and Technology (*www.abet.org*), four years of relevant work experience, and successful completion of a state examination.

The Bottom Line

Because of the growing interest in this field, the number of students graduating with a degree in biomedical engineering has increased. So biomedical engineers, particularly those with only a bachelor's degree, may face competition for jobs.

THE PAYCHECK

Median annual earnings	$81,120
Highest 10 percent earned	>$121,970
Lowest 10 percent earned	<$47,640
Best-paying states	Massachusetts, Minnesota, California, Connecticut, Illinois

Web Links

www.biomedicalengineer.com
www.bmecareer.org
www.bmes.org
www.bmenet.org

KNOCK 'EM DEAD TIP

The 1974 TV show, *The Six Million Dollar Man*, was about an ex-astronaut who was bionically rebuilt after a crash. Bionic implants were made to his right arm, both legs, and left eye, allowing him superior powers. The cost of his surgery in 2010 would be $26,225,089, according to the inflation calculator at *www.westegg.com/inflation*.

Business Services Professions

The jobs profiled in this section are an amalgamation of finance, law, entertainment, and global services, with expected growth rates between 22 and 33 percent. This represents the long-term shift from goods-producing to service-providing employment, which is expected to continue. Service-providing industries are expected to account for approximately 15.7 million new jobs generated through 2016, while goods-producing industries will see overall job loss.

The jobs that will be added by 2016 will not necessarily be evenly distributed across major industrial and occupational groups. Changes in consumer demand, technology, and workforce demographics will contribute to the continually changing employment structure in the U.S. economy.

Financial Analyst and Personal Financial Advisor

Day-to-Day

Financial analysts and personal financial advisors provide both personal and organizational investment analysis and guidance. Both types of specialists gather financial information, analyze it, and make recommendations based on their client's needs. However, their job duties differ because of the type of advice they give and their relationships with investors.

Financial analysts assess the economic performance of companies and industries for firms and institutions with money to invest. They work for investment banks, insurance companies, mutual and pension funds, securities firms, the business media, and other businesses. Financial analysts read company financial statements and analyze commodity prices, sales, costs, expenses, and tax rates in order to determine a company's value and to project its future earnings. They often meet with company officials to gain a better insight into the firm's prospects and to determine its managerial effectiveness. This information helps them advise the company they work for about whether or not to invest in a particular industry or company.

Financial analysts either work on the "buy" side or the "sell" side. Analysts on the buy side help companies that have a great deal of money to invest decide where to invest it. These companies, called institutional investors, include mutual funds; hedge funds; insurance companies; independent money managers; and charitable or nonprofit organizations, such as universities and hospitals, with large endowments. Conversely, analysts on the sell side help securities dealers such as investment banks and securities firms to sell their products. The business media also hire financial advisors to provide an impartial view of current economic events.

Financial analysts generally focus on a specific industry, region, or type of product. Within their areas of specialty, analysts assess trends in business practices, products, and competition. They must keep abreast of new regulations or policies that may affect the investments they are watching and monitor the economy to determine its effect on earnings.

Personal financial advisors help individuals with their financial needs. Advisors use their knowledge of investments, tax laws, and insurance to recommend short- and long-term financial plans. Planners help clients with financial goals such as retirement planning and funding college education. Many also provide tax advice or sell life insurance. Although most planners offer advice on most topics an individual or family would encounter, some specialize in areas such as retirement and estate planning or risk management.

Personal financial advisors usually work with many clients, and they often must find their own customers. Many personal financial advisors spend a great deal of time making sales calls and marketing their services to get new clients. Many advisors also meet potential clients by giving seminars or lectures or through business and social contacts. Finding clients and building a customer base is one of the most important aspects of becoming successful as a financial advisor.

Financial advisors begin work with a client by setting up an in-person meeting where the advisor obtains as much information as possible about the client's current financial condition and future goals. The advisor then develops a comprehensive financial plan that identifies problem areas, makes recommendations for improvement, and selects appropriate investments compatible with the client's goals, attitude toward risk, and expectation or need for a return on the investment.

Financial advisors usually meet with established clients at least once a year to update them on potential investments and adjust their financial plan to any life changes—such as marriage, the birth of a child, or retirement. Financial advisors also answer clients' questions regarding how potential life changes, such as purchasing a house or taking a pay cut, would affect their financial state. Financial planners must give their clients realistic expectations about the outcomes of their suggestions.

Most personal financial advisors buy and sell financial products, such as securities and life insurance. Fees and commissions from the purchase and sale of securities and life insurance plans are major sources of income for most personal financial advisors.

The Big Picture

Employment of personal financial advisors is expected to grow 41 percent through 2016; over the same period, employment of financial analysts should grow 34 percent.

Personal financial advisors are projected to grow at a rate much faster than the average for all occupations through 2016. Growing numbers of advisors will be needed to assist the millions of workers expected to retire by 2016. As more members of the large baby boom generation reach their peak years of retirement savings, more people will seek the help of experts. Many companies also have replaced traditional pension plans with retirement savings programs, so more individuals are managing their own retirements than in the past, creating jobs for advisors. In addition, people are living longer and must plan to finance longer retirements, and the economic downturn has left some people insecure about managing their finances on their own. They may feel that the fees associated with using a personal financial advisor are worth it, given the challenges of investing and retiring during an economic crisis.

Employment of financial analysts is expected to grow by 34 percent through 2016, which is also much faster than the average for all occupations. Primary factors for this growth are increasing complexity of investments and overall growth in the industry. As the number and type of mutual funds increase, mutual fund companies will need more financial analysts to research and recommend investments.

Training Track

A bachelor's or graduate degree is required for financial analysts and is strongly preferred for personal financial advisors. Most companies require financial analysts to have at least a bachelor's degree in finance, business administration, accounting, statistics, or economics, and many require an advanced degree and certain licenses based on the type and responsibility level of the job.

The Financial Industry Regulatory Authority (FINRA; *www.finra.org*) is the main licensing organization for the securities industry. Depending on a financial analyst's work, many different licenses may be required, although buy-side analysts are less likely to need licenses.

The majority of licenses require sponsorship of an employer, so companies do not expect individuals to have these licenses before starting a job. Licensed workers who change jobs need to have their licenses renewed with the new company.

Almost all personal financial advisors need the Series 7 and Series 63 or 66 licenses, which are issued by FINRA as well. These licenses grant the right to act as a registered representative of a securities firm and to give financial advice. Because the Series 7 license requires sponsorship, self-employed personal financial advisors must maintain a relationship with a large securities firm. This relationship allows them to act as representatives of that firm in the buying and selling of securities.

Financial analysts can earn the Chartered Financial Analyst (CFA) designation, sponsored by the CFA Institute (*www.cfainstitute.org*). To qualify for this designation, applicants need a bachelor's degree, four years of work experience in a related field, and a passing score on three examinations.

Personal financial advisors may obtain the Certified Financial Planner credential, often referred to as CFP. This certification, issued by the Certified Financial Planner Board of Standards (*www.cfp.net*), requires three years of relevant experience; the completion of education requirements, including a bachelor's degree; passing a comprehensive examination; and adherence to a code of ethics.

The Bottom Line

Continuing upheaval in the financial services industry is expected to spur demand for personal financial advisors in the banking industry. In recent years, banks and insurance companies have been allowed to expand into the securities industry. Although Congress is currently considering legislation to regulate the industry, we can foresee that financial services firms will continue to invest widely. Many firms are adding investment advice to their services and are expected to increase their hiring of personal financial advisors.

Despite overall employment growth, competition for financial analyst jobs will be intense because of the number of people who want to enter the occupation, given its high salary potential. A strong academic background is absolutely essential for those aspiring to financial analyst jobs. Good grades in courses such as finance, accounting, and economics are very important to employers. An MBA or certification is helpful in maintaining employment.

Personal financial advisors will also face competition, as many other services compete for customers. Many individuals enter the field by working for a bank or full-service brokerage. Most independent advisories fail within the first year of business, making self-employment challenging. Because the occupation requires sales, people who have strong selling skills will ultimately be most successful. A college degree and certification can lend credibility.

Both occupations must overcome customers' fear of fraud and investment mismanagement —bolstered by recent Ponzi scheme stories (particularly Bernard Madoff) and the collapse of some of Wall Street's most well-known financial institutions.

THE PAYCHECK

Median annual earnings of financial analysts	$66,590*
Highest 10 percent earned	>$130,130
Lowest 10 percent earned	<$40,340
Best-paying states	New York, Connecticut, California, Illinois, Washington
Median annual earnings of personal finance advisors	$66,120**
Highest 10 percent earned	>$145,600
Lowest 10 percent earned	<$32,340

Best-paying states for both positions	New York, Massachusetts, Connecticut, Alaska, Colorado

*The bonuses that many financial analysts receive in addition to their salary can be a significant part of their total earnings. Usually, the bonus is based on how well their predictions compare to the actual performance of a benchmark investment.

**Personal financial advisors who work for financial services firms are generally paid a salary plus bonus. Advisors who work for financial investment or planning firms or who are self-employed either charge hourly fees for their services or opt to earn their money through fees on stock and insurance purchases. Advisors generally receive commissions for financial products they sell, in addition to charging a fee. Those who manage a client's assets may charge a percentage of those assets. Earnings of personal financial advisors who are self-employed have not been included in these figures.

Web Links

Financial Analysts

www.finra.org
www.wallstjobs.com
www.sifma.org
www.aafm.us
www.cfainstitute.org
www.efinancialcareers.com

Personal Financial Advisors

www.cfp.net
www.fpanet.org
www.imca.org
www.jobsinthemoney.com
www.efinancialcareers.com

Gaming and Surveillance Officer

Day-to-Day

Gaming surveillance officers typically work at a casino or casino hotel. (Some state and federal agencies employ a limited number of surveillance agents or officers to observe whether casinos are following state and federal gaming laws, but these jobs are not plentiful.) The casino gaming surveillance officer's main priority is to prevent cheating and theft by casino employees and patrons. Gaming surveillance officers are also responsible for making sure that the company adheres to state gaming regulations.

Gaming surveillance officers may also be known as surveillance agents or gaming investigators. These individuals act as security agents for casino managers and patrons. Using primarily audio and video equipment in an observation room, they watch casino operations for irregular activities, such as cheating or theft, and monitor compliance to rules, regulations, and laws. Some casinos use a catwalk over one-way mirrors located above the casino floor to augment electronic surveillance equipment. They are also responsible for keeping security recordings in case they need to be used as evidence in police investigations.

The Big Picture

Expected to grow 34 percent through 2016.

Casinos will continue to hire more surveillance officers as more states legalize gambling and as the number of casinos increases in states where gambling is already legal. Casino security forces will likely employ more technically trained personnel, as technology becomes increasingly important in thwarting cheating and theft.

Training Track

Gaming surveillance officers and investigators usually need some training beyond high school but do not necessarily need a bachelor's degree. Several educational institutes offer certification programs, which can make a candidate more attractive to an employer. Classroom training usually is conducted in a casino-like atmosphere and includes the use of surveillance equipment. Employers prefer either individuals with casino experience and significant knowledge of casino operations or those with law enforcement and investigation experience.

Background checks and drug screening are typically part of the hiring process.

The Bottom Line

Gaming surveillance officers spend considerable time on their feet, either assigned to a specific post or patrolling buildings and grounds. They can develop eyestrain from constantly monitoring computer and television screens.

THE PAYCHECK

Median annual earnings	$27,130
Highest 10 percent earned	>$45,940
Lowest 10 percent earned	<$18,720
Best-paying states	Pennsylvania, Indiana, Connecticut, California, Nevada

Web Links

www.casinocareers.com
www.worldcasinojobs.com
www.americangaming.org
www.gamingfloor.com
www.casinosurveillancenews.com

> **KNOCK 'EM DEAD TIP**
> According to the American Gaming Association, the casino workforce has increased nearly 80 percent over the last two decades. It has grown from 198,657 employees in 1990 to 357,314 in 2008.

Court Reporter

Day-to-Day

Court reporters prepare verbatim transcripts of speeches, conversations, legal proceedings, meetings, and other events. These jobs are important, as they record spoken words for correspondence, records, or legal confirmation. Though they are most well known for their role in the court system, they are also essential wherever a spoken word needs to be translated into a written document. In addition, court reporters provide closed-captioning and real-time translating services to people who are deaf or hard-of-hearing.

There are several methods of court reporting. The most common is called stenographic, in which stenotypists document all statements made in official proceedings on a stenotype machine. The machine allows them to press multiple keys at once to record combinations of letters representing sounds, words, or phrases. These symbols are electronically recorded, translated, and displayed as text. In real-time court reporting, the stenotype machine is linked to computers for simultaneous captioning, often for television programming.

Another method of court reporting is electronic reporting, in which the court reporter monitors an electronic recording (on either analog tapes or digital equipment), takes notes to identify speakers, and listens to the recording to ensure clarity and quality. Electronic reporters and transcribers often are responsible for producing a written transcript of the recorded proceeding as well.

The third method of court reporting is voice writing, in which a court reporter speaks directly into a voice silencer—a hand-held mask containing a microphone. As the reporter repeats the testimony into the recorder, the mask prevents the reporter from being heard by anyone else. Voice writers record everything that is said by judges, witnesses, attorneys, and other parties to a proceeding, including gestures and emotional reactions, and later prepare transcripts.

All reporters are responsible for accurate identification of proper names and places. Electronic reporters ensure that the record is discernible, and stenographic reports make sure the computer-generated translation reads properly.

Although the courtroom is the main workplace for court reporters, some also work in business, the media, and government agencies. Court reporters who specialize in captioning live television programming for people with hearing loss are commonly known as broadcast captioners. They work for television networks or cable stations, captioning news, emergency broadcasts, sporting events, and other programming.

The Big Picture

Expected to grow 25 percent through 2016.

Despite an anticipated growth in the number of court proceedings, the demand for court reporter services will be spurred largely by the growing need to create captions for live television and by the need to provide other real-time broadcast captioning and translating services for the deaf and hard-of-hearing. Federal legislation dictates that all new television programming and all Spanish-language programming be captioned for the deaf and hard-of-hearing. In addition, the Americans with Disabilities Act gives deaf and hard-of-hearing students in colleges and universities the right to request access to real-time translation in their classes. These factors are expected to continue to increase the demand for court reporters who provide "Communication Access Realtime Translation" services (captioning for deaf and hard-of-hearing people). Although these services differ from traditional court reporting, they require a similar skill set.

Court reporters with certification and those who choose to specialize in providing CART, broadcast captioning, and/or webcasting services should have the best job opportunities. The favorable job market also reflects the fact that fewer people are entering this profession, particularly as stenographic typists.

Further, because of the shortage of court reporters and in efforts to control costs, many courtrooms have installed tape recorders that are maintained by electronic court reporters and transcribers to record court proceedings. But these electronic reporters and transcribers are used in a limited capacity, so traditional stenographic court reporters will continue to be used in felony trials and other proceedings. Court reporters will continue to be needed to produce written legal transcripts and proceedings for publication.

Training Track

The amount of training required to become a court reporter depends on the type of reporting. It usually takes less than a year to become a novice voice writer, but it takes at least two years to become proficient at real-time voice writing. Electronic reporters and transcribers learn their skills on the job. The average length of time it takes to become a real-time stenotypist is approximately three years. Training is offered by about 130 postsecondary vocational and technical schools and colleges. The National Court Reporters Association (NCRA; *www.ncra online.org*) has certified about seventy programs, all of which offer courses in both stenotype computer-aided transcription and real-time reporting.

Some states require voice writers to pass a test and to earn state licensure. As a substitute for state licensure, the National Verbatim Reporters Association (*www.nvra.org*) offers three national certifications to voice writers: Certified Verbatim Reporter (CVR), Certificate of Merit (CM), and Real-Time Verbatim Reporter (RVR). Earning these certifications is sufficient to be licensed in states that permit the voice method of court reporting.

Court reporters need both speed and accuracy, and must have excellent listening skills and hearing. They also need a command of English grammar, vocabulary, and punctuation in order to effectively produce the transcriptions. Those who work in courtrooms should have an expert knowledge of legal terminology and judicial procedure.

The Bottom Line

Work in this occupation presents few hazards, although sitting in the same position for long periods can be tiring, and workers can suffer wrist, back, neck, or eye strain. Court reporters also risk repetitive stress injuries such as carpal tunnel syndrome. In addition, the pressure to be accurate and fast can be stressful.

THE PAYCHECK

Median annual earnings	$45,610
Highest 10 percent earned	>$77,770
Lowest 10 percent earned	<$23,430
Best-paying states	Oregon, New York, California, Washington, Rhode Island

Web Links

www.aaert.org
www.ncraonline.org
www.nvra.org
www.getcourtreporterjobs.com

KNOCK 'EM DEAD TIP

Both the federal government and the National Court Reporters of America require prospective reporters to record a minimum of 225 words per minute. A champion court reporter has clocked in at 280 words per minute.

Actuary

Day-to-Day

Through their knowledge of statistics, finance, and business, actuaries help businesses assess the risk of certain events occurring and then create policies that minimize the cost of that risk. For this reason, actuaries are essential to the insurance industry. In that field, actuaries estimate the probability and likely cost of an event such as death, sickness, injury, or loss of property. Actuaries also address specifically financial questions, such as advising how a company should invest its resources to maximize return on investments in light of potential risk.

The Big Picture

Expected to grow 24 percent through 2016.

Employment growth in the insurance industry—the largest employer of actuaries—is expected to continue at a stable pace, due largely to the rise in popularity of annuities, a financial product offered primarily by life insurance companies. In addition, the risk of terrorism and natural disasters has created a large demand for actuaries in property insurance.

More significant job growth for actuaries is likely in the health care and consulting industries, as health care issues and Medicare reform continue to receive attention. Increased regulation of managed health care companies and the desire to contain health care costs will continue to provide job opportunities for actuaries. In the health care field, actuaries will also be needed to evaluate the risks associated with new medical issues, such as genetic testing.

Training Track

Actuaries need a strong foundation in mathematics, statistics, and general business. They usually have a bachelor's degree and must pass a series of exams in order to become certified. About ten colleges and universities offer an actuarial science program, and most offer a degree in mathematics, statistics, economics, or finance.

Two professional societies sponsor programs that certify different paths within the actuarial field: the Society of Actuaries (SOA; *www.soa.org*) and the Casualty Actuarial Society (CAS; *www.casact.org*). The SOA certifies actuaries in the fields of life insurance, health benefits systems, retirement systems, and finance and investment. The CAS certifies actuaries in the property and casualty field, which includes car, homeowners, medical malpractice, workers compensation, and personal injury liability.

The Bottom Line

Most actuaries work a traditional forty-hour week. Consulting actuaries, however, may experience more erratic employment, be expected to work more than forty hours per week, and may spend more time traveling to meet with clients. Actuaries should stay aware of national and global news; current economic and social trends and legislation; and developments in health, business, and finance in order to analyze how those events could affect insurance or investment practices. While many may be more comfortable working solo armed only with a calculator, good communication and interpersonal skills also are important, particularly for consulting actuaries.

THE PAYCHECK

Median annual earnings	$82,800
Highest 10 percent earned	>$145,600
Lowest 10 percent earned	<$46,470
Best-paying states	New Mexico, Pennsylvania, Indiana, Colorado, Delaware

Web Links

www.soa.org
www.actuary.com
www.actuary.org
www.beanactuary.org
www.actuarialgrads.com

Interpreter and Translator

Day-to-Day

Globalization has made the work of interpreters and translators integral across many industries, as they enable cross-cultural communication by converting one language into another. They must have a mastery of the subject matter in which they work in order to accurately convert information from one language (the source language) into another (the target language). In addition, they must be sensitive to the cultures they work with so as to understand nuances.

Interpreters and translators are often discussed together because they share some common traits. For example, both must be fluent in at least two languages—a native, or active, language and a secondary, or passive, language; a small number of interpreters and translators are fluent in two or more passive languages.

Interpreters convert one spoken language into another—or, in the case of sign-language interpreters, convert spoken communication into sign language. There are two types of interpretation: simultaneous and consecutive. Simultaneous interpretation requires interpreters to listen and speak (or sign) at the same time, meaning that the interpreter begins to convey a sentence while the speaker is still talking. Consecutive interpretation begins after the speaker has verbalized a group of words or sentences.

Translators, on the other hand, convert written materials from one language into another. They must have excellent writing, editing, and analytical ability. Translators need to be sensitive to colloquialisms, slang, and other expressions that do not translate literally so they can be explained fully to the intended audience. Today, nearly all translation work is done on a computer, and most assignments are received and submitted electronically. A large percentage of them work from home, given this flexibility.

The Big Picture

Expected to grow 24 percent through 2016.
Strong demand for interpreters and translators is a result of the broadening of international relations and the increase in the number of foreign language speakers in the United States. Growth will be particularly strong in health care settings and in work related to homeland

security. For example, homeland security will continue to need interpreters and translators of Middle Eastern and North African languages.

Current events and changing political environments, though often difficult to foresee, will increase the need for people who can work with other languages.

Demand will remain strong for translators of the languages referred to as "PFIGS"—Portuguese, French, Italian, German, and Spanish; Arabic and other Middle Eastern languages; and the principal Asian languages—Chinese, Japanese, and Korean. Demand for American Sign Language interpreters will also grow rapidly.

Training Track

The educational backgrounds of interpreters and translators vary, but they must have a thorough knowledge of at least two languages. Although it is not necessary to have been raised bilingual to succeed, many interpreters and translators grew up speaking two languages. Many interpreters and translators have a bachelor's degree in something other than a language, but then receive postgraduate certification. Most organizations seek candidates who have worked in the field for three to five years or who have a degree in translation studies or both.

There is currently no national certification required of interpreters and translators in the United States, but there are a variety of different tests that workers can take to demonstrate proficiency, including those given by:

- The American Translators Association (*www.atanet.org*)
- The Translators and Interpreters Guild (*www.ttig.org*)
- The National Association of Judiciary Interpreters and Translators (*www.najit.org*)
- The U.S. Department of State (*www.state.gov*)

- The National Association of the Deaf (*www.nad.org*)
- Registry of Interpreters for the Deaf (RID; *www.rid.org*)

The Bottom Line

Because many interpreters and translators freelance, their schedules are often erratic, with extensive periods of no work interspersed with very busy periods. Freelancers are also likely to spend a lot of time looking for their next job.

The work can be stressful (due to tight deadlines) and exhausting, and translation can be lonesome. However, interpreters and translators may use their irregular schedules to pursue other interests, such as traveling or working a second job.

THE PAYCHECK

Median annual earnings	$43,130
Highest 10 percent earned	>$69,170*
Lowest 10 percent earned	<$22,170
Best-paying states	District of Columbia, Virginia, New York, New Jersey, Michigan

*Note: Limited information suggests that some highly skilled interpreters and translators—for example, high-level conference interpreters—working full-time can earn more than $100,000 annually. Individuals classified as language specialists for the federal government earned an average of $76,287 annually in 2007.

Web Links

www.atanet.org
www.bilingualcareer.com
www.languagejobs.com
www.multilingualjobs.org
www.proz.com

Paralegal and Legal Assistant

Day-to-Day

Paralegals play a key supporting role to many types of lawyers. In fact, paralegals—who are also called legal assistants—have been assuming more significant responsibilities in legal offices, although they must work under a lawyer. They are explicitly prohibited from carrying out duties considered to be the practice of law, such as setting legal fees, giving legal advice, and presenting cases in court, but they can contribute in a number of other ways.

The paralegal is particularly vital when helping lawyers prepare for closings, hearings, trials, and meetings. They might investigate the facts of cases and ensure that all relevant information is considered. They also identify laws, research past judicial decisions, find legal articles (using the Internet and special computer software), and locate other materials that could come into play during a case. After they analyze and organize that information, paralegals may prepare written reports that attorneys use in determining how cases should be handled. If a client files a lawsuit, paralegals may help prepare the legal arguments, draft pleadings and motions to be filed with the court, obtain affidavits, and assist attorneys during trials. Paralegals also file all-important case documents so attorneys can access them quickly and accurately.

In addition to this preparatory work, paralegals help draft contracts, mortgages, and separation agreements. They also may assist in preparing tax returns, establishing trust funds, and planning estates. In smaller practices, paralegals may also maintain financial office records.

Paralegals are found in all types of organizations, but most are employed by law firms, corporate legal departments, and government offices. They support lawyers who practice many different facets of law, including litigation, personal injury, corporate law, criminal law, employee benefits, intellectual property, labor law, bankruptcy, immigration, family law, and real estate. As the law becomes more complex, paralegals become more specialized. For example, paralegals specializing in labor law may concentrate exclusively on employee benefits.

The Big Picture

Expected to grow 22 percent through 2016.

Private law firms employed seven out of ten paralegals and legal assistants; most of the remainder worked for corporate legal departments and various levels of government. Within the federal government, the U.S. Department of Justice is the largest employer, followed by the Social Security Administration and the U.S. Department of the Treasury. Some paralegals freelance, contracting their services to attorneys, corporate legal departments, or legal staffing services.

Demand for paralegals is expected to grow as the expanding population uses more legal services, especially in areas such as intellectual property, health care, international law, elder issues, criminal law, and environmental law. The growth of prepaid legal plans should also contribute to the demand for legal assistance.

Private law firms will continue to be the largest employers of paralegals, but a growing array of other organizations, such as corporate legal departments, insurance companies, real estate and title insurance firms, and banks also hire paralegals. Corporations in particular are expected to increase their in-house legal departments to cut freelancing costs.

Training Track

People entering this career either have an associate's degree in paralegal studies or a bachelor's degree coupled with a certificate in paralegal studies. (Only a small number of schools offer a bachelor's and master's degree in paralegal studies.) Some employers will train paralegals on the job. The most common method of training, however, is through a community college paralegal program that leads to an associate's degree.

Although most employers do not require certification, earning a voluntary certification from a professional society may offer job seekers advantages in the labor market. Certification is offered by the National Association of Legal Assistants (*www.nala.org*), the American Alliance of Paralegals (*www.aapipara.org*), and the National Federation of Paralegals Association (*www.paralegals.org*).

The Bottom Line

During recessions, demand declines for some discretionary legal services, such as planning estates, drafting wills, and handling real estate transactions. Corporations are less inclined to initiate certain types of litigation when plagued by falling sales and profits. As a result, certain companies affected by the downturn may actually lay off or reduce the hours of their full-time paralegals.

However, during recessions, corporations and individuals are more likely to face problems that require legal assistance, such as bankruptcies, foreclosures, and divorces. Paralegals, who provide many of the same legal services as lawyers at a lower cost, tend to stay busy for that reason.

THE PAYCHECK

Median annual earnings	$43,040
Highest 10 percent earned	>$67,540
Lowest 10 percent earned	<$27,450
Best-paying states	District of Columbia, New York, California, Alaska, Illinois

Web Links

www.abanet.org
www.nala.org
www.paralegals.org
www.aafpe.org
www.aapipara.org
www.nals.org
www.paralegaljobs.com
www.lawcrossing.com
www.lawjobs.com

Educational and Social Services Professions

In the next ten years, more than three out of every ten new jobs created in the U.S. economy will be in either the health care and social assistance or public and private educational services sectors. Employment growth will be driven by increasing demand for health care and social assistance because of an aging population and longer life expectancies. Also, as more and more women enter and remain in the labor force, demand for childcare services is expected to grow. Public and private educational services will grow by 10.7 percent and add 1.4 million new jobs through 2016. Rising student enrollments at all levels of education will create demand for educational services.

The six professions highlighted expect growth rates between 22 percent and 51 percent—again, these are all considered much faster than average by the Bureau of Labor Statistics.

Personal and Home Care Aide

Day-to-Day

Personal and home care aides help people who are elderly, ill, and/or have a physical or mental disability. They may make it possible for those people to live in their own homes or to live comfortably in residential care facilities instead of in health facilities or institutions. Most personal and home care aides work with patients who need more extensive personal and home care than family or friends are able to provide. Some aides work with families in which a parent is incapacitated and small children need care. Others help discharged hospital patients who have relatively short-term needs while they recover from an illness or injury. Personal and home care aides—who may also be called homemakers, caregivers, companions, and personal attendants—sometimes also provide housekeeping and routine personal care services.

The Big Picture

Expected to grow 50 percent through 2016.

This field is expected to grow by about 389,000 jobs, due in large part to the rise in the number of elderly people. Elderly people face mounting health problems and some will need assistance with daily activities.

This trend is caused by several developments. First, the high cost of inpatient care in hospitals and nursing homes forces patients to return to their homes from these facilities as quickly as possible. (Patients who simply need assistance with everyday tasks and household chores rather than observational medical care can reduce medical expenses by returning to their homes.) Second, most patients—particularly the elderly—increasingly prefer care in the familiar environment of their homes rather than in nursing homes or other in-patient facilities. Third, better and more portable medical technologies have helped home care become easier and more feasible.

In addition to private home settings, personal and home care aides also work in residential facilities for the disabled, elderly, or mentally challenged.

Training Track

Most personal and home care aides receive short-term on-the-job training specific to the job they'll be doing, such as learning information on nutrition and special diets in order to properly cook for a client. They may be trained in basic housekeeping tasks and how to respond to an emergency situation. In some states, the only requirement for employment is on-the-job training, which generally is provided by employers. Other states may require formal training, which is available from community colleges, vocational schools, elder care programs, and home health care agencies.

The National Association for Home Care and Hospice (NAHC; *www.nahc.org*) offers national certification for personal and home care aides. Certification is voluntary, but shows an employer that the individual has met industry standards. Certification requires the completion of a seventy-five-hour course, observation and documentation of seventeen skills for competency assessed by a registered nurse, and passing a written exam developed by NAHC.

Personal and home care aides must have a desire to help people and not mind hard work. They should be healthy, responsible, compassionate, patient, emotionally stable, cheerful, and discreet (because they work in private homes). Some employers may require a physical exam, criminal background check, credit check, and good driving record for employment. Additionally, personal and home care aides are responsible for their own transportation to reach patients' homes.

The Bottom Line

A home health aide's work setting and environment differs from case to case. Some homes are neat and pleasant, whereas others are messy and depressing. Some clients are pleasant and cooperative; others are angry, depressed, or difficult. Some aides form close attachments to their patients and must deal with the emotional difficulties of a patient's deteriorating health and even death.

Aides may spend a large portion of each day traveling between clients' homes. About 33 percent of aides work part-time, and some work weekends or evenings to suit the needs of their clients.

THE PAYCHECK

Median annual earnings	$19,690
Highest 10 percent earned	>$25,650
Lowest 10 percent earned	<$14,230
Best-paying states	Alaska, New Jersey, Massachusetts, Minnesota, District of Columbia

Web Links

www.hahc.org
www.carepathways.com

KNOCK 'EM DEAD TIP

The U.S. Census Bureau estimates there will be 57.8 million baby boomers living in 2030. That year, boomers will be between the ages of sixty-six and eighty-four years old.

Social and Human Services Assistant

Day-to-Day

Social and human services assistants help social workers, health care workers, and other professionals provide services to people. "Social and human services assistant" is a generic term for workers with a wide array of job titles, including human services worker, case management aide, social work assistant, community support worker, mental health aide, community outreach worker, life skills counselor, or gerontology aide. They are usually supervised by nurses, psychiatrists, psychologists, physical therapists, or social workers. This career encompasses a wide variety of job titles, including: case worker, youth worker, social services liaison, child advocate, residential counselor, eligibility counselor, gerontology aide, juvenile court liaison, intake interviewer, community outreach worker, group home worker, and rehabilitation case worker.

The amount of responsibility and supervision they are given varies a great deal. Some have little direct supervision—they may run a group home, for example—while others work side by side with their manager. Social and human services assistants assess clients' needs; determine their eligibility for benefits and services such as food stamps, Medicaid, or welfare; and help them to obtain those benefits. They also arrange for transportation, provide emotional support, and report progress to supervisors and case managers.

In a community setting, social and human services assistants may organize and lead group activities, assist clients in need of counseling or crisis intervention, or administer food banks or emergency fuel programs. In halfway houses, group homes, and government-supported housing programs, they assist adults who need supervision with personal hygiene and daily living skills. They ensure that clients take their medication, educate their family members, and confer with medical personnel and other caregivers to provide insight into clients' needs.

In psychiatric hospitals, rehabilitation programs, and outpatient clinics, social and human services assistants work with psychiatrists, psychologists, social workers, and others to help clients master everyday living skills, communicate more effectively, and maintain healthy relationships. They support the client's participation in a treatment plan, such as individual or group counseling or occupational therapy.

The Big Picture

Expected to grow 34 percent through 2016.

Job prospects in this career are expected to be excellent, particularly for applicants with relevant education. Demand for social services will expand with the growing elderly population, who are more likely to need adult day care, meal delivery programs, support during medical crises, and other services. In addition, more social and human services assistants will be needed to provide services to other people in need, such as pregnant teenagers, people who are homeless, people who have a mental or developmental disability, and people who are substance abusers.

As social welfare policies shift focus from benefit-based to work-based programs, there will be more demand for people to teach job skills to the people who are new to, or returning to, the workforce.

The number of people who have a disability is increasing, and many need help to care for themselves. More community-based programs and supportive independent-living sites are expected to be established to house and assist the homeless and those with mental or physical disabilities. Furthermore, as substance abusers are increasingly being sent to treatment programs instead of prison, employment of social and human services assistants in substance abuse treatment programs also will grow.

Opportunities are expected to be good in private social-service agencies. Employment in private agencies will grow as state and local governments continue to contract out services in an effort to cut in-house costs. Also, some private agencies have begun hiring more social and human services assistants in place of social workers, who are more educated and more highly paid.

Training Track

Many employers prefer to hire people with certificates or associate's degrees in subjects such as human services, gerontology, or one of the social or behavioral sciences. Depending on the particular job, an employer may require a bachelor's or master's degree in human services or a related field, such as counseling, rehabilitation, or social work.

Human services degree programs train students to observe patients, record information, conduct patient interviews, implement treatment plans, employ problem-solving techniques, handle crisis intervention matters, and use proper case management and referral procedures. Many programs also offer internships to give students hands-on experience, and most also teach specialized courses related to addictions, gerontology, and child protection.

The kind of work social and human services assistants are assigned and the degree of responsibility that is given to them depends largely on their level of education. For example, workers with no more than a high school education are likely to receive extensive on-the-job training to work in direct-care services—helping clients to fill out paperwork, for example. Workers with a college degree, however, might conduct supportive counseling, coordinate program activities, or manage a group home. Social and human services assistants with proven leadership ability, especially from paid or volunteer experience, often have less direct supervision. Regardless of the academic or work background of employees, most employers provide some form of in-service training to their employees such as seminars and workshops. It is becoming more common for employers to require a criminal background check, and in some settings, workers may be required to have a valid driver's license.

The Bottom Line

The work, though satisfying, can be emotionally draining. Understaffing and relatively low pay may add to the pressure. Working conditions vary as well—some work in offices, clinics, and hospitals, while others work in group homes, shelters, sheltered workshops, and day programs. Some traveling may be involved to see clients. Some clients can be potentially dangerous, though most agencies do everything they can to ensure their workers' safety. Most assistants work forty hours a week; some work in the evening and on weekends depending on clients' needs.

Many human services jobs involve direct contact with people who are vulnerable to exploitation or mistreatment. Social and human services assistants must have a strong desire to help others, effective communication and time-management skills, and a sense of responsibility; employers value patience and understanding.

THE PAYCHECK

Median annual earnings	$25,580
Highest 10 percent earned	>$40,780
Lowest 10 percent earned	<$16,180
Best-paying states	Connecticut, Maryland, California, District of Columbia, Alaska

Web Links

www.cshse.org (see section on Human Service Practitioner)
www.nationalhumanservices.org
www.socialservice.com
www.hscareers.com
www.getsocialhumanserviceassistantjobs.com

Health Educator

Day-to-Day

Health educators teach individuals and communities about behaviors that promote healthy living and prevent health problems. They attempt to prevent illnesses by informing and educating people about topics such as proper nutrition, the importance of exercise, how to avoid sexually transmitted diseases, and healthy habits and lifestyles. Although programming is a large part of their job, health educators also serve as a resource on health topics.

Before starting a training session, they assess the needs of their audience, which helps them determine which topics to cover and how to best present the information. For example, they may hold programs on breast self-examinations for women who are at higher risk for breast cancer or teach classes on the effects of binge drinking to college students. Health educators must take age and cultural norms of their audience into account—they cannot run a program targeted at the elderly in the same way they would run one for a college-aged population. Also, health educators must plan programs that are consistent with the goals and objectives of their employers. For example, many nonprofit organizations educate the public about just one disease or health issue and, therefore, limit their programs.

After assessing their audiences' needs, health educators must decide how to meet those needs. They may organize a lecture, class, demonstration or health screening, or create a video, pamphlet, or website. Often, planning a program requires working with other people in a team or with their coworkers.

Next, health educators need to implement their proposed plan. This may require finding funding by applying for grants, writing curriculums for classes, or creating written materials that will be made available to the public. Also, they must solve basic logistics problems, such as finding speakers or locations for an event.

Generally, after a program is presented, health educators evaluate its success. This could include tracking the absentee rate of employees from work and students from school, surveying participants on their opinions about the program, or other methods of collecting evidence that suggests whether the programs were effective. These evaluations help them and the organization they work for improve plans for the future by learning from mistakes and capitalizing on strengths.

The basic goals and duties of health educators are the same, but their jobs vary greatly depending on the type of organization in which they work. Most health educators work in medical care settings, colleges and universities, schools, public health departments, nonprofit organizations, and private business.

The Big Picture

Expected to grow 26 percent through 2016.

The rising cost of health care has increased the need for health educators. As health care costs continue to rise, insurance companies, employers, and governments are trying to curb the cost by teaching people how to live healthy lives and avoid costly treatments for illnesses. They often emphasize awareness of a number of illnesses—such as lung cancer, HIV, heart disease, and skin cancer—that may be avoided with lifestyle changes. In addition, many illnesses, such as certain types of cancer, are best treated with early detection, so it is important for people to understand how to detect possible problems on their own.

This emphasis on health education has led to a growing demand for qualified health educators. In the past, it was thought that anyone could do the job of a health educator and the duties were often given to nurses or other health care professionals. However, in recent years, employers have recognized that those trained specifically in health education are better qualified and more successful.

Training Track

Entry-level health educator positions generally require a bachelor's degree in health education. More than 250 colleges and universities offer bachelor's programs in health education or a similarly titled major. These programs teach students the theories behind health education and the skills necessary to implement programs. Courses typically include psychology, human development, and a foreign language, and many programs offer internship or other volunteer opportunities.

Graduate health education programs are available; often under titles such as "community health education," "school health education," or "health promotion." These degrees can lead to a master of arts, master of science, master of education, or a master of public health degree. Many students pursue their master's in health education after majoring or working in another related field, such as nursing or psychology. A master's degree is required for most health educator positions in public health. Once hired, on-the-job training for health educators varies greatly depending on the type and size of employer.

Health educators can also become a Certified Health Education Specialist, a credential offered by the National Commission of Health Education Credentialing, Inc. (*www.nchec.org*). The certification is awarded after passing an examination on the basic areas of responsibility for a health educator.

The Bottom Line

Health educators work primarily in two industries, with 20 percent working in state and local government and 53 percent working in health care and social assistance. In addition, a small percent of health educators work in grant-making services and social advocacy organizations.

374 KNOCK 'EM DEAD

Demand for health educators will increase in most industries, but their employment may decrease in schools, which are facing budget cuts. Many schools are instead asking teachers trained in other fields, such as biology or physical education, to teach the subject of health education.

The work environment of a health educator is based on the industry, but is usually an office or a classroom. Many spend a lot of time away from the office implementing and attending programs, meeting with community organizers, speaking with patients, or teaching classes.

THE PAYCHECK

Median annual earnings	$41,330
Highest 10 percent earned	>$72,500
Lowest 10 percent earned	<$24,750
Best-paying states	Maryland, District of Columbia, Georgia, Rhode Island, Nevada

Web Links
www.aahperd.org/aahe
www.sophe.org
www.publichealtheducation.com

Postsecondary Teacher

Day-to-Day

Postsecondary teachers instruct students in a wide variety of academic and vocational subjects beyond the high school level. Most of these students are working toward a degree, but many others are studying for some kind of certification to improve their knowledge or career skills. Teachers at this level include college and university faculty, career and technical education teachers, and graduate teaching assistants. Professors at this level working at four-year colleges and universities typically perform a significant amount of research in the subject they teach.

Nowadays, postsecondary teachers use computer technology, including the Internet, e-mail, and software programs, to broaden and expand upon their classroom learning sessions. They may use computers as teaching aids during lectures and may post course content, notes, syllabi, and other information on the Internet. The use of e-mail, chat rooms, social media sites, and other technology is now critical to student-teacher communication.

The use of computers in postsecondary schools even extends to what is known as distance learning, where instructors use the Internet to teach courses to students at remote sites. Faculty who teach these courses must be able to adapt existing lectures or material to make them successful online or design a new course that takes advantage of the format.

Most full-time faculty members serve on one or more academic or administrative committees, which could deal with the policies of their institution, departmental matters, academic issues, curricula, budgets, equipment purchases, and hiring. Some work with student and community organizations. Department chairpersons are faculty members who teach fewer courses because they have heavier administrative responsibilities.

The Big Picture
Expected to grow 23 percent through 2016.

Because of the size of this occupation and its much-faster-than-average growth rate, postsecondary teachers will account for 382,000 new jobs through 2016, which is among the largest number of new jobs for an occupation. Projected increases in college and university enrollment over the next decade will be the main source of the growth.

Higher enrollments and the need to replace the large numbers of postsecondary teachers who are likely to retire over the next decade will create job openings across the nation. Many postsecondary teachers were hired in the late

1960s and the 1970s to teach members of the baby boom generation; they are expected to retire soon and will need to be replaced.

Training Track

Four-year colleges and universities usually require candidates for full-time, tenure-track positions to hold a doctoral degree. However, they may hire candidates with a master's degree or doctoral candidates for certain disciplines. Doctoral programs take an average of six years of full-time study beyond the bachelor's degree; this includes time spent completing a master's degree and a dissertation.

Training requirements for postsecondary career and technical education teachers vary by state and subject. In general, career and technical education teachers need a bachelor's or graduate degree, plus at least three years of work experience in their field. In some fields, a license or certificate may be required.

Most postsecondary school faculty strive to achieve tenure, which protects the ability to teach and conduct research without fear of being fired for advocating controversial or unpopular ideas. The process of attaining tenure can take approximately seven years, with faculty moving up the ranks in tenure-track positions—instructor, assistant professor, associate professor, and professor—as they meet specific criteria. Tenure may be also granted if the individual maintains an exemplary teaching record, contributes outstanding research to the field, and plays an active role on the campus.

The Bottom Line

Postsecondary professors often face the time-management challenge of teaching students while conducting research and publishing their findings. They have also found their workloads increasing due to recent cutbacks in support workers, the hiring of more part-time faculty, and the fact that many now have to teach online classes. Many find that developing the courses to put online is very time-consuming, especially when learning how to operate the technology and answering large amounts of e-mail.

THE PAYCHECK

Median annual earnings	$56,120
Highest 10 percent earned	>$113,450
Lowest 10 percent earned	<$27,590
Best-paying states	Massachusetts, New York, New Hampshire, Virginia, Illinois

Web Links

www.collegenet.com
www.acteonline.org
www.preparing-faculty.org
www.hireedjobs.com

KNOCK 'EM DEAD TIP

In 2007, the five colleges with the highest enrollment were: Community College of the Air Force (332,095), City University of New York (CUNY) (261,602), University of Phoenix/ Online (239,912), Miami-Dade College (86,292), and Florida Community College at Jacksonville (80,000).

Instructional Coordinator

Day-to-Day

Instructional coordinators—who are also known as curriculum specialists, personnel development specialists, instructional coaches, or directors of instructional material—try to improve the quality of education in the classroom. They develop curricula, select textbooks and other materials, train teachers, and assess educational programs for quality and adherence to state and federal regulations and standards.

They also help implement new technology into classrooms.

At the primary and secondary school level, instructional coordinators usually specialize in specific subjects, such as reading, mathematics, or science. At the postsecondary level, coordinators usually branch out and may work with employers to develop training programs that produce qualified workers.

Instructional coordinators begin a project by evaluating how well a school or training program's curriculum meets students' needs. Based on their research and observations of current operations, they recommend improvements. To aid in their evaluation, they may meet with teachers to learn about certain subjects and explore how curriculum materials meet students' needs and relate to occupations. Coordinators also may develop questionnaires and interview school staff about the curriculum. Then they research teaching methods and develop procedures to ensure that instructors are implementing the curriculum successfully and meeting program goals.

Some instructional coordinators also review textbooks, software, and other educational materials and make recommendations on which to purchase. They monitor the ways in which teachers use materials in the classroom, and they supervise workers who catalog, distribute, and maintain a school's educational materials and equipment.

Some instructional coordinators find ways to use technology to improve or expand the current curriculum. For example, they might recommend installing educational software, such as interactive books or fun math exercises. Instructional coordinators may invite experts—such as computer hardware, software, and library or media specialists—to offer their insight into programs.

In addition to developing curriculum and instructional materials, many instructional coordinators also plan and provide education for teachers and administrators. They may also mentor new teachers and train experienced ones in the newest instructional methods. This role becomes especially important when a school district introduces a new curriculum or testing policy. For example, when a state or school district introduces standards or tests that students must pass, instructional coordinators often explain the standards to teachers then show them how best to teach their students the necessary information.

The Big Picture
Expected to grow 22 percent through 2016.

Job growth for instructional coordinators will stem from the increasing emphasis on continuing education for teachers and on programs for students with special needs, including those for whom English is a second language. These students often require more thorough educational resources. Those with experience in math and reading curriculum development will be the most in demand.

Although budget constraints may limit employment growth to some extent, a continuing emphasis on improving the quality of education will mean that these workers should maintain a steady level of employability. In addition, the emphasis on accountability should cause more schools to focus on improving standards of educational quality and student performance. Growing numbers of coordinators will be needed to incorporate the new standards into existing curricula and inform teachers and administrators of the changes.

Training Track

A master's or higher degree—usually in education—plus a state teacher or administrator license is the educational standard for instructional coordinators. Certain employers may require a master's degree, depending on the setting and program particulars.

Instructional coordinators should also have specific training in the specific field for which they are responsible, such as mathematics or history. Courses in research design teach how to create and implement research studies to determine the effectiveness of a given method of instruction or curriculum and how to measure and improve student performance.

Instructional coordinators usually must take continuing education courses to keep their skills current, as they are responsible for making sure others know of the latest trends. Topics that are perennially popular for continuing ed classes include teacher evaluation techniques, curriculum training, new teacher induction, teacher support, and observation and analysis of teaching.

The Bottom Line

Instructional coordinators who specialize in subjects targeted for improvement by the No Child Left Behind Act—namely, reading, math, and science—will be preferred by employers.

Many instructional coordinators find their work rewarding because they are able to specialize in areas that interest them and contribute to educational improvement, yet not be subjected to the typical daily classroom stress.

THE PAYCHECK

Median annual earnings	$52,790
Highest 10 percent earned	>$87,510
Lowest 10 percent earned	<$29,040
Best-paying states	Connecticut, California, District of Columbia, New Jersey, Virginia

Web Links

www.astd.org
www.ascd.org
www.academiccareers.com
www.chronicle.com/jobs
www.jobsineducation.com

Social Worker

Day-to-Day

Social workers help people cope with issues in their everyday lives, maintain healthy relationships, and solve personal and family problems. Some social workers work with clients who face a disability or a life-threatening disease or a social problem, such as inadequate housing, unemployment, or substance abuse. Some assist families that have serious domestic conflicts, sometimes involving child or spousal abuse. Other social workers conduct research, advocate for improved services, or go into planning or policy development. Many social workers specialize in serving a particular population or working in a certain setting.

Child and family social workers provide social services to improve the social and psychological functioning of children and their families and to maximize the well-being of families and improve the child's academic experience. They may assist single parents; arrange adoptions; or help find foster homes for children who have been neglected, abandoned, or abused. Some work with senior citizens by running support groups for them; advising them and their family members about housing, transportation, long-term care, and other services; and coordinating and monitoring these services. Through employee assistance programs, social workers may help people cope with job-related pressures or with personal problems that affect the quality of their work.

In schools, social workers serve as the link between students' families and the school, working with parents, guardians, teachers, and other school officials to ensure students reach and maintain their academic and personal potential. In addition, they address problems such as misbehavior, truancy, and teenage pregnancy and advise teachers on how to cope with these situations.

Child, family, and school social workers may also be known as child welfare social workers, family services social workers, child protective services social workers, occupational social workers, or gerontology social workers. They often work for individual and family services agencies, schools, or state or local governments.

Medical and public health social workers provide psychosocial support to people, families, or vulnerable populations so they can cope with chronic, acute, or terminal illnesses, such as Alzheimer's disease, cancer, or AIDS. They also help plan for patients' needs after discharge from hospitals, such as arranging for at-home services, such as meals-on-wheels or home care. Some work on interdisciplinary teams that evaluate certain kinds of patients—geriatric or organ transplant patients, for example. Medical and public health social workers may work for hospitals, nursing and personal care facilities, individual and family services agencies, or local governments.

Mental health and substance abuse social workers help individuals with mental illness or substance abuse problems, including abuse of alcohol, tobacco, or drugs. They may set up individual and group therapy, crisis intervention, social rehabilitation, and sessions to teach skills needed for everyday living. They also may help plan for supportive services to ease clients' return to the community. Mental health and substance abuse social workers usually work in hospitals, substance abuse treatment centers, individual and family services agencies, or local governments.

Other types of social workers include social work administrators, planners, and policymakers, who develop and implement programs to address issues such as child abuse, homelessness, substance abuse, poverty, and violence. These workers research and analyze policies, programs, and regulations, then suggest legislative and other solutions. They may help raise funds or write grants to support these programs.

The Big Picture
Expected to grow 22 percent through 2016.

Social workers who specialize in the aging population or work in rural areas will see the largest potential for growth. The increasing elderly population and the aging baby boom generation will create greater demand for health and social services, resulting in rapid job growth among gerontology social workers. Employment of social workers in private social service agencies may increase, but agencies may also restructure services and hire more social and human services assistants, who are paid less, instead of social workers. Employment in state and local government agencies may grow somewhat in response to growing needs for public welfare, family services, and child protective services, but many of these services will be contracted out to private agencies. The number of social workers hired for public social services agencies may fluctuate, depending on the economy and government funding levels.

Opportunities for social workers in private practice will probably expand, but growth may be somewhat hindered by restrictions that managed care organizations put on mental health services. The growing popularity of employee-assistance programs is expected to spur demand for private practitioners, some of whom provide social work services to corporations on a contractual basis. However, companies may not fund employee-assistance programs well or at all during recessions.

Among the areas of social work that will see the biggest percentage increase is mental health and substance abuse, which is expected to increase 30 percent through 2016. In particular, social workers specializing in substance abuse will experience strong demand because substance abusers are increasingly being placed into treatment programs instead of being sentenced to prison. Also, growing numbers of the substance abusers who *are* sentenced to prison or probation are also being required by correctional systems to have substance abuse treatment added as a condition to their sentence or probation. As this trend grows, demand for social workers will strengthen, as they will be needed to help these people fulfill the terms of their sentencing.

Additionally, growth of medical and public health social workers is expected to be 24 percent. Hospitals continue to limit the length of patient stays, so the demand for social workers in hospitals will grow more slowly than in other areas. But hospitals are releasing patients earlier than in the past, so social worker employment in home health care services is growing.

Training Track

A bachelor's degree in social work (BSW) is the most common minimum requirement to qualify for a job as a social worker; however, majors in psychology, sociology, and related fields may qualify for some entry-level jobs, especially in small agencies. A master's degree in social work (MSW) is typically required for positions in health settings and is required for clinical work as well. Some higher-level jobs in public and private agencies (supervisors, administrators, and staff training positions) may require an advanced degree, such as a master's degree in social services policy or administration. College and university teaching positions normally require a doctorate in social work (DSW or PhD).

The National Association of Social Workers (*www.socialworkers.org*) offers voluntary credentials that may help prospective job seekers. Social workers with a master's degree in social work may be eligible for the Academy of Certified Social Workers (ACSW), the Qualified Clinical Social Worker (QCSW), or the Diplomate in Clinical Social Work (DCSW) credential, based on their professional experience.

The Bottom Line

A social worker's hours can be long and they often witness social injustices such as abuse, rape, incest, and more. It requires a balance between empathy and some level of detachment. Social workers must resign themselves to not winning every battle and taking heart in those that do get won. It is a career that requires tenacity and patience. Problems cannot be righted at once; often it takes time and tremendous effort. People typically go into social work for the reward of helping people rather than the money. They must also be able to tolerate the administrative frustrations of the system.

THE PAYCHECK

Median annual earnings	$43,580
Highest 10 percent earned	>$68,500
Lowest 10 percent earned	<$25,540
Best-paying states	South Dakota, Mississippi, West Virginia, New Jersey, Rhode Island

Web Links

www.socialworkers.org
www.cswe.org
www.aswb.org
www.socialworkjobs.com
www.socialworker.com

KNOCK 'EM DEAD TIP

According to the National Association of Social Workers, the Department of Veterans Affairs is the largest employer of social workers in the country. It employs more than 6,000 social workers to assist veterans and their families with individual and family counseling, client education, substance abuse treatment, crisis intervention, and other services.

The Current Employment Scene and the American Recovery and Reinvestment Act (ARRA)

The goal of the ARRA is to bring relief to America's unemployed through the creation of approximately 3.5 million jobs. President Obama's economic stimulus plan in 2009 targeted four strategic sectors to receive funds for direct or indirect job revitalization: energy (459,000 anticipated jobs), infrastructure (377,000 anticipated jobs), education (250,000 anticipated jobs), and health care (244,000 anticipated jobs).

Revitalization has been slow in coming, but that doesn't mean that those people who are out of work, or others who are thinking about beginning a career or changing professions, should discount the stimulus plan as they make their current or future employment choices. Two websites will help you stay current of where the spending is being allocated and which projects are moving forward: *www.recovery.gov* and *www.stimuluswatch.org*.

For example, Recovery.gov reports that the five largest proposed stimulus projects according to number of jobs to be created are as follows:

1. Solar LA Program, Los Angeles, California (energy): 32,243 anticipated jobs
2. Newark Elizabeth Light Rail, Newark, New Jersey (transit): 20,000 anticipated jobs
3. North Corridor Light Rail System, Columbus, Ohio (transit): 11,000 anticipated jobs
4. North Corridor Rail Line, Charlotte, North Carolina (transit): 9,380 anticipated jobs
5. South Florida East Coast Corridor Transit Extension, Miami, Florida—(transit): 6,000 anticipated jobs

Stimuluswatch.org will tell you the status of each project.

Relocating

Are you thinking about relocating to a city with a promise of better job opportunities? The website *www.NewGeography.com* has published a list of cities that are well positioned to receive stimulus funding and therefore are likely to have good employment outlooks. The top ten cities are:

1. Atlanta, Georgia
2. Austin, Texas
3. Boston, Massachusetts
4. Columbus, Ohio
5. Denver, Colorado
6. Des Moines, Iowa
7. Indianapolis, Indiana
8. Madison, Wisconsin
9. Minneapolis/St. Paul, Minnesota
10. Nashville, Tennessee

Tomorrow's Careers

Anyone new to the job market and anyone already in it but seeking a career change should make plans for the future with an informed outlook. Do your homework regarding employment prospects for the next decade and what you need to succeed in a particular profession. Keep pace with those areas gaining momentum and attention because of technological innovation and/or cultural attitudes. For example, here are some new and emerging occupations that are expected to take a firmer hold over the next decade:

• Cancer registrar
• Transplant coordinator
• Genetics counselor
• Distance learning specialist
• Victim advocate

• Resettlement coordinator for disaster recovery
• Search engine optimization analyst
• Ergonomics engineer

Then there is also the clean energy boom, which is expected to produce more than 4.2 million new green jobs through 2038, according to a study by the U.S. Conference of Mayors released in October 2008. Under assumed scenarios and with government commitment and investment, the report projects green jobs could contribute 10 percent of new jobs through the next three decades, representing the fastest growing segment of the U.S. economy.

Green jobs fall into two core categories: jobs that directly impact the environment and interact with our natural resources, and those that are at eco-friendly employers that want to be good corporate citizens through sustainability initiatives.

U.S. Secretary of Labor Hilda L. Solis reported before the U.S. Senate Committee on Health, Education, Labor and Pensions regarding green job skills training for workers. She said, "Green jobs play an important role in our economic recovery. The promise of green jobs is not only to help restart the economy and put Americans back to work, but also to help make America more energy-independent. Investment in our nation's clean energy future will not only secure America's energy supply but will do so in ways that promote economic stability and the advancement of our communities."

Here are some new and emerging occupations that are expected to be outcomes of the green workforce.

• Energy efficiency builder
• Solar power installer
• Wind turbine fabricator
• Conservation biologist
• Sustainability officer
• Corporate waste compliance coordinator
• Storm water technician
• Aquatic ecologist

Here are some web resources for green jobs:
www.greenjobs.com
www.sustainablebusiness.com
www.greenbiz.com

KNOCK 'EM DEAD TIP
Believe it or not, saving the planet isn't new. On April 22, 1970, Earth Day was launched and celebrated by nearly 20 million people who made their voices heard by demanding a healthy, sustainable environment.

Links to More Lists

The following links provide lists for other high-growth jobs defined by different criteria than I've used in the section above. Consult them for other possible options.

www.bls.gov/news.release/ecopro.t03.htm
www.bls.gov/news.release/ecopro.t07.htm
www.bls.gov/news.release/ecopro.t06.htm
www.bls.gov/news.release/ecopro.t04.htm
www.bls.gov/news.release/ecopro.t10.htm
www.bls.gov/news.release/ecopro.t08.htm
www.sustainlane.com/green-jobs/jobs
www.greencareersguide.com/
www.indeed.com/q-Green-jobs.html

INDEX